Interpreting Management –
Exploring Change and Complexity

Interpreting Management – Exploring Change and Complexity

Derek Furze
Chris Gale

INTERNATIONAL THOMSON BUSINESS PRESS

I ⓣ P An International Thomson Publishing Company

London • Bonn • Boston • Johannesburg • Madrid • Melbourne • Mexico City • New York • Paris
Singapore • Tokyo • Toronto • Albany, NY • Belmont, CA • Cincinnati, OH • Detroit, MI

Interpreting Management

First published by International Thomson Business Press

 I(T)P
A division of International Thomson Publishing Inc.
The ITP logo is a trademark under licence

British Library Cataloguing-in-Publication Data
A catalogue record for this book is available from the British Library

First edition 1996

Typeset by WestKey Ltd
Printed in the UK by Clays Ltd, St Ives Plc

ISBN 0-412-71770-0

International Thomson Business Press
Berkshire House
168–173 High Holborn
London WC1V 7AA
UK

International Thomson Business Press
20 Park Plaza
13th Floor
Boston MA 02116
USA

http://www.thomson.com/itbp.html

Contents

Acknowledgements

As is always the case we are indebted to many people for their contributions, feedback and support that has sustained us during the writing of this book.

We would firstly like to thank International Thompson for the opportunity to put some of our thoughts into print, and Ingmar Folkmans and team for their patience, and for their flexibility in supporting our approach to the subject.

A major source of inspiration has been and will continue to be the many managers and students we have worked with on management development events over the years. Their ideas, stories and challenging viewpoints ensured we learned a great deal through sharing their experience of management.

Likewise our colleagues at Horizon, and those consultants and organisations we network with, have provided support, generous comments and perceptive criticism that have added greatly to the finished text.

The most valuable contribution of course has come from our partners and families who have had to tolerate the highs and lows and the diversion of time and energy associated with any project of this kind. Our thanks to Yvonne and Sue.

How to use this book – a navigation aid

Objectivity gets in the way of truth.

James Cameron

Life comes to us whole. It is only the analytical lens we impose that makes it seem as if problems can be isolated and solved. When we forget it is 'only a lens', we lose the spirit of openness.

Peter Senge

Introduction

The purpose of this brief introduction is twofold. Firstly, it provides you with some information about how the book is structured, and the way in which we have presented ideas and material so that you can make choices about how you use it and 'find your way' around the chapters as easily as possible.

Secondly, we are keen that you use this book as a learning tool in whatever way suits you. It is intended to be a working document – a source of ideas, questions and discussion – rather than a series of recipes to be slavishly followed. You may find it productive to highlight sections of particular interest or add notes and comments in the margins as appropriate. In addition, those of you undertaking management learning might find value in cross-referencing sections and topics to other course materials as you work through the book. Similarly, there will be ideas put forward that you wish to challenge, or which raise issues which do not reflect your own experience of management; we hope this provokes reflection on alternative perspectives and models.

We would ask that you approach the ideas presented here with a reasonably open mind, using them to challenge your own thinking, and the beliefs and values on which this is based, and to challenge our thoughts in return in the spirit of exploration and learning. The only real way of abusing this material is to treat it as 'the answer' – the 'truth' about management – or to dismiss the ideas it contains without any thought or reflection.

Structure

In writing a book about 'management' we have set out to explore a vast and complex subject that is full of contradictions and conflicting opinion, in which topics are all interlinked or related in some way, and where rapid change is becoming a constant feature. The first chapter, 'Interpreting management', sets out our approach to management development in outline, and provides a summary of some of the major themes that underpin much of the material to follow.

A book presents some real limitations as a means of communicating the richness and diversity of a subject such as management. A text demands a linear structure for example, while our experience of management activity is that it is inherently 'unstructurable' in this way. A book is only a 'one-way' form of communication, so at odds with our view that management is fundamentally about interactions between people, with all the confusion and wonderful opportunity this brings.

Whilst recognizing that any of the subject areas covered here are intrinsically related and overlap significantly, the book does follow a broad structure. It begins with a focus on the individual, moves on to look at managing within groups and teams, and then finally addresses some contemporary organizational issues. It is not necessary to read through the book in the order in which it is presented, but you should recognize that the divisions into chapters and subject headings is primarily to aid referencing and for ease of use. In any case each particular topic can rarely be studied in isolation, without most of the other aspects of management being raised at some point; in fact the interrelatedness of the various subjects covered is one of the key themes upon which this book is based.

Content

One of the difficulties in writing a book which covers such a huge and often controversial subject is what to put in and what to leave out. We have tried to maintain a balance between some of the useful ideas traditionally found in a textbook on management, and some of the more exciting ideas that are the subject of contemporary debate. The choice of material is inevitably subjective – like everyone else our own agendas influence this choice – but we have endeavoured to be guided by our experience of working with managers and students and what they seem to find interesting or valuable. In particular we have sought to avoid simply listing as many theories as possible on a particular subject, thus leaving the student or manager drowning in a sea of often contradictory ideas and models. In this respect we have omitted a range of useful theories that are extensively covered elsewhere. We have aimed to try and achieve a reasonable balance between the theory and concepts that abound in many textbooks, with discussions, cases and stories that show their application in the workplace on a practical level. Perhaps this is an unrealistic aim, since the right balance may well be different for each reader. We have attempted to treat ideas and theories as working tools, to be adapted by the manager to suit practical ends, rather than as vague memories that remain stored in some 'management training' file on the shelf. In the end ideas have the most value if they 'ring some bells' and get used in action.

Navigating a chapter

This section provides a brief guide to the approach we have followed in structuring each chapter. All of the chapters, with the exception of the first one, follow this standardized format, for both comfort and ease of reference.

In addition to the text, each chapter contains the following.

Quotes

Each chapter starts with one or two quotations chosen to inspire, provoke thought or just for fun. They come from a wide range of sources, not simply management related texts. If you find them interesting or amusing you could always pin them up at work, or quote them in a futile effort to impress people.

Objectives

Objectives are simply and clearly stated at the beginning of each chapter as a guide to the learning contained therein. We would encourage people to be aware of their own personal objectives when approaching a particular subject, perhaps noting these down as an aid to evaluating the ideas we have presented.

Learning activities

Learning activities are spaced about the text, and are designed to encourage the reader to explore ideas through their own experience, either at work, through general experience, or within a learning environment. It is for you to choose to what extent these are used, but the need to reflect on your own understanding and practice of management is a recurring theme of this book. The activities are useful in helping to embed this reflective approach, which is a crucial management skill in itself.

Developing ideas

At various points in the text we have introduced additional or more complex ideas inside 'concept boxes'. These are not crucial to the themes presented in the text, but build on them for those wishing to explore the subject in more depth or from a sometimes different perspective. They are ideas which we hope you will find both challenging and stimulating, and may wish to follow up either through management education, or via the references given.

Case notes

Rather than include lengthy case studies to illustrate particular points, we have chosen to scatter short examples of current practice and anecdotes about 'typical situations' throughout the text. The purpose here is to show how some of the ideas and theories presented apply in practice in a general way that relates to a wide range of readers. Stressed throughout the book is the need for managers to reflect on their approach to management in the context of their own situation. Case notes provide interesting insights into how some organizations have approached particular issues, but do need to be used with caution. There is an ever-present danger from trying to apply the ideas and strategies out of context – in an organization with very different people, history and culture. That it 'worked for Hewlett-Packard' is no guarantee that it will work for you.

The short cases or examples we have included aim to reassure readers that some of the more challenging and contemporary ideas about management included here are not simply 'nice ideas', but that they are being successfully used in a wide range of real business settings.

With case studies we have taken the view that managers cannot afford to wait for particular ideas and approaches to be 'proven' and become accepted wisdom. The nature of management as a complex, fluid and dynamic subject suggests that waiting for such a state of agreed understanding to arrive condemns people to a very long wait indeed. In simple terms our advice is 'if it feels right to you – try it', then use the opportunity to reflect on the outcomes of your experience in order to learn.

Language and definitions

It is common for writers to spend time with each new subject trying to define the meaning of specific terms they use to describe an idea or topic. In practice individuals create their own meaning for terms such as 'leadership' or 'perception', and use the words and ideas freely on a day to day basis with little reference to precise meanings. What we have stressed is the need for people to explore and clarify their own understanding of these terms and ideas in their own context. We have also encouraged the reader to recognize that an important aspect of communicating with others about any topic or idea, is that their understanding will inevitably be different. This provides an opportunity both for clarification and for people to explore meaning together, learning from this process.

'Academic' references

EG: Schein, E.H. (1987) *Process Consultation,* Vol. 2, Addison-Wesley.

We have put references directly related to the material alongside the text to avoid breaking up the flow of the writing. This makes the references easy to use for those who wish to do so, and acknowledges our debt to the original work of the many writers and thinkers that have contributed to our current and future understanding of management issues.

Summary

Each chapter also has a short summary at the end, that reinforces key points from the text. It also provides you with a quick reference to the topics covered and approach taken in that particular chapter.

Further reading

At the end of each chapter we have suggested books that we feel will be of particular interest and value, and commented on their style and content. We have chosen these primarily on the grounds that they are both inspiring and accessible. Of course this choice is inevitably subjective – there are many more books and ideas out there that we are yet to come across. In some cases we have also suggested books that provide material and ideas that we have not found space for here. This is particularly the case with some of the more traditional or historically significant theories.

We recommend spending time in libraries or bookshops to search out further material at a level and in a style to suit you. If you are attending a management course or training session, tutors and colleagues can provide valuable leads on books and materials that they have discovered or found inspiring. There are many contemporary journals, such as *The Harvard Business Review* or *Management Today*, that include invaluable comment on current initiatives and case studies.

In addition, many colleges, universities and business organizations are increasingly linked up to the Internet. This gives an opportunity to access up-to-date information, such as research papers or business data, with the potential to establish dialogue with other interested parties.

General references

Also at the end of each chapter are lists of all the works referred to in the text as well as sources of ideas and reading beyond those selected for 'further reading'. These references vary enormously in their style and approach, ranging from straightforward 'how to' booklets through to detailed texts with a more 'academic' flavour. You might like to add to each list material and references that you find useful or inspiring as you go along.

We hope that you find the ideas presented here valuable, and use them positively to challenge and explore your own feelings about the practice of management. As a 'subject' for study, and more importantly as an art, management offers boundless opportunities for learning and development through action – a lifelong journey of growing understanding and experience.

We would be happy to receive any comments you might care to make either about this material or your own experiences of managing in your organization. You can contact us through the publishers – or directly at:

Horizon Development Training
14 Springbank Road
Chesterfield
Derbyshire
S40 1NL

And finally, a word of encouragement for anyone engaged in the art of managing:

Walking on water wasn't built in a day.

Jack Kerouac

1

Interpreting management

How much we are the woods we wander in.

Richard Wilbur

A managerial reality

Perhaps our opening lines should really say something profound or deeply perceptive about management, but we have chosen instead to begin by recalling our conversations with people about their work as managers.

We spend a fair proportion of our working time exploring management issues with people from a wide range of organizations, positions and working cultures. It is during these management development events, or more often in the bar afterwards, that we hear from people their 'truth' about the practice of management. We listen to the stories and anecdotes managers share about their working lives – the people they work with, and the things that happen. These stories ring a lot of bells from our experience of management, and in the problems we face in our own organization – the notes may be different, but the tunes they play are familiar.

The picture they paint about their 'managerial reality' is a vibrant and colourful one. As with any other aspects of our lives it is full of triumphs and disasters, laughter and stress, tales of progress made and of setbacks suffered. There are many common threads to their stories and observations despite working in very different fields and in different organizational cultures. Perhaps one of the most inspiring 'threads' is a genuine concern to find better ways of working effectively together, driven by the need to develop positive working relationships focused around real achievements and shared success.

There are a great many other clues to an optimistic view of making progress in the workplace – of managing more effectively. People tell us enthusiastically about their jobs, and of the developments that have brought real benefits to both people and their organizations – the friendships they have at work, the fun and the humour, and the excitement and satisfaction that comes from developing new products or services, for example. They point to personal achievements, the things they have learned, and above all to their hopes for the future. The desire and commitment to a better life and more productive workplaces is there in abundance.

But there are often other stories being told alongside the hopeful ones related above. These are stories of frustration and misunderstanding – of unfulfilled needs, conflict and disillusionment. The picture includes ineffectual initiatives, plans that went wrong or the upheavals triggered by major change. They come across in situations that will be familiar to many of us – here are some short examples:

- A common storyline relates the introduction of new systems or initiatives designed with well-meaning intent to address particular problems or pursue improvements in performance. Here the enthusiasm that surrounds the introduction of such developments meets with cynicism – the 'seen it all before' or 'it won't make any difference' response. The effort falters and fades away – it loses momentum. A contribution has been made, but the outcome is less than successful. Perhaps expectations of failure are a self-fulfilling prophecy.

- Most managers can recognize the damage blaming others or 'passing the buck' causes, both to individuals and to organizational performance – and yet in so many workplaces this behaviour becomes the norm and goes unchallenged. 'Keeping your head down' and 'covering your back' are the games to play 'for survival'.

- Then there are the endless examples of 'communication difficulties' – the misunderstandings, lack of clarity, differing interpretations, hidden agendas and politics, and unspoken needs. There are those who are accused of not listening, who don't appear to trust others, or who don't consult and involve. Yet others seem to say one thing and do another – they get labelled as being 'inconsistent'.

These are common enough stories of course – but they raise some interesting questions in any search for managerial wisdom. We have got used to applying a huge range of 'solutions' to the problems faced in managing people and organizations; some are followed with evangelical fervour and others dismissed as just the latest management 'fad'. Organizations have at their disposal a vast range of sophisticated tools for handling information, for planning and decision-making, and for worldwide instant communication. There are initiatives and systems galore to choose from – Total Quality Management, Investors in People, team-based working, performance management systems – the list is a long one. They all have real and valuable contributions to make, in the right circumstances, to productivity and managerial effectiveness, and many of them will be covered in this book.

But despite this plethora of management tools and systems, managerial reality remains both complex and confusing to the managers and students we work with. It retains its mixture of excitement and frustration, achievement and missed opportunities. It is not that established management techniques are a failure exactly – they have a valuable contribution to make – but any observer of organizational life cannot fail to notice that simple, rational solutions do not always seem to work.

Somehow, organizations end up producing the unexpected. A new quality system generates dissatisfaction and lowers motivation. A planned strategy ends up being overtaken by events. A kind word mistakenly causes offense. Throughout organizations, good intentions and actions can have unintended consequences. Of course these consequences can be both positive and surprising. Yesterday's crisis leads to real opportunities, a chance conversation solves major problems, or one person's idea becomes the next innovative and successful product or service.

Organizations are complex social systems, where cause and effect are sometimes hard to unravel, and where a shifting and changing environment makes predicting outcomes difficult. At the heart of these complex systems are people – it is the way people behave and interact that provides energy and inspiration at work, but which also introduces uncertainty and confusion to the management equation. We do not come to work and operate in a rational, consistent and open manner, we do not behave like machines or other corporate 'assets' – we bring along our emotions, our history and our unique personalities. It is the difficulties we have in understanding the ways in which people work together and interact that lies at the heart of the stories quoted above, and which form the basis of our approach to the subject of *Interpreting Management*.

Interpreting management – some key themes

Every book, no matter how seemingly 'objective' the authors try to be, is written from some form of perspective. It is born from the understanding the writer has of a subject at a particular point in time, and reflects to a greater or lesser extent their own values and attitudes shaped by past experience.

To attempt to write a management 'textbook' from a detached and analytical point of view we felt to be unhealthy on two grounds. Firstly the idea is simply a lie – it is not possible to be 'objective' in covering a subject such as management: even decisions about what to include and exclude, for example, require us to make personal judgments about the value of particular ideas or theories. Secondly, to try to do so would be to deny our own desires to be engaged in the 'management debate', to be involved in influencing others positively and, most importantly, to try to get across our enthusiasm for the subject.

Having stated that it is not possible to be completely objective in our coverage, it is also very much the case that the perspectives on management presented in this book do not represent necessarily 'the right approach' nor provide definitive answers to the question 'What is the right way to manage?' Ours is just one contribution, designed to encourage reflection, debate and challenge. Ultimately you must decide for yourselves how to manage in a way that suits you, your colleagues and the situation in which you manage. It is the complexities of management – the lack of a checklist of 'right' answers – that make it such a fascinating and absorbing subject, and which provides endless opportunities for learning and discovery.

We have included below some of the key themes or viewpoints that form the basis of our approach to *Interpreting Management*. These serve the need to both clarify our own perspectives, and to introduce important themes and ideas that underlie the book as a whole.

Understanding self and others

Understand that what we believe precedes policy and practice.

The starting point in developing managerial effectiveness must lie in developing our understanding, not only of the way other people behave and interact, but of ourselves. Without a genuine commitment to developing this understanding, the unthinking application of otherwise valuable management techniques will flounder on the rocks of ignorance. This is perhaps the strongest theme in this material and is reflected in its clear focus on the management of people.

A desire to understand ourselves and others provides links between the professional development of managerial skills and our basic beliefs about the value of people. In this respect, we have worked from our own personal perspective that people have unbounded potential to act with integrity, commitment and humanity. It is through liberating this potential that organizations can create a future full of hope, energy and meaning.

It is this view of people that supports the recurring references in the book to the importance of trust, openness and honesty as primary goals in establishing positive working relationships and, ultimately, productive and successful organizations.

Management – a complex process

We have already referred to management as a complex process, particularly with respect to the behaviours displayed by people and the relationships they develop. Part of this complexity lies in the way each aspect of management – communication and change, or leadership and empowerment, for example – is interrelated. Actions taken in one area potentially build effects in all of the others. This suggests the need to develop a holistic approach to your understanding of management, and a readiness to think widely about the issues and opportunities that present themselves.

We have also introduced important ideas such as the need to step outside of linear and rational approaches, the importance of exploring different 'paradigms' or ways of thinking, or the value of paradox – holding opposing ideas in 'tension' – as essential components in any understanding of management. A further dimension must be the need to reject a static view of the social systems in which we work – the 'dynamic' element has always been important, but never more so than in rapidly changing work environments.

Learning and development

Another common thread throughout the book is the value of learning. This is not simply acquiring better skills or more knowledge, though these are important, but learning as a driving force for developing more productive and inherently satisfying workplaces.

One of the key skills in improving managerial effectiveness is the ability to reflect on our own behaviour and its effect on others as part of the learning process, and to embed this reflection in our approach to managing. Throughout the book we emphasize the value of learning through discussion, dialogue and discovery as key features of a dynamic, hopeful and exploratory view of management.

Effective people and effective organizations

As we have already stated, the focus of this book lies squarely on the management of people as the key to managerial effectiveness. People are also the key to developing successful and effective organizations; they are the major differentiating factor between those that survive and prosper, and those that struggle or disappear.

Despite the current rhetoric along the lines of 'people are our most valuable asset', it is our view that in practice they are also the most underutilized and undervalued 'asset' an organization has. The potential contribution people can make to improvements in productivity and performance is immense. In an age where the availability of information about technical developments or new systems allows any organization access to the 'hardware' of running a business or providing a service, it is the people that offer the chance of real 'competitive advantage'.

That employees of an organization are vital to its current operation is all too obvious, but it is when we look to the future that their contribution must play a leading role. It is people that provide the energy and drive, the creativity and learning, and the flexibility to change and adapt. The potential is there also for people to enact a vision of a more productive and 'human' workplace, and to create direction and meaning for themselves and their organizations. It is not systems or directives that generate enthusiasm and commitment, nor is it rules and procedures that 'control' or determine the way an organization delivers its products or services – it is people who work there that can make the real difference. *Interpreting Management* focuses on people, then, not simply because they are the most challenging and complex part of a manager's role, but primarily because they have the major contribution to make to creating successful and fulfilling workplaces.

Action and engagement

Works of the mind exist only in action.

Above all, management has to be about action, about doing things, about getting engaged in the process, in order to effect change and have influence. This is the need to use your management skills, your understanding and your commitment to improve the way you work, to develop positive relationships and to contribute to organizational success. Throughout the book we will be encouraging managers and students to put their learning into practice and actively to seek to change and develop the way they manage on a day-to-day basis. Each chapter will include a range of suggestions about using ideas or skills in a practical setting, should they be appropriate to your own situation.

Our approach suggests that people do have the opportunity to influence others and to change things for the better, whatever position they hold in an organization. It is optimistic about the possibility that people want to and can change the way in which they work together, and can create meaning and direction through their actions. It implies that passively waiting for improvements to be handed to you, placing all responsibility for a 'better' organization with senior people, is an understandable but ultimately unfulfilling strategy.

Looking forward – optimism and opportunity

The real quest isn't where ideas come from, it's where they go and how they get there.

We have tried to maintain a balance between a realistic appraisal of the difficulties and complexities of management, and one which is enthusiastic and optimistic about the progress that can undoubtably be made on a personal and on an organizational level. Our own passion for the subject comes almost entirely from the managers and students with whom we work, and the optimism they display about their future.

Ultimately, learning about management, as with many other things, is a lifelong journey. It is full of adventure and opportunities for exploration. The potential is there for creating meaningful futures for ourselves and our colleagues.

Timid men prefer the calm of despotism to the boisterous sea of liberty.

Thomas Jefferson

Part One

Managing Individuals

2

Perception and perspectives

The most important thing for managers . . . to understand is what goes on inside their own heads.

Edgar Schein

Objectives

By the end of this chapter you will be able to:

➤ Explain how perceptions underpin management activity
➤ Describe how perspective shapes our understanding of people and events
➤ Describe the main sources of perceptual bias and their impact on managing
➤ Take steps to reduce the effects of perceptual bias on management activity

Introduction

All over the world, making interventions is the stuff of management. Wherever there are people or processes to organize, management is involved in taking action to improve the outcome. Often, managers make interventions that affect the context in which work takes place by designing systems or procedures to facilitate activity. Sometimes they intervene more directly by using visionary words to inspire others or by taking decisions that shape the direction of an organization. Even on a day-by-day level, managers make plans, review targets and solve problems, all of which intervene in organizational processes.

Making some critical intervention, such as investing in training or making a key appointment, doesn't just happen. Managers have first to assess the existing situation and make judgments about appropriate actions before they can take the necessary steps. Much of this takes place inside the manager's head, as a series of reactions and judgments made about the situation and information observed. The factors that influence this process are many, including both objective facts and subjective interpretations. In order for the whole process to be productive, managers need to recognize when their reactions might be based on their own view of reality rather than on what the situation might really demand. This chapter aims to develop an understanding of the key elements that affect our perceptions, and explores how we might build a more informed perspective on the interventions that we make. Part of this exploration will consider the ways in which people react to situations and events in an effort to uncover some of the causes of managerial behaviour.

A simple cycle for a complex process

All our interventions are based on an extremely complex process taking place as we interact with the situations around us. At the centre of this process is the brain, which works to gather and process data, while at the same time managing our actions. Unlike Spock of the Starship *Enterprise*, we humans have emotions and feelings, which the brain also has to manage interwoven with the data that it receives. While Spock is apparently (and amusingly) able to make logical calculations based on an accurate assessment of the facts, our processing system is inextricably bound up with our **self**. Incoming data does have an effect on our feelings and emotions, and causes a reaction that is driven partly by the data itself, but is also shaped by previous experiences, values and beliefs. To make 'rational' interventions, it is first crucial for managers to understand their own self, so they can assess how their perception of each situation is distorted by the baggage of their own perspective.

To understand this complex process it is useful to use a framework that allows us to focus on the elements that make up our actions. By looking at the process through a simplified framework, it is easier to assess how our perspective is built up and how we can check our perceptions of situations. To make interventions, the brain firstly has to make observations. These are followed, sometimes without much conscious thought, by feelings or emotional reactions.

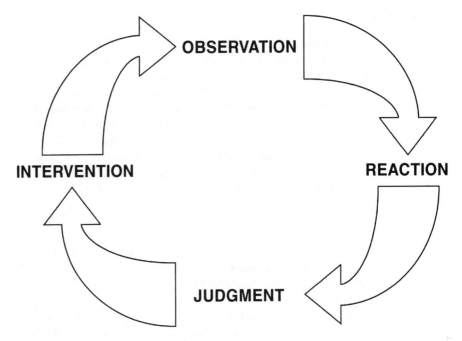

Fig. 2.1 The ORJI cycle. Adapted from Schein, E. H. (1987) *Process Consultation*, Vol 2, Addison-Wesley.

These lead in turn to judgments which enable us to make the interventions that seem to be appropriate. These simplified stages of the process can be represented as a cycle known as the ORJI cycle, as shown in Figure 2.1.

This cycle can be used to describe the process that takes place each time we act, and each stage is affected in different ways. This begins with the observations that we make of events, where we receive primary data from the environment around us. If we are to go on to make appropriate responses to events, then this stage should be free from error. However, studies of the way in which our psychology works show that this is far from being the case.

Problems with the stage of observation

Several factors affect the way we 'see' events, so that different people may experience the same event in very different ways and have different reactions to it. This happens because our psychology is geared up to do more than just observe events – instead it is a sophisticated processing tool that is able to analyse and infer from observations. However, these processes do not happen objectively, but are based on the experiences and learning that we have previously undergone. An example of this is the way in which different witnesses describe traffic accidents to police. Often these descriptions are vividly detailed, but contradictory, leaving the police with the job of trying to interpret what actually happened from a variety of reports. So, if I observe a road accident between a young driver and an old driver, my observations will be shaped by my experiences of how young and old drivers behave, and the mistakes that they are likely to make. I am likely to see 'aggressive yobbo' or 'blind old fool' according to my previous learning, however carefully I look.

Problems with observation are based on several features of our psychology, all of which are necessary tools to help us through life. While these features are essential aids to our role as a sophisticated animal, they are not always helpful to managing. Some of the more notable features are briefly illustrated and explained below.

Figure and ground

This effect is based on our ability to resolve information into 'figures' against a background. Figure 2.2 provides an example of this effect, where it may be initially difficult to pick up any pattern in the picture.

Fig. 2.2 Resolution of a 'figure' against a background.

Once the image of a Dalmatian dog has been spotted, the brain will lock onto the 'figure', and it will become impossible not to see this central figure in any subsequent exposure to the image. This ability to pick up and focus on important, central information has benefits in terms of spotting danger quickly, and in historical times performed a useful role in helping people to hunt for food or find shelter. However, it is less relevant to making sense of a complex package of information in a business environment. Here features of the 'background' may be crucial to success – think how necessary it is to understand the hidden agenda or to listen for the tone of a message as well as the words.

Adapted from Pascale, R.T. (1984) 'Perspectives on strategy: the real story behind Honda's success' in *California Management Review*, **XXVI** (3), 47–72.

Case note

Honda

An example of the importance of the background comes from Honda's entry into the US motorcycle market in the 1950s. Despite a lack of support from the Japanese trade body, the company pressed ahead with plans to sell large motorcycles. The plan did not work as there was no interest in the large machines, but the Honda staff in San Francisco noticed that people were interested in their own transport – small 50cc Super Cub bikes, primarily used for economy and to save valuable foreign currency! By focusing on this opportunity, Honda built a toehold in the States.

Against this background the giant General Motors did nothing. It had a market share of over 50% and paid no attention to the arrival of a one-shop motorcycle importer over in San Francisco. But from small seeds grow mighty trees, and Honda was a player that would change the face of the American market. On the back of success with motorbikes came the arrival of small cars, coinciding with the 1970s rise in fuel prices. By now General Motors were awake to the competition, and concluded that the customer wanted small, fuel efficient cars. Honda, meanwhile, had identified quality as the significant element in buying decisions. The game moved on, with General Motors adopting strategies to adapt its product line in the face of competition. In the 1990s, Honda has a climbing market share and manufacturing base in the US, while General Motors has seen falling profits and declining share.

This is not to illustrate cause and effect as the situation is too complex for those links to be made. The companies did adopt different strategies, but there were many other factors as well. With hindsight GM did the wrong thing, but they made decisions that seemed pretty rational along the way. Instead, the case illustrates the sometimes vital significance of tiny changes in the background of organizations. Different changes may have shaped a different future.

Closure

This feature explains our ability to close up the gaps in information in order to build a full and consistent picture. It is exampled by our readiness to make assumptions, to finish off other people's sentences and to depend on stereotypes

Fig. 2.3 Example of closure.

for our view of other people. Figure 2.3 provides a simple illustration of this feature, where the eye perceives a central white triangle even though no such feature has been drawn.

Primacy
This feature affects our treatment of information by ensuring that early information that we receive is regarded as more important than later information. Again, this is useful in terms of our animal behaviours, making us alert to danger and able to react quickly, but has damaging effects on the way we handle more complex information in organizations. In communicating with others, for example, primacy will tend to ensure that early information is picked up more readily than later information, whatever the relative importance.

Learning activity

A new colleague

Consider meeting a new colleague for the first time. In what way does the first information that you receive on an individual contribute to the first impression you form of that individual?

Perceptual set

This feature is based on our ability to learn, which ensures that our perception is influenced by our prior experience and upbringing. As we learn, we develop a particular perspective on events that is driven by the patterns and situations that we have been exposed to before. As a result, when we are in new situations, we see them from a 'set' perspective, driven by expectations and comparisons with previous experiences. This tends to mean that our impression of any situation is shaped and formed by ourself, rather than existing as an objective reality. Nevertheless, we usually rely on our impression as if it were true, and use it as the basis of our reactions and decisions.

Perceptual set seems to be easily influenced, with advertising being a commercial example of how it is possible to encourage people to take up a particular view. Figure 2.4 illustrates how 'set' can be developed, as the central figure is perceived as letters to fit with our expectations about what the words should say.

Fig. 2.4   Perceptual set – what words can you read?

It would seem that our basic systems for making observations are not entirely reliable at producing a consistent view. These effects are made worse by situations of pressure, as these produce anxiety and tend to make us depend more on our instincts, rather than on careful analysis. As our observations are the start of a process which ends in making interventions, it is important that we build better awareness of the kinds of errors that we can easily make at this stage of the cycle. Our psychology makes it impossible to develop a completely objective view of situations, as we each create our own interpretation of reality. However, by being aware of our own biases and distortions, and the impact of these on our management actions, we are better able to assess and counter the effects.

Exploring reactions

The important feature of this part of the cycle is that it often goes by without us being consciously aware that we have had much of a reaction. Quite often, in response to situations, our immediate reactions go unnoticed and we just get on with actions. However, when we observe situations there are always some inner feelings as the initial part of our response. These can include joy, anger, guilt, jealousy, excitement or anxiety, as well as a whole host of others depending on the situation. However, these emotional reactions are a part of everyday life, and our social upbringing teaches us that feelings should only be shared in certain circumstances, whereas in others they should be suppressed or hidden from view. Typically, work is a situation where feelings are not usually put on open view but instead are kept under wraps, as such reactions might detract from productive efforts and distort work relationships. Additionally, such feelings are thought to interfere with the rational processes that are needed to make judgments, and are therefore further ignored or controlled.

Such methods of dealing with our emotional reactions can prevent us from taking the time to explore this stage of the cycle. No amount of ignoring feelings or 'looking at things logically' will prevent them from occurring, because they are a fundamental part of our make-up. However, such strategies do make us less able to assess the effect that emotional reactions have on our judgments. By not taking time to examine and understand all of our reactions, we are succumbing to the unpredictable and poorly understood influence that they have on our actions. Emotions that are not surfaced and explored have effectively been buried alive, and it is difficult to assess the damage that they can do when hidden from view.

Learning activity

Exploring emotions

In what way might buried emotions of anxiety and anger affect people going through a major change at work?

Making judgments

At this stage of the cycle, judgments are being formed based on the observations made and the reactions that we have had. It is likely that our observations are not objective, in that they are driven by the perceptive system and its inbuilt features. Further, it is unlikely that there is much attempt to assess how our emotional reaction is affecting our view of the situation, making the process of making judgments less reliable than it may seem. Paradoxically, in an attempt to make the process more logical, we often attempt to rid ourselves of 'illogical' emotional reactions, despite the impact that these have on our judgments.

The judgments that we make can have far-reaching consequences, as human beings have a capacity to make complex plans that stretch into the future. However sophisticated the process of planning becomes, it is all undermined by a lack of objectivity or analysis at the information gathering and processing stage. Bias does exist, caused by our basic systems of perception and our feelings. Failing to acknowledge this is the source of considerable potential error in the seemingly rational processes of managerial interventions. Flawed observations and misunderstood emotional reactions are the basis of misguided judgments and interventions. We have a duty to other people to improve this process wherever possible.

Learning activity

Assessing the impact

Think about the various effects on the observation, reaction and judgment stages of the cycle. How might these impact on the daily interventions that a manager makes at work? How can a manager check that their interventions are not based on subjective, internal factors?

The impact of perception on the ORJI cycle

Taking account of the various influences and distortions discussed suggests that the ORJI cycle should be modified as in Figure 2.5 to reflect the real process taking place.

The key problems with the process are that:

- Errors in perception occur
- Emotional reactions are driven by poorly understood factors, including many that have nothing to do with the immediate situation being observed
- Analysis that seems to be logical and based on rational information is in fact influenced by errors and emotions to an indeterminate degree
- Interventions – managerial actions – can be poorly founded and irrational

Learning to cope with these problems provides management with much of its complexity and excitement. Countering the effects depends on building understanding of your own perspective and exploring that of other people. Before looking at some basic strategies that may help provide direction, it is worth looking at how the cycle affects the way we interact with other people. Much of our efforts at work involve other people either directly or indirectly, and anything that affects the quality of workplace relationships will have an impact on managerial success. The next section explores how the ORJI cycle affects the way in which we build and maintain working relationships.

The impact of the ORJI cycle on relationships

The way in which we observe and react to other people is just as likely to be influenced by perceptual distortions as any other situation or event that we experience. Indeed, the fact that other people are involved, each seeing the situation from their own perspective, brings in an added layer of dynamics. This is because our perspective is not fixed, but changes and evolves in response to the experiences that we have. In turn our observations affect our judgments and

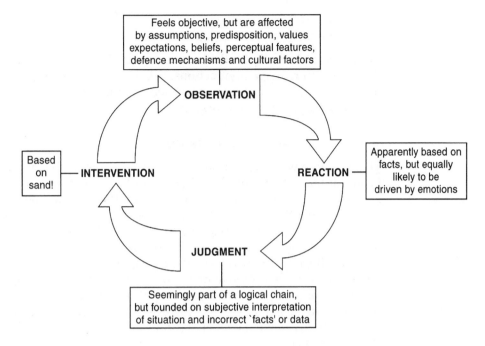

Fig. 2.5 The modified ORJI cycle.

the action that we take. This has an impact on the event that we observe and the ORJI cycle of other people involved. As a result, any interaction between people is a situation that shapes and forms reality as it moves along, based on history, expectations and interpretations of what seems to be happening. In this way, through our interpretation of events and our efforts to build meaning, we construct our 'objective' reality. Building understanding of how we construct our own part of that reality is the starting point for trying to manage the construction of a better one. Exploring some of the potential errors that we make in our observations of others is therefore a rich source of understanding for managers.

Errors of person perception

Systematic errors in the way we observe other people have been identified through various studies. It is hard to think of these as errors as they are firmly rooted in our psychological responses. Instead, they are like unintentional fouls which have a significant effect on the game of management. There are seven basic errors that bear consideration:

- Assuming behaviour is constant
- Assuming characteristics are consistent with each other
- Being over-influenced by first impressions
- Being too positive to people who are similar to ourselves
- Looking for negative features of others

- Relying on general views of others
- Not being interested enough in others

The seven sections that follow explore each of these errors and the impact that they have on management actions. It is important to recognize that these are not merely minor mistakes to be ironed out, but are part of the fabric of the way in which people relate and organize.

Assuming behaviour is constant

This is where we tend to assume that the way people behave will be the same in any situation that they enter. For example, if we observe a person displaying a 'lack of confidence', we tend to think that they will not be confident in most situations that they find themselves in. In making this assumption, we undervalue the influence of particular situations on the person's behaviour, and fail to acknowledge how people behave differently according to their circumstances. This kind of error leads the manager into self-fulfilling prophecies, for if they use this perception to help make judgments, they will be unlikely to put the person into situations that need confidence. They may even justify this as sensitive, caring management. However, the lack of exposure to new situations will eventually make the label accurate, all based on faulty observations at the start of the cycle.

This error is the basis of labelling, where we use labels such as 'aggressive', 'highly-strung' or 'moody' to describe other people's behaviour. Categorizing others' behaviour in this way prevents us having to work too hard to understand the often complex factors that explain the situation more accurately. It also places the responsibility for action firmly onto the other person, as managers of their own character, making it an understandable strategy. Understandable it may be, but positive management it is not, as it encourages managerial actions that do nothing to challenge the label or solve the situation.

Assuming characteristics are consistent with each other

This is where we try hard to build up a consistent view of the characteristics of other people, and is based on the psychological feature of closure. This means that if we observe a quality in a person – good looks for example – we assume that they will have other qualities to complete the package. We resist the idea that people are an inconsistent mixture of qualities, strengths and weaknesses and prefer to assume consistent character.

Learning activity

Type-casting

This effect is used regularly in the movies. How often is clean-cut Kevin Costner cast as an arch-criminal or psychopathic killer? How easily are we fooled by the old

Agatha Christie chestnut of always making the nicest people in the drama the ones that did the dirty deed? All too easily for these novels to merit the title of 'whodunits' apparently! As managers, our efforts to build consistent pictures often lead us to ignore evidence that contradicts the picture that we are trying to build up. How would this interfere with effective management? What actions could you take to minimize the damage of this effect?

This effect is very noticeable in interview situations, where it is an effective strategy for candidates to clearly show some qualities, safe in the knowledge that those doing the interviewing will build additional qualities onto the ones that have been observed. Indeed, the situation, with time pressure and the need to make a reasoned case, almost guarantees that this effect will occur to some degree. Studies show that interviewers will even try to evidence that these projected qualities exist after the interview is over and events have suggested otherwise. In many management situations, our efforts to build up consistent pictures can lead us to undervalue evidence about people that goes against the trend, with the potential to make our actions ineffective as a result.

Being over-influenced by first impressions

This error is where we allow the first impression we make of people to have too much ongoing influence over the way we relate to people. This is based on the psychological features of primacy, closure and perceptual set and also has clear benefits in situations of personal threat. Our ability to form an impression of people in a very short time is remarkable, often taking no more than a glance or a short exchange of words. However, while it is great for helping to avoid the nutter on the bus, it is inappropriate as an aid to managing people, where we need to recognize that people will change and develop.

Learning activity

Checking assumptions

Think of an occasion when someone has made a poor first impression upon you. Note down the factors in the situation that might have been the cause of this. Try to think how you might have behaved in their shoes.

Nevertheless, the first impression effect is very powerful and even causes trained interviewers problems. As a natural tendency, managers need to work hard to assess how this error affects their observations and actions. This is especially relevant when the first impression made is negative in tone, as this is likely to have a damaging effect on all subsequent interventions.

Learning activity

Exploring stereotypes

The ability to categorize other people quickly appears to be a highly developed skill. This is demonstrated when we recognize stereotypes, and the messages that they are trying to convey, even when they feature as characterizations in a 30-second TV commercial. How does this skill benefit you as a manager?

- What disadvantages does the skill have when managing other people?
- In what ways are people stereotyped in your workplace?
- What is done in your workplace to reduce the effects of stereotyping of staff?

Being too positive to people who are similar to ourselves

Another related error is that we overrate people who mirror our own qualities, and have a natural inclination to give them more attention than others. This means that we are undervaluing the qualities of people who are not like ourselves, which affects the way in which the strengths of various people are viewed and used. A person with different qualities will find it more difficult to obtain recognition and opportunity than one who is able to reflect our own characteristics.

 Learning activity

Looking for similarities

Consider your own environment.

- What positive effects are there from the similarities that exist between people?
- What limits do the similarities impose on the work team?

This error has useful social properties, as it means that we are likely to surround ourselves with people who will share our own interests. It also means that they are likely to have common aspirations, values and even background, which is perhaps helpful in terms of building lifelong relationships. However, in the world of business organizations, allowing this error to influence actions can have dangerous consequences as it leads towards a uniform approach. Organizations need a varied range of ideas and styles if they are to develop flexibility, responsiveness and creativity. This is difficult to develop in a one-dimensional organization that rejects the opportunities that radically different people may be able to offer.

Despite the dangers of developing uniformity, the error is quite powerful at drawing groups of people together through a shared approach. People can easily feel threatened in an organizational context by the scale of the society in which they have to operate and make their way. One of the ways of reducing the anxiety is to seek out people who are similar, and indeed having a shared objective and approach can bind teams together in common purpose. There is therefore a tension between these two forces which organizations have to confront – on the one hand are forces for unity and security which may lead to a lack of creativity, and on the other hand are forces for flexibility, change and dynamic ideas which nevertheless hold considerable threats for the psychological safety of people.

Learning activity

Friends in strange places

This effect has been tested in many situations! Think back to your reactions when you last met someone from your neck of the woods when you were away on holiday. What kind of reaction did you have?

Why is this type of reaction, based on perceived similarities, unhelpful for the manager?

This error is one that affects people while on holiday, with amusing consequences. For many people, getting away to foreign countries is an opportunity to experience the excitement of a different culture and language. However, this does have an impact on security, making some people a little anxious as they are cut off from the familiar surroundings of home. As a result, we have a disproportionate interest in people from our own 'neck of the woods' that we happen to meet while away, sometimes forming quite strong friendships where we have no natural affinity.

Looking for negative features of others

The fifth error is that we tend to notice negative features of other people rather than their positive qualities. This error is rooted in our defence mechanisms, whereby we are geared up to notice the threats and weaknesses in other people. It also has some value in helping to maintain a positive self-image – relative to the failings of people around us – but does not help us to build effective relationships that value the qualities of others.

This effect is so strong that it sometimes feels uncomfortable giving positive feedback to others, and it is common to find workplaces that accept routine criticism of colleagues as a normal part of work. It is also linked to a concept known as attribution error, where we readily blame other people when situations that they are involved in go wrong. However, when the situation involves us, we are more likely to blame factors in the situation itself. We are naturally skilled at blaming others and ignoring the factors that may have affected their performance, but equally skilled at using those same situational factors to excuse our own efforts. This is the management equivalent of having our cake and eating it and, objectively, the world just is not like this.

Relying on general views of others

The sixth error is that we tend to have a perspective on other people that is too general, and which does not allow for the difference in characteristics, values and qualities that actually exists. We are therefore likely to categorize other people into groups, based on general assumptions about the character of such groups. For example, people readily develop views about categories of people in society – politicians, the mentally ill, the unemployed – and use these views as if they were a valid way to describe the qualities of people within the group. In reality, any group of people will have such diversity as to make generalized descriptions a misleading simplification.

Case note

Organizational cultures

Such categorization is familiar in organizations where polarized views about 'management' or 'the workers' have been a feature of industrial relations bargaining and posturing over decades. Yet when Lucas needed to close manufacturing plant as part of a restructuring strategy, the union side developed a strategy to save the business that received widespread commendation for its vision and creativity. While it failed to gain ultimate approval, it challenged views that people on the shop floor side of the fence had little to contribute to managing organizations.

Since the closure of coal mines in South Wales, the success of mines taken over by worker/shareholders have been noticeable, again challenging previous perceptions of the group as a whole.

In forming general views of other people, we can only make reference to our existing experience and the perspective of people that we have developed. As the person we know best is ourself, our view of others is framed by our own self-image, which helps shape our image of acceptable and unacceptable characteristics. The general views which we hold of others, and the characteristics that we use to describe them, are likely to be based closely on our own. We therefore 'project' our character onto others, 'seeing' the reasons why they behave in certain ways according to our own responses. If we are a person that is driven by recognition and status, then we are likely to explain the behaviour of others as being motivated by similar forces. This error obstructs effective management, because relying on general views prevents us from making the effort to develop an accurate view of the characteristics of others. In turn this has an impact on our behaviour towards people, making it less likely that we will effectively relate to people with potentially very different needs.

A general view can be a powerful self-fulfilling prophecy. Take a manager who thinks other people 'need close supervision' or 'tight managerial reins'. Such a manager will develop control systems and checking procedures based on their general view of others. Under such a regime, self-motivated or free-spirited people will find work difficult to tolerate, and will leave to find more exciting jobs where they are given responsibility and freedom to move. Replacement staff may be difficult to attract, and are unlikely to be innovative individuals capable of self-directed work. Over time, the manager's perspective will become true – an example of how our perspective can create and shape an 'objective' reality and a managerial trap of the worst proportions. Indeed, given the way our views can become reality, it is probably best to assume positive general views of others, safe in the knowledge that the self-fulfilling prophecy effect will lead to a positive outcome.

Not being interested enough in others

The last error is simply that people do not take enough interest in others. This is perhaps obvious, for if we were sufficiently interested then we would not tend to make the assumptions that lead to the other six errors. This is not to say that we have no interest in other people as our social nature suggests otherwise, but that we do not maintain enough interest to develop a full understanding of others. As managers, this can prevent us developing the kind of knowledge and insight into other people that will help effective management.

The more we know about other people, their likes and dislikes, values and beliefs, the better we are equipped to manage effectively. Successful management depends on getting the best results from the resources that you have, including the people in the team. Understanding people's needs, and their strengths and weaknesses, helps to build the quality relationships that underpin successful organizations. Such understanding is not obtained from behind closed doors and polished mahogany desks but is the product of working hard to learn about the people that you work with every day. This depends on our willingness to suspend the prejudgments and assumptions that we make, and to accept that in their personality, all people have something unique to share with us. Other people are a source of unlimited opportunities for discovery, interest and growth. If managers are to reach out and use this opportunity, they must be prepared to make their observations, reactions, judgments and interventions reflect a more careful and complete view of people. Anything else fails to value the real potential of other people, and limits the lessons that they can give to us all.

Dealing with the effects

The ORJI cycle illustrates the way in which our perceptive system, with all its potential for error, has an impact on our management actions and our relationships. Even when we are highly aware of the effects, we may not be able to prevent the distortions in our observations, reactions and judgments from taking place. The psychological responses that we make to external events are sometimes operating below the level of conscious thought, driven by a deeply embedded perspective formed through our life experience. In many respects, the task is not to prevent the various stages of the cycle from happening, but to explore and try to understand the reasons why we make certain reactions, judgments or interventions. The object is not to reduce human behaviours to a uniform expression of perfectly objective and rational action, but to encourage people to work to bring to the surface the many complex influences over their actions. By understanding the subjectivity in our perspective, we can better assess the validity of various actions and act in a more considered and deliberate way as a result. The responses themselves should not be suppressed, for they are an expression of our personality and our human differences, and should be valued for their rich variety. However, there are particular influences that cause bias in our actions, which may have a general impact on people in the workplace. The next section looks at some of these influences and tries to assess how they can be corrected.

Dealing with our own perspective

One of the most significant influences over our actions is the vast store of past experience that we all have. This helps us in many situations, providing us with templates of behaviours that worked in similar circumstances, enabling us to respond more efficiently than if each situation was completely new. These templates are not stored as thousands of unique and detailed models, ready to recall and use in situations that exactly match previous experience. Instead, they are much more general, giving us working models of broad situations that are adjusted as new experiences show us important differences. In this way we may carry a template to help us manage an 'upset' child for example, but not the millions of combinations that would be necessary to deal with all kinds of upset and all kinds of children. Indeed, the process of selecting the 'right' template would become unwieldy if they were too specific, nullifying the point of carrying such a perspective around in the first place.

Learning activity

Challenging perspectives

What actions can you take to challenge your own perspectives?

The drawback with using templates is that it leads us to act on the similarities between situations and our past experiences, with the danger that important differences are ignored or undervalued. Yet the situations that we observe, and the people with whom we interact, do change, sometimes in radical ways. Indeed, with people this process of growth and development is always happening, making our past experience of their character a poor guide to their present or future behaviour. If management is to be based on real understanding, we should recognize that our perspective is something that was built in the past, and that we should be open to the possibility that it will be shaped by the present and challenged by the future. For this to happen, we need to look carefully at events and people, especially when our experience tells us that we already know exactly what to expect.

Challenging our own perspective is not without its difficulties. Rather than depending on the things that we already know to help us respond, we must look closely at situations to uncover their unique character. This opens up the possibility of learning from each situation, but it also means developing a more open approach. Instead of coasting through events using automatic responses based on the templates of our experience, we have to invest our energies in identifying and valuing the important differences that exist in situations and between people. Sometimes, quite minor differences will provide great insights, whereas on other occasions considerable effort will not add greatly to our understanding. However, while undoing the influence of our perspective is never easy, it does fill life with opportunity and interest where it sometimes seems there is none.

Perspective and self-worth

One particular reason why it can be difficult to challenge our perspective is that our own way of seeing things may be exactly what gives us our sense of uniqueness and self-worth. Indeed, holding a particular point of view can be the source of power and recognition, in that it may be exactly that quality that people admire in us. In such circumstances, where our role is linked with providing a certain point of view, perhaps to give a team balance, we can develop a high degree of faith in the correctness of our perspective. It is then difficult to be analytical about our observations, as the situation encourages us to demonstrate conviction and we feel valued if we do. Again, such faith in a particular perspective is a simplification of reality, but one that can have interesting effects in the wider world. Take the Barings Bank collapse, for example, where one of the traders in the Far East became so highly valued for his view of likely market movements that other traders would regularly follow his position. Given sufficient belief in the perspective of one person, the collective trading behaviour of others shaped the predicted outcomes until, eventually, faith held no more.

Dealing with our own defence mechanisms

Another important influence over our actions are the defences that we build to protect ourself from psychological threat. These defences help us to feel secure, and allow us to maintain our self-image, values and belief systems. If every interaction we had caused fundamental questions to be asked of our views of self and the world, we would find life very difficult, as we would not have a secure platform from which to approach situations or encounters. We need to maintain stability in order to provide a basis for our interactions, otherwise each interaction would be made unpredictable by the lack of coherence in our perspective. So, while we allow our perspective to be altered by new information, we assimilate it carefully, without allowing it to fundamentally undermine our particular point of view. Part of the way in which we protect ourselves from information that may radically shake the foundations of our perspective is our defence mechanisms, which work to filter out, or explain away, information that does not match our expectations.

Learning activity

Taking criticism

Think about a situation in which you have been criticized. What feelings did this develop about the person doing the criticism? What actions did you take as a result?

The way in which people respond to criticism provides a good example of defence mechanisms at work. When a person is criticized, they often react with angry justification of their position or hasty excuses based on external factors. Sometimes they will turn defence into attack, choosing instead to be equally critical of some aspect of the other person's behaviour or character. All of these responses help to prevent the criticism from reaching us, and help us to maintain our current self-image, even when the information contained in the criticism is valid. At an extreme, we sometimes avoid situations or people altogether to prevent ourselves from being exposed to information that threatens our viewpoint or self. A person who avoids situations that cause them anxiety, such as public speaking for example, is using this defence.

Controlling these defences, so that they protect us without obstructing our access to new experiences and information, means that we have to come to terms with the ways in which our own defences operate. These are unique to each of us, and surface only through careful observation of the way we react in a variety of situations. Even then, trying to manage without defences, or allowing them to be questioned, does open up the possibility of personal risks. It may mean that the mental models that make up our perspective become undermined or even dismantled, threatening our security and raising questions about ourself. Opening up our defences gives us better access to different perspectives, but these may come with a price. The cost of exploration may be the loss of innocence and the birth of self-doubt. The rewards are in opening wide the doors of understanding and discovery.

Dealing with our culture

Our culture exerts influence on our actions at a variety of different levels. On one level, our national culture might be expressed through the symbols of the nation – the Royal Family, the British 'way of life' or the national football team, for example. These symbols infuse our lives to some degree or another, developing a sense of what it means to belong to a particular nationality or culture. Our sense of belonging to an identifiable culture is then part of what governs our observations – politicians regularly express a 'British point of view' on issues, even though such a collective view is largely symbolic. Yet the national culture influences our reactions and judgments in many ways – witness the entirely subjective viewpoints built up nationally in times of a threat to national fishing rights or to a collection of sheep farms in the South Atlantic. Our culture affects our perspective, damaging our ability to see events objectively and introducing bias into the way we interpret situations where our collective identity is involved.

On another level, culture exists in organizations, where informal and unwritten codes govern acceptable attitudes and behaviour. This can work to encourage both positive and negative perspectives on all aspects of organizational life, according to the dominant influences over culture. So an organization may develop a culture that supports creativity, including the flexible systems and belief in the unusual that encourages such behaviour. Another might display intolerance of ideas that threaten the established power base or hierarchy, no matter how valuable the potential contribution to organizational success. These cultural influences can be highly visible, like the dress codes to be seen in the City of London or in the upper reaches of the Civil Service, but they can also be subtle and difficult to identify.

Features of the culture in which we work can therefore have an impact on the perspective that we hold and the interpretations that we put on events. This can be damaging to our management actions through the reactions we have and judgments that we make. Coming to terms with our own personal defences is difficult enough, but confronting the influence that culture has on management actions is even more difficult, because it involves swimming against the tide of organizational unity and security. Nevertheless, if management actions are to reflect considered interpretations of events, the impact of culture on our actions must be considered, and every effort made to encourage people to challenge the validity of the influences to which they are exposed.

Four basic strategies for dealing with the effects

There are no magic formulas for dealing with these various influences on our perceptions. Our viewpoint is unavoidably the product of our past, and our past should not be forgotten. Our history helps to make up our essence, contributing to our qualities and our failings without discrimination or favour. As it is impossible to get rid of our history, which in any case would be unhelpful, we must instead work to develop a better understanding of how it affects our daily interventions. By building greater insight, we can manage our interventions more effectively, and take better account of the many influences that affect each situation that we observe. Four basic steps will help this process forward and these are developed below.

Cultural defences

A particularly important example here is the unspoken acceptance of what have been termed **organizational defence routines**, where people collude in order to protect themselves from embarrassment, insecurity or anxiety. One way in which individuals protect themselves from these is by avoiding the issue, but for this strategy to work in an organizational context requires the tacit agreement of others. People are only able to avoid facing up to problems or failings at work if others also avoid confronting the issue by hiding from the results or pretending that problems do not exist. Very often, dealing with difficult issues, such as highlighting the poor performance of others, causes anxiety to all concerned, particularly as the complexity of organizations usually means that everyone has had some role to play in the mishaps. Such circumstances can make it easier for everyone to simply pretend that the problem does not exist, or that nothing can be done about it anyway, rather than face the potential anxiety of trying to deal with the issues.

So, factors that might be developing poor performance in the organization, such as misguided decisions, failing to solve problems or mismanaged operations, would therefore be blamed on external factors or some scapegoat in order to prevent public discussion of the real reasons for error. Such routines are effective in providing an outlet for anxiety, yet widely (if privately) acknowledged by the participants as inadequate explanations of events. Operating defence routines ensures that real problems do not get addressed openly, and that issues affecting organizational success become increasingly undiscussable, perpetuating a cycle of failure and incompetence. As the cycle continues, people build up their skill in operating the defences, leading to increasingly subtle avoidance strategies that prevent issues from being discussed and resolved. At this stage, the organization has become skilled at maintaining poor performance, with widespread – and deeply ingrained – acceptance of inadequate 'reasons' for poor results. As a cultural influence, these routines can become extremely significant, as they support people in the organization by reducing levels of real anxiety, making them feel more comfortable and secure, but only through a strategy that avoids confronting the issues. This makes the defences widely acceptable to people, yet potentially very damaging for organizations in terms of achieving success. Exposing defence routines by being prepared to examine explanations and test them against people's real understanding and beliefs is an important component of improving management actions.

Do everything possible to check your understanding

There are many ways in which the manager can test their understanding of situations and events. Firstly, they can encourage other people to share their views, developing a process which opens up different perspectives and reactions to events. The dialogue developed helps people to learn alternative ways of interpreting situations, and has the beneficial side-effect of demonstrating how each person's contribution is valuable. This process is particularly useful in building up a view of your own reactions, in that other people are sometimes better placed to 'see' how your emotional responses are interfering with an objective view of situations.

Secondly, it is useful to look closely at background features of any situation or event in order to test the various influences that may be well hidden from view. These features may well provide the key to a full understanding yet are ordinarily the least likely areas to get our attention. Making deliberate efforts to check that we have assessed the contribution of peripheral influences helps managers to develop understanding. This is particularly useful when trying to understand the behaviour of others, as it counteracts our natural tendencies to look for the faults in people and attribute blame.

Be prepared to ask about everything

This highlights the value of developing an enquiring approach to managing, based on the view that simple solutions are fine for simple problems, but that management is rarely blessed with simple problems. The management problem is full of complex elements, from the dynamics of markets and competitor behaviour to the sophisticated nuances of relationships between people in teams. Cause and effect in such complex, interrelated systems are uncertain and unpredictable making it simplistic for managers to apply models or templates to help understand events. Instead, such complex systems have to be managed with due regard for their unique qualities, with managers making an effort to interpret all that they can get from the flow of emerging information. This depends on recognizing that it is only possible to possess all of the answers if we reduce organizations to simple systems, populated by unsophisticated 'workers' with little inherent variety. Challenging this view means that management must be based on developing a belief in the value of enquiry. Ask and be prepared to learn from the whole range of answers that you get. In its own way every answer, even the 'wrong' ones, will have lessons for us all.

Recognize the value of pausing to think

This involves managers taking the time to think through the stages of the ORJI cycle, making considered interventions rather than those based on automatic and unthinking responses. By deliberately slowing the process down, it is possible to examine the influences that are building towards action, and to assess the relevance or validity of each along the way. This might seem like a recipe for thoughtful inaction, but is actually an effort that drives towards actions that are understood and valid within the context in which they occur. The alternative, of actions based on emotive and ill-considered reactions to distorted observations, feeds a cycle of managerial error that people and organizations deserve to avoid.

Ensure that you focus on people

A great deal of the source of distortions in the ORJI cycle is in the way we interpret the personality and behaviours of other people. These distortions then feed through into the way in which we manage, leading us to interventions that have not taken full account of all the relevant information. Often the effects of this are relatively minor – we manage to implement a plan but cause offence to someone who would rather have been consulted – but the effect can accumulate into more intractable management problems. Handling a minor change badly, for example, makes people less prepared to approach a more major change positively, and may develop a considerable attitude of resistance in an organization.

As people are at the root of many of our misunderstandings, it is essential to develop an approach that focuses on relationships of real quality. By continually striving to improve our understanding of other people, we can begin to learn how our views and reactions affect our management judgments and impact on the relationships we build at work. It is a process that provides a foundation for all of our management actions, and brings opportunities for self-understanding and personal growth that stretch far beyond the goals of improving our management interventions. There are no issues of management that cannot benefit from a better understanding of ourselves or the views that we adopt of situations and other people. Building this understanding is the key to management. It is the same key that unlocks our potential as a person.

Going forward

The world of management is a complex place, full of people that bring a unique and ever-changing perspective to work. The perspectives of people shape the nature of their interactions and drive forward a cycle of outcomes in the results of their labours. These interactions are not easily described or understood, yet they take organizations forward into the future, sometimes with hope and sometimes with despair. We can try to interpret human interactions using simple assumptions and generalizations, but this hides from our view the diversity that is at the heart of people. Reducing management to simple models that aid our understanding brings a certain security to our view, but it also brings strict boundaries to the potential of ourselves and others. Organizations are like oceans, sometimes appearing calm and serene, yet at times a torment of turbulent and crashing chaos. Beneath the surface there are hidden depths and dangerous currents, a world apart from life on the waves. Like oceans, organizations will never be understood by sailing on the surface alone, but only by those who are prepared to travel into the deeps. Within there are wonders and beauty, for what we find will be shaped by the strength of our hope and our imagination. Look forward to the future of management, for it is made by you.

Tsoukas, H. (ed.) (1994) New Thinking in Organisational Behaviour, Butterworth-Heinemann, Oxford.

Management is inescapably shaped by the ideas, meanings and interpretations that human beings have of themselves and of their surroundings.

Haridimos Tsoukas

Summary

This chapter has made the following key points:

➤ That all interventions are based on a particular perspective that we develop through our lives. This perspective is unique to ourselves, and ensures that everything we do is based on an interpretation of events. Understanding how this can be distorted and biased by our observations and reactions is essential to a real understanding of the process of management.

➤ That our view of other people is particularly open to error, making our management interaction with others prone to misunderstanding and misinterpretation.

➤ That challenging our perspective is the basis of developing a learning approach to management that enables us to base interventions on better foundations.

➤ That confronting our own defences and those that develop in the organization requires a commitment to openness and therefore involve personal risk. These risks are balanced by the potential opportunities for interest, excitement and personal growth inherent in the process of exploration.

Further reading

An interesting look at the nature of individual perspectives can be found in A. Schutz and T. Luckmann *Structures of the Lifeworld* (Heinemann, 1974). This examines how we each construct a personal perspective, based on our life experience, that helps us to interpret the events around us. However, we have a tendency to assume that other people have built the same perspective, or lifeworld, making us resistant to experiences that fall outside of our existing learning. Experiences or insights that challenge our lifeworld are a threat to the way in which we view the world, and are therefore in the category of high risk learning. Other writers (see C. Argyris (1970) *Intervention Theory and Method*, Addison-Wesley, and P. Senge (1990) *The Fifth Discipline*, Century Business) have looked at the limits to learning imposed by defence mechanisms, with Argyris identifying the need to engage in double loop learning while Senge uses the term 'metanoia' to describe the 'shift of mind' necessary to accomplish true learning.

Senge, P. (1990)
The Fifth Discipline,
Century Business,
London.

Real learning gets to the heart of what it means to be human. Through learning we re-create ourselves.

Peter Senge

References

Argyle, M. (1982) *The Psychology of Interpersonal Behaviour*, Penguin.
Argyle, M. (1983) *The Social Psychology of Work*, Pelican.

Argyris, C. (1990) *Overcoming Organizational Defences: Facilitating Organizational Learning*, Boston: Allyn & Bacon, Prentice Hall.

Schein, E.H. (1987) *Process Consultation*, Vol. 2, Addison-Wesley.

Stacey, D. (1993) *Strategic Management and Organizational Dynamics*, Pitman, London.

3

Building a platform for effective relationships

> *The best fortress that exists is to avoid being hated by the people.*
> **Niccolo Machiavelli,** The Prince

Objectives

By the end of this chapter you will be able to:

➤ Explain how effective relationships can contribute to achieving organizational success
➤ Describe the major factors contributing to effective relationships
➤ Use a range of strategies to develop personal power and influence
➤ Use techniques to help strengthen and maintain interpersonal links

Introduction

Managing involves making and sustaining all sorts of relationships. While there are management tasks that can be done by the individual in isolation, the effect of management activity nearly always involves other people. Indeed, in pursuing organizational objectives, the manager is actively trying to achieve results using whatever resources they have, including people that make up the workforce. It is also necessary to build relationships outside the organization, with a variety of partners forming essential links in the chain of organizational activity. In addition, organizations have a place in our wider societies, and may seek to develop relationships with outside agencies in order to help to achieve goals. This may involve building relationships with funding agencies, political parties, trade unions, employers' associations and other lobby groups. The common thread here is that management involves the coordinated effort of people across a whole range of activities, and is therefore based fundamentally upon the relationships that managers make. The object of this section is to look at ways in which managers can improve their ability to develop effective working relationships.

The basis of influence

Management actions are not always based on clear decisions and rational arguments. In a simple world, actions would always be based on a rational assessment of the quality of alternative ideas. However, making such a rational assessment assumes that all the chains of cause and effect are known, and that it is possible to predict all potential outcomes of a particular action. The world of management, even in the most basic interaction, is much more complex than this, with a web of interrelationships and causal linkages that make it impossible to know in detail what the end results of actions will be.

A common example of this is the changes that organizations often introduce as part of a process of rationalization. These can be carefully researched plans, with a wide number of efficiency gains, improvements to the structure of the organization and the work that people do. Nevertheless, they can still develop a whole range of unpredictable responses as people absorb the impact of change on their existing roles, relationships and vested interests. On occasion, the resistance that builds up and the emerging debate can radically alter the shape of change, giving an entirely different emphasis from the original plans. The complexity of management means that rational analysis can only contribute to actions; it is necessary, but not sufficient as a basis for action alone.

Instead, action is often the result of a process of considering alternatives, none of which are clearly better or worse than others. Reaching agreement in such situations is not only linked to the quality of the ideas or proposals that people have, but is also dependent on the influence of people taking part in the discussion. A proposal that is presented by a person who has widespread acceptance amongst colleagues, is likely to 'win' over that presented by a person without such personal support, whatever the relative technical quality of their ideas. This is not as irrational as it may seem, as the complex nature of the management environment makes it impossible to know which is the 'best' idea in any case. As putting an idea into action may involve gaining the commitment of many stakeholders, proposals that are supported by 'acceptability', however irrationally founded, may paradoxically have more chance of success than better ideas from elsewhere. Choosing actions that are based on a blend of technical quality and the proposer's ability to exert influence may be more rational than it seems.

Developing the ability to influence others is the engine of management progress. All the good ideas under the sun will not mean a thing unless a manager also has the influence to get those ideas onto the agenda and discussed. Securing budgets to move an idea along, or assembling the key personnel for a project, will not happen unless a manager is able to influence debate and win arguments. Similarly, gaining the commitment of a team or building openness into a work culture depends on more than just rational ideas. Reasoned points are not enough in a world that is full of people; instead managers need to build acceptability into their position through their ability to exercise influence over others. This ability is fundamentally based on the quality of the relationships and networks that they develop, nurture and maintain. Achieving managerial objectives depends not just upon the merit of ideas, but also on developing the personal qualities that support the use of influence.

Learning activity

Thinking about influence

Think about people who seem to be influential in your own networks, either working or social. On what factors is their influence based?

Think of using influential contacts to push ideas onto the agenda at the expense of others. Why might this seem objectionable to other people?

The idea of using influence, and developing the qualities that make it work, can seem uncomfortable to some people. It can conjure up images of manipulating the political strings of organizations in order to pursue their self-serving goals against a background of political manoeuvring, intrigue and deceit. Part of the problem lies in our perspective on organizational politics, which can view all attempts to develop influence as a sordid game of clambering up the ladder of personal success. This view is easily sustained in some organizations, where there is a cultural acceptance of the belief that people are motivated by self-interest. If such a perspective is held, then it leads to people **appearing** to behave in a self-interested way, whatever their real motivation. Eventually, the culture of the organization will grow to reflect expectations, and people will be forced to act in a self-interested way, merely to survive in a climate of political in-fighting and power struggles.

While such a negative use of influence, designed only to achieve narrow rewards, probably happens, it may not be as common as we think. Exercising influence in order to achieve organizational objectives necessarily involves building relationships and behaving in ways that takes account of the political aspects of the situation, such as seeking the support of key players for a particular plan. Viewed by other people, who may have seen their own ideas put to one side as a result, such behaviour is bound to be regarded negatively, and described in terms of self-interest and personal gain. The trick is in developing acceptance of the role of influence, and recognizing that it is an unavoidable component of human processes. As such, it is a skill to be cultivated and used openly, rather than consigned to the closet of political skullduggery where it may do much damage.

The use of influence is interwoven with personal power, as it is strategy that helps us to achieve our goals in an organizational setting. If we do not have the ability to persuade other people to give their support, then we are forced to rely on other sources of power to achieve objectives. These might include authority, force or threats, all of which have significant dangers – not least that people will be less restrained in using such powers in return! If managers are to have the personal power to manage effectively, it is best to rely on sources of power that do not involve demeaning other people along the way. People that have been pushed into a particular position rarely give it their honest commitment or work to their full potential. Instead, such use of power breeds petty rivalries and leads inevitably towards rule-bound organizational structures. Powerlessness in organizations, at whatever level, can lead to frustration and demoralization, as good ideas fail through an inability to energize people and obtain resources to meet goals. Exerting influence involves using personal power in a way that develops the commitment and consent of others, minimizing potential barriers to the process along the way. The basis of this influence is in developing key personal qualities that support our relationships with other people and enable our ideas to be accepted. The next section looks at how these can be developed and used in working situations.

Developing personal acceptability

The first important quality that contributes to influence is our personal acceptability. If we are liked and able to establish relationships based on friendship, then other people will be more open to our ideas and influence. This is not to say that it is essential for all work relationships to be built on deep friendships, but that the attributes that lead people to like us are useful in helping us to manage. Developing intense friendship may not be appropriate in a work setting, but the characteristics that attract people to us as friends will help us to exercise influence in a wide range of situations. Encouraging people to develop a liking that would, given time or different circumstances, result in friendship is therefore an aid to the process of management.

Certainly, professional constraints need to be borne in mind – friends might spend most of their time chatting about shared interests rather than on work –

but relationships based on mutual liking do oil the wheels of organizational influence. Understanding what factors lead others to develop liking is therefore a key component of management, as it is a source of influence that allows us to build bridges between people rather than encourage the erection of defensive walls.

Learning activity

Exploring likes and dislikes

Think about people at work or in social situations. What basic factors make you more inclined to:

- like them?
- dislike them?

What things could you do that would make people feel more positively about you?

The basis of liking

There is a considerable volume of evidence that links liking with influence. People who are liked are seen as trustworthy and impartial, which helps build basic acceptance of ideas. Further, the psychological effects discussed in Chapter 2 tend to mean that when we like someone, we also will attribute a range of additional qualities to them (principle of closure), project our own values and viewpoints onto them (principle of similarity) and also maintain a positive view over time, despite evidence to the contrary (principle of primacy). All of these make it particularly important to make liking the foundation of our work relationships, as initial liking will smooth the path of management through many potential difficulties. Liking is the foundation of a great deal of managerial influence, and it is important to develop awareness of the factors that build towards feelings of basic liking.

Appearance

The first factor leading to liking is physical appearance, with an attractive appearance being closely associated with positive acceptance by others. This may seem a difficult factor to adapt, as to some extent we are saddled with what we have got in terms of our appearance, but there are important qualifications that make this factor open to more active management than might initially appear.

A key qualification is that while our basic looks are the main elements of our attractiveness, the second most important component of appearance is the way that we dress. This is something that we can make considerable efforts to manage, by adapting our dress to improve our personal acceptability. It is worth recognizing that this is not simply a matter of changing our basic appearance to suit some fixed ideal of attractiveness, but being prepared to think carefully about what would generate acceptability in the situations that we are in. For example, it is common for people to be advised to dress smartly for interviews, and this often leads people to dress in suits, following a fixed stereotype of 'smartness'. However, it is more important to be dressed appropriately by the standards of the people offering the post, and in a creative advertising agency this might well be far more casual and relaxed than in banking, for example. If we take the time to match the way that we dress to the role that we are expected to play, then we will find that it helps our acceptability in the situation. A good example of this is in Japanese manufacturing plants, where it is common to find that managers wear overalls rather than suits. This helps to build a sense of team identity, rather than making differences in status visually apparent, and also improves the personal acceptability of managers to the people making up work teams. There is no formula that can be adopted here, as appropriate dress is subject to differing interpretations and context. The point is that our dress is something that we can manage quite actively, subject to financial constraints, and that matching dress to the role we play and the expectations of those around us will help to develop increased acceptability and liking. By building aware-ness of our own appearance in various situations, we are able to manage this particular aspect of liking more effectively.

A second qualification is that while there are media ideals of male and female attractiveness in society, there is also considerable tolerance in our personal definitions of attractiveness. Fashion is an example of how definitions of what constitutes attractiveness shift and change according to the current vogue. Similarly, many of us would not put 'gothic' or 'punk' appearance high on our list of desirable characteristics, yet it plainly forms an acceptable definition of attractiveness to some sections of youth society. Another example is how some of the examples of previous fashions – the multi-coloured platform shoes and outrageously wide trousers of the 1970s for example – become dress that we wouldn't be seen dead in by the 1990s. Our definitions of attractiveness show a tolerance for a wide range of different appearances, making it easier to find a niche into which our own appearance can comfortably fit, without having to stretch too far towards the realms of the supermodel to find an image that is acceptable in gaining influence. Adapting our appearance is more manageable than it might appear, and paying attention to maintaining our standards is effective in providing a basic source of liking that will help underpin our personal acceptability.

A third qualification is that these aspects of 'superficial' appearance are most relevant to the early stages of relationship. While appearance continues to have implications, a mature relationship generally moves towards a broader accept-ance of individual qualities, based on a more complete understanding. So, while it can be important to manage appearance early in relationships, we can expect people who know us well to allow us some leeway in our basic dress and appearance as time goes by. Similar effects apply to our use of language, where our initial caution and attention to social norms becomes relaxed in close company, allowing us to experiment with a wider range of expressive language as familiarity grows.

The first impression

The second factor that develops basic liking is the first impression that people make upon meeting. The principle of primacy ensures that the early observations made in any relationship tend to weigh heavily in the overall impression that people form of each other. This effect is quite persistent, and will lead people to ignore or play down observations that later show that the initial impression was wrong. Undoubtedly, first impressions are a potentially misleading source of information – after all, initial encounters can be full of apprehension and anxiety caused by the circumstances and people's preconceptions about the agenda. Managers need to challenge themselves whenever they are relying on a hastily formed first impression of another person, as they are missing many possibilities and pitfalls that lie hidden in the situation. Paradoxically, however, managers also need to work hard at giving a positive impression, or they will be saddling themselves with a persistent and damaging handicap at work if they do not. This is a situation where it is important to build the best possible start to a relationship, developing firm foundations of liking, by ensuring that everything possible is done to manage the first impression. That said, it is crucial that we also recognize the limitations of such an impression, and use the good start to go on to build better foundations for a relationship by developing our understanding of people through shared interaction and meaningful dialogue.

While the initial contact we have is vital to our liking for others, there is a similar factor at work on a daily basis. In our greetings and initial exchanges of pleasantries, it appears that we go through a similar, though less aware, process of forming an impression. This is guided by the views that we have already formed in our relationship with the other person, but nevertheless does have an impact on our future impression. It is as if our initial contact each day is used to reaffirm our views about others, to check that they fit our continued expectations about them. In a small way, each day can be regarded as a fresh start to any relationship, bringing a daily opportunity to make a new impression on others.

The effect of our initial contact with other people is probably something that we have all observed. Most people will have experienced days when, for some reason, other people have been sensitive to changes in behaviour. Typically, when we are preoccupied with an issue from our home lives and perhaps less attentive to our colleagues than usual, people will soon ask questions about what might be troubling us. Similarly, arriving at work full of the joys of spring has an impact on others, and soon leads people to remark on the change and speculate on the causes. People do form an impression of our daily mood based on the initial contact that they have with us, and this is something that can be actively managed to improve the quality of our work relationships.

 ## Learning activity

Openings

Think back to your arrival at work or college today. Describe your first moments with the first three people that you came across. How could you improve the initial impact of these encounters?

Think of someone that you find 'difficult' in some way. How could you change your first contact with them each day to improve the relationship?

If we spend some time observing our own initial interactions with others, at work and at home, we are likely to find that we have autopilot techniques to get us through these moments. By exchanging a few words about the weather or the traffic on the motorway we can get through the exchanges without a great deal of effort, conscious thought or risk. Of course, adopting such patterns soon means that these exchanges become meaningless in terms of genuine interaction, neither adding to or subtracting from the existing relationship. By making neutral statements and engaging in trivial patterns, we maintain the relationship in its current pattern. However, as the first impression has the potential to build a platform for our daily relationships, it is worth investing a little time and effort into creating a positive foundation. By focusing on a few key points in our initial interaction, we can take steps towards generating a positive work climate for our work relationships and develop a basis for liking that will support our attempts to exert influence.

The implication here is that it is worth preparing more carefully for the initial interaction that you have with people each day, based on the assumption that this will help establish a positive framework for relationships. The idea is attractive in that it requires no special skills, and the necessary preparation can be an ideal way to while away the journey to work. It is based upon challenging your existing comfortable patterns and trying to establish a more interesting and valuable interaction. The key points to the process are:

- Ensure eye contact
- Smile
- Recognize and reward people by always using their name
- Maintain open body language
- Make your opening words valuable, not trivial
- Show interest by listening carefully to other people – talk in terms of their interest

These points are generally easy to put into practice, although it may be somewhat removed from normal routine. Perhaps the biggest step to take is in changing the nature of conversation, moving away from trivia towards exchanges of value. This is not to imply that our greetings should be replaced by earnest discussion of the meaning of life, but that what we say should be focused more precisely on the person to whom we are talking. It is not enough to make a general enquiry – 'how are you today?' – that could apply to anyone, but instead we should aim to make our conversation person-specific and linked to shared interests. Take the time to ask after their children, using their names and showing an interest in their progress at school. Rather than ask whether someone 'enjoyed' their holiday, ask about the experiences that made it up. Similarly, try to avoid the standard lines that we all adopt; 'did you have a good weekend?' must be the first words of thousands on a Monday morning!

Case note

Changing patterns

A specialist personnel unit is staffed by a small, very committed team of people headed by a charismatic, hard-working leader. She is dedicated to the field and focused on pushing the agency agenda, and as a result often appears preoccupied with the tasks of work. In the past, this has led some other staff to feel that she is not interested in anything other than work, making it difficult for them to maintain the human side of the relationship.

Small changes can go a long way. Recently, the leader has softened and takes time to share other interests, breaking the preoccupation with work and engaging in less purposeful conversations. A lighter atmosphere has come along, and with it has come more sharing of concerns and the workload. Projects now benefit from people's willingness to get involved and recognize that problems with work are easier to share when people share part of themselves.

Adopting this approach is simple and has little risk. By choosing to demonstrate a more considered interest in other people, making our initial interaction more meaningful, we demonstrate how much we value others. As a technique it is remarkably powerful, being very easy to apply and to observe the effects. Concentrating on creating a positive impression each time we meet people can have the effect of dissolving barriers between people, helping work relationships to become cooperative and constructive. It requires little effort, yet opens up channels between people that are built upon meaning and value rather than necessity and politeness.

Remembering names

Using people's names is an important part of the process that can be difficult early on in relationships, or when getting to know larger groups of people. However, using names has a double benefit – firstly, people feel recognized and rewarded that you have taken the trouble to make a personal connection with them, and secondly, it is unusual enough for people to do this that it actually gets noticed and remarked upon. Using names brings you rewards and extends your personal acceptability. This is an important enough skill to consider what steps will actively help to improve our name learning ability. The techniques below will help overcome embarrassing forgetfulness, and enable you to cope in situations where you are meeting a number of people at once. Learning a lot of names can seem insurmountable, but several tips can make the task seem easier.

- **Take time**. This is something that cannot be rushed. Time spent learning names will probably be time saved later, and taking time demonstrates your commitment to beginning an effective relationship. It helps people feel valued.
- **Place your initial focus on learning the names, not just on the object of**

the meeting. Trying to absorb too many of the other aspects of the person or situation distracts from the purpose of learning names, and that provides real barriers to achieving objectives. If you learn names well, it will smooth the progress of the relationship and end up being a sound investment of effort. Give it your full attention.

- **Use the name immediately in a few words of conversation**. Getting over the hurdle of using the name once takes some of the anxiety out of the situation. Remember to make the conversation valuable by encouraging the person to talk about their interests. This helps you to remember them and makes them feel valued.
- **Use the name again on closing the conversation** and moving on.
- **Try to notice a particular feature of each person** as you finish to associate with the name – 'Bill is very tall' or 'Jane seems very knowledgeable'.
- **Make a mental return to each person several times** in the next few minutes – it does only take a second – to reinforce your memory. Concentrate your effort on the people who have made least impact on you as these are the ones that you will find hardest to remember.

These techniques offer a reliable way of picking up names. Failing to learn names is an expression of your lack of interest and effort or your preoccupation with other, more important issues. Show people how much you value them by doing this simple thing well.

Similarity

A third factor that leads to liking is the similarity between people, supporting the popular view that 'birds of a feather flock together'. This factor is based on the positive regard we hold for people who are similar to ourselves, and has been discussed more fully in Chapter 2. Building relationships on the basis of similarity has dangers, in that it can lead the manager to be more accepting of ideas that come from people with similar qualities to themselves, eventually providing a predictable, dull, yet easy to manage workplace. In many respects, dissimilarity provides a foundation for tension and challenge, but it is also a source of innovation and excitement. The paradox for the manager is that similarity is undoubtedly a basis for liking, making it important that a manager is able to reflect the qualities of others if they are to build a platform for liking and influence.

Learning activity

Your similar side

Think about some of the people that you work with on a daily basis. Try to identify similarities that you observe between yourself and them.

How can you use these similarities to build influence?

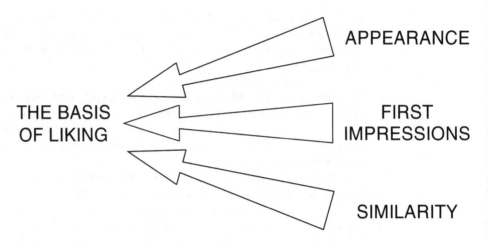

Fig. 3.1 Factors in the basis of liking.

Showing similarity might not seem very easy to do, especially when the need to exert influence is based on clear differences of opinion! However, one of the benefits of working with people is that their complexity means that there is always some facet of their personality, values or interests which has similarities with our own. Once these similarities have been identified, it is possible for the manager to highlight these and reinforce the common ground on which a relationship can be established. Showing similarity therefore depends on taking time to observe and learn about the qualities of other people, in order to understand where these qualities overlap with and reflect our own. Adopting this approach forms a useful two-pronged approach to relationships, building a fuller understanding of other people while at the same time helping us to share and acknowledge our similarities. Together these help to demonstrate the value which we place on other people and the effort to which we will go to help put the relationship onto effective terms. This process helps to establish empathy and works to develop our personal acceptability to others, building solid foundations for liking to grow and influence become established.

In combination, the three factors above provide the basis of liking, as shown in Figure 3.1. Of course, there will always be some people who we like for very different reasons, particularly once we have established a relationship and begun to find out more about their personality, interests and values. However, as a platform for work relationships, the factors identified help to develop a basic liking that provides the foundations of personal acceptability. Without liking, it is difficult to develop the positive means of exerting influence that are at the heart of effective management. While all of these factors may initially seem to be inborn features of our personality, they can be managed to maximize our personal acceptability and effectiveness. By taking responsibility for actively trying to develop relationships based on mutual liking, managers help to create a framework for work that is positive and engaging, valuing people as individuals rather than for what they can contribute to the organization. Much of the discussion has highlighted the importance of building relationships as a demonstration of how we value other people. This, in itself, by showing liking and the wish to be liked, provides reward in relationships and provides the basis of success with people. It is a powerful source of influence, without which managers become increasingly dependent on other sources of personal power and influence. The next section explores some of these in more detail, and tries to assess how these can be developed.

Sources of personal power and influence

Expertise and competence

Another source of personal power that is linked to our own characteristics is our level of expertise or competence in performing our role. This source of power and influence becomes more relevant and acceptable in an environment that is technologically dependent. As the level of reliance on technology rises and the systems in place become increasingly sophisticated, expertise in a particular role becomes more critical for the organization. Developed expertise is then an essential component of the organization's strategy in pursuing its objectives, and people with particular competences can become almost indispensable as a result. In this way, the expert knowledge that a person holds, or the particular skills that they bring to a critical situation, can become a source of power and of influence. Other people have to recognize perspectives based on expertise, and this opens up the possibility of exerting influence.

Personal power and influence based on expertise or competence can be a useful thing for a manager to develop. One reason for this is that competence, skill and expertise are all regarded as positive attributes by others, and this helps to increase personal acceptability and liking. The complex nature of activity in most organizations means that it is usually possible for people to find some small niche in which they can develop their particular skills or specialism, opening up opportunities to build some basis for power. The danger is that specialization can be pursued too far, leaving the person with a narrow expertise that does not readily transfer elsewhere in the organization. Worse still, expertise and skills can become redundant if there is a change in technology or structure within the organization, leaving highly specialized staff both vulnerable and without any effective source of personal power. So, while developing some particular skill is a useful strategy for building a basis for influence, the manager needs to be aware that acquiring broad-based knowledge and expertise are also important.

 ### Learning activity

Using expertise

Expertise can be a productive source of personal power when it is used effectively. Think about people you work with who have particular knowledge and skills. How do they use these to build influence? Are there any problems with using expertise as a basis for personal power?

The way in which expertise is used is also important in terms of creating influence. A person who uses expertise destructively, by withholding essential information or using knowledge to undermine others, may find that people respond by building their own niche of expertise, or simply going elsewhere to find what they need. This can breed an atmosphere of empire building, where people invest their energies in creating impregnable fortresses of expert knowledge upon which the organization depends, but which is released only reluctantly into the common pool of knowledge. The way in which skills, competence and expertise are made available to others is critical to organizational success and to its acceptability as a source of personal power and influence. Only those managers that can use their special expertise constructively, freely giving it to the common good without overtly manipulative goals, will find that it provides a useful basis for influence. Managers that share their expertise widely, enabling others to take on their role, will paradoxically find that this gives access to more influence than the original expertise.

Cited in Maccoby, M. (1976) *The Gamesman.*

Case note

Brian Wheatins

Wheatins was a manager who decided to offer formal classes to his staff on how to do his job. These took place after work and most people attended. They soon built the skills to take on more of the manager's work, and developed understanding of the pressures and constraints under which the manager worked. Staff were grateful for the gain in skills and valued the commitment being shown to their development. Learning projects were self-selected, leading to higher levels of enthusiasm and motivation. Departmental productivity rose and the manager became free to accept more challenging projects, so the organization began to direct new initiatives towards this vibrant and dynamic team. The team became recognized for its breadth of skill, commitment, cooperation and energy. The manager became recognized for innovation and moved quickly upwards to a position of greater influence. Sharing expertise became a source of influence for all in the team.

Effort

The amount of effort that a manager puts into their work provides another source of personal power that is linked closely to personal characteristics. By making a lot of effort with work, there are several basic effects that build towards increased potential to exert influence. Firstly, extra effort leads to increased knowledge on whatever topic or project the manager is working on. This gain in knowledge provides a source of expertise, meaning that other people will seek to access the manager's opinions on issues related to the work. Secondly, the more senior person who has commissioned or delegated the work will have seen a positive response, supporting them in achieving their objectives and justifying their trust in the manager. If this is openly recognized by the senior staff, then this will also implicitly confer expertise on the manager. Again, this leads to increased opportunities for influence. Thirdly, managers who work harder than the organizational norm, putting in longer hours on projects, are usually seen as dedicated, committed individuals. Effort over and above that required is seen by others as something that should be rewarded rather than rejected. While other people may be seen less favourably by comparison, they will find it hard to acknowledge their own performance as less than good – accordingly, it is more comfortable to view the extra effort as extraordinary. The alternative, of persuading a colleague to work less hard, is not easily acceptable because it carries its own implicit admission of failure.

It is worth recognizing the ultimate futility of pursuing an 'effort' approach to influence. Making an effort soon becomes a cultural norm, as evidenced by surveys showing the rising average number of hours being worked by British managers. Once people start to conform to the expected norms, effort becomes less and less valuable as a source of influence.

Support for organizational values

Engaging in actions and espousing views that uphold organizational values can provide a further source of personal power that can help support influence. This is because conforming to such values enhances the collective sense of security that is felt throughout the organization by reinforcing the perspectives that have been built up through the organization's history. In contrast, challenging the organizational values can develop uncertainty as long-held beliefs are undermined. This leads to widespread feelings of anxiety and as a result people making such challenges are commonly given little support. Obtaining acceptance and exercising influence often means 'toeing the party line', rather than making proposals that upset existing values.

There is a notable danger that in the search for influence within the organization, people will recognize the personal gains to be had if they provide support for existing values and beliefs. In doing so, the individuals ensure that they maximize their own ability to exert influence. Paradoxically, however, by failing to challenge the accepted perspective, the actions and ideas that they pursue will maintain the existing direction of the organization rather than provide new inspiration or opportunities for adaptation. In building influence, managers commonly find that challenging the values of the organization is counterproductive. As a direct result, the influence that they exert can end up creating stagnation. An awkward tension exists whereby managers have to reflect existing values in order to develop effective influence, but then use the acceptability gained to focus their efforts on creating new values that challenge the existing perspectives.

This is another example of the way in which organizational defence routines can develop, providing a very real barrier to organizational impetus. Uncertainty does create real levels of anxiety in people, and one of the ways of dealing with this is to find elements in the situation that are certain and dependable. An obvious source of certainty is the existing organizational values, and the perspectives that they uphold. The process of building certainty is further supported by group dynamics, which ensure that when faced with a situation that develops anxiety, one of the classical responses is to seek unity. In an uncertain situation, one of the only certain things to unify behind is the existing position, and this reinforces the defensive behaviour.

Boulding, (1964) 'Further reflections on conflict management' in R.L. Kahn and E. Boulding (eds), *Power and conflict in organizations*, New York, Basic Books.

An interesting example of this defence routine in action comes from a study by Boulding. Groups were given the task of generating solutions to a range of problems. In some of the groups, one member was briefed to play the role of 'devil's advocate', challenging the group processes and assumptions in an effort to encourage a more considered approach to the problems. At the end of the problem-solving tests, the groups that contained a 'devil's advocate' had generated both higher quality and a wider range of solutions. The groups were then asked to reduce their membership by one for a further series of tests. In every case where the group had a person playing a challenging role, they were the person who was rejected – a clear example of how group behaviour organizes in a way that reduces the level of uncertainty and anxiety, even when it proves to be a disadvantage.

Working in ways that reflect organizational values is therefore important to the overall acceptability of a person and their ideas. If a person is to build this source of power, they need to recognize that failing to conform to existing perspectives will encourage resistance to influence. As a result, the rising levels of anxiety that uncertainty creates have to be carefully managed as part of the process of making proposals or introducing new thinking. How effectively this can be managed is partly dependent on a further factor affecting personal power – the position that an individual has in the organization.

Learning activity

Reflecting values

Think about your own work groups. How do people reaffirm organizational values through their interactions? What is the reaction when people express views outside of the mainstream of organizational thought?

Position in the organization

In addition to the sources of personal power and influence that are linked closely to personal characteristics, including effort, conformity and expertise, an important source is also found in the position that the individual occupies in the organization. To some extent it is obvious that influence is hard to exert from the far-flung reaches of the organizational empire, however much local expertise is developed. In order to contribute effectively to personal power, there are five key aspects of the position that need to be considered. Each of these are briefly discussed below.

- Firstly, if we think of the organization as having a hub through which information and decision-making flows, then any position at the centre of organizational activity will enhance personal power. Such a position is not necessarily determined by job title, but can be developed through building an informal network of relationships throughout the organization. A network allows access to information and skills that may be difficult to obtain through any other means, and provides a short-cut means of moving things along, far removed from the ponderous processes of official channels.

- Secondly, personal power will be affected by the importance of a position to organizational processes and objectives. This is most easily exampled through expertise, where a uniquely qualified expert to a key organizational objective has a critical role and considerable associated power. However, any person can increase the critical nature of their position by involving themselves in a wider range of work, and by taking on tasks that need specialist skills. Similarly, because influence ultimately depends on a political process of discussion, developing an informal network that connects to the 'right' people can lead to a manager becoming 'critical' to new initiatives or projects. Here, the power depends not upon critical technical skill, but on critical political or personal expertise allied to the strength of the network.

- Thirdly, personal power is more easily built in any position where there is a higher degree of freedom and need to use judgments. The act of using discretion to make management judgments demonstrates initiative and the ability to handle situations that are out of the ordinary. In a more restricted work environment, surrounded by procedure and rules, it is difficult to do anything other than follow established patterns, and this rarely attracts attention or power. An important point is that new projects and initiatives tend to be situations with more flexibility and freedom, simply because patterns are not evident at the outset of a new process or task. By their nature, these are the very situations that encourage a flexible approach, with considerable freedom of manoeuvre for managers to display initiative and ideas, as well as move beyond the bounds of their basic role.

- Fourthly, if position, task or process becomes more visible in the organization, then it will develop increasing personal power. Good deeds that are performed quietly in the background will sink anonymously without trace, or even be claimed by someone with more visibility and political insight. Building influence means being noticed, and this is largely developed through direct contact with people that move the organization along. It is important to be a face that people know and associate with particular events, not just a name on the payroll.

- Lastly, when management actions are directly linked to organizational objectives and processes, power will be greater as a result. If the position a manager occupies is immediately relevant to the current preoccupations of the organization, then the increased relevance of their role becomes a source of personal power. As organizational concerns shift according to internal and external factors, a manager needs to be aware of the changing climate and focus. Moving with the tide of organizational opinion helps a manager to maintain and develop personal power.

Learning activity

Your own position

Think about the position you hold in your own organization or college. What aspects of the position develop influence?

The various factors that develop personal acceptability and the sources of personal power do not of themselves guarantee influence. Instead, these go together to build a **potential** for influence, without which it would be hard to gain support however hard the individual tried. Whether that potential is translated into actual influential behaviour depends on the style that the individual chooses to adopt in particular situations. The following section considers the various styles of influence available and how these can be applied to best effect.

Putting influence into practice

People can try to achieve influence in a variety of ways, according to their personal style, the particular context within which they work and the behaviours of other staff. In many respects there are as many ways of achieving influence as there are managers. However, all of these can be categorized into three basic strategies. The first strategy is based on **reasoning**, where the manager is trying to achieve influence through discussion and appeal to the basic facts of the matter. The second strategy is based on **reciprocity**, where the manager tries to achieve influence by making some form of trade with other people in the situation. The third strategy is based on **retribution**, where the manager attempts to exert influence by making threats or pressurizing other people in order to gain compliance. These categories are known as the **3 Rs of influence** (see Figure 3.2) and can be observed taking place in many human interactions, from children at play to politicians at work. Each category is considered in turn below, exploring how each influencing strategy works in practice and its particular drawbacks. Attention is also given to the impact of each strategy on the manager's style and the consequent effects on staff.

Reasoning

Exerting influence through reasoning involves two basic patterns. The first pattern is that influence can be achieved by the logical statement of facts and

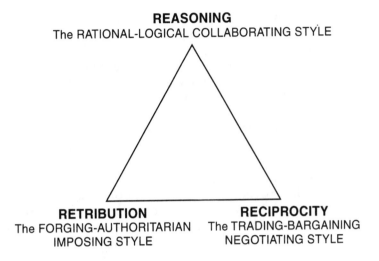

Fig. 3.2 The 3 Rs of influence – various positions or blends can be used by any particular individual according to circumstances or personality.

reasoned debate about alternatives. This allows anyone involved in the situation to share information and expertise before making any decision. As it is based on direct statements of evidence, influence through this pattern enables others to contribute to their maximum ability, as there is open sharing of relevant detail. As a result, this simple sharing of facts, expertise and open persuasion is empowering, allowing others to share in some of the elements that build power, particularly knowledge. This approach is particularly appropriate when the manager is sure of the facts in the case, and where there is time available to bring other people up to speed on details. It is also relevant where the commitment of others to an initiative is important, as it allows for decisions to be agreed rather than imposed. As an approach, it encourages an open style of management, with information and expertise becoming the common property of all. As it is based essentially on factual information, using this pattern alone does not allow the manager much scope to exert influence based on their personal acceptability, though it will have some effect on other people's willingness to accept the facts.

Learning activity

Reasoning without the facts

How can a reasoning approach to influence be used when the issues are related to values, beliefs or perspectives, rather than facts?

The second pattern is a less direct variation of reasoning, where the facts of the case are no longer clear or sufficient to convince others of a particular argument.

In organizations, the complexity of cause and effect and the unpredictable influences of a wide range of factors make many issues indeterminate. Presenting the facts may not be enough to exert influence, as the case rests on interpretations of those facts and judgments about the effects of any particular course of action. In these circumstances, reasoning has to be based on more than just presenting facts and logical analysis. Instead, influence has to make some appeal to basic values by persuading people that a particular course of action supports common goals and ideals. For example, in an organization where existing values supported financial efficiency above all else, a manager would base arguments for moving to a flat organizational structure around the potential cost savings that would result. In an organization based more clearly on valuing people, the same change might be presented in terms of offering opportunities for devolving decision-making and empowering people. By making an appeal to shared values, influence can be developed that is not based purely on sharing facts and expertise, but is instead rooted in supporting organizational truths.

Using reasoning that is based on an appeal to values allows considerable scope for the use of personal acceptability. Shared values, by their nature, are subjectively held constructs rather than objective facts – 'efficiency is best' or 'the customer is king' are judgments, not facts. As a result, using these to support influence depends on the manager's ability to maintain the value as credible and convincing. For example, persuasion based on an argument of 'we must drive costs downward' becomes intrinsically less convincing when half of the people present are having doubts about the effect on morale of the last efficiency savings. Accordingly, this pattern of influence depends on increasing the persuasiveness of a case using interpersonal skills. The ability to communicate with passion, or inspire people with vision and trust, becomes a useful element that adds strength to a case based on an appeal to values. This is particularly true wherever the case is not convincingly rooted in shared values, but instead involves shaping values to support a new direction. Convincing people from an 'efficiency' culture that devolving financial control to an empowered workforce has benefits requires an ability to appeal to a completely new way of attaining 'old' values. The source of this influence is in the power of the individual to shape the values that people hold, despite the defences that this might surface.

This pattern of persuasion is used to support a case where the facts alone do not provide influence. The discussion above highlights the political nature of reasoning in these circumstances, with arguments based on subjective interpretation, personal qualities and the strength of alliances rather than just upon facts. Nevertheless, while political in nature, the discussion of issues is open and visible, making a direct appeal to shared values and therefore involving people in decisions. Such a pattern takes time to discuss issues and resolve uncertainty, but does work to build positively upon existing relationships as a foundation for action. As a strategy, it is effective in building levels of commitment and a sense of shared purpose, partly through the process of reaffirming or restating values publicly.

It is important to add that putting the emphasis on a reasoning approach does not necessarily suggest that management can be reduced to logical analysis of facts and figures. Sharing these concrete things in a complex environment still gives rise to a variety of alternative interpretations, as well as developing differing emotional reactions. The reasoning approach merely defines a process by which people are involved in the process of influence, and valued as part of that process. It allows for open sharing of a variety of information, but maintains the possibility that there may be divergent solutions. Reason, in this case, becomes a search for mutual understanding, but one that fully recognizes the absence of any ultimate answers.

Case note

Looking at politicians

The House of Commons provides an interesting example of the reasoning approach. Here rational 'facts' are used extensively, in the form of statistics, to build influence across the floor of the chamber and in media exchanges. However, the statistics often relate to complex issues (economy, law and order) and are subject to many different interpretations of cause and effect. Yet, rather than move the debate onto issues of values in an effort to persuade, most politicians continue to base their case on the 'concrete' facts. Ultimately, these are inadequate to sustain the point and arguments crumble or dissolve into arcane debate over the 'real' facts. The values underpinning the points are often lost, and little real movement or influence is felt as a result.

Reciprocity

Using the strategy of reciprocity to develop influence also falls into two basic patterns. The first is where direct bargaining takes place between parties, allowing particular outcomes to proceed as the result of an open trade. For this particular pattern to be exercised, each party must possess the power to offer something of interest to the other, otherwise there is no clear basis for bargaining to take place. Exerting influence in this way involves using personal power to make something happen, rather than to present the facts of a case effectively or with persuasiveness. The influence occurs because of the trade 'if you do . . . then I will . . .' rather than through the use of persuasion or argument. The advantage of this type of influence is that it is quicker than using reason, as there is no need to justify a particular case or point in full. Instead, through a process of open bargaining, making direct offers and receiving clear compensation, a particular decision or course of action is achieved.

This pattern involves the manager in negotiation and depends heavily on their ability to achieve suitable outcomes for others. Making trades that cannot be supported by results eventually leads to managerial impotence, as people will become unwilling to bargain if they do not gain the specified outcomes. In some senses the strategy is expensive, as it involves the manager using their power to obtain an outcome. While this may be relatively easy for the manager to achieve, any use of power is likely to have some impact on other people, incurring a cost in terms of changing loyalties, expectations or trust. Using this strategy can also lead other people to expect to trade whenever an issue arises, even in situations where reasoning would ordinarily provide sufficient influence. This can lead people to withhold commitment because the situation holds potential gains, even though they are persuaded by the arguments. As a pattern of influence, direct bargaining makes demands on negotiating skills, and develops a style of managing based on exchange, rather than on commitment, trust and cooperation.

An alternative form of reciprocity works through indirect trading in loyalties, favours and obligations, rather than with bargaining around the outcomes of the issue. For example, influence is exerted by 'calling in favours' that have been built up through previous activity. Several points are worth examination here, as this form of trading is a more subtle and complex exchange. Firstly, by implying obligation rather than offering a direct and open bargain, this use of trading has hidden elements. There is no longer a clearly visible link between taking an action and gaining a reward. Instead, by seeking to gain influence on the back of some past deeds, there exists an invisible and unpredictable link between past rewards and the actions that may be required in the future. Secondly, obligation can be implied after the event by reflecting on situations where help or support was given to another person, even if it was given freely at the time. The strength of influence gained then depends on the extent to which people 'feel' indebted. This means that this pattern of influence can appear very open-ended, with no clear limit to the 'debt' that is owed. Thirdly, while bargaining of this nature has hidden elements, it nevertheless still depends on a basic exchange, and is based on mutual benefits. The significant difference over open bargaining is that the value of the exchange is not agreed before it takes place, making it open to abuse and manipulation in certain circumstances.

The open-ended nature of obligation makes the success of this pattern of influence dependent on the style of the manager. For example, people will be more open to this influence if they find the person exerting it personally acceptable. In this instance, the basic elements of liking serve to keep the exchange within the boundaries of a trusting relationship. Similarly, if a manager seeking such influence enhances feelings of value, importance and self-worth in the other person, then influence is more likely to be powerful. It may also serve to sustain the relationship, despite the hidden power that has been exercised, as the focus has been on the mutual nature of the relationship. This is easier to achieve from the basis of a relationship built upon personal acceptability, making it important for managers to continually keep in mind the factors that help develop liking between people. In an atmosphere of dislike, or even ambivalence, trying to use influence based on reciprocal exchange can lead to a situation where people only value the outcomes of each deal. Dislike, or a lack of personal acceptability, also lead to poor bargaining and upward pressure on the 'cost' of each exchange. Other people, faced with an attempt to buy their support, are unlikely to be persuaded to give it easily to a person who has a poor level of personal acceptability.

Retribution

The last influencing strategy is based on using retribution to secure support. Again, there are two basic patterns that the strategy can follow. Firstly, direct threats can be used to obtain support on a specific issue, with a clear link between compliance and avoiding the threat. This kind of direct approach takes the form of 'if . . . then' or 'if you do not . . . then', and ensures that the use of retribution is clearly linked to a specific situation. This type of influence can achieve outcomes quickly, without the manager needing to justify the position or make some compensating exchange. This advantage is offset, however, by the fact that influence based on threats invariably develops a lack of commitment and covert resistance alongside the necessary compliance. People tend to respond by giving the minimum possible support to avoid retribution, as their personal rights have been unfairly overridden by the process. Additionally, this type of influence can only arise in situations of unequal power between parties, otherwise some form of retaliation would almost certainly occur.

The second alternative is where the threat of retribution is indirect, unrelated to any particular issue. This occurs when a manager maintains an overwhelming sense of intimidation that leads people to comply on all issues. Such influence might easily lead people to respond with their own threats, so it can only be achieved by provoking an atmosphere where people feel powerless, either individually or collectively. The necessary conditions to make this type of influence effective also lead inevitably to a lack of inspiration, commitment and initiative, making this strategy very damaging for the organization if it is used extensively. As a method to cope with particular crises, the strategy can secure compliance and achieve specific objectives, particularly if time constraints are critical and the issue is important. Against such a background, the manager might find this approach effective, though it is also likely to cause unpredictable levels of resentment and opposition. Using this type of influence to obtain short-term results may be at the expense of long-term damage to trust and commitment that will be hard to repair.

Learning activity

Using retribution

What are the dangers associated with using retribution as a strategy for influence?

This effect is worsened by the fact that the strategy has an impact on a manager's personal acceptability, as using threats and intimidation inevitably leads to a decline in general liking. Though some people may admire the toughness, most will find the behaviour a distasteful infringement of rights, and will therefore find the manager less personally acceptable. As the manager's acceptability provides an important source of personal power and influence, the manager finds it increasingly necessary to rely on other means of gaining compliance.

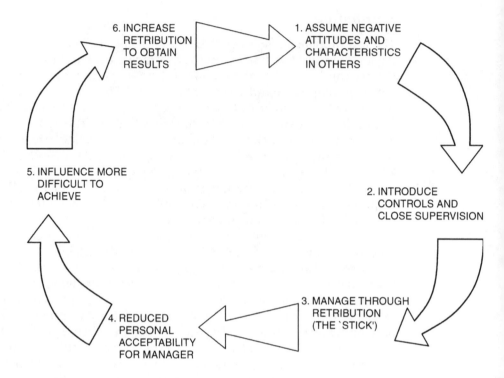

Fig. 3.3 Retribution as self-fulfilling prophesy.

Paradoxically, using retribution as a basis for gaining influence means that the manager will have to use it more in the future, as the options for other more personal styles of influence diminish.

This provides another example of a self-fulfilling prophecy effect, illustrated in Figure 3.3. Managers who feel that other people are basically lazy and untrustworthy will be reluctant to use any influencing strategy built on trust. For them, the only way to get staff to comply is to use threats and intimidation and this rapidly means that they become less personally acceptable to others. This decreases the options that they can use to gain influence, as people respond less and less to any attempts at influence based on forming relationships of genuine liking. Soon, the only way that managers can gain influence is through retribution, which justifies the perspective originally held at the outset. This sort of cycle is surprisingly common, where actions that we take because of our beliefs end up reinforcing our perspective, making our essentially subjective view of the world surprisingly well-supported by the observed 'facts'. Adopting a negative perspective on other people might seem a dangerously prophetic thing to do, whereas sustaining a positive perspective might be both optimistic and empowering of others.

An important qualification in discussing strategies for influence is that no matter what the relative strengths of any particular approach, some people appear to respond to a particular style. For example, a person who has analytical skills may prefer an approach based on reason, whereas someone who values the cut and thrust of relationships might enjoy bargaining. If these preferences do exist then it is obviously sensible to use a strategy that will have some inbuilt appeal for the person that you are trying to influence. This reflects our earlier points about acceptability, where basic liking is enhanced by similarity. Adopting a style that demonstrates similarity can enhance the effectiveness of influencing attempts, and this should be taken into consideration by making an effort to understand preferences. However, as our assumptions about other people can be self-fulfilling, it is important to take care to establish 'real' preferences, rather than make assumptions based on unchecked impressions.

Looking at the other side of influence

Handling the influence of others

Part of the skill of developing influence lies in resisting the direction in which other people are trying to exert influence. This is particularly important when they have a great deal of positional power to lend weight to their cause rather than useful ideas. In these circumstances, it is helpful to know some basic strategies that help focus the debate onto points of merit, rather than allowing it to be locked up by the manipulative use of personal power. Some ideas are listed below.

- **Create networks of mutual dependence**. As the ability to exert pressure through retribution depends on unequal power, it is helpful to work on options that develop interdependence. A person is less likely to try to threaten or intimidate when they recognize that they are dependent on maintaining goodwill.

- **Be prepared to openly challenge threatening tactics**. To some extent these unpleasant tactics of bullying can become acceptable in organizations despite the infringement of personal rights that they represent. They can also become undiscussable, being the accepted way of 'getting things done', continuing without ever being questioned. Be prepared to state that this is wrong, and encourage discussion of a more equitable and valuable arrangement instead. Such tactics are only effective with the acceptance of the victims.

- **Be aware of the potential costs of transactions with others**. Other people can develop influence through pressuring for favours to be returned. If the exchange has not been openly agreed, then it is possible that more than is justified will be claimed back. The best defence against this is to create open understanding in transactions. There is nothing intrinsically wrong with trading, but it is better if it is open and agreed, with full awareness of potential costs at the outset.

- **Be prepared to challenge pressurized trading behaviour.** Exchange can work well to facilitate influence, but is far more effective as an open process of negotiation. When others are resorting to tactics that pressurize the situation, such as imposing a deadline on action, the negotiation process becomes overburdened with 'extra' detail. It can become difficult to assess the true value of an exchange under such circumstances. It is important to take the time needed to consider the issues and facts carefully, and this may mean openly challenging behaviour that ratchets up the tension in the situation.

- **Be prepared to use reason to enhance your power.** Other people may well bring reason into their case, making persuasive arguments for a particular course of action. Indeed, this approach to influence is intrinsically the most acceptable, as it implies interdependence and value. However, it is most equitable when both parties are able to present effective arguments built on solid understanding. This is easiest to achieve given time to consider issues and prepare a case, and you should exercise your rights to take time. Further, even a reasoned case may not take account of your personal rights or the pressures that you may be under. It is important to take the opportunity to state your position clearly, even if this means declaring feelings about abuse of your good nature.

The overview of influence strategies highlights the significant benefits of adopting an approach based on reason. This strategy alone, by involving open discussion of facts and values, allows an opportunity to build understanding of other people at work. The insights gained in this process enhance personal relationships and build mutual acceptability, creating a spiral of improving personal power and influence between people. Basing influence on reason is an involving strategy, empowering others to take part in shaping outcomes through the sharing of knowledge and discussion. Putting reason at the basis of influence is a strategy that enables others to feel that they are worth persuading, and regarded as reasonable, committed and positive people who are important to a cause. While offering to bargain at least gives some benefit for giving support, the rewards of an approach based on reason are in the lasting sense of value, equality and commitment that shared understanding can develop. It takes time to build up the trust and understanding that helps the reasoning strategy to be effective, but it is an investment in people and personal learning that enables the foundations of open, honest and trusting management to grow deeper and spread wide.

The foundation of success with this and other strategies is the strength of the relationship that managers develop with the people that they need to influence. While compliance can be gained through threats and intimidation, they provide a pathway to a damaged form of relationship based on fear and control. Strategies based on strong relationships depend on the factors that build a manager's personal acceptability and develop basic liking. Maintaining behaviours that encourage liking takes a willingness to understand how other people view the world in an effort to understand how they will best relate to you. It also takes a genuine commitment to relate positively to all types of other people in the belief that everyone has something valuable to share. Above all, it needs an acceptance that it is possible to find qualities in everyone, and that understanding them is the key to learning how best to influence and manage other people.

Going forward

Adopting a positive approach to building personal power and influence is an important step for the manager to take. While there are many other skills that go to make up the complete manager, the basic ability to move things along depends on influence. There are managers who operate through flexing their positional muscles, making full use of intimidation and threats to develop compliance. Their progress through some organizations can be dramatic, as it can develop both results and a highly visible style. The downside is that others will tend to show limited commitment, delivering according to coercion and leverage rather than interest or enthusiasm. Progress and innovation, key themes of the modern world, will be limited by the imagination of the person barking the orders or making the threats. However, an approach to influence that builds on qualities and enhances the value of people opens the doors of management opportunity, throwing wide the limits of creativity and progress by empowering others to join in strength rather than submission. Along the way it provides a limitless education.

Effective relationships are at the heart of all successful management. Without the ability to influence other people, our wildest management dreams can only end in dust. Without the personal skill and style to make this a positive process, built upon personal liking and the valuing of others, our dreams may become nightmares, twisted by the abuse of personal power. We can never control the reactions of other people, yet we can always do our best to ensure that they are positive. Above all, we can try to understand the real value of other people in helping to achieve our goals, and work closer with them to make our vision come true.

Summary

This chapter has made the following key points:

➤ That effective work relationships are an essential path to achieving management goals

➤ That developing relationships based on personal acceptability and liking enables influence to be developed. The factors that promote acceptability and liking include our basic appearance, the impression that we create and the similarities that we show to others. In particular, the benefits of creating a fresh impression each day, based on simple, personal attributes, were emphasized.

➤ That personal power can be developed through a variety of other means, all of which have potential uses. These include expertise, effort, support for the values of the organization and the position of the manager in the organization. Each of these sources of power can be enhanced by the personal acceptability of managers.

➤ That putting influence into practice can be achieved through strategies based on reason, reciprocity or retribution. The success of these strategies depends on the context in which they are used. The personal skills and acceptability of the manager also have a significant effect on success.

Further reading

Carnegie's book above provides a simple, energetic and impassioned approach to developing influence based on his experiences as a salesperson. It is full of anecdotal advice and is written in a light and optimistic manner.

Another book listed below (Rosenfeld, Giacalone and Riordan, 1995) provides a more academic treatment of the subject area. It is based on contemporary views on the concept of managing the impression that you give, and provides a good overview of the literature in this field. There are convincing discussions of ideas such as **ingratiation** and the way in which people in organizations **protect** the impression that they have built. The book is very practical and includes many case examples.

References

Berscheid, E. (1985) Interpersonal attraction, in Lindzey, D. and Aronson, E. (eds), *Handbook of Social Psychology*, Academic Press.

Carnegie, D. (1973) *How to Win Friends and Influence People*, Pocket Books, New York.

Kanter, R. (1979) Power failure in management circuits in *Harvard Business Review*, July–August, p. 57.

Packhard, V. (1982) *The Hidden Persuaders*, Penguin.

Rosenfeld, P. Giacalone, R.A. and Riordan C. (1995) *Impression Management in Organizations*, International Thomson Business Press, London.

Schein, E.H. (1987) *Process Consultation*, Vol. 2, Addison-Wesley.

Schmidt, S. and Stitt, C. (1981) 'Why do I like thee?' *Journal of Applied Psychology*, **66**, 324–8.

Whetton, D., Cameron, K. and Woods, M. (1994) *Developing Management Skills for Europe*, HarperCollins.

4

Making sense of communication

Organizations talk in order to discover what they are saying, act in order to discover what they are doing.

Karl Weick

Only connect.

E.M. Forster

Objectives

By the end of this chapter you will be able to:

➤ Recognize the complex processes that take place during communication
➤ Enhance the basic quality of communication through focusing on interpretation
➤ Improve the quality of your listening
➤ Take steps to improve the value of your communication

Introduction

Communication is the stuff of organization, the means by which information, opinion and direction ebbs and flows through the body of business. The process of communicating underpins management activity, providing the basic means by which people organize and coordinate their actions and enabling the pursuit of common goals. Planning for an uncertain future, that uniquely human activity, is built upon a framework of communication, making it possible to collect information, analyze possibilities and share insights or objectives. In addition, the essence of our social interaction is communication, an endless web of half-interpreted signals and messages that go together to bind people in shared purpose through life. Communication is fundamentally a part of our social processes, helping to define our relationships and shape our interactions through a continuous cycle of interpretation and reaction. Ultimately it is a process that is filled with ambiguity and potential outcomes that differ from our intent, because however clearly we communicate, our meaning is made up in the minds of other people. This chapter aims to explore ways of improving the process of communication at work, in the belief that achieving high quality communication is a foundation for constructive and productive human processes.

In working with a range of organizations, we hear that 'improving communication' is one of the commonest goals that people hold. Wherever people are in the organization, they nearly always describe communication as a problem that provides a real barrier to achieving greater organizational success. Sometimes this is a simple lack of crucial information to enable effective decisions, but often a more complex problem of inconsistent or contradictory messages is described, with an understandable confusion and lack of clear direction the predictable result. One of the problems in addressing issues of communication is that it is a skill that we all possess, having spent a lifetime developing our ability to communicate. As a consequence, while individuals often recognize the problem exists in organizations, they rarely feel that it is related to their own ability to communicate. More often, communication problems are perceived as being caused elsewhere, by other key individuals, management as a whole or, more simply, the 'system'. This kind of analysis leads to collective inaction, with individuals believing that they are communicating better than everyone else and are therefore not a part of the problem. Yet face-to-face communication is responsible for a great deal of our organizational time, and the quality of this process is the foundation of successful interpersonal relationships. High quality relationships are not only the basis for a comfortable and enjoyable work life, but are the most significant determinant of organizational success. As such, developing a communication process that builds interpersonal relations is a key step towards enhancing the process and outcomes of management itself.

More than just messages

A second problem in addressing communication issues is the tightly woven interplay between the quality of communication and the quality of our relationships. Poor communication results in inaccurate messages, but it also has an unavoidable impact on interactions between people. Whatever we intend, the way in which we communicate carries a great deal more than just the bare content of our messages. Other people use our communication as a basis for developing opinions about us as people, and continually make inferences about our values, meaning and intent according to their own perceptions of the situation. This social interplay is impossible to separate out from our messages, and is to a great extent out of our direct control, as we have no immediate way of accessing or understanding the reactions and interpretations of others. A poorly delivered message, hastily assembled in the maelstrom of a busy day, can therefore lead others to make assumptions about our motives that do not reflect our real position or intent. In turn, those assumptions can develop suspicion, mistrust and defensiveness between people, causing a spiral of worsening relations and avoidance that is all sparked off by simple errors in communication. The poor communication itself causes a barrier between people that grows beyond the limits of the message, and actively stands in the way of efforts to put things right. It becomes part of the history of the relationship, unavoidably dampening the quality of the process of interaction. Making an effort to improve communication is a worthwhile aim for any manager, but the skill is inextricably bound up with the process of building and maintaining relationships. As such, it is a complex, dynamic and unpredictable area to explore.

The social aspect of communication provides a great deal of the difficulty in the process, but it also brings much potential for interest and reward. If, for example, we communicate with a machine, such as a computer or industrial robot, then the machine will faithfully execute the required actions with considerable efficiency. Indeed, it can be interesting to watch novice computer users as they grapple with the literal requirements of the machine. Computers merely execute instructions, they do not make interpretations, and some novices find it immensely frustrating that the machine fails to understand what they really intend it to do. However, when we communicate with other people, the process is dramatically enriched by powers of observation and interpretation, and the basic messages that we convey become a means by which people construct a sophisticated understanding of us. Our communication is the only way in which people can come to understand us, our values, beliefs and attitudes, making it a rich and rewarding process of discovery that can never be entirely separate from the nuts and bolts of our messages.

Communication is always about more than just the bare bones of the message. In addition to the basic content of the words, there are a whole host of other signals passing back and forth, all of which may contain vital information. For example, when a message is unpalatable or discordant with beliefs, people subconsciously display feelings of defensiveness or discomfort through their body language. These signals themselves vary according to circumstances or relationships – a person is unlikely to display unease with company policy in the presence of the managing director, whereas it may well surface when briefing the team. Similarly, in the context of a 'poor' relationship, people become more guarded about revealing their feelings, naturally dampening their body language and paradoxically making their messages less complete and more difficult to fully interpret. Against a background of such variety, it is not surprising that the process of communicating is inclined to break down on occasion. It also explains why the problem of poor communication is very difficult to cure by simply adding more communication – such a response often just adds extra misunderstanding and chaos because it fails to develop a more complete process first.

There are a number of things that can be done to try to improve communication, but the process will always depend on the quality of relationships between people. It is therefore a skill that has to be developed and managed in context, by applying effort and understanding to the situations and people with which you work. There are no universal rules that will magically improve communication. Instead, it is a process that demands continual attention, sensitivity and a willingness to work with people to get mutual benefits. The rewards of better communication are many, including organizational goals of increased effectiveness and efficiency. More significantly, it is at the heart of the process that allows our collective action to be more than what we can achieve on our own. As such, it is a pathway to opportunity and insight beyond those that we find within ourself.

Learning activity

Bare communication

Try to think about how you can communicate an instruction without revealing something of yourself. Would this help or hinder the message?
  Would this help or hinder the development of workplace relationships?

Harris, S. (1981)
'Know yourself?'
It's a paradox, 6
October,
Associated Press.

In order to know oneself, no amount of introspection or self-examination will suffice. You can analyze yourself for weeks, or meditate for months, and you will not get an inch further – any more than you can smell your own breath or laugh when you tickle yourself. You must first be open to the other person before you catch a glimmer of yourself. Our self-reflection in a mirror does not tell us what we are like; only our reflection in other people. We are essentially social creatures, and our personality resides in association, not isolation.

S. Harris

An interactive process

However carefully a message is crafted, ultimately its success depends on whoever receives the communication. If other people are uninterested, too preoccupied or reluctant to accept your point of view, then the message will be lost or distorted. Put bluntly, other people control the outcomes of your communication. Accepting this is the basis of skilled communication, for it encourages us to focus attention on managing the receiver in order to develop an improved relationship that will allow better quality to communication. This also helps to move attention away from an approach based on trying to improve the basic accuracy of the content – while this is worthwhile as part of an overall approach, it will do little by itself to deliver more effective communication. It is difficult to improve communication without firstly considering the context in which it takes place; like a badly-timed joke, many a well-designed message has been lost to the moment.

Learning activity

The meetings process

Think about a conventional meeting at work. Traditionally, meetings are used to exchange information, discuss ideas and strategies, make decisions and plans. All of this involves communicating. What things are normally done to help 'manage' the interaction so that the communication is maximized?

What aspects of communication cannot be managed simply through the formal structures and procedures?
    How do you as an individual manage these instead?

These points are illustrated by considering a common scene at meetings. In many organizations these are intended to allow efficient communication and effective decision-making, particularly on issues that require a wide range of expertise. To help this process they are often structured to allow attention to be focused on the key issues, and various rules and procedures are employed in some degree to ensure full and relevant contributions. Information concerning key items is often circulated in advance, and the use of an agenda allows others to prepare their thoughts on issues ahead of the meeting. This ought to help ensure that meetings are an opportunity to communicate essential information and ideas clearly and simply.

However, the reality of the experience often differs from this ideal. Despite the structure and form of meetings, most people know that meetings do not necessarily provide ideal conditions for presenting ideas and proposals. In practice, the context of meetings is often overlaid with political manoeuvring in many shapes and guises, where the play that is being enacted bears little resemblance to the script that people are supposed to follow. For example, impressing senior people with support for their favoured projects can stand in the way of accepting a valid idea from a colleague, while providing a vigorous defence of a department's role in some mishap can limit consideration of proposals to prevent it happening again. In such circumstances, putting effort into crafting an accurate message may well be wasted, as it is more important to pay attention to the background features of the interaction if productive communication is to take place. Pressing on with a well-prepared presentation, in the face of a political intent to avoid the message, is not effective communication, but naive and misguided effort. Instead, it is more important to develop an overall ability to understand and manage the interaction in order to influence the process of communicating. This demands that the focus of effort should be on managing the listener to ensure that they are best placed to receive the message we intend to deliver.

Focusing on the listener and the interaction

 Learning activity

Tuning in

Since skilled communication depends on managing the listener, what can you do to ensure that your messages are well received?

If the results of our communication are ultimately governed by the responses of other people, it follows that our attention should be on the overall process, rather than just on our end of the exchange. Shifting the emphasis of our effort to the interaction and the listener helps us to focus on communication as a holistic process, and to pay attention to the interdependent elements that go together to make up effective interactions. By building the process upon inter-personal relationships, we are explicitly including and valuing the social elements of the exchange. There are three basic steps that can be used to help ensure that we approach communication with an initial focus on the listener and the interaction:

- Monitor attention
- Maintain inherent interest
- Engage emotions

Each of these is considered below.

Monitor attention

The first step to take is to try to look actively for attention in the recipient. It is all too easy to become preoccupied with delivering the message, particularly if it has a theme close to your heart, and to fail to assess how it is being received. By looking closely for signals of interest it is possible to assess the effectiveness of the communication as it takes place, rather than when the results become apparent at some later stage. The process of monitoring attention helps us to adjust our communication immediately, enabling us to improve the quality of the interaction as it proceeds. Further, the very process of monitoring the exchange closely sends positive 'attentive' signals about the relationship to the other person; it helps to demonstrate your commitment to the exchange and the value which you place upon the other person's reactions and views. It is important to look for signs of attention and interest, such as eye contact, encouraging verbal responses, attentive posture (leaning forward with open stance) and positive body signals such as nodding. These contrast with signals of disinterest, such as a lack of eye contact, particularly when listening, routine verbal responses ('Oh really') and a posture that appears to be in retreat. Noticing these signals, and making an appropriate response, demonstrates your interest, involvement and commitment to the exchange. This, of itself, helps to set up a process that values the quality of the relationship, rather than simply delivering a message.

Maintain inherent interest

While monitoring attention is a valuable skill that can be applied universally, the second step of maintaining communication of inherent interest is far more difficult. Each of us has our own particular interests, and naturally enjoy communicating about those particular topics more than other subjects. If we are to maintain interest in our communication, it implies that we have to adjust what we say to appeal to the particular interests of each unique recipient, which may begin to sound like saying different things to different people. Several points are worth making here, as maintaining interest is a crucial aspect of making the interaction effective.

Firstly, because communication is the means by which our relationships are maintained, making space to talk about topics of inherent interest to others is not simply time-wasting. By engaging in conversation about fishing, golf or children we can help to reinforce the social connections upon which relationships are built. This helps to reaffirm the value we place on others, by showing our commitment to their interest as a person, and lays firm foundations for subsequent communication. Good managers are often reported as people who take an interest in others as people, and this is easily built by taking the time to reinforce social ties through focus on conversations that reflect people's interests.

Secondly, it is impossible to engage in such conversations without showing an interest in other people. A manager has to take the trouble to find out about their staff's interest, values and ideals if they are to hold such conversations at all, and this stage of the process inevitably sends positive signals to people about their worth. As a step towards more effective communication it is self-reinforcing, helping to provide an understanding of other people's interest and values that makes it easier to develop interest in future exchanges. This is not to say that messages have to be dressed up in small talk about hobbies, but that expressing genuine interest in others will help maintain their interest in what you have to say.

Thirdly, our own interests are a natural source of verbosity for ourselves. Taking care to monitor the attention of others will help keep in check our enthusiasm for particular topics which may not be shared universally. However, there are some topics that seem to provide basic interest for most people, and provide safe ground for establishing communication. The marketing machine that surrounds us all gives a good guide to how effective these topics can be, as they serve to maintain our interest in some relatively dull items – cat food, breakfast cereal and lager to name a few. Using these subjects of common interest serves to gain attention and build initial links with people.

Common interest

Ourselves
Whatever we do in life, we are always at the centre of our own particular world. As a consequence we have a natural interest in expressing ourselves and our views to others, and in hearing or seeing these views reflected. Marketing images allow us to recognize stereotypes readily, enabling us to identify easily with particular lifestyles and products. Allowing people to talk about themselves, and reflecting their views, is the easiest way to develop communication linkages.

Relationships
However sophisticated an animal we become, we still value relationships and sex highly, making them topics that awaken our interest very easily indeed.

Highlighting the relationship aspect of communication, ahead of the content of the message, is an effective means of establishing interest. This can easily be achieved with relatively simple signals. For example, using people's names and involving them directly helps – it is better to say 'I would value your opinion on this' than 'I am interested in opinions on this'. Similarly, open body language helps to reinforce the value of the relationship as do positive gestures.

Money and power
As the launch of the lottery or the diary pages of the press illustrate, many people have a basic interest in these topics. The stereotypes are that women also appear to be interested in other people and in the emotional sharing of common experience, while men appear to maintain higher basic levels of interest in sport and technology.

Taking the second step of working towards maintaining inherent interest involves approaching communication through understanding of other people. As such it demands effort and acceptance of other people, and a willingness to explore their interests ahead of our own. The third step towards focusing on the interaction is also an expression of commitment and belief, for it involves being prepared to engage emotions.

Engage emotions

Communication that makes an effort to reach our emotions is more likely to be successful than that which merely states the message in a matter-of-fact way. This effect is one that we are commonly exposed to in many forms of media, with films and novels often attempting to reach well beyond conveying basic information into the realms of stirring an emotional response. We have probably all seen films that we remember with a lump in our throat or a tear in our eye, and the messages that they carry tend to remain with us for longer than those that do not manage to engage our emotions. This does not mean that we need to communicate dramatically or in poetic phrases, but that we should recognize that if our messages excite or inspire people then they are more likely to be remembered. Communication that attempts to involve people's emotions simply has more impact.

 Learning activity

Emotions

How can you engage people's emotions during a contribution to a meeting?

The obvious difficulty with this is that not many messages at work appear to have much inherent emotional appeal. However, if work is viewed as a place for discovery, filled with opportunity and learning, then there appears to be more that is worth getting excited about. In a complex environment, conversations about day-to-day decisions on apparently mundane issues hide a plethora of outcomes and effects, all waiting to be discovered. A piece of routine delegation might be seen as a gateway to opportunity by a less experienced colleague, particularly if it is presented as such. To some extent this is a case of looking for the positive aspects of all your messages and driving the communication forward with those aspects as the heart of the emotional appeal. Recognize also that the language we use is part of what shapes our reality – being prepared to get excited about things helps to draw other people along on a wave of collective emotion. Again, advertising is full of examples of this technique, with the Andrex puppy adding emotional appeal to toilet paper, while the Dulux dog brings interest to watching paint dry.

The three basic steps of monitoring attention, maintaining inherent interest and engaging emotions provide a basic framework for communicating. Through managing the interaction fully, the steps help to build a relationship within which communication takes place. Making time to develop interests with other people in a manner that provides mutual enjoyment and reward, helps to establish and sustain positive workplace communication. The benefits of giving attention to the quality of the interaction go far beyond that of successful messages, bringing a sense of support and opportunity to people involved. The next section identifies some principles that work to develop a communication style that aims at further supporting and enhancing interpersonal relationships.

Complete communication

The idea that communication is a process that is ultimately under the control of the listener is important, and highlights the need for the manager to develop their own abilities as a listener. This is particularly relevant as organizations move towards ideas of empowerment and self- direction, as essential information will appear from all corners of the organization, rather than be disseminated from above. People who make time to listen to others are always regarded as good communicators, making the argument in favour of improved listening persuasive. The first principle of complete communication is that listening must be at the core of the interactive process of communicating.

Developing listening skills

 Learning activity

Identifying skills

Think back over your career and identify a few people who you think were 'good' managers.
Generally speaking, how would you describe their communication skills?

What actions did they take that demonstrated their ability to listen?
What were the effects of this active listening?

Improving listening skills has significant advantages for managers. While it develops our basic ability to absorb information and understand the communication of others more fully, a great deal of the potential gain is in the messages that it sends to other people. When active listening is practiced, others will feel recognized and valued, even when the message they give is subsequently rejected as unworkable or impractical. We are sometimes quick to make up our minds about the value of other people's communication, but making the time and effort to listen pays off in terms of building a better interaction with people. Managers who listen well develop respect in others, and this has benefits for their work relationships and subsequent interactions.

Taking time to assess your own listening patterns is a worthwhile exercise. Many managers are very critical of their own listening skills, and studies generally show that we absorb as little as 25% of what we hear. (Given that managers typically spend 80% of their time in face-to-face communication this is a worrying amount of information loss!) A common discovery from self-assessment is the impact that pre-judgment has on our listening patterns – there are people who we do not listen to well because we have decided that they are not worth listening to! When we consider why we are making these judgments, we often find that the reasons are not related to the current situation at all, but are based on previous experience and prejudice. Rejecting the communication of some people based on historical evidence, dislike or difference of opinion is a good way to ensure that there will be growing rifts between staff. Worse, it provides an example of management pigeonholing that undervalues the potential of people to grow beyond their history, and helps to fulfill the prophecy that they cannot.

The active listening checklist

1. Remove the pressure that other people feel by giving them time and space to communicate

Work pressures affect us all, and people can be sensitive to the burdens of management. It can be difficult to bring issues and ideas to the attention of managers in a busy environment, and this can only be overcome if managers make a deliberate effort to send a clear message that time and space is available.

2. Work hard to reduce your spoken contribution

Good communication has a rhythm that reflects an equality in the relationship. This helps to reinforce the worth of each person's statements, by allowing a share of conversational time. This can be developed by ensuring that you take time to develop other people's contributions, by asking questions and allowing them the opportunity to amplify or clarify their points. It is also useful to draw clear links between your own contribution and what has gone before, maintaining a clear flow. Statements that build on, or qualify, previous comment demonstrate acceptance and validate the contribution of others, whereas comment that is unrelated to the flow of the exchange is destructive of the process of communicating. In a similar way, long pauses in the flow have a disruptive effect on dialogue, and these can occur when points are repeated unnecessarily.

3. Give messages that you are listening

Of all the items in this checklist, this one is probably the most powerful. It is easily put into effect through body language, with listening being demonstrated through the three simple steps explored below. Controlling body language takes concentration, as it is an unconscious, natural part of our expressive behaviour. However, listening provides an opportunity to focus on these simple points and the effort of concentrating improves listening as well.

- Maintain eye contact when listening
- Nod at appropriate moments and make encouraging facial signals
- Mirror the other person's body language

This last is a simple technique that helps to develop a sense of empathy between people, provided it is done with discretion. It simply involves adjusting your own posture, facial expressions, hand signals and emotional state to reflect those that the other person is displaying. While some judgment is needed to avoid making this too obvious, it should be noted that people who are communicating well do this without thinking – it is an observable feature of our behaviour. As such, introducing mirroring deliberately tends not to be noticed, as it is subconsciously assumed to be a sign of positive acceptance and empathy. It may seem difficult to reflect an emotional state, but what is meant is that you should try to reflect the state that is being outwardly portrayed. If the other person displays excitement, then responding with excited signals would effectively mirror the communication and demonstrate a state of empathy. It is important to note that the effect of mirroring is to amplify communication by strengthening the connection between people, so it is important to reflect positive signals only. Reflecting anger – a commonly observed behaviour during disputes – works to heighten the differences between people and may well make things worse.

 Learning activity

Exploring mirroring

Try to observe the communication and behaviour of two people in your team who appear to work well together. Note any instances of mirroring of body posture, facial expressions, hand signals and emotional state.

Next time you communicate with someone you find difficult try to practice mirroring techniques. What effects does this have?

When trying to establish a new relationship with anyone try out your mirroring techniques. What effects does this have?

4. Use the words of the other person to reflect messages

Using the words of the other person has several effects. By reflecting their use of language it demonstrates listening and acceptance while also mirroring back the message that has been heard. This process helps to clarify and paraphrase communication, and enables the speaker to accept or qualify the meaning that has been received. While it is useful to use some of the key words of the speaker, it is important that the process is not simply repetition. Rather, a good listener will add depth and substance to the reflective process, providing an amplification of what is being said. The key to this process is in identifying key aspects of the communication and in focusing the reflective phrases on those elements. Peripheral information that might distract the speaker from their chosen topic is left out of the reflective process.

Guidelines for reflective comments

- Make it a priority to reflect feelings as these are more difficult to communicate. Similarly, reflect personal aspects of the communication rather than impersonal facts or details.
- Try to add to the conversation even though the speaker provides the topic and guides the conversation. This can be through simplification, clarification or adding depth and resonance.
- Demonstrate acceptance by using their key words. Use mirroring of body language to reinforce feelings of empathy. Avoid 'objective' detachment which creates a sense of superiority. Avoid both disagreement and agreement, as these can appear confrontational or patronizing and add little to the communication.

5. Take time to paraphrase and summarize

This is a highlighting technique that helps the other person identify the key points that you have understood. It allows them the opportunity to recap, qualify and enlarge upon what they have said. It helps the communication to remain a shared process and reinforce the interaction, even when the topic is controlled by one party. It also helps to provide communication with simple reference points, helping to keep complex issues manageable.

6. Encourage people to develop thoughts and feelings

This technique aims to encourage full expression of views, beyond the simple bounds of factual content. By seeking to develop understanding of thoughts and feelings, the communication includes both emotional and conceptual elements, bringing depth and understanding to the process. This helps to strengthen the social aspects of communication, and builds quality and value into the interaction.

7. Beware of responses that evaluate or pass judgment on the content of the communication

The speed with which we think enables us to form opinions on issues far faster than we listen to information. Making early evaluations has the drawback that it tends to be a response that closes down conversational options and directs the progress of the interaction. It therefore has the danger that vital information, not yet revealed, will be lost in a hasty conclusion. Particularly with difficult issues, people use conversation to help them work through their thoughts, and passing judgments can inhibit this process of exploration. These responses may become more appropriate during the course of dialogue, as facts, thoughts and feelings become clear, but in general, our impulse to provide evaluation limits the value of the interaction. An early judgment often fails to allow the potential of the exchange to develop and sends negative signals about the worth of the speaker's communication.

Moving communication beyond words

Improving listening skills and managing the interaction helps to ensure that communication is more complete. Rather than being a simple transfer of information between people, adopting this approach allows a process that values the wider, human aspects of communication. Developing active listening enables a manager to learn to appreciate the ideas and perspectives of other people. Focusing on interests and allowing communication to involve emotions also helps to improve the scope of a communication agenda, giving depth to the contributions that people bring to the process. Communication becomes valued for the opportunity to connect with other people in shared endeavour, rather than merely an exercise in data processing. Communication is a pathway to the hearts and minds of other people, whether or not we intend it to be so. As such, all communication is important, with an impact beyond simple words. It needs to be valued as such, with continual effort to stay in touch with the changing interests and values of the people around us. The following section develops some additional principles that help our communication to be complete, supportive of interpersonal relationships as well as a flowing channel of valuable information.

Enhancing the worth of people

A key principle of effective communication is that the aim should always be to develop and maintain the other person's sense of worth. This principle is based on the view that even negative communication can be delivered in a way that enhances the basic relationship between people and enables people to maintain their core value. This is made possible by considering several related points.

Firstly, it is easier to achieve positive outcomes from the process if an effort is made to identify and share areas of **common ground**. Ultimately, the differences between people are part of what helps establish our own unique identity, but sharing similarities of views, values or behaviour does help to create basic acceptance of others. It is difficult to reject or dismiss communication when it comes from someone whose beliefs, approach or attitudes are congruent with your own. By identifying and highlighting these aspects, it enables a core of common ground to form a platform for dialogue. This process helps to support the self-worth of people by demonstrating the value placed on areas of agreement, and also highlights the possible pathways that exist between points of view.

The process of building congruence is made easier in an environment of **openness**. If people communicate with some hidden agenda, there will be a difference between what they are saying and what they think or feel. This is likely to be evident through a difference between the content of their communication and their apparent emotional state. They may state that they are comfortable with a particular idea, yet appear distressed. This creates hidden ground in the relationship, and ensures that the interaction will become distracted by trying to identify hidden motives, thoughts and feelings. It also makes trust more difficult to establish, leading to guarded communication that attempts to deal with a variety of possible outcomes. At the least, this brings confusion and it can easily lead to communication that is misleading and misinterpreted.

Basing communication on a platform of common ground also helps people to feel recognized and accepted. It begins a process of interaction that involves shared contribution and responsibility for involvement, promoting a two-way flow of dialogue between equal partners to the exchange. By emphasizing the value of each contribution, it helps to cultivate a **sense of equal worth** in the participants, breaking down the conventional barriers to effective communication that can exist in rigid hierarchies. Status, rank and projections of superiority can all interfere with the open flow of information, or revealing thoughts and feelings, and any strategy that helps the manager to demonstrate the equal status of others as people is helpful to genuine dialogue. By focusing on the building blocks of the exchange, it is possible to promote a sense of potential progress that is more difficult to achieve when barriers or differences are to the fore.

Making progress in communication, particularly when differences are being explored, involves **adopting a flexible position**. Presenting opinions as facts, or ideas as received wisdom, does little to encourage open debate or sharing of reactions. It is important to signal which elements of the dialogue are open to change, by clearly presenting them as options or possibilities that can be adapted according to subsequent information. This opens up the possibility of debate, rather than closing down areas where agreement can be sought, and encourages full contributions to be made in areas that remain to be resolved. This helps to prevent a 'horse trading' approach to communication, where interactions become a marketplace of concessions rather than a genuine attempt to establish agreement through understanding. Encouraging contribution puts further value into the interaction, building the worth of the other person and enhancing the social content of the communication.

All of these strategies help to make people feel as if they are holding a valid perspective, even in situations where there are apparent differences of view. Allowing communication to embrace the differences between people, rather than adopting an approach that tries to deny or ignore variety, encourages people to feel comfortable giving their own thoughts and values to the process. In a complex world, maintaining flexibility in thinking is one way of responding effectively to the varied demands that emerge, and the key to flexible thinking is through encouraging a broad spectrum of views to be shared. Any behaviour that fails to acknowledge other views as valid will ultimately narrow the options that are available to the enquiring manager, as well as providing a gulf of misunderstanding that becomes increasingly difficult to cross.

Maintaining a positive process

The pace at which communication can proceed makes it difficult to adhere to some principles. After all, there are no guarantees that all the communication that you face will be so sensitively presented, and even the calmest of managers can be tempted to respond to attack with anger or criticism. Managing the detail of a communication interaction is also made easier with some basic principles to offer as a guide. All of these are aimed at making sure that the communication proceeds in a manner that gives the best chance of enhancing the relationship at the same time as conveying information accurately.

Firstly, to reinforce a point that has already been touched upon, our communication is likely to be more open and positive in nature if it is descriptive rather than evaluative. This helps the manager to avoid passing judgment, and allows dialogue to remain open-ended, which encourages further contribution. Evaluations close down the need for further communication by indicating that enough information has already been obtained. Other people are forced to directly challenge this conclusion if they wish to contribute, and are likely instead to withdraw their potential ideas. The problem is that they may also withdraw their commitment.

Secondly, descriptions that are specific are more helpful and complete than general ones. Making a general point, such as 'you performed well in the meeting today', may well convey some positive sense of worth, but is less empowering and rewarding than a detailed description – 'I felt that you handled the issues with balance and were very fair in the way you sought contributions.' Giving people more detail allows them to respond to specific points, whereas general information leaves them trying to work out exactly what was meant.

Thirdly, communication that tries to focus on the particular problems of a situation is better than communication that attempts to state problems in terms of personality. Communication that implies that fault lies in the personality merely leads people to feel attacked – after all, it is difficult to do anything about the personality that you have, at least in the short-term. However, by stating problems in terms of detailed outcomes, it allows people to recognize that a particular aspect of their behaviour has caused difficulties. For example, 'I feel that your interruptions today made it difficult for me to complete my project' is far more problem-centred and useful than 'you spoiled my day'. While the first example is conveying negative information, it is at least constructive, giving direct information about a behaviour that can subsequently be adjusted. It is even more valuable to follow this process through by describing problems in terms of three basic stages:

- **Stage one**. State the problem giving a detailed description of the specific situation.
- **Stage two**. State your own reaction to the problem – share how it made you feel.
- **Stage three**. State how the situation can be corrected by detailing what needs to be done to put things right. Then seek a response or reaction.

This highlights the strength of communication that avoids causing defensive responses. Once an interaction has caused one person to feel defensive, much of the effort of their communication goes into strategies to avoid further threat, and to provide a robust defence against the points being made. In such circumstances they are unlikely to listen well, or to accept legitimate points that are being made. Worse, the interaction itself is likely to lead to a decline in the quality of the relationship, making subsequent communication more difficult. Even where the matter under discussion is not controversial, the history of the relationship is likely to overlay the communication with suspicion and a lack of trust.

Some simple guidelines

There are several useful guidelines that help to reinforce the process of communicating and help to ensure that the interaction has the best possible chance of success.

1. Begin communication with the clearest possible understanding of the receiver

By developing understanding and appreciation of the perspectives of other people we are better able to connect with their interests and values. This helps establish and reinforce a relationship, building the social content of the process. This provides a solid foundation for dialogue and makes difficult issues easier to confront.

2. Try to establish your own objectives before communicating

Defining objectives is valuable in that it helps communication to move towards common targets. If the objectives are declared honestly, it also helps to keep the agenda open and removes the threat of hidden aims. Thinking about objectives requires a certain integrity – saying 'I would like to reach agreement on how to proceed with this project' is very easily undermined if the real objective is railroading through your own view. Good communication is built upon flexibility and a willingness to allow the process to shape your views.

3. Think about all points of view before you start

The exercise of thinking through all of the issues and exploring possible alternatives helps to develop a flexible approach. By anticipating potential difficulties and alternatives, the possibility of resolving them positively increases. It also means that new ideas are seen as an extension to the discussion, rather than something that undermines the message. This makes a defensive reaction less likely.

4. Invest time in clarifying ideas

A simple lack of clarity is a short-cut to misunderstanding. Time spent restating ideas to help understanding is rarely wasted as it demonstrates a recognition of the needs of other people. Clarity is an essential step to maximizing the contribution of others.

5. Try to understand and value a critical response rather than act defensively

A common response to critical comment is defensiveness, but this rarely improves the quality of the interaction. However, criticism must be founded in something, even if it is misunderstanding or dislike. Trying to understand the source is a positive step towards absorbing any valid points that criticism contains, and ensures that the interaction continues to build positively by demonstrating the value placed on the person giving the comment. Despite the personal threat that criticism contains, accepting our own fallibility helps us to remain open to the possibility that our reasoning may well be misjudged.

6. Take responsibility for your communication by talking in terms that are clearly owned

Using statements that express your own views or beliefs are more powerful and easier to respond to than statements that are presented as impersonal. Saying something in first person terms such as 'I believe' reveals something of yourself and your commitment. Presenting the same point in an impersonal way – it is believed that – does not reveal your own view, and can leave people unclear about where your own feelings lie. This can make communication vague, as the lack of ownership leaves open a maze of escape routes in the conversation, allowing people to disown the comments that they have made.

Going forward

However hard you try to connect with other people, it is ultimately an error-prone process. There are many factors that have an influence on the success of any interaction, including the pressures of work and the diversity of people, and that make it difficult for communication to be reliable or precise. By concentrating on interacting, it is possible to develop a process that is positive and rewarding, even though a potential for misinterpretation still exists. Effective communication becomes something that is not measured in terms of outcomes, but in terms of a process that builds and maintains work relationships. By appreciating the complexity at the heart of any process of interpretation, we can learn to focus on the social aspects of the exchange, and embrace communication as a process that is fundamental to our humanity. Communication is more than just a message, it is the process by which we understand and shape our world. It can never be made simple, but it can be simply valued.

Summary

This chapter has made the following key points:

➤ That communication underpins all social and organizational processes.
➤ That communication is unavoidably about more than just messages.
➤ That communication is an interactive process that is shaped by the recipient.
➤ That a simple, three-step strategy of managing the listener contributes to effective communication.
➤ That listening skills enhance effective communication.
➤ That effective communication is a foundation for valuing people and enhancing people's sense of self-worth.

Further reading

The 3M management team have produced good practical material on meetings. Try their 1987 work *'How to run better meetings'*, McGraw-Hill, New York. Also useful are the pamphlets published by Video Arts Ltd., designed to supplement their training videos. The pamphlets are actually a useful guide to meetings practice and presentations. Try 'Meetings, Bloody Meetings' and 'More Bloody Meetings' for guidance on structuring meetings and effective chairing skills. Also useful is 'Making a Case' on presentation techniques, though watching the videos is a more complete aid to identifying appropriate behavioural skills.

References

Alberdi, L. de (1990) *People, Psychology and Organisations*, Cambridge University Press.
Athos, A. and Gabarro, J. (1978) *Interpersonal Behaviour*, Prentice Hall, New Jersey.
Burley-Allen, D. (1982) *Listening; the forgotten skill*, Wiley.
Eisner, J. (1986) *Social Psychology*, Cambridge University Press.
Haney, W.V. (1979) *Communication and Interpersonal Relations*, Irwin, Homewood, Ill.
Hanson, G. (1986) Determinants of firm performance: An integration of economic and organizational factors. Unpublished doctoral dissertation for University of Michigan Business School, sourced in Whetten, D., Cameron, K. and Woods, M. (eds), (1994), *Developing Management Skills for Europe*, HarperCollins.
Heylin, A. (1993) *Putting it Across*, Michael Joseph, London.
Packhard, V. (1982) *The Hidden Persuaders*, Penguin.
Whetton, Cameron and Woods (1994) *Developing Management Skills for Europe*.

5

Putting communication to work

From the vantage point of the symbolic frame, organizational structures, activities and events are secular theatre. They express our fears, joys and expectations. They arouse our emotions and kindle our spirit. They reduce our uncertainty and soothe our bewilderment. They provide a shared basis for understanding events and for moving ahead.

Lee Bolman and Terence Deal

Objectives

By the end of this chapter you will be able to:

➤ Apply communication principles to a range of formal communication scenarios
➤ Describe how communication quality underpins new management processes
➤ Identify, analyse and break down some of the key barriers to quality in communication
➤ Identify and describe the organizational and social benefits arising from informal communication networks

Introduction

The world of organizations is filled with opportunities to communicate. Under the mission of shared endeavour, organizing people involves a whole raft of structures, activities and events where communication is the point of the process. Meetings, briefings and presentations are all events where communication runs deep at the core of the process, while the informal networks are built upon interactions. These situations are unlike the face-to-face exchanges of the office corridors, and different processes are often at work. This chapter looks at how people can make the most of these settings, developing communication with real impact as a platform for moving organizations forward.

Creating communication with impact

Creating communication with impact begins with grabbing attention. A useful guide to this can be gained from an evening spent viewing adverts on TV, all of which use basic techniques to grab our attention. The lavish budgets certainly help advertisers to reinforce their messages in appealing ways, but they nevertheless have to overcome the initial problem of getting and maintaining the interest of the viewer.

Learning activity

Watching the commercials

Spend an evening paying close attention to the commercials. Try to identify which adverts grab your attention the most. What techniques are used to hook your attention?

Think about some of the adverts that fail to spark obvious interest. What techniques are used to get their messages across? Why is this an effective use of an expensive advertising medium?

While a variety of techniques are used to help get the messages across, there are two basic principles used which are relevant to all communication settings. The **first principle** is that unexpected and unusual images, patterns or sounds are constantly used as a means of triggering attention. Differences always stand out, just like when we notice changes to road signs or landmarks in the middle of a familiar journey. Many commercials rely heavily on this technique – think of the Rutger Hauer series for Guiness, the Boddington's 'cream of Manchester' series involving Gladys or the Halifax Building Society adverts using people to form construction art. In some respects, adverts are a background feature of TV viewing, yet they manage to excite interest and deliver effective communication in a very short time. The cost of screen time is a good indication of the success of the medium, and the fact that adverts often feature in conversations is evidence of the level of interest that they develop in people.

The **second principle**, also used in nearly all commercials, is best exampled by soap powder adverts. This type of advert often does little that is unusual, but instead delivers a predictable, routine pattern. This is often embedded in an instantly recognizable and stereotypical version of normality. Examples of this genre include the Danny Baker series for Daz, Fairy Liquid's well-worn theme or the 'nine out of ten owners said . . .' style of pet food commercials. Even adverts that contain unusual elements – Hamlet cigars or Carling Black Label – also deliver predictable patterns, even if only in the theme music or general style.

Combining the two principles forms an effective basis for communication with impact. Firstly, use the unusual, unexpected, surprising or even shocking as a trigger for awakening interest, and secondly, use routines, patterns and predictability to reinforce and carry messages. Even Guiness adverts, famed for their weird and wacky characteristics, contain enough familiar elements in the colours, tones, music and basic style to be recognizable almost without thinking. The first principle is known as using **entropy**, while the second is using **redundancy**.

Using entropy attracts our attention because of our basic survival mechanisms. We are readily placed in a state of alertness by unusual or unexpected events, in order to take evasive action if they turn out to be threatening. As a result, we quickly tune in to behaviours that are away from those we expect, and this response can be used to develop attention when we communicate. However, maintaining a state of alertness involves physical and mental preparedness, with increased levels of breathing, heart rate and adrenaline, and is therefore tiring. Entropy cannot therefore form the core of communication – think how tiring it is to concentrate on alternative films or theatre: nice for a change, but hardly a recipe for relaxation. It is here that redundancy shows its value, with communication that fits into expected patterns and routines. The familiar and predictable nature of the message makes it easier to absorb, in much the same way that following the plot of soap operas rarely strains our levels of concentration. Some losses of detail can occur as attention begins to wander, making it necessary to repeat the message and reinforce it in different ways. Hence the term, as a lot of the communication is actually redundant.

Put together these two principles work to maximize the appeal and effectiveness of communication. The next section looks at how these principles can be used to improve the quality of communication in some common management scenarios: giving presentations and conducting meetings.

Presenting skills

Learning activity

Presentations at work

Think about the manager's role at work. What management situations are likely to depend on effective presentation skills?

The ability to present well can improve the management of many work situations, not just the public speaking role of presenting to an audience. Speaking in meetings, making an impression on new clients, dealing with outside agencies, conducting interviews and training sessions are all situations that benefit from good presentation of facts and ideas. In most of these situations, the interaction differs from face-to-face communication in that structure is introduced, placing responsibility for the exchange on the person delivering the point. In one-to-one interactions, time can be spent listening and developing the other person's themes, but in most presenting situations there are less opportunities for this to occur. Accordingly, the pressures upon presenters to communicate effectively are higher than in less formal roles.

Presenting to an audience

Making a formal presentation to an audience is one of the least natural communication tasks facing managers. Often presenters are expected to speak on a particular topic of expertise, at some length and without interruption or feedback. Presentations expect great things of the listeners – that they will be interested, willing to keep their thoughts and views to themselves, and able to concentrate and remain involved when they have no opportunity to express themselves as people. In addition, the formality of presentations gives an atmosphere that many managers find uncomfortably stressful, and as a result they often fail to give their best performance. Many otherwise good managers fail to thrive in this situation and often people will seek to avoid situations where the focus is so firmly upon them. However, there are several strategies that can be used to create dynamism and add vitality to the most mundane of topics, enabling all managers to approach the situation with confidence. Presentations, for all their formality, offer managers important opportunities to build influence and networks. With a few reliable techniques, they can become situations to relish.

Learning activity

Using entropy and redundancy

Think back to the two key principles discussed earlier. What could be done to bring each of these crucial elements into a presentation:

- **Entropy**, which is needed to grab attention?
- **Redundancy**, which is needed to reinforce messages through repetition?

It is worth basing your ideas here on yourself, as it is no good thinking of wonderful ideas to introduce surprise that you would not feel confident enough to carry out. A useful source of ideas is to watch other people who seem to be effective presenters, and try to adopt things that would work for you. Just as we all have different personalities, it is important to allow your own qualities and style to come through – following a set of presentational rules is ineffective when the rules are designed for someone else.

Introducing redundancy is much easier, as it basically just requires simple repetition of the message using varying formats. Table 5.1 should give some ideas as to how and where you can introduce these essential principles of high-impact communication.

The significant thing about the list in Table 5.1 is that it is easier to prepare the items on the right-hand side of the list than those on the left, and so naturally people will work tirelessly on producing professional material to support their

Table 5.1 The essentials of high-impact communication

Entropy	Redundancy
Open with something that people will remember. While arriving in a puff of smoke is difficult, it is worth trying to grip people at the outset. 'What I plan to cover today' is predictable and expected, whereas 'I believe . . .' is not. Show commitment, energy and something of your emotions and people will give you more attention.	Use flipcharts, overhead projector slides and audience contributions to ensure that the messages are reinforced in different ways. By simply ensuring that the message is delivered repeatedly through different routes there is more chance of it striking home.
Make an effort to use language that appeals to the emotions. If you want people to notice something, colour it brightly with language that is vivid. Add in humour – having fun helps us to connect.	Support presentation material with handouts that cover the points made, perhaps using the opportunity to add some useful detail. Try to link these visually to the points made in the presentation.
Use your feelings. Don't just give facts – say how you feel, but make an effort to look as if you mean it. Commit your emotions.	Repeat points in summary form at regular intervals. Use recapping points as an opportunity to get audience feedback and questions.
You are on stage and giving a performance. People will find it difficult to concentrate on a routine presentation, but will remember a performance that excites and inspires. Think about how to **act** the part that you play with energy and innovation.	Restate ideas in different ways. Use metaphors, anecdotes and imagery to convey points in several different ways. Remember that these have more power to connect with people and convey the basic message than figures and graphs. These details have an important place, but it is rarely at the heart of a presentation.
Use silence before key points. Five seconds will grab everyone's attention.	Where possible, use exercises and audience participation to add experiences that reinforce the key ideas.
Introducing the unexpected. Ad libs do bring involvement because people feel that they are helping to create something fresh.	Introduce objectives clearly. Provide regular signposts to content and give a final overview at the end.

points. However, while redundancy is helpful in ensuring that communication is complete, it is important to note that it can be wasted effort unless entropy is used to gain attention first. Using entropy may be less natural or intuitive, but the effects on communication are powerful, provided it is not used to tiring and irritating excess.

It must be emphasized that these ideas rely on expressing something of yourself. The natural temptation, faced with such daunting situations, is to rely on structure and the formal skills to get you through. However, having the confidence to try to build a relationship across the floor helps presentations enormously, and this is best done through showing people characteristics and personality that they can relate to in some way. It helps to:

- Talk to people, not at them
- Recognize that conversations with people can add understanding and warmth
- Use humour and stories to make human contact and bring things to life
- Smile – it helps you and others relax

Putting together a structure

Presentations that follow a recognizable structure contain inbuilt redundancy in that the audience will get to see and hear things when they expect to. At the most basic level, a presentation that has an identifiable beginning, middle and end will satisfy people's expectations and make the communication easier to accept. This sets the presentation apart from the usual rhythms of conversation, or the ebb and flow of debate, and makes it important to impose a clear structure on the event.

Learning activity

The role of structure

What advantages does a structure bring to a presentation:

- For the presenter?
- For the audience?

What key features do you think a structure should provide?
   What disadvantages might be associated with structure?

Providing a clear structure is analogous to giving the audience a map. In the same way that a map helps you to find your way in unfamiliar territory and gives you some idea about the features that lie ahead, so a structure helps an audience to find their way through a presentation. Any journey into unfamiliar territory without a map is a journey full of entropy – tiring, full of surprises and with the potential to end up anywhere. A presentation without structure can lead to a similar experience, perhaps full of wondrous surprises, but with a high potential of leaving you lost at the end.

Fortunately, providing structure is relatively easy to do using a simple, standard framework. When preparing your presentation, check that it provides the following sections.

Introduction

This should be where you present the theme and title of the presentation so that the listeners are clear about what to expect. In map terms this is rather like telling people which part of the world they will be visiting. Aim to be brief here, as this gives an opportunity to restate the theme and style when providing the listeners with a more detailed map as the presentation proceeds. It is also the first opportunity to give signposts that show both your own style and the basic approach of your presentation, making this an opportunity to use the principle of entropy.

Value

This section is where the value of the presentation is made clear and the map equivalent is in describing the positive benefits of the particular place that people will be visiting. To the listener, the value is made up by a combination of the intrinsic interest of the subject, coupled with a style of communication that connects with them effectively. This section should certainly try to explain why people should listen by highlighting links between the presentation and the issues facing the audience. The stronger these links to people's concerns, the more the presentation will reflect their own experience and the more intrinsic interest the presentation will contain. Look hard to identify these links when designing the material and use every opportunity to signpost links regularly as this will remind people of the intrinsic value of the material.

Despite the basic worth of the presentation, two people, using identical material, can have a very different impact on an audience according to their particular style. The style you use, if it succeeds in connecting with the audience, adds value to the basic material. There is some use in highlighting your own worth as a presenter, by showing the links between yourself and the issues or concerns of the audience, but in general most of this message will come from the communication style and technique that you use.

 Learning activity

Providing the map

How can you provide an audience with a clear map of a presentation?

In general this is simple to achieve by describing the various stages that you intend to cover and reinforcing this with an overview on screen or flipchart that clearly identifies the key elements of the presentation. The most logical method of structuring almost all material for presentations is to use an approach based on the **four Ps**:

> 'First I shall describe the current **position** in our industry. Then I would like to highlight some of the main **problems** that are causing concern, before going on to look at some of the **possibilities** for moving things forward. Lastly I shall be presenting a **proposal** for action which I hope will gain the approval of this forum.'

This basic approach works for a surprising range of situations and can be used to help structure presentations across many issues. It is worth including some surprises to attract interest, and reinforcing where possible with visual aids, handouts or audience participation.

The main section

Learning activity

Using signposts

Good presenters help you to follow the direction easily, taking much of the work of following the map and moving along through the presentation away from the listener. This allows them to concentrate on the ideas and gives them space to think about issues and choices that arise. What techniques can you list that would help to make clear the changes in purpose and direction at various stages of a presentation?

The ability to signpost clearly at every junction of the presentation is a critical skill, enabling the audience to follow the route that you have planned through the material. It is no use having a structure that is clear to you if the audience is lost at the first change of direction. Be prepared to provide very clear signposts by making the changes deliberate and obvious. Don't be frightened to say things simply – 'We have now **finished** our look at the issues surrounding restructuring **and the next section** is going to work out how we might approach these more productively.'

Useful signposts

- Provide clear, deliberate oral links.
- Reinforce change points by reintroducing a screen or flipchart overview.
- Provide summaries at the end of longer or more complex sections to clearly signal the section end and ensure people keep pace with progress.

Summary

While there is likely to be a need to present summary points at various stages of a presentation, it is important to provide an overview of the key ideas, arguments and points that have been established. A powerful presentation will carry the audience along and allow them to follow the arguments, but recapping allows the presenter to add emphasis and simplicity to the overall message. Ideally, any negative reactions that have been sensed or expressed can also be built into the summary – 'The reservations held about the direction of policy are perfectly reasonable, but I believe that we would be in a better position to exercise influence if we express our interest in shaping policy from the outset.'

Conclusion

In many senses the hard work has already been done and all that remains is to convincingly present your proposal to conclude a successful presentation. However strong the case has been up to this point, it is crucial to recognize that it can all be wasted if the audience misses your proposal. Remember that entropy suggests that the offbeat, new or futuristic proposal will be more engaging and have more potential impact. If nothing else, it may fire people's imagination and start productive discussions.

Learning activity

Memorable conclusions

What would you do to ensure that the audience notices and remembers your proposal?

In different circumstances drums would roll and the audience would gasp because this would be the point of the show. Make sure that the audience can see your commitment to the proposal you have built and the conviction that you have for the arguments. Be prepared to engage emotions, both your own and those of the audience, by showing excitement, raising your voice, getting up on your soapbox and even being prepared to thump the table if it helps to get the point across. This is the climax, the point of the whole event, and everyone should feel that they have arrived there together.

Using visual aids

Visual aids such as flipcharts and overhead projector slides can greatly enhance the message by reinforcing points that are made and adding detail that cannot be readily communicated without a picture or diagram. However, they are not a replacement for good speaking, and if they are used badly they can be a barrier to making connections with the audience. Poor visual aids are worse than no visual aids at all, and even the best presenters have regretted some of the things that have been thrown up onto the screen as they spoke. The following guidelines should help you check whether your own visual aids are an aid or a distraction.

Vibrant visuals

Flipchart

- Using the flipchart maintains informality and intimacy with smaller audiences.

- Try to write large, clear points. Gain acceptance before paraphrasing audience contributions.

- Use different colour pens for impact and clarity.

- Stick up completed sheets in the room to allow people to refer to them later.

Projector

- Use a linking visual to highlight the common theme – this can be colour, logo or a slide frame.

- Support written information with pictures to reinforce your theme and add interest – slides that merely repeat what you say are missing an opportunity to put the same message across differently.

- Use a common style and format if possible – computer presentation packages have made this very much easier though using the same typeface, logo and colour produces a similar effect.

- Slide colours need contrast. Pastels may look nice in your dining room, but look wishy-washy on screen. Graphs and diagrams need strong colour to be effective.

- Give slides a number and a label that help you to identify them quickly.

- Avoid handwritten slides as it sends messages about your preparation.

- Use another person to help proofread – mistakes on a screen can be amusing, but they can also be embarrassing.

Making the point at meetings

Meetings vary in their style, purpose and process, but whatever the particular type of meeting, they can be a difficult setting in which to make points and communicate effectively. There are many possible reasons why meetings can become unproductive, awkward or difficult, often related to a variety of team or organizational issues. However, whatever the background or team culture that surrounds meetings, the situation is not helped by poor communication. This section is intended to look at how communication can be strengthened in a meeting setting.

Learning activity

Making the point

Consider the meetings which you attend. What factors make it more difficult for effective contributions to come:

- From you?
- From others?

Think about the people who seem to communicate successfully in the meetings. What factors do you feel contribute to their success?

Meetings can be seen as an organizational drama in which members of the workplace gather to perform. The bare bones of a plot are often put together in an agenda, but the details of the script are something that depends on the performances of the people who take to the stage. Often the absence of an influential actor can radically alter the form of the drama, turning dark tragedy into a light-hearted and inconsequential sketch, or allowing an opportunity for the bit-part players to show their skills in leading roles. Often, a part of the drama in meetings has nothing to do with organizational objectives, but is rooted in the social networks and individual agendas of the people who make up the cast. Communication is not only strained by the goldfish bowl atmosphere that meetings can develop, but by the intent of people to communicate more than is required by the bare bones of the business agenda. It is worth recognizing this aspect of the drama and being prepared to play your role accordingly.

Some ideas to help you share the limelight

The lack of a script can make it particularly difficult to put ideas across effectively, though sometimes an opportunity exists to 'present' to the meeting on particular topics. More often, the agenda provides the only guidance as to the intended plot, and the contribution that you make will depend upon your interpretation of this and your ability to improvise. This is a skill that depends heavily on personal attributes and influence. It is useful to spend time considering the agenda points in some detail – there will be issues on which you have a point of view, strong feelings or expertise, and others on which you have little interest or comment. Try to think about your own arguments and ideas, but also consider what outcomes you would like to achieve as a result, as it is very easy for outcomes to be lost in the midst of interesting debate. Having a plan of your line of argument and your intended outcomes helps you to see the process through to a conclusion. Of course, other people may still persuade you otherwise, but it won't be through your lack of preparation.

To help prepare

- Think about how people with different views might see the issue. Try to think about how such objections can be accommodated. If accommodation is impractical, how can the objections be countered? Think of reasoned arguments related to facts where possible.
- Put your arguments in a series of key points. This makes it easier to recall and helps to develop the ability to provide a summary or restatement when necessary.
- Recognize where it might be useful to negotiate or concede. Showing that you are able to compromise can help build support and helps lessen the build-up of tension.
- Use the time leading up to key meetings productively by building support with those people who share your views and by trying to establish and work on common ground with those with whom you disagree.

Learning activity

Taking to the stage

What can you do to make a positive impression in the meeting itself?

There are a number of ideas here that help, some of which depend on your own particular circumstances. To summarize:

- Use entropy and redundancy.
- Be aware of the processes taking place in the meeting – remember that much of what goes on is motivated by considerations other than the raw business in hand.
- Choose your time and place carefully – if other people have a burning issue to get off their chest, then their attention to your ideas will be limited.
- Avoid attacking people who make objections. Be prepared, especially if your idea is not easily supported by facts, to engage emotions – feelings are surprisingly persuasive.
- Gain commitment to your position by encouraging others to participate and openly working on process issues.

Communication and new management processes

Improving communication may be an obvious aim for organizations to adopt, yet it also can seem a difficult goal to achieve. In principle, better quality communication helps build the social fabric of organizations, and also underpins the success of a whole raft of practical objectives. Indeed, there are a number of 'new' management processes that have gained increasing acceptance in recent times that depend absolutely on the quality of communication an organization can develop and maintain. The basic thrust of these new processes is an emphasis on gaining the involvement and commitment of people, as opposed to a model of organizing that is founded on hierarchy and control. By developing a sense of individual value and shared ownership, the aim is to build real commitment and purpose into people's work, enhancing self-motivation and providing opportunities for initiative, learning and growth. Implementing this approach implies several important changes for the management of people, and these illustrate the core role that quality communication has to play in organizational progress.

One key change is in placing more reliance on individual responsibility at the heart of the organization. Rather than a conventional reliance on clear lines of authority and mechanisms for decision-making, instead there are increasing efforts to design systems that support individual initiative, autonomy and empowerment. While this opens up possibilities for creative solutions, flexibility and responsiveness, by allowing people to use their full range of capabilities, it also changes the nature of management communication. The need for systems that allow the clear flow of directives from the decision-makers to the implementors disappears, to be replaced by a communication web that allows for a multi-directional free-flow of information and ideas. The emphasis shifts towards a style of communication that transcends functional boundaries, chains of command and narrowly defined responsibilities, with management involved in a role of support, enablement and enquiry, rather than control and direction.

A second important change is in the growth of team-based styles of working. This again reflects a shift in management values towards a belief in the potential of people to contribute to organizational success. By designing approaches that allow teams to take on a broader range of responsibilities, the locus of communication shifts away from management towards the team. Important decisions on a whole range of technical and strategic issues can become part of the team responsibility, ensuring that important communication happens amongst the team, blurring traditional functional boundaries and levels as it happens.

Alongside this shift in responsibility comes a change in the nature of work itself. In a conventional environment of hierarchy and control, it is necessary to provide clearly defined duties, targets and boundaries within which people can perform. However, as self-direction grows, a flexible and open-ended definition of duties become essential, to allow people the opportunity to pursue their initiatives and goals in the most appropriate way. Communication is again an important vehicle for this process, allowing people to negotiate and redefine their role dynamically, outside of the conventional constraints of a narrowly-defined job description.

The changing emphasis on new processes has emerged through recognizing the limitations of approaches based purely on improving the efficiency of conventional methods of managing. Organizational life is littered with examples of control systems that do not appear to exercise control, project managers who fail to give direction or drive to key projects and administrators who build empires and erect barriers rather than provide for seamless background administration. Strategic planners regularly produce plans that disappear onto dusty shelves or are swept aside by events, while the regular rounds of evaluation fail to identify and deal with issues that are apparent to everyone. Of course, there are many examples where these things do contribute to productive effort, but it is increasingly apparent that organizations need to reach beyond doing conventional things better. Instead, alongside the search for improved efficiency, they need to reach within themselves to release the potential that resides in people. The next section looks at the way in which informal communication networks provide dynamism and direction in organizations.

Valuing networks and dialogue

Informal social groupings and communication networks grow and develop in all organizations in response to people's need for relationships. Often the formal organization regards the cliques and grapevines that form as a damaging feature, standing in the way of efficient communication and order. However, by understanding the reasons why the informal organization develops, and looking at some of the positive aspects of their behaviour, the next section highlights the valuable contributions that networks can make.

Learning activity

Networks and need

Think about the informal linkages and groups that have grown up in your own organization. What needs do you think these fulfil?

The need for networks

Networks grow and develop in response to individual needs that stretch beyond what the organization can formally provide. On a simple level, an individual might build friendships outside of the boundaries of their accounts office, for example, purely and simply because they cannot find people within the office who seem suitable for a friendly, sharing relationship. As long as people have needs to share their thoughts, concerns or ideas with other people, they will seek to build relationships that enable that to happen. Wherever people cannot meet these needs within the formal organization, they will seek networks that allow them to do this informally. This would be trivial except that organizations create some of the concerns and anxieties facing people, while at the same time they may not provide systems to allow these things to be resolved. This is particularly relevant because of two key points.

Firstly, organizations develop the features of bureaucracy in order to help them become technically efficient. Surviving in a competitive environment often depends upon doing things well, and significant effort goes into designing systems pursuing ever more effective methods of working or tighter control of processes and costs. Becoming an efficient organization involves pursuing clearly defined objectives through carefully planned methods using narrowly defined roles. The rewards of success are profitability and survival, key aims for most organizations and their members.

However, immersing people in an environment that is necessarily bureaucratic has a damaging impact. The very things that lead bureaucracies to be highly organized and efficient human systems also impact negatively on the people that make up the organization. Narrowly defined roles place limits on people's creative expression and confine them to a certain amount of dull routine. Social contact with people becomes subsumed in the need to pursue organizational aims, leading work to become a means to achieving corporate ends. Such features alienate people and feelings of isolation, insignificance, dissatisfaction and frustration can grow as a result. In addition, a bureaucratic, procedure-bound culture can easily lead people to develop feelings of not being trusted or valued, as they sink beneath the morass of a deadening and robotic structure.

Further, the development of procedures, systems and rules has significant effects. Greater efficiency may be one, but people will also become increasingly bound by the bureaucracy, with limits on the flexibility, variety and scope of work. People are driven in the direction of responding to the guidance and norms provided by the system, with little opportunity to design their own roles or approaches. This encourages passivity and dependence, and has a damaging effect on motivation. It also leads to deskilling, as people become increasingly dependent on implementing procedures with less and less scope for unique or creative action. Work can become removed from people's values, where they end up performing repetitive or routine tasks that have no cultural significance for individuals. This leads people into work that has no personal meaning and which devalues their personal commitment. They can end up feeling that anyone could perform their role, leading to behaviours that kick against the dehumanizing aspects of the system. In extremes, they can end up sticking slavishly to the procedures, with the familiar consequences of a system that cannot cope with the unforeseen or which seems trapped in a spiral of designing ever more rules to cope with ever more insignificant variations on the theme of becoming efficient.

Bureaucracies then are a positive response to the need to organize and work productively in a complex and competitive environment. Nevertheless, the impact of bureaucracy on people is not wholly positive, and in an effort to provide for needs that the bureaucracy cannot meet, people seek satisfaction in the informal networks that they design.

Secondly, even if these damaging reactions do not occur, the nature of bureaucracy is such that it places limits on the ability to cope with organizational life. The more complex or unpredictable the environment, the less it is possible to design a system or procedure in advance that can provide efficiency. Worse, when uncertain or unique events arise, the system has no inbuilt capacity to cope, nor does it have the potential to respond quickly. In a system driven by procedure and control, the formal system cannot adapt without using the established channels of communication and approval. A response may be designed, but it is characterized by a process of working through the hierarchy in a ponderous and cautious way. This is only prudent, as an organization does not hastily dismantle the very things that make it efficient merely because the unexpected arises; more likely, it uses the system to refine its approach only reluctantly.

Further, bureaucracies place value on particular functions, such as monitoring of current performance against standards, maintaining information flows, investigating deviations from the norms and refining policy. These functions are exercised through the formal organization, in meetings and through circulation of reports, in ways that reaffirm and maintain the system. This is most productive and conveys a greater sense of success and worth when the process is concerned with issues within the system, as these are issues that are bounded by the known procedures and policies. This builds up a tendency for bureaucracies to become self-referential, concerned with the tried and tested means of confronting standard organizational problems, partly because the culture supports this as the successful strategy. As a consequence, within the formal organization issues that are ambiguous or open-ended are sidelined, as the system does not have the means to cope and these issues are not legitimized by the dominant culture.

Case note

Barings Bank

The response to the collapse of Barings Bank provides an interesting example of this process in action. Following the collapse, the City review of the situation highlighted the need for better controls and procedures as a means of preventing similar situations from occurring in the future. While the particular incident did illustrate the inadequacy of controls in Barings, possibly leading to further prosecutions of other staff, the review fails to address more difficult issues. In a world of growing complexity, where derivatives appear to provide ever-more intricate investment instruments, managing risk becomes increasingly unbounded. One approach is to refine controls, but the system grows slowly and can become too unwieldy for the fast-moving world of financial trading. As traders respond to the mission of making money, taking risks becomes culturally dominant, reinforced in certain circumstances through the self-referential framework of the network. Controls can only provide part of the solution to these situations; the informal organization has a role to play in designing a new set of values to help. The informal organization provides a place where dialogue about the issues can occur, changing perceptions and cultural norms as it takes place. The most effective route to change is through people changing their values and beliefs, which in turn will alter their trading behaviour and their willingness to engage in actions outside of the acceptable framework.

Faced with uncertainty, ambiguity and open-ended problems, people have to find a means of resolving the issues. As the formal organization is not equipped for this, they turn to the informal organization for help. By establishing networks they can discuss the problems that fall outside of the framework of the system, yet continue to play their role in maintaining the formal organization. In doing so they can build alliances and take actions that ultimately threaten the organization. They are responding to concerns and anxieties that the organization cannot deal with, and which may lead to a change in the shape of the formal organization. Fulfilling human needs to resolve uncertainty and deal with the unexpected helps to move bureaucracies forward in situations where they are ill-equipped to move of their own volition. Networks fulfil some of our human needs, but also display characteristics and lead to results that can have fundamental consequences for organizations. The next section looks at some of these key characteristics and outcomes of the informal organization.

Characteristics of the informal organization

The informal organization has some key characteristics that are very different from those of the formal organization. Firstly, networks are self-organizing, consisting of people who come together to pursue a particular interest or share a set of common beliefs. These may be in response to concerns about organizational direction and policy or because particular issues have brought to the surface problems that cannot be resolved using the usual channels. They may simply arise because people want social connections or wish to acknowledge the alienating effects of bureaucracy and provide themselves with a form of mutual support and understanding. As a result, the agenda they pursue and the means by which they do so are decided within the network, and are not subject to the ordinary controls or approval of the formal organization.

Second, as networks operate outside of the formal systems, behaviour within them is primarily political. Issues and conflicts are resolved without reference to the hierarchy, systems or authority, but instead are addressed through influence, persuasion and negotiation. This gives networks the capacity to confront complex, ambiguous and conflicting issues, and to provide a stimulus to the design of new beliefs and values. As a result, networks can be viewed as a source of instability, seeking to deal with issues and provide new frameworks in areas that the formal organization fails to address. This instability can be damaging to the organization's conventional views, but is also a positive force for change, innovation and dynamism.

Thirdly, because networks provide a forum for discussing issues that fall outside those which the formal organization addresses, they become a source of organizational learning. The dialogue surrounding complex and uncertain issues, removed from the routine and mundane, offers opportunities for imagination and wonder. The informality of networks brings dialogue that is free of the pomp and circumstance of formal channels, enabling a freedom of expression with roots in the values and beliefs of people rather than the constructs of the system. As a result, the network is characterized by anecdotes and story telling as a means of relating experiences and sharing common understanding. This might on the surface seem far removed from the goal of organizational efficiency, but it actually provides a fundamental basis for passing on knowledge and resolving contradictions in organizational life.

Orr, J. (1990) 'Sharing knowledge, celebrating identity: war stories and community memory in a service culture', in Middleton, D.S. and Edwards, D. (eds), *Collective Remembering: Memory in Society*, Sage, Beverley Hills, CA.

Case note

Learning through networks – the value of going beyond the system

A classic case study of the learning potential of networks comes from Orr. This study details the work practices of photocopier service technicians, and examines the processes by which they resolve uncertainty, doubts and confusion.

The technicians are people who service and repair photocopiers in response to customer calls. These are sophisticated machines with complex electronic and mechanical components, and the company has therefore designed service manuals that give detailed procedures for correcting faults. They also run training programmes that teach the procedures and upgrade technicians in the procedures required by new machines. The manuals are comprehensive with step-by-step procedures for all recognized problems, reflecting the company drive for efficiency in customer service. Repair is expected to follow the prescribed procedures, and failure to do so is regarded as both mistaken (deviates from proven system) and unacceptable (challenges company aim of efficiency).

The system described reflects the aims of organizational bureaucracy in trying to improve efficiency through standardization of procedures and detailed technical support in a complex area. It also illustrates some of the problems, in that it limits creativity, enforces routine and apparently de-skills the role of technician. Potentially, such a system creates dependence on procedure and demotivates individuals.

Problems occur when the machines develop faults that are not described in the manuals, leaving technicians ill-equipped to proceed technically and in a potentially embarrassing situation with the customer. The procedural solution is to replace the machine, but this technical solution ignores the other significant aspects of the problem. For example, replacing machines makes the company's products look increasingly suspect and places the technician in an ineffectual role as the bearer of bad news. Further, it leaves the customer with piles of photocopying and without a machine. The practical solution adopted by the technicians is to improvise repairs using their store of experience, and then to hide the fact that this has happened from the company. They appear to work by the procedures of the company, yet in practice adopt methods that the company would not condone.

The process by which the technicians improvise is through dialogue between themselves, the customers and other technicians. Faced with an unexplained fault, the manuals are abandoned and diagnosis proceeds through recounting anecdotes about other repairs and the characteristics of customer use. As the tales continue, various experiments are prompted which eventually result in repair and the salvaging of individual and corporate pride. Customers are impressed with the on-site repair of an intransigent problem and the skills of the technician. New skills, beyond those taught in company courses, are assimilated into the technician's repertoire and another story is born.

Within the network of service technicians this has led to a growing exchange of stories about repairs. These reflect both technical aspects of problems (what the manual did not contain about the machines), but also develop understanding of the other factors (harassed office workers, third call this month or simple misuse). In swopping stories the technicians contravene their training and written procedures and move their actions outside of the formal organization. Yet within the network they learn about how to create solutions to problems that are unexpected or idiosyncratic. Paradoxically, the network approach builds skills, restores motivation through shared endeavour and reinforces the sense of self-worth that the manuals erode. This is dialogue that should not happen in formal terms, yet actively delivers an improved corporate practice. Informal story telling, a knock-about dialogue, is a key to progress and innovation.

This learning aspect of the network has been observed on our outdoor management development programmes. Faced with a manual that gives technical solutions to problems such as abseiling down a cliff, delegates set to work. In the course of their efforts they discover that abseiling hides other problems (height, slippery rocks, overhangs) that the manual does not cover. They begin a process of swopping experiences that move from the closely related ('I remember abseiling in Wales . . .') to the tangential (It's like the feeling you get waiting outside the boss's office . . .). In exchanging anecdotes, uncertainty and doubts are reduced, and anxiety falls as the group proceeds to solve a problem that extends beyond the boundaries of the manual. In the process they learn more than technical solutions to specific problems; instead they produce a new story that conveys a breadth of human experience and insight. In its turn,.the new abseiling story will help design solutions to some other issue where the formal organization cannot find a way forward.

The reader is referred to the case on air traffic control in Chapter 8. This also highlights the role of networks and the informal organization in the real practice of work.

The informal organization has a lot to give. It is a place where, despite the apparent lack of structure, objectives or control, many valuable things can happen. Through the social contact of networks people can feel a sense of purpose and place that can be entirely absent from the routine humdrum of their work role. The dialogue that occurs can help resolve issues that are difficult to place on the agenda of the formal organization, often because they challenge much of what is good and worthwhile in the parent body. Yet this is not just challenge for the sake of challenge, but a real response to the inconsistencies, frustrations and alienation thrown up by successful bureaucracy. In making the response, the network becomes a source of both accommodation and change, where ideas and perspectives are shaped by a political society into a new order. Networks provide innovation, drive and dynamism alongside destruction and destabilization. In doing so, they are a place where people make meaning, tell stories, find soul, and learn.

Managing the informal organization

The very nature of networks makes them difficult things to manage. They can plainly serve a valuable purpose, though they can also become the hotbed of subversive activity. However, they cannot be designed or formalized without losing the qualities that make them attractive and useful to people and organizations. Planning to establish a network runs counter to their core strength – that they are self-organizing in response to the needs people themselves identify. Yet there are conditions, such as a rule-bound and authoritarian culture, that we might expect to generate networks that are subversive and resistant to the messages of the organization. It should be possible, therefore, to design conditions that encourage the development of networks and support positive, learning outcomes from their activities.

Creating conditions

Developing new perspectives on control

Stacey, R. (1993)
Strategic Management and Organisational Dynamics, Pitman, London.

Exposing the organization to the uncontrolled and unpredictable consequences of network behaviour is a concern to many senior managers. The informal organization cannot be formalized without losing its potency, yet the potency also poses threats to existing good practice. However, direct involvement and monitoring is only one form of control – and sometimes an ineffective one at that, especially in the face of strong informal networks. Instead, organizations need to recognize that control can be built through political influence and through ensuring that power is dispersed rather than concentrated. This helps to provide a 'checks and balances' means of control, where subversive behaviour by networks can only proceed to real change if political alliances are developed to allow formal support and resourcing to happen.

Designing the use of power

The way in which power is used has a significant impact on the working of networks. If power is concentrated and highly visible, then networks will have little opportunity to drive change and may put their energies into resisting authority. If power is widely dispersed and rarely visible, then people will struggle to identify channels through which influence can be brought to bear. Again, the results of the informal organization may well have more to do with releasing frustrations than driving genuine innovation. Instead, the use of power needs to be designed so that it is seen as something which responds as conditions dictate, applied to pursue particular ends. Only then may networks grow to recognize that they might influence corporate direction, given the right conditions.

Establishing self-organizing groups

By making the effort to establish self-organizing groups, organizations can be a catalyst for the development of genuine networks. However, in order to maintain distance from the formal organization such groups need to be given genuine flexibility over how they operate, the issues that they address and the people that they choose to involve. Organizations can attempt to kick-start the network, but thereafter need to allow the group to develop its own direction. Making continual interventions, setting objectives or checking progress will bring the network firmly into the realms of the formal organization, responsive to all of its procedures and norms.

Adapted from Peters, T. (1992) *Liberation Management*, BCA, New York. On pp. 201–2 Lars Kolind comments on the spaghetti organization of Oticon: 'Shaping jobs to fit the person instead of the other way round. Each person would be given more functions and a "job" would be developed by the individual's accumulating portfolio of functions.'

Case note

Project working at Oticon

There is a formal 'computer job offer board'. Switch on any terminal and use the 'Jobs' icon to scroll through the different projects 'on offer'. You'll also find the project leader's name, a description of the job with a list of some of the tasks the leader thinks will be involved, and the project's expected duration. Usually, though, project leaders informally search out key people for their tasks. And vice versa: if a 'secretary' wants to tackle a marketing project, then she or he is wisest to informally chat up the appropriate project leader. Theoretically, a person could write an application, but . . . 'it's so much easier just to walk across the room and ask'.

Encouraging new cultural perspectives

Bringing in new perspectives helps prompt the exploration of contradictions and tensions in organizations. This can be done through the formal organization by moving people around departments and bringing in outsiders.

Opening up challenges and encouraging risk

People can be encouraged to form networks if they are presented with challenges to resolve. This conflicts with the conventional advice that people need clear objectives to work towards if they are to be productive and efficient. By presenting contradictions and unclear concepts, it can encourage networks to form to try to make sense of the challenges. In doing so new directions may emerge. The difficulty here is that the organization needs to model risk acceptance by demonstrating that it is alright to take on difficult issues and confront the norms. By allowing and encouraging networks to take on challenges, the organization takes a risk itself, as the outcomes are unpredictable and potentially destructive of the status quo. In the search for dynamism and innovation, such risk taking is vital.

> **Case note**
>
> *General Electric's 'work out'*
>
> General Electric adopt a novel method called the 'work out'. Senior figures present ideas to ad hoc groups of employees, who then retire to consider implications and issues. After this, they give feedback and ideas to the senior managers, who must respond openly. The process is designed to involve people, encourage challenge and bring issues to the surface across the company.

Developing group learning

Providing people with opportunities to openly engage in group learning may also provide valuable seeds for the growth of networks. By bringing issues and differences in perspectives to the surface and creating conditions where these can be legitimately explored, organizations can provoke new and challenging agendas. Part of this process will involve managers in exposing the game-playing, defence routines and covering-up that provide obstacles to organizational learning. Group learning provides a foundation for the openness, honesty and trust that is needed to inspire solutions to these issues.

Ensuring sufficient resource slack

In the end, addressing these issues takes time and effort. The potential gains of a flourishing informal organization highly committed to a positive organizational future are goals worth striving towards, full of hope and inspiration. Avoiding the uncontrolled and potentially damaging effects of a subversive and destructive network is also worthwhile. Conventional bureaucracies support a paradigm of efficiency and cost-saving, yet these arguments suggest a need to invest time and effort in less tangible processes that are well outside the framework of shareholder returns and measureable improvements to profit. Managers need to know that their efforts are valued more widely than the ten-hour day culture suggests; they need to know that they are valued for being the seeds of an unknowable future that with their best efforts will be enlightened, hopeful, uplifting and engaging.

Going forward

Our communication helps us to define and label the events that happen in the world around us. Within a process of sharing dialogue, we can invent descriptions and interpretations that provide meaning, sense, hope and vision. Engaging in the process provides opportunities that are enormously uplifting, challenging ourselves to design solutions in a world that presents uncertainty and ambiguity. Along the way we create a human drama that weaves faith and excitement amongst the patterns of making things work. We legitimize our actions and reward our success. The world moves forward and all the while we change.

Old conflicts, new blood, borrowed expertise, and vital issues are attracted into the arena of change where they combine to produce new myths and beliefs. Change becomes exciting, uplifting, and vital. The message is heartening and spiritually invigorating. There is always hope. The world is always different. Each day is potentially more exciting and full of meaning than the next. If not, we can change the symbols, revise the drama, develop new myths, or dance.

Bolman and Deal (1994)

Summary

This chapter has made the following key points.

➤ That creating communication with impact is based on using entropy and redundancy.
➤ That successful presentations are built upon using your personality.
➤ That communication in meetings must acknowledge and value the social and political aspects of the exchange.
➤ That communication underpins many contemporary management processes and initiatives.
➤ That dialogue and networks are a fundamental resource for organizational dynamics and change.

Further reading

Ralph Stacey has written an accessible and very interesting book that reflects themes developed in the source quoted above: *Managing Chaos* (1992, Kogan Page, London). It provides many insights into the complex world of organization change and develops the idea that organizations need to maintain a state of tension between 'ordinary' excellence and 'extraordinary' destruction and reshaping if they are to survive and develop.

   R.T. Pascale's *Managing on the Edge: How successful Companies use Conflict to stay ahead* (Viking Penguin, London, 1990) develops a fascinating model of the 'vectors of contention' which looks at the areas of the organization that need to be held in tension as a source of dynamic change. Many of these find their outlet through the informal organization and are inherently unplannable.

References

Bolman, L. and J. Deal, (1994) 'The organization as theatre,' in Tsoukas H. (ed), *Thinking in Organizational Behaviour*, Butterworth-Heinemann.

Heylin, A. (1993) *Putting it Across*, Michael Joseph, London.

Morgan, G. (1986) *Images of Organizations*, Sage, London.

Orr, J. (1990) 'Sharing knowledge, celebrating identity: war stories and community memory in a service culture', in Middleton, D.S. and Edwards D. (eds), *Collective Remembering: Memory in society*, Sage, Beverley Hill, CA.

Peters, T. (1992) *Liberation Management*, BCA, New York.

Stacey, R. (1993) *Strategic Management and Organizational Dynamics*, Pitman, London.

Part Two

Groups and Teams

6

Valuing and motivating others

Ignoring differences . . . not only supports the fiction of a homogenous workforce, but it leads to the potentially dangerous conclusion that differences are unacceptable.

Barbara Walker

Objectives

By the end of this chapter you will be able to:

➤ Explain how differences underpin organization progress
➤ Introduce strategies to help the organization to value diversity
➤ Describe the differences that affect the motivation of people
➤ Identify factors that lead to change in motivation
➤ Use strategies to maximize motivation at work

Introduction

Many would recognize that differences between people provide potential for both interest and discovery in organizations. Exploring and analyzing our differences provides a foundation for questioning our beliefs and values, and enables us to define our approach to work and to life. However, though differences can be the font of insight, innovation and wisdom, any realistic view must recognize that potential conflict is buried within different perspectives or approaches. Differences between people are therefore a source of both opportunity and conflict, and your task as manager is to help to create an environment where effective use is made of the diversity that exists in the team. Diversity is the key to organizations surviving in a world of changing patterns and pressures. An organization that fails to realize the variety and potential that exists in people is an organization that cannot match the pace of change and opportunity that fills the environment. Valuing differences is about creating dynamism and distinction; it is the source of organizational energy and progress. Real competitive advantage is rooted in difference and the ability to adapt more quickly than others. This section looks at the benefits of actively valuing differences and develops an approach that uses differences as the cornerstone of organizational and individual success.

The value of differences

Differences between people are all about us, notably in some of the persistent conflicts between various interest groups across the world. Some of these conflicts dissolve into violence or intransigence, as grounds for negotiation or compromise disintegrate in a struggle against the perceived threats embodied in differences, prejudice and ignorance. Undoubtedly, for many people, differences can be immensely threatening, despite the potential value in exploring alternative views. As a result, people are often more comfortable in their similarity, and strive to identify 'common threads' and shared purpose in their approach. This is reflected in the way that managers and organizations try to develop strong cultures and norms that dictate the boundaries of acceptable behaviour and approaches, placing limits on the diversity that can legitimately be expressed. A simple example can be seen in the unwritten dress codes that permeate many organizations and which help provide uniformity and consistency, but at the expense of limiting people's freedom of expression.

Learning activity

Shared purpose

What things are done in your organization to develop a sense of shared purpose? What things are done to develop common approach to the work itself?

Organizations often try to develop a shared sense of direction through visionary statements about goals or mission. These have the effect of providing a diverse set of people with an overall goal or approach, binding people together in common pursuit of the same objective. In addition, the effort to focus attention on similarities often goes further – indeed, job titles, responsibilities and gradings all express ways in which organizations identify similarities rather than actively manage differences. Of course, there are pragmatic reasons for this, but the point is that there are many ways in which organizations identify and focus on similarities between people, rather than choose to manage the real level of diversity that exists. Challenges to these norms can lead to sanctions, both through the official reactions to 'breaking rules' and the unofficial ostracizing of people that exhibit behavior beyond conventions.

Case note

Graduate trainees

Working with graduate trainees in an agricultural machinery business has highlighted this paradox. The trainees are regarded as an important source of dynamism and new direction in an organization that operates conservatively in mature markets. They are encouraged through a variety of projects to network across the organization, making links with colleagues operating in different countries to develop initiatives and ideas that will bring innovative products to the marketplace. This role is reinforced through giving the graduates time to work in a variety of plants and familiarize themselves with many aspects of the organization's business. They are also given special training and little expense is spared in emphasizing their status as a potent source of change.

However, despite the commitment of senior staff to the ideals of the scheme, graduates report that in practice it is difficult to carry ideas forward. When they present initiatives in meetings, they meet resistance from senior executives and other practising managers, largely because they challenge the unwritten conventions of the organization by confronting orthodox methods and bypassing the usual development mechanisms. Executives and managers find that part of their role is being overtaken and their political power is being threatened. As a result, despite the organization's commitment to developing diversity by tapping the energy and ideas of people who are not yet immersed in the conservative culture, the differences threaten existing structures and roles. This can be very frustrating for the graduates and the organization's attempt to generate change.

Despite the value of a pragmatic response, in the real world people **are** different. More particularly, our differences – as we perceive them – are part of our essence. They are, in some circumstances, the very thing that makes us feel unique and valuable. Ignoring differences, or trying to minimize the occasions when they surface, can have the effect of making people feel like cogs in a machine – similar in design, purpose and easily replaced. It can develop stress between the differences people feel and the cultural norms that the organization imposes. For people who feel that their differences are important, such an approach will devalue their contribution, and may have the effect of alienating them from the organization.

Learning activity

The value of difference

Think about organizations. List the ways in which differences between people can make a positive contribution to effectiveness at work.

One obvious area in which differences can make a very positive contribution is in customer care, or in indeed any area where success depends on the quality of the relationship between people. Some staff will be able to form better working relationships with particular clients, and will have a natural advantage in terms of achieving business objectives. Whatever the basis for the strength of the working relationship – a shared enthusiasm for football or a similar sense of humour – it is likely to mean that a particular staff member is able to obtain better results. The differences between people in terms of their ability to form and maintain a particular working relationship can therefore be used to advantage. Making use of the affinity that exist between customers and staff is therefore one way in which the differences between staff can be valued.

Learning activity

Differences and fairness

Making active use of the differences in this way might lead to a situation where workload reflected the particular strengths of each staff member. One staff member may end up doing a lot of administration work, while another did far more face-to-face work with customers.
  What potential problems might this approach bring?
  How can these be managed?

Making use of simple differences is no more than valuing as a positive asset people's strengths in an organization. Part of the barrier to making this process effective is that there is often a sense that the only way to maintain equality of opportunity is to treat people as if they are the same, by giving them an equal share of the same work. While such an approach has the advantage of being

Case note

Breakthrough

This effort to recognize differences is exampled by many of the modern approaches to customer care. We are probably all familiar with the customer care formula exhibited by fast food services and the carefully scripted lines of 'have a nice day' or 'enjoy your meal'. While this is better than the surly attitudes that may have prevailed in the bad old days, it soon becomes little more than lip-service, and very rarely makes a real connection with the individual customer. British Airways have developed a different strategy in their 'Breakthrough' programme, and are training cabin crew to make individual observations of boarding passengers, aimed at developing the skill to make a genuine connection with each passenger. While this approach carries the risk that the greeting comments made may be wide of the mark, it does also carry the potential rewards of them genuinely arousing the passenger's interest as an individual. By recognizing the differences, and being prepared to meet diversity with diversity, the airline tailors its customer care to each passenger, forming the basis of real one-to-one service.

even-handed, it does not recognize and use the very real differences that exist between people. As these are potentially a source of organization success, the manager is missing an important opportunity in an attempt to be fair. Moreover, it is a doomed attempt, because it is ultimately impossible to be even-handed, so the potential for staff to feel unfairly treated is always there anyway. It is better to work to value and manage differences by allowing strengths and weaknesses to surface and be explored in an open forum rather than to attempt to pretend that differences do not exist or are unimportant.

This approach carries implications for many aspects of the organization, requiring positive regard for all individuals and a supportive work environment. In particular, as work tasks undertaken begin to reflect strengths and a negotiated workload according to individual needs, reward systems need to grow to reflect shared success rather than individual job roles. Continuing to manage with a reward system that is based on grades or performance inhibits the acceptance of differences – people who are paid according to their merit are less likely to reveal strengths or differences that do not fit with the narrow measures used by the reward system. Experience with merit pay systems has in any case uncovered real problems in measuring performance, and the difficulties staff face making judgments about people's contribution, suggesting that reward systems are not simply resolved by moving from grades to performance. Valuing differences implies that rewards need to be revisited and systems designed that accept the diversity of contribution that people can make wherever they are in the organization. Genuine acceptance of differences needs a reward environment that supports shared success and mutual acknowledgment of the positive value that individual people can make.

Recognizing key differences

Learning activity

Exploring differences

Think about your own working situations. What are the major sources of differences that exist between people? What are the positive effects of this? What negative effects can be attributed to differences? How would you suggest that these could be managed to make more use of the differences?

Some of the key differences between people are based on the values and beliefs that they bring to work. These factors affect our whole approach to work – whether it is something we undertake through a well-developed work ethic or pursue because of its intrinsic interest. People can approach work with a deep-rooted suspicion of all things hierarchical, or they can have highly political aspirations to make it to the top. Our values, developed through our upbringing and experiences, underpin all of our actions and reactions, making them a fundamental difference that arises in the workplace that has a significant impact on our approach to working life.

Our experiences affect our style, attitude and preferences, all of which are brought to the surface through our work tasks and our interactions with those around us in the work environment. They affect the way we adopt roles within teams, based on our skills, interests and personalities. All of these differences are shown up in team settings, where people are working towards common objectives together. Differences in teams actually make a strong contribution to a team's ability to deal with a diverse range of tasks and situations, as different strengths can complement other weaknesses. However, simple differences in preferences and style can also be a potent source of misunderstanding, disagreement and conflict.

One last set of differences is worth particular mention, partly because they are surrounded in legislation designed to prevent the differences being exploited. Age, gender, disability and sexuality all provide obvious differences between people that can be the cause of misunderstanding and even discrimination at work and in the wider society. As with other differences between people, it is critical that these are valued as part of a fundamental positive regard of others rather than allowed to become a means of dividing or labelling people at work.

Accepting differences begins with individual people being willing to accept their own prejudices and challenge their own perspectives on others. All people, whatever their role, bring preconceptions and stereotypical views about others into the workplace. By recognizing that our judgments about others are based on our own experiences and reactions, we are able to begin the process of challenging our views of people who display uncomfortable differences in appearance, values or behaviour. By encouraging this process to be acceptable at work as part of the way in which people learn to understand more about what other people have to offer, the organization can support diversity and benefit from the rewards that differences can bring.

Case note

The fourth age

Both supermarkets and DIY chains in Britain have recognized the strengths of using older people to fill many roles in the workplace, including packing and restocking. Employers have found people who are keen to be valued as employees and who do not react to the apparent lack of opportunities in mundane work. Surveys have found that customers find staff more experienced, helpful, polite and better with advice.

Similar opportunities have been observed with the employment of disabled persons. An American food manufacturer, Carolina Fine Snacks, began employing disabled persons in packing and shipping. Productivity has increased, reliability of attendance has improved and employee turnover has reduced.

Adopting an approach that aims to encourage and value differences is essentially based on recognizing the real diversity that exists in people. By using the diversity as a source of innovation and as the basis for a productive approach to organizing work, it is possible to make better use of the skills and strengths that exist in a group of people. Problems may arise as differences in work type or role lead to conflict between people, but the discussion that arises is an opportunity to develop further understanding and acceptance of differences. It is important to recognize that the issue of differences is an unavoidable feature of people in groups, and that it is an issue that can open up pathways to a more interesting and productive organization. Attempting to avoid the issue by concentrating on similarity undervalues the contribution that diversity can make and the qualities of the people that make up the team. When people do not feel that their particular qualities are used or valued, then they are unlikely to be motivated to contribute to the best of their abilities.

A key area of difference is in the things that motivate people. For the manager, part of the skill in building a successful team is in ensuring that people are motivated to use their full potential constructively at work. If people merely turn up at work to do the narrow requirements of their job to predefined standards, then the opportunity is being missed to set new standards and work beyond simple job descriptions in areas where our strengths can make a significant contribution. While the former may be all that is required, a well-motivated person will bring added value to work and will gain personal satisfaction and reward through doing so. Understanding and valuing the differences in motivation between people is therefore a useful thing for a manager to develop within the context of their own team. As a foundation for this, it is worth exploring the basic needs that people have, as allowing people the opportunity to satisfy needs is a step towards realizing their potential.

The basis of motivation

Learning activity

Motivation at work

Think about your own experiences of school, college or work. From your observations, what things tend to motivate the people you know to give of their best?

Motivation of individuals is a complex aspect of management, partly because there are great differences in the things that motivate various individuals and these can change according to circumstances. However, people do have aspirations or goals of some form in life and use work to help achieve those that are important to them. For some people, these are long-term goals, whereas for others they are very immediate, often as a result of the particular circumstances that people face at the time. People suffering economic hardship, for example, may be less concerned with providing for their retirement than those who are reasonably well off. By observing people and listening to the things that they say, it is possible to understand something about the things that they aim to achieve. This gives some insight into the things that may help to motivate them to give their best. If the broad needs of people can be identified, and some of the likely changes to these needs predicted, then the manager is better placed to design work and tasks that will link into people's personal aims. If this link is clear, it should help achieve better motivation. This section aims to explain some of the key categories of goals or needs which people aim to satisfy through their efforts.

Work by John Hunt (1986) has identified six basic categories of need which individuals may pursue during their lives. These are:

- Physiological or 'comfort' needs
- Security or structure needs
- Social or relationship needs
- Recognition needs
- Power needs
- Growth needs, including the need for autonomy and creative expression

Learning activity

Thinking about your own needs

Consider the basic categories of needs listed above, and try to note down:

- Which categories seem to be important in terms of motivating you in your current role and stage of life?
- An example of when you feel other categories were particularly important to you. How do you explain any differences?

1. Physiological or comfort needs

˙This need is based on the interest that individuals have in physical comfort levels. This includes the day-to-day comfort afforded by a particular lifestyle or standard of living, as well as health, fitness and freedom from stress. This need is very variable across individuals, depending to some extent on their socio-economic circumstances and the context in which they live. People from a poor background may be driven to satisfy this need, as might individuals who have suffered some setback to their normal standard of living.

 ## Learning activity

Changes to comfort needs

What things in general do you think would have an impact on people's need for physical comfort?
How can a manager provide opportunities for these needs to be met?

This need is highly dependent on context, being easily affected by things that threaten or affect an individual's level of physiological comfort. These can, for example, include redundancy, restructuring, illness or accident. In addition, changes to the circumstances of close associates or family can also have an impact on an individual's drive to satisfy physiological needs. As a consequence, a restructuring programme that involves redundancy or downgrading will inevitably affect the motivation of other, unaffected people by driving them to re-assess their basic comfort needs.

While many of the factors that impact on this need are outside of the work environment, and very much beyond the influence of managers, some are more readily influenced. Any significant change in the workplace is likely to raise questions concerning people's ability to earn a basic living, making it more likely that meeting basic physiological needs will become more important as a driving force to them. This has important implications for change management, emphasizing the need to offer continuous reassurances over future job security if people are going to contribute effectively to the change.

Similarly, if managers are able to keep in touch with people's circumstances, then they are better able to recognize when external events are likely to influence needs, and so able to offer appropriate support. For example, it may be appropriate to consider moving people to more routine work during times of serious changes to family circumstances as it is likely that people will want to satisfy basic comfort needs as easily as possible.

2.   *Security or structure needs*

This need is based on the individual's need for psychological safety. It is very closely linked to the physiological needs already discussed, but is concerned with meeting those needs in the future. For example, someone with a high need for security will be more interested in professions with stability and a reliable career path, whereas a person with low needs for security will be able to accept work with a higher risk attached.

People with high need for security are likely to respond to uncertainty by building structure and order into work. In doing so they reduce uncertainty and build predictability through a systems-based approach. While this can produce improved levels of security, the systems so designed are to meet their needs, and are not necessarily to the benefit of the organization. Larger organizations tend to attract people with high needs for security, as do departments such as administration or accountancy, and these sections can begin to take on a purpose of their own.

External factors in the individual's family and personal circumstances will have a significant impact on this need. It is again important for the manager to keep close to their staff and in touch with their circumstances in order to continue to understand what things may be affecting their motivation and achievements.

 Learning activity

Threats to security

What factors might lead individuals to seek more security and structure in life?

This need is affected by very similar events to the physiological or comfort needs. Major change at work, domestic upheaval or threats to our relationships can all have the effect of driving people towards security and structure needs. Again, this is important in a changing environment, as people may tend to pursue the very things – systems, order and procedures – that the change may be trying to alter. The reaction of individuals in these situations is driven by their own needs, and may well be counter to the needs of the organization, inhibiting the process of change.

3.   *Social or relationship needs*

This need reflects the interest of people in finding a network of relationships within which they belong. While all people have this need in some degree, it can be satisfied in a wide variety of different ways according to individual personality and circumstances. For example, some individuals may find that their need for relationships is satisfied within the family, leading them to have little motivation in pursuing these needs in the work environment. Others may find that their personal circumstances do not lead to these needs being satisfied, and they may instead find that work is an opportunity to build networks of relationships that make them feel wanted as individuals. These two examples illustrate how different motivation can be, with people in the same team being driven by similar needs but seeking very different things from their working situation.

A high need for relationships can lead people towards jobs that have a natural emphasis on people, and where the work gives opportunities to build significant relationships. These include jobs in personnel, sales and training. To some extent, the value of relationships can appear higher in situations of dependence, where other people are forced to depend on us as individuals, so nursing and caring roles are particularly likely to attract people with a high concern for relationships. However, the modern emphasis on team-based styles of working gives more opportunities to satisfy these needs in almost any job role, so people with relationship needs are found throughout all organizations.

Learning activity

Developing relationship needs

What changes to personal circumstances may lead people to seek opportunities to satisfy this need at work?

What changes may lead people to be less interested in satisfying this need in the work environment?

How might the culture of the organization affect this need?

This need may change significantly as people move through various stages of life. In early adulthood, for example, many people are seeking to establish their place in life, and much of this revolves around social ties as well as work success. Accordingly, people at this stage can either appear very motivated by outside social opportunities, or they can appear to need to find these networks at work. Forming a significant relationship, through marriage or otherwise, is also an event that is likely to affect the way in which this need is met. Typically, people will go through a stage where the need is very much met by their main relationship, and those within their new extended family, leading them to be less motivated by opportunities to satisfy these needs at work. A similar effect can often be observed with the birth of a first child.

This particular need may also be strongly influenced by cultural factors. A work culture that values relationships highly and which encourages people to develop networks as a basis for understanding and learning may alter the cultural perception of this need. This effect is evident in Japanese society, where the sense of belonging is strong and reinforced by the way in which companies organize strong links to their employees' families and the community. Similarly in Britain, with its long history of industrial relations division, there appears to be less natural acceptance of work as an important part of our lives, particularly as a source of significant relationships. While this culture seems to be receding, the relatively high mobility in British society may be one legacy of the lack of importance attached to organizations as a basis for satisfying our relationship needs.

4. Recognition needs

This need is based on our concern to have our achievements recognized by other people. While most people feel this need to some degree, it is linked closely to factors in our upbringing, and is rather less dependent on current events and circumstances. People who have not received recognition and praise as a child, either through their parents or through schooling, are likely to feel this need strongly in adulthood. As a consequence, they will seek working situations that allow them to experience the attention of others. Work roles that have high visibility, such as policing, teaching, selling or the military, are all attractive to people with high needs for recognition.

Learning activity

Providing recognition

As this need is less affected by circumstances, once identified, a manager should be able to apply strategies to meet the need. How would you suggest that a manager can provide recognition for people at work?

This need is one of the easiest for managers to meet, as recognition is straightforward to give by praising individual or team successes. The only real difficulty with doing this is that praise is not necessarily easily given, as cultural barriers can develop in some organizations that work against such positive and supportive behaviours. Also, even where people give praise, others do not always accept it as a genuine attempt to recognize their qualities or their contribution. In some organizational cultures, there is a reluctance to accept that praise is anything other than political manipulation.

People can also give recognition through genuine acceptance of the concerns of others, or the problems they have in trying to achieve their goals. By taking the time to listen to concerns, demonstrating the value in which the other person is held, recognition takes place. This is useful in circumstances where praise is not necessarily warranted, or where there are strong norms that resist praise. Here, by giving recognition for the individual by discussing or acknowledging their particular concerns, it is possible to strengthen mutual acceptance and lead towards a situation where praise is more acceptable.

5. *Power needs*

This need is based on the individual's interest in exercising power and influence over people or events. Again the need is dependent partly on factors in a person's upbringing, such as exposure to 'powerful' role models, or experience with power roles such as captaining sports teams in young life. However, contemporary experiences continue to shape power needs, and promotion to managerial posts, experience in leading projects or success with influencing others may well lead people to seek power through work.

Of all the needs identified, this one appears most frequently in the profiles of successful individuals and is closely correlated with achievement in organizational life in terms of position, salary and other indications of personal performance. Some of this may be because people develop power-seeking goals through their position, but undoubtedly some of the factors underpinning success relate to people having a need for power from an earlier age. This does not suggest that other people, with different needs, cannot be successful, but that power needs are a significant factor in achieving success in organizations. It also tells us nothing about how that search for power is best conducted; exercising power ruthlessly, with little regard for the needs of others, may not be the heart of the message here. Power needs to be exercised in ways that are acceptable to others, and this varies according to the context and culture that people are operating within. Seeking power may be a factor in achieving personal success, but it does not reduce the need for people to manage thoughtfully, with proper regard for the people and situations they meet.

Learning activity

Power and people

Power is often closely tied up with position in organizations, and this is sometimes symbolically reinforced using executive car parking spaces, separate dining areas and more comfortable offices. This has the effect of linking power with recognition, even though the two needs may be quite separate and distinct to the individual. Yet power may be an important need for people throughout the organization, and this may even emerge negatively in the form of intimidation and harassment. How can all people in the organization be given positive opportunities to exercise power?

6. *Autonomy, creativity and growth needs*

These needs grouped together represent the individuals's concern for self-fulfillment or self-actualization. Linked together they are an expression of growth – an ideal towards which the individual aspires and strives. The separate elements can be pursued individually, though people tend to pursue all three strands of self-fulfillment at the same time, as they are to some extent interdependent.

- Autonomy needs are an expression of the individual's concern for independence and control over their self. Achieving autonomy allows the individual to make choices for themselves, based on fulfilling their own needs, rather than be dependent on the choices and control of other people. This opens up more options for the individual, and allows choices that reflect personal aims of self-fulfillment.

- Creativity needs are an expression of the individual's search for originality and innovation in the activities that they pursue. The greater freedom that autonomy brings opens up the possibilities for creative choices, but the two needs can be separately pursued. For example, it is possible to be creative in a team setting, even though choice and control remains with the team leader.

- Growth needs are an expression of the individual's pursuit of challenge, opportunity and new situations or experiences. Pursuing these needs implies a requirement to develop creativity in order to deal with new situations that are encountered. Similarly, while autonomy is not necessary for growth needs, it certainly allows more options to be taken up in working situations.

People who value self-fulfilment highly tend to have initiative and are often interested in exploring problems and designing lateral solutions. They are less interested in routine, and indeed often lose interest in projects when they have moved towards completion, well beyond the exciting phase of exploration and innovation. They can be restless, always on the lookout for new and interesting challenges, but rarely finding sustained satisfaction in the here and now. People who pursue self-fulfilment through autonomy, creativity and growth have a great deal to offer organizations, as they can be a potent source of ideas, initiatives and innovation. However, despite their suitability for entrepreneurial or creative roles, they tend to have little interest in or need to depend on other people, systems or structure, and this can make them difficult people to manage in a typical organizational environment.

 Learning activity

Thinking about self-fulfilment

People with high needs for self-fulfilment are potentially a valuable asset for teams. How can the best use be made of the creative potential of these people? What problems might they bring to a team? How can self-fulfilment opportunities be provided for other people?

Motivating others

Identifying these basic needs or goals that people hold is a useful step towards motivating others. By understanding the things that people aim towards, or feel the need to fulfil, it is possible to design work or tasks that allow people to meet their own needs as well as those of the organization. People can either find opportunities to fulfil their needs at work, or they will invest some of their energies elsewhere, on activities where those needs are better met. Unless organizations make an effort to understand and value the different things that motivate people to work towards their needs, they will fail to release the potential energy and inspiration that lies within their people.

The motivation of individuals is based on understanding their unique needs, and managers need to develop the relationships that allow them to understand the factors that drive each person. These are likely to vary according to time and circumstances, and managers need to be wary of making assumptions based on previous experiences. A constant dialogue, based on genuine exploration and expression of needs, gives the most reliable information and ensures that staff can achieve their personal goals alongside those of the organization. However, there are several useful guidelines which can help to give people opportunities to meet needs through their work, and these are explored in the following sections.

Provide more complex work assignments

Complex work is inherently more challenging than simple tasks and therefore affords more opportunities for fulfilling growth needs and achieving recognition. It can also increase the need to build relationships in order to achieve outcomes. However, providing more complex assignments can be demotivating unless sufficient structure is associated with the task, and managers need to be careful to help define objectives that enable people to approach complex tasks with confidence.

A useful way of providing opportunities for complex work can be found through job swap, job shadowing and multi-skilling initiatives. These all have the advantage of adding to motivation possibilities and also building the skill base of staff. Coaching and making use of the variety of informal development opportunities that arise in the work environment – team discussions, dealing with exceptions or delegation – all add to the range of ways in which challenging work can be provided.

Ensure that work is arranged in identifiable and complete units

Work that forms a part of an unseen whole, such as assembling components or operating a stage of a process, is inherently less meaningful than work that gives identifiable and complete results. Work should be organized to allow individuals or teams the opportunity to see real results, thereby increasing the significance of the task, highlighting structure and allowing recognition, ownership and growth needs to emerge.

Develop opportunities for customer contact

By encouraging real contact between people at work and the customer, both internal and external, the organization builds the possibility for relationship needs to be satisfied through work. Providing the opportunity does not mean that people have to make work relationships the source of satisfying social needs, but allows those who wish to do so a framework in which these goals can be achieved. Contact with customers and other outsiders also provides opportunities for feedback to be obtained, and helps people see the external value of the work that they do.

Devolve the authority for work-related decisions to the people doing the work

Encouraging people to take control over the way in which they approach tasks and organize their work allows them to maximize autonomy, creativity and growth. It also provides opportunities for recognition to emerge, and for power to be developed. At the same time some people will value the possibility of defining their own structure under which the task will be organized and executed. Others may require more initial structure, and this is an opportunity for managers to negotiate a framework that meets the needs of both the organization and the individual.

Develop and maintain open feedback systems

Providing feedback improves the potential for recognition to be gained, and in an open, two-way framework will also allow power to be explored in the relationship. Dialogue gives a basis for negotiating objectives and structure, and for ensuring that performance satisfies both the aims of the organization and the individual. This is a crucial process in terms of building understanding of needs between people, and helps to overcome the tendency to project our own needs and drives onto others. Many of the motivational difficulties in organizations are related to the fact that tasks and work are often allocated by people with needs associated with management and achievement. These typically include power, recognition and autonomy, and often do not include as much focus on relationships, structure and comfort. This causes problems when staff do have these needs, yet have little opportunity to express these or ensure that they feature in job design.

Another advantage of open feedback systems is the opportunities they provide for individuals and teams to give and receive praise. This practice can develop cultural acceptance of the value of praise and constructive comments, and highlight the value of recognizing individual differences. It also enables collective celebration of successes and helps generate stories that enable people to pass on valuable anecdotes.

Model enthusiasm and commitment

Providing a model of energetic and motivated behaviour is inspiring of itself, particularly if people are able to identify and share the positive outcomes that it generates. Energy levels vary from person to person according to many factors, but people who bring visible energy into the workplace and achieve results do provide others with the confidence to follow the model.

Help people to understand the context and purpose of work

Making an effort to help staff see the big picture gives an overview of the broader context and reinforces the value of the work that people do. This brings structure to work, and helps develop feelings of security in the organization's objectives. By ensuring that this takes place in a forum that allows challenge and exploration of goals, values and ideals, people can also pursue power, recognition and growth needs.

Strive to develop a positive regard for others in all circumstances

Beginning with the assumption that all people are driven by positive intent and able to make a worthwhile contribution helps to enhance motivation. Positive regard helps us to seek explanations for mishaps and failures in systems and complexity, rather than in the performance of individuals. It helps us reinforce the belief that sometimes things will go wrong despite the best efforts of people rather than because they have deliberately, or misguidedly, contributed their worst. Above all, it accepts that people are imperfect, yet values the imperfections as an expression of our differences, a sign of the potential diversity and value that surrounds us in other people.

Case note

The Pygmalion effect – the Dov Eden studies

Helping others to achieve their full potential is at the core of effective management. The Pygmalion effect is a type of self-fulfilling prophecy whereby holding positive expectations about other people's potential actually leads to them improving their performance. The name comes from the mythical Greek sculptor who brought a beautiful statue to life through the power of belief.

Professor Dov Eden has done a series of experiments into the effect at Tel Aviv University. In one experiment Eden gave instructors working with the Israel Defence Forces different expectations about the potential of 104 soldiers attending a training course. Although the ratings he gave – high, regular or unknown – were actually randomly assigned to names, the instructors believed the ratings were based on actual knowledge of the soldiers. By the end of the course, the soldiers who had been allocated a high rating were consistently receiving higher grades from their instructors across a range of activities. Further, the soldiers expressed greater enjoyment of the course and were keen to do further training. Raising the instructors' expectations about randomly picked soldiers appeared to lead the soldiers to expect more of themselves, and this led to them deliver better performances.

In a second study Eden randomly chose 25% of soldiers enrolled on a course and told them directly that they had high potential. Again, by the end of the course it was found that instructors had rated these people higher across a range of tests and examinations, despite being unaware on this occasion of which soldiers were rated highly. Raising soldiers' expectations about their own ability seemed to lead to improved performance, regardless of the actual potential of the people in the target group.

Eden suggests that these effects are probably relevant in the workplace, and that challenging negative perceptions of people is a fundamental basis for improving performance. By developing a high expectation culture that ignores the evidence of past failure or poor performance and continues to set challenging goals, people will be motivated to perform beyond themselves. Holding such expectations about people is positive, optimistic and empowering, enabling people to break free from the barriers imposed by a culture of poor performance and low expectations.

Going forward

Exploring differences is the key to better understanding of people and a crucial component of organizational dynamism. By searching for the things towards which people aspire, we learn about values and find ways of challenging our own perspectives. The process helps us to design workplaces where corporate purpose can be pursued with energy and people can find personal fulfilment in the effort that they make. Work can become a source of identity, affiliation and support, a place that encompasses the whole of human aspirations for growth and development. Above all, it can make a place where people construct meaning and purpose through their endeavours that enriches their lives.

Summary

This chapter has made the following key points:

➤ That differences between people are a vital expression of personal identity.
➤ That differences between people are a valuable source of system diversity that enables organizations to maximize their adaptability.
➤ That the motivation of people is linked to the personal goals that inspire individuals to effort.

➤ That personal goals include six broad categories of aspiration, including;
   (a) physiological or comfort needs;
   (b) security or structure needs;
   (c) social or relationship needs;
   (d) recognition needs;
   (e) power needs;
   (f) autonomy, creativity and growth needs.
➤ That providing motivation is based on improved understanding of individual needs and differences.
➤ That a range of strategies can help to develop a work environment that maximizes the potential for motivation.

Further reading

Motivation is about finding inspiration and ultimately the sources of this are unique to each of us. Though management books can give us theories, genuine desire can come from novels that touch our heart and soul. We can seek inspiration in the dawn of each new day, or in the light that seeps through autumn leaves. We may find energy in the crackle of conversations or in the passionate rage of arguments. We may see hope in the innocence of children or the splendour of the world around us. We live with places and people that are full of wonder and beauty; finding inspiration is about breathing it in.

Try Tom Peters, *The Pursuit of Wow* (Vintage Books, New York, 1994), for passion, enthusiasm, ideas and challenge. It is tearing apart with energy and vitality.

References

Cartwright, R., Collins, M., Green, G. and Candy, A. (1993) *Managing People*, Blackwell, Oxford.

de Alberdi, L. (1990) *People, Psychology and Business*, Cambridge University Press.

Hunt, J.W. (1986) *Managing People at Work*, McGraw-Hill, Maidenhead.

Walker, B. (1994) Valuing differences: the concept and a model, in Mabey, C. and Iles, P. (eds), *Managing Learning*, International Thomson Business Press, London.

7

Building the team – 'groupwatching'

*You think that because you understand one, you must understand two –
because one and one makes two. But you must also understand 'and'.*

Sufi teaching

Objectives

By the end of this chapter you will be able to:

➤ Describe some of the major processes at work in a team or group
situation
➤ Recognize and respond to behaviours commonly found in
group settings
➤ Apply an understanding of team development and group processes to your workplace

Introduction

It is hard to talk or read about management today without coming across teams and teambuilding in some form or another. We hear of project teams, management teams, cross-functional teams, self-managed teams to name but a few. It seems that teamwork is fast becoming the accepted way of organizing ourselves in the workplace in an effort to find more productive and effective working structures.

But simply labelling a group of people who work together as a 'team' does little by itself to improve their effectiveness, nor will it result in instantly harmonious working relationships. Managing and developing effective teams requires a real understanding of the complex way in which people interact, and an environment or culture which supports a team-based approach. It also vital to consider under what circumstances teamworking provides a 'better', more productive way of working, so that valuable or more appropriate alternatives are not cast aside in the rush to set up teams.

This chapter starts by looking at the value of a teamworking approach and notes situations in which it can sometimes become a barrier to effective working. We then set out to explore some of the group processes that you will need to be aware of to manage teams effectively. Finally, we draw attention to some of the behaviours commonly found in team or group working situations. The intention here is to help the manager develop an understanding and awareness of what is going on inside a team or group through observation, dialogue and reflection. The ways in which a manager can actively intervene to help 'build the team' at a practical level forms the focus of Chapter 8.

As with topics covered in other chapters, there are no 'right' or even 'easy' ways to build a team: once again the processes at work are both complex and dynamic. Understanding something of the way we work and behave in teams is only a starting point. It will not be possible to manage a team situation from a position of isolated observer, rather the need is to build understanding by actively engaging in the processes described and sharing your understanding with the team. It is this practical action – working with the team on issues of behaviour and how you work together – that will help you develop productive relationships with your colleagues at work.

Lastly it is important not to see teamwork as the sole answer to, for example, how to manage change or improve performance – it must be seen as part of a web of developmental working practices and ideas. These parallel ideas are developed in other chapters on, for example, empowerment, continual development and making conflict work.

Working in teams

A team or a group?

A great deal of serious thought has gone into trying to define what we mean by 'team' and by 'group'. In practice though, not only are these terms used interchangeably on a day-to-day basis, but the processes and behaviours explored here are common to both formal team settings and informal groups at work.

On the sportsfield the idea of the team should be fairly clear to us all, but in the workplace it can be difficult to distinguish the team from the collection of people you happen to be working with. It might be useful to consider the following criteria. A 'team' has:

- Common aims and goals and a sense of shared purpose
- Individuals who perceive themselves to be members of 'the team'
- Members who communicate and interact with one another
- A level of interdependence – members need each other to achieve common goals effectively.

Note that, at this stage, the criteria above say little about how well the team works together or whether or not the team is effective. They do, however, illustrate that the key difference between groups and teams lies in the sense that teams have an agreed and overt sense of purpose and membership. It is this recognition of themselves as part of 'the team,' and a shared commitment to it, that is important in adopting some of the strategies for team development recorded in the next chapter.

Though we will use 'teams' generally throughout this section, as we have noted many of the processes we will describe apply just as easily to group situations. In many respects the less formal groups we identify with, such as social groups, friendships and networks, have a very significant impact on the way we work together. They can provide valuable arenas for generating support, motivation and information, as well as enabling us to meet many of our social and psychological needs that create our desire to work with others.

While work teams often have organizational objectives, it is important to recognize the social value of teams in helping people to meet their individual needs. Individual needs provide much of the complexity in team processes and have to be actively managed if the team is to be truly effective.

The value of working in teams

There is a danger that, as teamworking becomes the 'norm' in terms of workplace organization, we assume that it is the most effective way to organize people at work, without pausing to challenge this assumption. Teamworking can provide real benefits for both individuals and for the organization, but it is important to be clear about what these benefits are, and what some of the 'downsides' of teamworking might be. Let's look firstly at how working as part of a team can meet the needs of both the individual and the organization for which they work.

Meeting our personal needs

Teamworking builds upon some basic psychological needs we all have as human beings to live and work as part of a group. These might be summarized as:

- The social need to be with other people, sharing experience and history
- To develop and maintain self-image, self-esteem and status
- Reinforcement of shared beliefs, perceptions and values
- The need for security and the support of others
- To enhance opportunities for growth and learning.

Handy, C.B. (1985) *Understanding Organisations,* Penguin Books, London.

These individual needs are also met in some of our commonest social groupings such as the family, the class at school, and clubs or societies. They are also common to the many types of informal groups to be found in the workplace. These informal groupings will occur whether or not formal teams have been established, reflecting the importance of the psychological needs listed above. Teamworking as a method of organizing people, works **with** these basic human needs rather than imposing other work regimes which may, for example, isolate individuals from their colleagues.

It is important to remember here that these needs will vary considerably from one individual to the next. In practice some members of your team may demand close working relationships while others may prefer to work more independently most of the time. This issue is further complicated by the degree to which these needs are met outside of work. In managing these differences, it will be necessary to develop a shared understanding and acceptance among team members about what each person requires from the team. Since individual needs will also vary over time and in response to different situations, working towards a shared understanding must be an integral and ongoing process for the team. This raises again the need to develop open and honest inter-group communication – guesswork and assumptions will not provide adequate information about complex personal needs however sensitive we may think we are.

Teamworking for the organization

Teamworking is fast becoming the norm for many companies and organizations in response to the increasing complexities of their tasks and the need to respond quickly to changing circumstances. Witness the transformation in major car manufacturers from the old production-line approach where each person did only one simple job to the modern team-based approach where work teams operate together, in some cases with a team building complete cars. There are many benefits for the organization to be gained from using teamworking – try thinking these through in the activity below.

Learning activity

Organizations and teams

Think about the value of teamworking for organizations, and try to list some of these benefits.

Some of the key benefits of teamworking you may have thought of might include:

- Deal with complex tasks that are beyond the capabilities of individuals
- Provide a focused channel for communication
- Share ideas, skills and expertise
- Provide a support mechanism and a learning environment
- Improve some types of decision-making and problem-solving
- Facilitate change and innovation by encouraging the sharing of differing approaches and ideas
- Provide a structure for networking and developing influence
- Help to break down functional or hierarchical barriers
- Support devolving responsibility or empowerment programmes
- Provide continuity – when members leave or are unavailable.

There are many others! But creating teams, with a common purpose and defined membership, will not by itself guarantee to improve factors such as communication, decision-making, problem-solving or the sharing of skills and ideas. We shall return to these topics later as they are very much the product of effective and well managed teams. Simply calling a group of people who work together a 'team', will not magically generate any of the benefits listed above. Gaining these benefits requires an effort to build understanding and challenge our own perspectives. Accessing the ideas that other people offer requires us to question and confront our own thinking and assumptions and adopt a climate that encourages challenge within a supportive framework.

Life outside teams

Finally, it is very important to be clear that teamwork is not always the most appropriate form of organization. Whether or not teamwork is a useful tool may depend upon things like the type of task being undertaken, the working environment, and the culture and management style of the organization. Here are some examples where teamwork might not be the most appropriate way of organizing work:

- For routine or non-complex decisions
- Some creative roles – e.g. artist
- Where the management style is particularly rigid and authoritarian
- Where individuals are physically isolated and work predominantly alone
- Where individuals work most effectively or prefer to work alone most of the time
- Where the organizations culture emphasizes self-interest and competition between individuals.

In these and other situations, imposing a team approach may be counter-productive. The issue of managing 'remote' teams, where members work on their own in distant locations, is an interesting one. Even with good communication systems the lack of frequent face-to-face interaction limits opportunities to build mutual understanding and develop the levels of openness and trust associated with effective teams. This presents managers with a paradoxical situation in that remote working may well demand higher levels of trust and shared responsibility as frequently decisions are taken by the lone team member. It makes the task of developing mutual support mechanisms, and the social relationships so useful for teams, a difficult one.

Kanter, R.M. (1994) 'Dilemmas of Teamwork' in Mabey, C. and Iles, P. (eds), *Managing Learning*, Routledge.

It is also important to remember that teamworking does not in itself remove our affiliation for hierarchies. In an organization where hierarchies are strong, there is a tendency to duplicate these within a team environment, leading to the most 'senior' person having more influence and 'speaking time' in group situations. In our work with teams of managers the presence or otherwise of the team leader or 'boss' is often an important influence and can greatly affect the level and type of participation, as well as the degree of openness and challenge within the team.

The above examples do not preclude teamworking as such, but serve to illustrate that the nature of this approach will need to be adapted in the light of the tasks being done. Thinking about the value of teamworking in relation to the task at hand also applies within a team environment.

Group processes

This section explores some of the approaches to understanding how teams or groups function. The emphasis here is very much on 'how' a team works rather than on the task it actually does. We will be looking at the stages of group development, ideas about the roles individuals have in teams and the need for managers to invest time and energy on the way the team works together.

In focusing on these group processes, the key skill for the manager is the ability to use the ideas as an aid to understanding their own particular situation, rather than as complete explanations for group behaviour. Since our subject here is how people interact, it presents us with a very complex and constantly changing changing picture, an area with few 'off-the-peg' solutions.

It is worth noting at this stage that while we would encourage managers to observe and reflect upon the workings of their team, it is important to remember that managers are equally part of the team being observed, and that a willingness to reflect upon their own role and involvement is crucial. It cannot be stressed enough that the team will be greatly influenced by your actions (or inactions) and that understanding your own impact on the processes discussed is vital.

Viewing team processes

So where do we begin in looking at how our team operates? A useful start can be made by splitting processes – 'how the group does things' – into those

Schein, E.H. (1988) *Process Consultation*, Vol. 1, Addison-Wesley.

relating to the **task** and those concerned with group **maintenance**.

- **Task processes** are concerned with getting the job done. The task could be anything from introducing a new service or product to organizing the Christmas party. The processes involved here can include setting objectives, timekeeping, decision-making, planning and anything else that works directly towards the achievement of a particular goal or the completion of the task in hand.

Maintenance processes on the other hand focus on promoting good working relations, providing support to team members, creating a positive and productive working atmosphere and generally maintaining group communications and cohesiveness. These are also vital for the achievement of the task but relate more generally to the team's ability to work effectively together.

To discuss these processes further, let's look at how we might recognize them in a practical 'team' situation – the team meeting – by thinking about commonly observed behaviours or comments. Some typical examples of 'task' expressions might be:

'We need to decide . . .'	(clarifying goals)
'The deadline is . . .'	(providing information)
'What about this idea . . .'	(giving opinions)
'Can we get back to the issue'	(refocusing)

While it is clear that these behaviours focus on completing the task, they also contribute something to team maintenance. That there is no absolute dividing line can be illustrated by the statement: 'Have you got any ideas on this?' Seeking ideas from others is a maintenance behaviour as it encourages participation and involvement. Depending upon the situation, it could also be task-focused effort to find a way forward or a solution.

Maintenance behaviours in a meeting situation might be illustrated by expressions like:

'That might be an opportunity for Dave to learn . . .'	(development)
'That's a useful idea'	(encouragement)
'Is everyone happy with that?'	(checking)
'Is there a way to meet both these concerns?'	(seeking compromise)
'Could you brief everyone on . . .'	(seeking information)

Again while these examples focus on team cohesion and participation, they nevertheless have a vital contribution to make to completing the task. It is not crucial that you are able to categorize every behaviour in terms of task and maintenance – it is in any case difficult to do so without reference to things like context and situation, existing relationships within the team or body language for example. The distinction simply presents us with a useful way of discussing the way in which the team interacts.

We can summarize common task and maintenance behaviour as in Table 7.1.

It is not important to memorize the list in Table 7.1 but it is useful to grasp the value of both task and maintenance processes to the effectiveness of your team. The crucial idea here is one of **balance** between the two. We can think through the effects of an imbalance between task and maintenance in the activity below.

Table 7.1 Common task and maintenance behaviours

Task	Maintenance rules
Plan/coordinate	Set the climate
Give information	Seek information
Give opinions/ideas	Seek ideas/opinions
Clarify	Seek to resolve conflict
Summarize	Seek ways of making decisions
Structure the task	Compromise
Make decisions	Support
Time keeping	Encourage
Elaborate	Diagnose
Keeping on target	Set and test codes of behaviour
Solve problems	Encourage openness˙

Learning activity

Looking at balance

The value of balance:

- If your team focuses entirely on the task, what might happen to working relationships, and ultimately the service you provide, in the medium to long term?
- If your team spends all of its time on relationships, support and encouragement, what will happen to the work you need to get through?

This activity looks at the effects of an imbalance between task and maintenance. Let's look at these scenarios in a little more detail.

Totally task-focused

This is a common form of 'imbalance' sustained by the short-term need to complete tasks to deadlines, deal with crises and meet the day-to-day demands of customers or senior management. It is further compounded by our tendency to measure our progress and effectiveness primarily in terms of achieving measurable goals and targets. Clearly at a time when managers and staff are all being asked to take on more work, the pressures of the 'task', short deadlines and crises can push even the most aware manager in this direction. Putting off the need to 'maintain' the team can, however, lead to the deterioration of relationships, increased levels of frustration, demotivation and poor communication. This lack of 'maintenance' feeds rapidly back to the team's ability to tackle tasks effectively and creates a sort of spiraling inability to move forward, particularly over the medium to long term, as illustrated in Figure 7.1 overleaf.

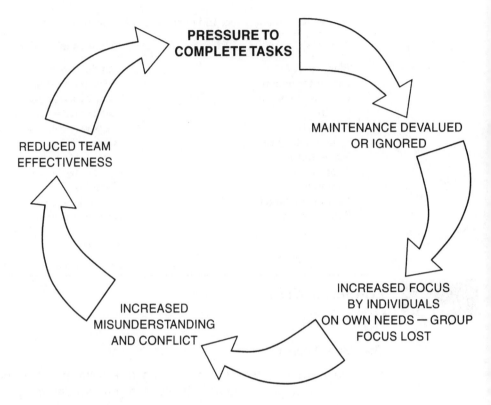

Fig. 7.1 The 'task-trap'.

In this situation the manager must recognize that this 'imbalance' is simply not sustainable without serious consequences for both the team's output and the individuals within it. Focusing on the 'people' orientated aspects of a team's processes is not a luxury but the crucial element in 'getting the job done.'

A further issue here is that team members will, even in this situation, carry on their own maintenance activities through informal and social groups. The danger here is that these may become a destructive focus for disaffection and grumblings, and that a busy task-obsessed manager will have little opportunity to influence the way in which the team's maintenance processes operate.

Totally maintenance-focused

This extreme scenario suggests a group developing a very cosy way of working who may find difficulty in reaching decisions quickly or completing a reasonable workload. In some circumstances, elaborate consultation processes or oversensitivity can lead to missed opportunities or 'ducked' issues, and make tough operational decisions hard to implement.

It should be clear then that for a team to perform effectively there needs to be a balance between task and maintenance, and that ensuring this balance in a team is an important part of a manager's role. This balance, of course, is something to aim for over a period of time, and may tip one way or another as current circumstances dictate.

We have talked so far about the 'maintenance' needs of a team as if its members all responded to situations in a similar way and act 'as one'. We need now to consider a third dimension – the needs of individuals within the team.

Meeting individual needs

In addition to the balance between the need to complete the task and look after the team as a whole, managers must consider the needs of individual team members. Most team members will not continue to contribute constructively to the team's work if their own needs for involvement, development and support are not being met to some degree. It is as if people apply a sense of 'give and take' when working together – they contribute fully to the team if they in turn feel they are valued and supported.

While these needs will vary greatly from one person to the next, the following list provides a general view of some common 'individual needs':

- Friendship and time for social interaction
- Encouragement, support and advice
- To be respected, valued and trusted
- To have achievements and contribution recognized
- Learning and development opportunities
- To be listened to and consulted
- To get involved
- To be given or take responsibility
- To have control over their own work.

We might add to this list things that individuals might not want or expect from a teamworking environment, such as intimidation, being ignored or put down, or being the victim of prejudice or misplaced humour.

The important point for the manager here is that the needs of the individual must be recognized and taken seriously, in balance with the task to be done and the maintenance of the group. A failure to do so can greatly reduce the contribution individuals make and reduce the team's performance. Think about your own reaction to a situation in which you have not had a chance to contribute, your ideas have been 'put down' or you have been assigned yet another undemanding role in a new project. It would not be surprising to feel a loss of commitment and enthusiasm, or even anger, in this position.

To consider 'individual needs' as a manager, it helps to have an idea about what they are. This is certainly difficult if you choose to rely solely on your own observation or on lists like the one above! You are in effect basing your actions on guesswork and assumptions. A preferable way to access these needs is clearly to create a climate where needs and concerns can be expressed directly and openly. This requires team relationships to be based on trust and a belief in the value and practice of mutual support.

Putting the picture together

This simple division of team processes into 'task' and 'maintenance' provides a useful starting point for observing and understanding what is going on in a team or group. As we have seen in discussing these processes it provides a glimpse of the complexity and dynamic nature of group behaviour. It demonstrates the need for managers to cope with the tensions between the demands within a team that can sometimes appear to be in direct conflict.

We must also be aware that additional tensions arise from within each individual from our own conflicting needs, which can often feel contradictory. In a team situation an example of this 'paradox' might be our need for close working relationships, friendships and belonging, conflicting with our need for independence or personal recognition. (This tension can be seen vividly in many personal relationships as the battle between our need for intimacy and independence.) In the workplace this conflict manifests itself in 'inconsistent' behaviours which add to the difficulty of managing your understanding of an individual's needs. Again an acceptance and understanding of the complexity of this issue can help managers to engage in this apparently confusing arena.

However, it need not be the manager's responsibility alone to manage and balance out these many and changing needs. It is a valuable exercise to share this perspective on group processes with your team, so that they are aware of the tensions created between the task and more people-based concerns. The recognition by all staff of these three areas of concern could provide the manager with a useful team development exercise and reinforce the practice of shared responsibility.

Group processes – stages of development

Another useful tool in looking at the way in which your team works is to see the development of a team as a kind of 'lifecycle'. This sees the team 'growing' through various stages of development from its formation to a mature stage where it performs most effectively. Again it simplifies what actually happens in a team, but it provides a valuable way of assessing the team's development. Known as the 'ormings', the model below sets out five stages in the development of a group or team.

- **Forming.** This is the 'getting together' stage. Group members get to know each other, and early views on group objectives and norms are generated. Communications are generally polite, even formal. Members may try to create good impressions or at least 'play safe', forming views about other team members before committing themselves.

- **Storming.** This is the stage where initial understandings of the group's purpose, the roles of members, leadership and norms regarding work and behaviour are challenged and clarified. It is often characterized by conflict or hostility, often hidden, as personal agendas and styles move to centre-stage. Common behaviours include forming alliances, withdrawal or even sabotage. Moving beyond this stage can be a key moment in the development of the team, putting the level of trust and openness in the team to the test.

- **Norming.** The group establishes agreed working processes having dealt with or worked around any major conflicts or differences. It agrees how it should work, how it takes decisions, what is acceptable behaviour, and what level of trust and openness is appropriate.

- **Performing.** Although the group will 'perform' to some degree in the other stages above, it is only at this 'mature' stage that the group will perform fully and effectively, and can concentrate on its objectives rather than internal issues.

- **Mourning.** This is a stage reached by some groups whose real purpose is no longer there, or whose task may have finished. There may be a reluctance to admit that the group should be disbanded.

Although real life is inherently more complex than this model suggests, there are some valuable lessons that can be drawn from it that will aid a manager in building an effective team.

Firstly it suggests that in order to reach the 'performing' stage, the team will need to devote energy and time to establishing, very overtly, ways of working that are agreed and accepted by all team members. That members all know the purpose of the team and the roles they play cannot be taken for granted – particularly as these will be constantly changing. It is crucial that the team makes the time to discuss the way they work together openly. If this does not happen, individuals will create their view of others and the team only from their personal perspective, based on unchecked assumptions. Without open discussion, misunderstandings and tensions will flourish, preventing the team from establishing positive working relationships of any depth. Of course we can only hope to reduce misunderstanding through open and constructive communication, rather than banish it altogether. Importantly, though, it provides the team with a positive mechanism for handling misunderstandings that will inevitably still arise when any group of people work together.

It is worth noting in this respect the value of informal situations, both at work and often socially, in developing understanding and getting to know each other. This is most obvious in the forming stage but plays a vital role in many aspects of the team's development and needs to be supported at all stages.

Riding the storm

Perhaps the most helpful aspect of this model is what the 'storming' stage shows us about group dynamics. It is very common that teams get 'stuck' before this crucial stage in group development. This is often because of the perceived difficulties in handling differences or conflicts should they be brought to the surface. It is very natural for people to try to put differences and concerns to one side – the idea of open conflict or opposing opinions does not sit comfortably with our image of 'good teamwork'. The fear that outpourings of emotion and conflict could wreck the team or be painful to handle leads team members to collude in denying the existence of such 'monsters' in their midst.

What actually happens, of course, is that the 'monster' just goes underground, the storming continues and festers in the background with hidden agendas, politics, disquiet and frustration continuing to damage team performance and relationships.

These internal differences, lack of consensus and agreed working styles, and conflicts of interest provide a significant barrier for teams in their search for a more effective way of performing. They manifest themselves in any number of ways – grumbling about decisions, increased frustration, withdrawal or silence, feelings of disquiet or anger about certain individuals for example. The opportunity for the team to move forward is greatly reduced by these behaviours, and in order for the team to reach the real 'performing' stage they must come to an agreed understanding that some 'storming' or surfacing of their concerns needs to take place. If the 'storming' does not take place, a blockage is created and reinforced through a sort of vicious circle as illustrated in Figure 7.2.

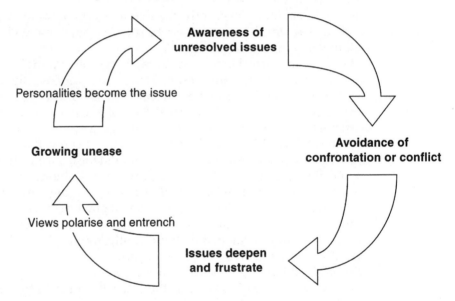

Awareness of unresolved issues

Personalities become the issue

Growing unease

Avoidance of confrontation or conflict

Views polarise and entrench

Issues deepen and frustrate

Fig. 7.2   Avoiding difference and contention.

The manager's role at this point is quite crucial. He/she must resist the temptation to avoid tackling the differences and conflicts, and raise them with the team. This may require some groundwork in raising awareness of outstanding issues and developing a shared commitment to move forward together. As noted above, the degree of trust and openness in a team will be critical in tackling this hurdle – a lack of trust will prevent members taking the risk of being open and honest about the differences and their own needs and feelings. Working with the team on an agreed way of giving constructive feedback will also provide a useful practical way to approach this process.

One of the difficulties with the storming process is that people tend to view conflict as always negative, something to be avoided at all costs. It may prove worthwhile to work with the team on the positive things that conflict and differences can bring to the team, and the dangers of sidestepping these differences. Conflict in particular needs to be seen in perspective as a valuable part of the process of moving forward and of developing healthy and open working relationships. This issue is dealt with directly in Chapter 13 on making conflict work.

A dynamic process

Finally, although the 'ormings' model necessarily shows a simple progression from forming to performing, the manager should not relax when the team reaches the performing stage. Many situations, such as a new team member or a major change in the task or organization, may require working through the stages again. The group will need to regard 'forming – storming – norming' as a **continuous process** as people and situations change and develop almost on a day-by-day basis.

In this respect it is worth considering that the stages of development could only be applied in a simple linear way if the task at hand is relatively straightforward. In practice, of course, as tasks become more complex with fewer clear boundaries, team members may adopt a wide variety of behaviours designed to reduce anxiety and impose structure onto their work and relationships. In this situation, behaviours such as suppressing conflict or accepting unwanted decisions can lead to the illusion that the team is 'performing' effectively, at just the time when 'storming' would be most valuable.

The 'ormings' model helps us to understand the growth process of teams, and gives insights into some of the driving forces behind general team or group behaviours. One of the key determinants of team effectiveness and group behaviour are the team roles that emerge and are acted out as part of the team dynamic. The next section takes a more detailed look at the roles people adopt in a team or group setting.

Team roles

We all understand, in general terms, what a 'role' is in everyday life and most of us take on a number of these – the teacher, the shop assistant, father/mother, friend, tea-maker, etc. Our understanding of these roles gives us a sense of identity and security, and helps us to decide (often wrongly) how to behave towards others. Roles appear in the workplace too, and are commonly identified by job title and/or place in the hierarchy. With these job roles come expectations about what an individual should do, and how they should behave.

But what about roles in teams? Job titles may still apply here, team leader/manager or secretary for example, but this tells us little other than their formally designated position. In teams or groups, members take up more informal roles, relating to their personality, skills and attributes, and importantly to the situation in which the team operates. These roles are often far more influential than those suggested by job title or rank. These 'informal' roles present powerful ways of establishing who we are and how we contribute to the team. Developing an awareness of informal roles can greatly help us to understand the complex nature of the contributions we make to the team's work and processes.

Belbin, R.M. (1981)
*Management
Teams – Why They
Succeed or Fail*,
Butterworth-
Heinemann,
Oxford.
There are a number of different ways of looking at team roles, but one of the most widely used is the work of Meredith Belbin. Belbin has moved away from identifying roles on the basis of position or status and looked at the roles people take up in the more democratic atmosphere of a modern team. His roles are therefore based on the contribution that an individual's behaviour makes to the work of the team.

Belbin's team roles

Belbin's team roles are listed in Table 7.2. This displays some of the common behaviours associated with each role and what are termed 'allowable weaknesses' – in other words the downside of each role. Note that these roles do not describe the functional or 'job' role of a team member but rather the tendency of an individual to behave and contribute in certain ways. Before discussing the value of this approach to team roles, think about how it might apply to your own team in the workplace.

Table 7.2 Belbin's team roles (Adapted from Belbin, R.M. (1993) *Team Roles at Work*, Butterworth-Heinemann, Oxford)

Role	Contribution	Allowable weaknesses
Plant	Imaginative and creative, an ideas person. Enjoys difficult problems – uses unorthodox approaches.	Can be too involved to communicate effectively, not good on detail.
Resource investigator	An explorer, uses contacts and ideas from outside the group. Enthusiastic and extrovert.	Can lose enthusiasm or get bored after a while.
Coordinator	Good chairperson, confident manager of people resources. Clarifies goals and delegates well.	Not necessarily the most dynamic or creative member of the group.
Shaper	Challenging and dynamic. Keeps up group momentum and pushes through obstacles.	Can provoke conflict, a little insensitive.
Monitor evaluator	Careful and analytical, aware of all options, a good judge.	Can be seen as over-critical, and lack ability to inspire others or move things forward.
Teamworker	People-orientated communicator, focuses on team relationships, cooperative.	Can be indecisive in difficult situations and is easily influenced.
Implementor	The 'do-er', gets the task done, practical and reliable.	Inflexible – not the first to take on new challenges or opportunities.
Completer	Pays attention to detail, meticulous, conscientious and meets deadlines.	Over-anxious, finds it hard to delegate. May annoy others with too much detail.
Specialist	Provides skills or expertise otherwise absent from the group.	Can be too focused on their specialism and not see the big picture.

Learning activity

Understanding team roles

- Looking at the each of the Belbin's roles, try and identify which of your team members or learning group might supply these strengths to your team.
- Are there any roles that are not covered well? If so, what might be the implications for your team's performance?

Try to focus on Belbin's team roles rather than job-related ones.

Relating each of these roles to individual team members is not always easy. This is partly because all of us have the capacity to operate in each of the roles; we can all, for example, be creative or help to develop good relationships within a team. Belbin suggests that while this is the case, most people have strong preferences for one or two 'roles', and will operate most effectively in that way. In practice this is unlikely to be clearly demonstrated at a team level, as the strength and style of other people's contribution and the task being done will ensure that the 'roles' people take up will change and adapt to circumstances.

It may also be the case that there are roles in your team that are not well covered. Looking down the list you will no doubt have realized that all of the roles have an equally important contribution to make to the effectiveness of a team. A team without people who can effectively build relationships (team-worker), or finish off work and check the detail (completer), could find its performance limited.

Take an example of a project team that is set up to develop service improvements or a new product line. This team would need people who can generate great ideas (plant) and push them forwards (shaper). Unless there are also people around who can fulfill the other roles, such as liaising with other parts of the organization or getting the job done, a potentially valuable idea may flounder through want of someone to check legal implications or overcome the day-to-day problems of implementation.

In practical terms, Belbin's work can provide a useful tool for developing teams which can be summarized as:

- Providing a way of improving understanding of the differing roles needed in a team if it is to be successful – the value of diversity
- Helping to identify some of the team's strengths and weaknesses
- Encouraging individuals to understand and value their own style and contribution to the team, and the differing contributions of others
- Helping to challenge our expectations and perceptions of ourselves and others
- Helping to bring to the surface development opportunities.

Belbin's roles are particularly useful in highlighting the need for diversity within a team for it to function effectively. Members need to value each other's contribution and working styles as a positive asset. This raises questions for managers who find different working styles a source of conflict and work well with those 'out of the same mould'. While this may be an understandable response, managers have a lot to gain from stepping back and looking at the spread of roles taken up in the team as a whole. In looking at the spread of roles in any team, it may be necessary to 'fill the gaps' by bringing in people from outside the team, either for particular projects or on a regular basis depending on need.

It is also important to take account of the type of work the team is involved in and how this relates to the sort of contribution members make. A creative team working in advertising or marketing, for example, may well need a higher proportion of 'plants', than a team carrying out routine work or one engaged in detailed financial tasks.

Finally, a word of caution. As the work we have done on perception and perspectives suggests, there will be a tendency for people to label themselves and each other according to their preferred roles. There is a danger that once someone decides that they are a 'completer' for example, they may assume they have no creative or coordinating abilities. This can easily lead to stereotyping themselves (or others), restricting the potential of both the individual and the team. In using team roles as a method of developing understanding and valuing difference, it is important to guard against these ideas becoming a barrier to growth and development by applying this knowledge too rigidly. Adding to this it is inevitable that some roles will be perceived as more 'glamorous' than others, and managers will need to stress the value of all roles in the important contribution they make to the team's success.

A word about 'experts'

In some ways everyone is an 'expert', particularly about the job they currently do, and most teams will have personnel that bring distinctive knowledge or skills to the team. The value of having specialist contributions from within a team are obvious – they can take on technical tasks, advise the team during decision-making and planning, or share their knowledge and skills with colleagues. The specialist, though, can pose particular problems for the manager and the team.

- Firstly it is important not to confuse 'expert' knowledge with the ability to manage a project or service, or coordinate a team. The knowledge that specialists bring to the team is a resource to be shared and used, not necessarily a passport to leadership.

- Without careful management, communication can become an issue with experts, especially with technical or legal topics. They are likely to introduce specialist terms and ideas or jargon that can easily turn off the rest of the team. Try thinking about some of the problems in communicating with, say, computer specialists, accountants or car mechanics when they use technical language.

- Finally, there is sometimes the tendency for experts to withhold information in the mistaken belief that not sharing it freely somehow makes them indispensable. In fact the opposite is the case, as colleagues will notice this is happening (causing damage to team relationships) and quickly find other ways to get the information or advice that they need.

Margerison, C.J. and McCann, D.J. (1985) *How to Lead a Winning Team*, Bradford University Press.

There are a number of other ways of looking at roles in a team apart from Belbin's work that are equally helpful. One of the most valuable ways of approaching team roles is to work with your team to create your own ideas. Technical language and academic rigour are not important here – you might wish, for example, to create your own terms for the roles members play using more familiar language such as 'the ideas person' or 'the compromiser'. The value of this exercise lies in the fact that the process of discussing and refining your own idea of 'team roles' in an open way promotes a shared awareness of each other's style and contribution. People have the opportunity of looking at how their own team operates by sharing expectations and understanding through feedback and disclosure.

Remember that looking at roles in a team is only one of the ways you can improve your understanding of how the team – and the individuals in it – work together. It helps to demonstrate the need to value and respect the differing contributions your colleagues bring to their work.

Is size important?

The number of people in a team clearly has an impact on its ability to function effectively, and at either extreme (too big or too small) there are additional challenges for the manager.

Small teams, say of under four people, may find the lack of a good range and mix of skills, experience and approaches a limiting factor when it comes to tasks such as decision-making or a search for creative solutions to problems. Small teams may be able to bring in additional people with the necessary experience or approach on the occasions when these attributes would be useful, using them as 'associate' team members.

In larger teams, for example over ten people, it becomes increasingly difficult to manage the maintenance aspects of the team. Maintaining close relationships, ensuring effective communication or involving everyone all become more demanding as the team size increases. Large teams may be able to make more progress by creating sub-teams or working groups around particular issues or functions. This situation would require careful management to ensure that the smaller units remain focused on the same goal and aware of the work, support and needs of other sub-teams.

In our own work with teams of managers or students undertaking team-building exercises we observe that there comes a point at which the benefits of working in a group on, for example, decision-making become outweighed in larger groups by the difficulties of handling group management and process issues.

From processes to behaviours

In the first half of this chapter we have looked at some of the processes that aid our understanding of the dynamics of working with others in a group or team.

These included task and maintenance processes, the team 'lifecycle', and using team roles to develop an understanding of each team member's contribution.

Inevitably dealing with human relationships is a sophisticated area to explore. In the next section we go on to discuss some of the more common behaviours that you will encounter in everyday group situations. Though some of these behaviours relate to individuals in the team, there is of course no clear-cut division between individual behaviours and the collective actions of a team or group.

Behaviour in teams

In the second half of this chapter we will explore some of the common behaviours you will need to be aware of when trying to understand what's going on in your team or in any that you belong to. Crucially these are not simply behaviours to be 'observed' in others, but ones which require a great deal of personal reflection on the part of the manager as well as team members. It is also an important part of the team's development that these ideas can be shared and developed by all team members – understanding behaviour is not simply a 'management' tool.

These topics should be put in the context of the work you have already done on building relationships, communicating and valuing others, and cover behaviours that are common to other situations and to informal groups. The aim here is to alert the manager to some common group situations and discuss their implications.

It is difficult if not impossible in practice to observe such behaviours in isolation, as people's relationships are inevitably complex. In any one situation you will need to remember that there will be a wide range of variables affecting what is happening and as a manager you cannot be aware of them all. In particular, any group will have a 'history' – how people have worked together in the past, reacted to each other, or formed friendships and dealt with difficulties.

These behaviours are also interlinked in complex ways where, for example, small incidents can act as triggers for larger issues, or actions are followed by reactions which lead to escalation. This difficulty goes some way to explaining why prescribed solutions to teamworking issues do not always yield the expected results, since it is not possible for the manager to accurately predict the effects of any one intervention.

What is possible, however, is to develop a positive and open working atmosphere in the group, one which will support a constructive approach to tackling team issues.

We shall begin by looking at one of the most common of these issues – hidden agendas.

Hidden agendas

A·hidden agenda is an aim or objective that a person or sub-group has that is not revealed to the team and which is often at odds with expressed or agreed

Non-linearity

An important aspect of the way we think about actions and solutions is the idea of linearity. Linear thinking – a simple process of linking directly cause and effect – permeates the way Western cultures approach problems, that is from a mechanistic point of view. For example, if we press the gas pedal in our car (cause), we expect acceleration (effect). Our actions lead to predictable results except in rare cases of breakdown. This is fine for driving or operating machines but unfortunately fails miserably when applied to complex human systems such as the workplace. The difficulty comes when we try to apply linear thinking to teamwork or other complex people-focused situations. Teams do not respond to simple cause and effect linear approaches – the dynamics of the situation, and the complex relationships therein, will wreck most attempts to intervene in this mechanistic way. Take a team situation where its members agree that meetings would be more productive if structured and controlled by 'the chair'. In simple terms it is tempting to think that taking such action (controlling the meeting – the 'cause') will lead to the desired effect (more productive meetings). In practice, however, applying control may generate all sorts of responses, even from those who agreed to the action in the first place. People may find control stifles debate, prevents personal needs being aired or leads to rushed decisions. This can raise frustrations and lead to missed opportunities and even conflict. The point is that it is difficult to predict with any certainty the outcomes of the actions taken – we cannot safely establish all of the 'effects'. It is important therefore to grasp that the dynamics of group behaviour are complex and non-linear in nature. Do not be surprised if there are unexpected results from your efforts to 'build a team'.

team objectives or decisions. Examples in a team situation might be individuals seeking promotion or favour with the manager, or a small group of people deciding quietly to do things their own way. People behaving like this are sometimes said to be 'playing games or politics' because they are not clear or honest about their real motives or needs. There are also situations in which individuals have hidden agendas that they would like to share with the team but feel for a variety of reasons that they are unable to do so.

So what are the effects of hidden agendas and what can you do about them? In a team rife with hidden agendas, the opportunities for confusion and conflict rise dramatically. Team members may argue their case in line with their own objectives rather than those of the team as a whole, with the real reasons for their position being hidden from others leading to ineffective decision-making. Conflict or tensions between members may use unrelated topics as a battleground, leaving the rest of the team wondering what on earth is going on. It is clear that team performance will suffer badly while team members continue to operate in this way, with growing levels of frustration and declining involvement.

The presence of hidden agendas are a useful indicator to the manager of the lack of maturity and health in a team, denoting a low level of trust and openness between members. It suggests that people see colleagues as opponents, or at least as barriers to their needs and aspirations; that somehow the team cannot be trusted to understand or deal with their needs, feelings and thoughts. Fear of open conflict can also be a significant reason for an individual to hide their views and feelings from others, particularly if it involves confronting aggressive individuals in the team.

The result of this lack of openness is that any understanding of each other's needs or views is based on assumptions and guesswork. It is common for the group to be aware of the presence of conflicting 'agendas', but to carry on working with an unspoken agreement not to confront the issue through fear of the potentially destructive consequences.

Like many aspects of team development there is no 'magic wand' to wave at the problem of hidden agendas. A range of useful strategies are outlined in the next chapter, but of particular importance here must be the development of a working atmosphere based on openness and trust. It has already been noted that this requires building gradually through action – it must be demonstrated as well as agreed by the team.

During the process of building trust, introducing the careful use of constructive feedback can begin to give the team a practical method of disclosing and discussing some of their previously hidden agendas. Team building events can also provide a focused opportunity to air some of these issues.

Hidden agendas can also be viewed as conflicts of interest within a group that are not made public or expressed in any obvious way. As we have noted above it is often the fear of the conflict that might follow should these agendas become open that keeps these differences underground.

Conflict

Conflicts arise in groups, as elsewhere, from a tension created by differing opinions, feelings, beliefs, goals or behaviours. The stunning range and variety of ways in which conflict can be expressed make it difficult to categorize, or even to decide whether such conflict is healthy or destructive. That there will be conflict in any given group is inevitable. The key point to retain from this is that 'removing' conflict from a team situation is not a realistic goal; rather the manager will need to develop strategies for the acceptance and constructive use of conflict.

The idea that conflict can be valuable to a team might appear to run against our image of how an effective team should work together. But conflict can provide a vital source of energy and emotion, as well as encouraging creativity and the release of tension. The difficulty lies in recognizing when conflict can be used constructively or when the potentially destructive effects need to be challenged directly.

Hunt, J.W. (1986)
Managing People at Work,
McGraw-Hill.

We will be looking in detail at the issue of conflict in Chapter 13 on making conflict work, but it would be worth looking here at some behaviours that might signal conflict in a group situation. John Hunt has identified the following behaviours to be found in group situations, in the form of tactics or strategies that people use to avoid confronting differences directly.

- **Restricting information**: a team member implies that they have a solution or idea but do not disclose it to the group,
- **Pairing**: forming sub-groups rather than tackling conflict as a group.
- **Lying**: deliberate distortion of the facts or partial disclosure to defend a position.
- **Put-downs** (self or others): usually verbally and often disguised as 'banter'. Serves to stifle challenge and difference. Self-put-downs diffuse opposition – the 'poor me' game.
- **Fight**: getting locked into win–lose conflicts that are hard to resolve.
- **Flight**: withdrawal in its many forms – leaving the room, sitting back, sulking, silence or expressing non-interest.
- **Making noise**: speaking to be heard rather than to contribute, a delaying tactic.
- **Expertise**: using jargon, science or contacts to stop contrary views or impress.
- **Suppressing emotion**: demands for logic and rational thought to block emotions. Concentrating on facts to avoid the 'messy' realm of feelings and values.
- **Changing the topic**: changing the focus between topics or people. Another delaying or avoidance strategy.

You may well be able to add to the list from your own experience as there are many different versions of similar behaviours. It is important to acknowledge that these are tactics that we all use on occasions, sometimes without 'thinking' – they are not necessarily used to deliberately obstruct. We have developed these tactics through long experience of what has worked for us in the past. Watching children interact with their parents is a good way of observing some sophisticated strategies in action, and indicates that we learn all about avoiding conflict at an early age. Watching politicians in action lets us see avoidance and deflection elevated to an art form – albeit a pretty transparent one.

While these behaviours can readily be observed in others, it is helpful for managers to reflect on their own use of such strategies to avoid conflict situations. This is particularly important given many a team's tendency to expect the manager to take the initiative in confronting conflict in the group. If you are observed avoiding issues, the chances are that they will need little encouragement to do exactly the same.

In practice, dealing with conflict can be a very difficult area for some managers, but the acceptance and constructive use of conflict represents a major step forward for most teams.

Blaming others

Blaming others, finding fault and deflecting criticism away from ourselves are common in all walks of life, and we probably all experience these behaviours in the workplace. Attributing blame 'elsewhere' has become a routine defence for us all, not only for individuals, but also for teams, departments and even whole organizations. As a defence mechanism, blaming others seeks to protect our sense of self-worth and competence. We do not wish to be seen to be responsible for mistakes, misunderstanding, and worst of all, failure. It is a behaviour that is deeply ingrained in our language and our culture.

While the use of 'blame' is understandable in these terms, how a team or individuals use and react to blame can tell the manager a lot about the way people work together. Furthermore, it is one of the most useless and destructive behaviours that survives unchallenged in many teams and organizations.

In a team situation it is relatively easy to spot this type of behaviour, often through obvious comments like: 'It's not my fault, it was . . .', 'He didn't give me the right information', or 'it would have been OK if . . .' Blame can also be more subtly expressed in the form of excuses, or more casual comments like 'I'm just waiting for (these parts) then I will (finish the job)'.

The crucial indicator is whether people use mistakes or failures constructively, or whether they look for someone or something to blame. Organizations often develop an elaborate 'system' for passing the blame for errors from one person to the next, with no one accepting responsibility and nothing being done to rectify the situation – it has been termed a 'blame culture', a case of 'the buck doesn't stop anywhere'. Of course this requires that everybody in the organization colludes in this blaming process, and it is a good example of an unhealthy organizational 'norm'.

To help us explore the value and the dangers of allowing blame to become acceptable in a team, work through the activity below:

Learning activity

Analysing blame

Think of a situation in your team where a mistake has been made and one individual is being singled out and blamed for it by the rest of the team. For each of the following questions, note down in a list as many points as you can think of:

- What are the benefits for the team from blaming the individual?
- How might the individual feel in this situation and how might they react?

Hopefully your list for the first question will be very short. There may be some temporary relief to other team members along the lines of 'I'm glad it's not me' (we have avoided punishment – this time), and there may occasionally be an unhealthy satisfaction at seeing someone else suffer. Generally there is no lasting benefit to anyone from blaming people in this way. Interestingly the same would apply on a larger scale to placing blame outside the team – in another part of the organization for example. Managers must challenge attempts to blame people wherever they work, and resist building their team through supporting an 'us and them' attitude to other people in the organization – the 'bigger team'. Apart from other damaging effects, blame doesn't help to make progress on outstanding issues. It is a strategy of accepting situations rather than moving them forward.

The effects of blame on those receiving it, however, can be disastrous. The individual could feel some of the following – uneasy, useless, stupid, unhappy, ridiculous, demotivated, unconfident or incompetent (the list is endless) – all of which are actively destructive. They may react by blaming others or the situation, getting angry or being defensive. Again, while these are understandable, they are far from helpful reactions and work against your efforts to build an effective team.

In addition to the damage it causes to those deemed 'at fault', blame – or the fear of it – supports a climate that is hostile to trying new things, taking risks and being creative. All of these can be difficult enough without the threat of ridicule or punishment, yet are crucial to organizations wishing to promote learning or be innovative for example.

Blame then is a largely destructive behaviour – worse than that, it crucially fails to deal with the mistakes made or to use them constructively as a learning opportunity. Where blame is used frequently in a team it might indicate a lack of positive commitment to improving services or going forward, a fear of punishment, or a lack of trust and support.

In tackling blame in a team the manager will find most of the teambuilding 'actions for progress' in the next chapter useful. However, there are a few additional ideas that you might find helpful.

Firstly you might try the activity you have just done with your team, adapting it to your own circumstances and using a flipchart or board to record the team's lists. Ask them how they feel when they are blamed for making mistakes, using examples (carefully!) if necessary to prompt a response. The bigger the list of 'bad' feelings, the stronger the point! Discussing the results can be interesting so allow plenty of time for this. You may reach agreement across the team that blaming in this way is no longer acceptable, or the discussion may widen to include issues of responsibility, your management style and the prevalence of blame in your organization, so be prepared to accept this, learn from it and use it to discuss ways forward.

You may also wish to introduce or, better still, produce with the team a simple formula for handling mistakes or failures. This looks at mistakes constructively through a two step process:

- Work together to put the mistake right – take whatever action is needed to rescue the situation. Be honest and direct about the mistake you have made.

- Learn from it! Work together to ensure the same mistake is not made again. Remember reviews must be followed by action. Share the learning with the team.

In working to reduce the use of blame in a team it is important to remember that it takes place alongside other team development approaches – they are all interlinked. Managers cannot expect to make progress in this area if, for instance, staff still fear retribution for their errors, or if the team has not developed ways of acting constructively in these situations. It requires a working environment based on mutual respect, where errors are seen as just mistakes and not deliberate acts of sabotage, and on a willingness to learn together. It would be useful if a blame-free environment can be adopted as a group norm or unwritten 'rule' towards which the whole team can work.

Group norms – getting to know the rules

Group norms are a series of usually unspoken 'social rules' that indicate what is and is not acceptable behaviour within the group. They may range from a view about standards of dress through to powerful norms concerning performance at work. They are not 'rules' as such, but more an 'understanding' that the group has about how to behave at work.

Groups develop norms that cover a wide range of behaviours including those about:

- The task or job and standards of performance
- Social matters – about interests, sport, breaktimes, humour and other people
- Controls within the group – using language, power, timekeeping
- Opinions, beliefs and attitudes – about unions, management, politics, or religion for example
- Physical appearance – for example, dress codes, use of safety clothing.

Accepting the norms of a group can bring friendship and support from colleagues. Challenging the norms, however, can lead to being the butt of jokes or, more seriously, conflict and non-cooperation. This presents an extremely powerful form of informal social control, and one which has the potential to override individual views and the wishes of managers or the organization.

Understanding what the norms are in a team is particularly important to the manager looking to improve performance and develop the team. While norms play a valuable part in team cohesion and identity, they can also present barriers to changing 'the way things are done around here.'

For example, if there is a poor relationship between management and staff, norms may develop about low levels of cooperation and mistrust or about how long it should take to do a certain job that are based more on an 'us and them' approach. New team members will quickly learn to operate according to these norms and underperform, even if it means lowering their own standards. The tendency of some managers to crack the whip in such a situation will only reinforce these norms and make the situation more difficult to retrieve.

Developing good relationships with colleagues, on the other hand, can give the manager the opportunity to influence group norms, either directly or through some members of the team. With teams that have a positive and open approach to their work it is possible to discuss what the norms of the group are and how they feel about them (a 'norming' process). This not only helps to clarify group expectations about behaviour, but provides the opportunity to agree new 'norms' that are acceptable to the team as a whole and challenge existing behaviours that are deemed unhelpful.

Conformity – the need to 'fit in'

There is undoubtedly pressure in any group situation to behave like other group members, to hold similar views, to reinforce group norms and to avoid 'rocking the boat'. This is known as conformity. It is particularly noticeable with new employees who need to 'fit in' with their colleagues, but it is also likely that some of us have a stronger need than others to go along with the group. Conformity is the way we respond in trying to meet some of the personal needs we have for working with others, and involves us, consciously or otherwise, in adapting our behaviour in return for the rewards of acceptance.

There is nothing wrong with a degree of conformity – we all conform to a large extent most of the time, and we need some rules, boundaries and norms to give our work and relationships some structure. It is a valuable process that helps to support teambuilding efforts and provide a secure atmosphere in which to work. In some respects it is part of the 'bargain' we strike between our personal needs to be individual and to gain the benefits of working alongside others in a team. But there are difficulties in conformity for the team's performance and development that a manager needs to be alert to.

The major difficulty for the team is that if everyone conforms totally then things will not change or improve, new ideas or ways of doing things would not be put forward, and the team could stagnate or at best move forward only slowly. Conformity works against the group tackling differences or conflict for fear of destroying a superficially comfortable working atmosphere. Everyone in the team has the ability to offer ideas and be creative, and this is a valuable resource to be encouraged and utilized in the search for greater effectiveness and involvement.

Janis, I.L. (1972) *Victims of Groupthink: A psychological study of foreign-policy decisions and fiascoes,* Houghton-Mifflin, Boston.

Taking this one step further it is possible that groups can develop 'over-conformity', a state known as 'groupthink'. In this situation people are so attached to the need for a cohesive group that the desire to conform prevents any meaningful attempts to appraise ideas, options or plans. When this happens the quality of decision-making is reduced and a healthy level of challenge and criticism fades away.

As a manager you will need to promote an atmosphere that actively supports the involvement of your team members in challenging (constructively) current methods, solving problems creatively, and allowing free expression of ideas and concerns. When this happens, it is important that your response is positive and demonstrates that you value these contributions. This is about setting new norms, and using the power of conformity to reinforce these within the group. Again, it is important to work with the effects of conformity, rather than against it.

Taking an active part

We must all have experienced being members of groups where a few people seem to do all the talking and all the decision-making, and where others sit quietly and allow this to go on happening. Or perhaps a situation where some team members seem to be involved in tackling problems and moving the team forward while others contribute little more than completing the tasks delegated to them.

It is relatively straightforward for the manager to observe variations in the degree to which people 'take an active part' in the team. Some common behaviours which might indicate non-participation at a group event, for example, could be:

- Silence – non-contribution of ideas or opinions
- Whispered conversations to one side
- No signs of active listening
- Non-verbal indications of boredom, frustration or anger
- Saying 'That's OK with me' when it clearly isn't!
- A general lack of energy or enthusiasm.

The difficulty lies not in the observation, but in trying to understand what is going on here and why, or to decide what to do about it – if anything. There are real dangers in trying to interpret people's reasons for not participating simply from observation. Attempting to 'explain' people's behaviour in group situations is dependent upon the complex interaction of factors such as relationships with others in the team, how they are reacting to the current situation, what's going on 'at home', and their own established patterns of behaviour, among others.

In this part of the section we shall illustrate this complexity by working through a commonly observed example of 'non-participation', and follow this by looking at ways to encourage participation and the benefits of 'taking an active part'.

Non-participation

To illustrate the difficulty in drawing conclusions from observing a group in action, let's take the common example of a team meeting. As the team's manager you notice that several people are not contributing at all, while others speak up, often loudly, with their views and ideas.

One interpretation could be that those speaking out are 'naturally' talkative, or aggressive, argumentative, control-seekers, people who don't listen – while the non-participants may have nothing to contribute, are unconfident and powerless, even intimidated by the behaviour of others in the team. There may well be some truth in this, particularly if this pattern is observed over a period of time. But there are also many other ways of understanding this scenario. For example, non-participants may:

- Be happy with the decisions/discussion and have nothing to add
- Have other more important things (to them) on their minds
- Be uninterested in this topic
- Be unwell or tired.

Those who speak up may simply be:

- Confident and assertive
- Have a great deal to contribute
- Displaying real enthusiasm and energy.

The key thing here for managers and teams is not to speculate about participation by making assumptions or jumping to conclusions which may lead to inappropriate actions. It is important to move beyond 'telepathy' and to check openly with each other about their contributions and about the way the team works together. This needs to happen in an atmosphere where the team agrees that participation is valuable, and where there is sufficient openness to share observations through feedback and disclosure.

The above discussion implies that participation is necessarily a valuable thing to encourage in a team. We need to look now at some of the benefits to be gained in a team where everyone 'takes an active part', and ask whether there are not situations in which participation is unnecessary or counter-productive.

The benefits of participation

There are many benefits that make striving for increased participation worthwhile, including:

- Improving the quality of some decisions
- Access to a greater breadth of ideas and experience
- Encouraging interest, involvement and commitment
- Developing skills and confidence
- Sharing ideas and information
- Supporting empowerment and 'ownership'
- Reducing frustration, withdrawal and defensive behaviours
- Improving communication within the team
- Promoting equal opportunity.

The main thrust of these ideas is to improve team performance by maximizing the opportunity to use the skills, ideas, views and commitment of all of the members of a team. Not taking this opportunity at a time where most organizations are being asked to achieve more, often with less 'resources', only increases pressure on current ways of working.

You would be right of course to challenge the idea that all participation is necessarily a useful thing! It is a common concern that full participation can be a very time-consuming way of doing things and can lead, for example, to some decisions never being taken at all. A lot will depend upon applying participation appropriately – a team of 12 people meeting to discuss the colour of pencils to be ordered for the office is probably not a useful exercise!

But the most important point here is that time spent on promoting participation, with all its benefits of involvement, breadth of ideas, ownership and commitment, cannot be seen as 'wasted' time, even if some decisions in the short term take a little longer. You could ask what is the value of a quick decision when the benefits of participation listed above are lost?

It is worth noting in a broader context that many successful and progressive businesses are investing a great deal of time and money in promoting a more participative and people-orientated way of working, a move which is seen as having sound commercial or 'bottom-line' returns.

Participation, above all, begins with a belief in the potential of people. Participative management without a belief in the gifts people bring to organizations is a total contradiction in terms.

In this chapter we have begun to explore some of the ways in which people work together and behave in team or group situations. The aim has been to help you to develop your understanding of the very complex interactions that are the inevitable product of working relationships.

Being aware of these processes and behaviours provides support for your efforts to think through and share what is happening in your own team and to reflect upon team management issues generally. But crucially management is about action; it is about being engaged wholeheartedly in the very processes and relationships we have been discussing.

It is not enough then to become an aware observer of team issues – the need is to move on and think about how this awareness can be shared and developed through action. The following chapter sets out to do just that. It suggests practical strategies for building and developing your team based on the understanding gained here in looking at group processes and behaviours.

Summary

In this chapter we have focused on developing an understanding of team/group processes and common behaviours, and have endeavored to underline the complexity of exploring personal behaviour and relationships in a group setting.

The value of teamworking

The chapter has looked briefly at the benefits of working in teams for the individual and for the organization. In particular it has stressed the personal needs we have – social experience, self-image/esteem, security, support and opportunity – that we meet through working with others. It reminds us that teamworking is not always the only or most effective way of organizing people at work.

Group processes

This section discussed a number of tools which a manager might use to view the way in which the team works together. These included the division of team processes into those relating to the task and those seeking to maintain the team, and the importance of balancing these together with meeting individual needs. We examined the 'stages of development' model and stressed the value of working through difficulties and conflicts as a way to move the team forward. Lastly team roles were discussed using Belbin's classification, with the emphasis on a fluid and developmental approach to their use.

Behaviour in teams

The last section looked at developing an understanding of a wide range of common behaviours that managers may encounter in groups or teams. These included hidden agendas, conflict, blame, group norms, conformity and non-participation.

The emphasis throughout the chapter has been on the need to explore an understanding of these processes and behaviours overtly with the team, and to accept the innate complexity of group relationships and personal behaviour.

Further reading

John Hunt's *Managing People at Work* provides useful and readable discussion on the subject of behaviour in organizations, including chapters on individuals and groups, power and motivation. Of particular relevance regarding this chapter, his material on conflict in groups and group behaviours will be of interest.

For further exploration of group processes and individual behaviour, Edgar Schein's *Process Consultation* looks at these areas to a depth we could not cover in this text. It is directed at practising managers as well as consultants, and his ideas are delivered in a clear and accessible style. Perhaps more than the subjects covered though, his facilitative approach to management processes is well worth taking an interest in.

References

Argyris, C. (1990) *Overcoming Organisational Defences*, Prentice Hall, London.

Belbin, R.M. (1981) *Management Teams – Why they Succeed or Fail*, Butterworth-Heinemann, Oxford.

Belbin, R.M. (1993) *Team Roles at Work*, Butterworth-Heinemann, Oxford.

Berne, E. (1964) *Games People Play – The Psychology of Human Relationships*, Penguin Books Ltd.

Chaudhry-Lawton, R., Lawton, R., Murphy, K. and Terry, A. (1992) *Quality: Change Through Teamwork*, Century Business.

Hunt, J.W. (1986) *Managing People at Work*, McGraw-Hill.

Makin, P., Cooper, C. and Cox, C. (1989) *Managing People at Work*, British Psychological Society and Routledge.

Phillips, N. (1993) *Innovative Management*, Pitman.

Schein, E.H. (1988) *Process Consultation*, Vol. 1, Addison-Wesley.

Senge, P. (1990) *The Fifth Discipline*, Century Business.

8

Building the team – actions for progress

However outlandish a person's views may be, they will contain grains of truth embedded in his logic and prejudices. It is much more fruitful, much more productive to bring the differences out into the open, to extract these grains of truth and use them. It is in this way that you will build your team into the group that grows and develops, making each one a full participant in action.

Warren Bennis, Jagdish Parikh and Ronnie Lessem

Objectives

By the end of this chapter you will be able to:

➤ Describe the advantages of investing time in the way a team works together
➤ Recognize the value of developing open communication within a team and use strategies to facilitate this
➤ Describe a range of teambuilding tools and be aware of the complexity of teambuilding processes

Introduction

The previous chapter looked at some of the processes and behaviours commonly found in group or team situations with the aim of helping the manager to reflect upon the way people work together. This chapter goes on to explore some of the ways in which you can develop effective teamworking and improve the quality of team relationships at work. A few words first though about these 'actions for progress'.

We have chosen to put the work on group processes and behaviours and these actions for progress into separate chapters for two connected reasons. Firstly on a practical note, the interventions that a manager can make to develop effective teamwork are often not specific to one particular team issue. Building trust, for example, is a very valuable way to reduce misunderstanding, but it can also help to improve the quality of communication or to combat the presence of hidden agendas. More importantly, though, we hope to move well away from the idea that the team issues discussed in the last chapter respond to a simple 'cause-and-effect' analysis. There is a temptation to link a particular team issue with a given solution – 'If this is happening, then I do that' – problem solved. But teams are not machines and do not respond in such linear and predictable ways. Adopting a strategy may work in one situation but make things worse in another seemingly similar one. This is not to say that simple, often 'commonsense' actions cannot be extremely effective, but to suggest that managers should think broadly about their actions or strategies in any particular situation and be prepared to change them as the need arises. In this respect these 'actions for progress' are not put forward as solutions or instant remedies but as actions you might consider adopting in working with your staff to develop effective teamwork.

Some key themes in this book have been developing awareness and understanding of yourself and others, learning to value the different skills, experience and styles of the people you work with, and accepting the confusions and difficulties that inevitably arise in our working relationships with others. Developing this understanding is a continuous process, one which is best progressed not just by observation and reflection, but by being actively engaged in trying things out and 'learning by doing'.

Adding to this need for active engagement is the understanding that the manager plays a key role in influencing how a team works together through his or her own activities, decisions, and behaviour. In fact the mere presence of the manager in team situations will affect the behaviour of the team members. In a team meeting, for example, members' expectations of what the manager likes to hear and how he or she likes to work will provoke changes in behaviour as members seek to influence events in what appears to be an 'effective' way. The crucial idea here is that it is not possible to separate out the 'observer' from the 'observed'. It is unrealistic to hope to manage a team without giving serious thought to the effects of your own behaviour on the interaction between yourself and your team.

Building the team is a complex project – many of the ideas noted here are interlinked, and running alongside these 'actions for progress' are issues like commitment, 'leadership', empowerment and learning that are explored in other chapters.

The ideas presented here range from practical suggestions through to approaches you could consider adopting in your search for effective teamwork. All, however, imply taking action – doing something positive to 'make it happen'. Taking action in this context means working with people to build a team, with a shared understanding that effective teamwork results from the efforts of all of the team. In this respect teambuilding is not something you can 'do to' your staff – they must value and commit to teamworking and its development as individuals.

Lastly, teambuilding is not a one-off activity, but a continuous and dynamic process. The environment in which the team works, the tasks to be done and even team membership will all change over time, introducing new variables and relationships to be managed. Team development needs to be a permanent item on the manager's agenda – there are always things to learn and improvements to be made in the way in which we work together.

How we work together

In order to 'build a team' and improve its effectiveness and productivity, we are essentially looking to change the way people work together. It is very difficult to make this change if team members do not have a common understanding of the way they work together at the moment, and about the way they would like to work in the future (a vision). This will require a real investment in time and energy on a continuous basis and by all concerned if it is to be successful.

To make this investment, individuals need firstly to see the value of spending time on how they work together. A common early barrier to team development is a tendency to focus on tasks or systems and to bypass or ridicule efforts to discuss process issues or even to deny that this approach is necessary or useful. Comments such as 'this is just navel-gazing – let's do some work' should be seen for what they are: understandable but defensive reactions to the perceived difficulties in approaching 'personal' topics in favour of the 'safe' territory of the job in hand. Tackling relationship issues in a team setting challenges the established working patterns and may result in anxiety or insecurity for some team members – a case of 'better the devil you know' being preferred to the uncertainty of exploring new ways of working.

The first step in looking at process issues, therefore, is to generate through discussion and example a genuine understanding of the value of exploring the way we work together. It is often appropriate to do this by reviewing particular events or tasks. Using practical work situations can demonstrate the powerful impact that team processes and relationships have on team effectiveness.

Another way to introduce the value of process work is to lead an open discussion on how the team would like to work together in the future, working towards a mutual understanding of how effective teams function – in effect a 'vision' about positive and supportive working relationships. This can be based on practical work problems or outstanding issues, looking at how the team can move forward and what people need to do to 'make it happen'. It is important here to ensure that the team takes responsibility for moving forward together. It is not possible for the manager or the organization to change team processes from the outside in any really effective way.

It is crucial that the whole team is involved in efforts to understand and develop its working style for three important reasons:

- They will all have valuable ideas and suggestions to make – contribution is a vital element in developing a sense of 'team'
- They need the opportunity to clarify situations, ask questions and correct any assumptions made by others about their behaviour. They will need to share their understanding of how the team works and learns, and express their views and feelings openly
- To develop effective teamworking processes the manager will need the team's commitment, involvement, enthusiasm and help. In stating these needs overtly, the manager 'models' an open expression of views and needs.

These serve to emphasize that a manager cannot implement a teamworking approach by order or by stealth. Indeed, moving towards a shared approach to team development raises important issues about what happens to the manager's traditional role of being in control and taking all the responsibility.

Spending time on processes

In addition to gaining commitment, discussing and challenging processes needs to become an accepted way of investing the team's time. Some practical approaches to creating opportunities for this investment might include:

- Set aside specific times to review and discuss issues concerning working together. This could follow on from or include teambuilding activities or training sessions. It might be useful to explore particular issues such as communication, team norms or decision-making methods at each event. It might be helpful here to use an external facilitator to question and prompt your explorations. You could allow time at the end of team meetings to discuss 'How could we do this more effectively', 'How did you feel when . . .', 'What happened here', etc. Add this item to the agenda regularly and be sure the team knows why this is important. These actions symbolize the team's commitment to improving working relationships.

- Openly support and reinforce behaviours which promote a teamworking approach, for example: thank people for their contribution, feedback or questions and encourage participation in decision-making or problem-solving. Show genuine concern for feelings and viewpoints. It is important that these interventions are authentic and sincere. (It is possible for comments like 'Thanks for that' and 'How are you feeling about . . . ?' to become part of a collective joke about a new caring language.)

- In taking process issues seriously and demonstrating their importance, you will be continually sending a positive message to the team. Modelling behaviour in this way is particularly vital in tackling difficult relationship issues or areas of potential conflict which have been avoided or have become undiscussable.

- Use an observer during team situations to give feedback on how you work together – provide a checklist for this initially, developed and updated by the team. Rotate this 'role' so that each member can see the value of an 'outsider's' view.

- Rotate roles at team gatherings, particularly that of the 'chairperson', so that team members get a different view of the processes they use and improve their understanding of the difficulties others might face.

- Use informal and social situations to open up discussion and generate ideas about better ways of working together, and to build relationships. Challenge the boundaries we construct between 'work' and social or informal exchanges.

- Ask a lot of questions. Questioning in an open and constructive way encourages people to think things through for themselves. Use questions to examine not just what to do, but widen this to look at 'how we go about it' (processes). Promote the exciting and positive aspects of learning together as a team.

- Use checking and summarizing on process issues too. Include a discussion on how the team will tackle a particular issue before ploughing into the task at hand – make this a learning experience.

While these suggestions are useful in themselves, we must stress the point about the context in which these ideas can bear the most fruit. We have already noted that people need to understand and commit to the value of looking at the way in which they work together. Building on this understanding, team development is more likely to be successful in an environment which provides support through the elements illustrated in Figure 8.1.

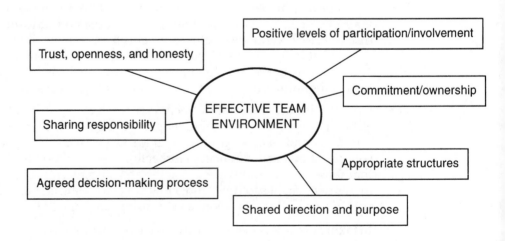

Fig. 8.1 Creating an effective team environment.

The comment about structure is important and needs to be carefully balanced and appropriate to team and individual needs. Too much 'structure' can lead to a rigid and inflexible approach, stifling opportunities and killing creativity. Too little structure can be equally a problem for many people – it is unusual for most of us to be able to operate effectively without some frameworks and boundaries. Of course the extent to which people find structure helpful will vary from one individual to another and the manager will need to continually balance and reappraise the structural needs of the team to avoid the pitfalls of either extreme.

Finally, a reminder that as a manager or team leader you are very much part of the team's processes yourself and it is not possible for you to become purely an observer and shaper of these processes. You will need to be aware of your own actions and behaviours and the influence these have on team processes.

This presents the manager with a useful starting point for process work. It is helpful if the manager is up-front with the team in acknowledging their own role and influence in shaping team processes and 'setting the tone'. This not only models open discussion and disclosure but by encouraging feedback and discussion about your influence, it keeps the focus on your behaviour which may be less threatening for some team members. It further demonstrates that you are prepared to act in an open and trusting way and not just talk about it in theory.

This section has looked at how we work together in broad terms, including the need to gain commitment and to find the time for exploring team processes. In order to make real progress and positive use of valuable team time it is important to develop open and honest communication between team members.

Being overt – get explicit!

In any team or group there is always a level of misunderstanding, assumption making, guesswork and ignorance that presents a real barrier to developing effective teamwork. It's not possible to eradicate these factors entirely from complex and ever-changing working relationships, but they are important issues to tackle if the team is to move forward. The team will not be able to change the way it behaves unless people are prepared to be open about issues, personal agendas and needs, and individual behaviour.

Various sources adapted from Luft, J. (1961) 'The Johari window' in *Human Relations Training News*, 5.

To reinforce the value of open communications in a teambuilding situation, it is worth looking at a model known as the 'Johari window'. This model is useful not simply as a justification for the manager to work on openness, but can be shared with the team to help build understanding of the need for openness and to support the use of feedback and disclosure. There are many versions of this model but we have illustrated in Figure 8.2 overleaf a simplified one relating to the value of open communication between an individual and a group or team. The 'window' has four boxes, each referring to a state where the group and the individual is or is not aware of certain pieces of information (i.e. facts, views, feelings, concerns). We will run through each of the 'boxes' first, giving typical team examples, and then look at how it helps us to support teambuilding through encouraging both disclosure and feedback.

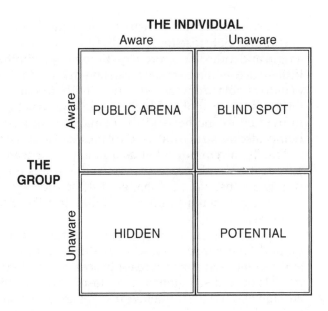

THE INDIVIDUAL

	Aware	Unaware
Aware	PUBLIC ARENA	BLIND SPOT
Unaware	HIDDEN	POTENTIAL

THE GROUP

Fig. 8.2 Simplified Johari window.

The **potential** box is the least useful in terms of 'being explicit', as it relates to things of which neither the individual nor the group are aware. This might, however, include undiscovered abilities or hidden strengths and assets that have not been explored or developed. The potential here can be the source of creativity and energy yet to be tapped. On the other hand it also includes subconscious thoughts and repressed feelings. For this reason it is perhaps an area best left unexplored in a team situation until an environment of support and trust is developed enough to deal sensitively with an individual's own forays into the 'box'. It is also possible that it might conjure up images of therapy sessions or 'encounter' groups that some of your team members may see as threatening.

The box labelled **public arena** relates to information that is known and expressed by both the group and the individual. It is **only** when issues, feelings or concerns are 'public' or 'common knowledge' that a team can begin to develop understanding and find ways to move forward. An example of this could be that of a team manager who finds it difficult to 'let go' of projects or tasks being delegated. If the group expresses this concern overtly and the manager recognizes and accepts the difficulties it can cause, then the issue becomes 'public'. At this point the team and manager can work together constructively to resolve the issue and improve the way the team operates to everyone's benefit.

The remaining two boxes represent the areas where there are real opportunities to develop open team communications. The **blind spot** is the area which represents information about an individual's behaviour that is known by the group but of which the individual is unaware. A common example is that of a person whose behaviour is perceived as noisy and aggressive by the group – they may talk together about this 'backstage', or illustrate their frustration through withdrawal or non-cooperation with the individual concerned. The individual in the 'blind spot', however, is unaware of the effects of his or her behaviour on the group and has no reason to adapt their behaviour as there is 'no problem' as far as they are concerned.

This situation and its damaging consequences will persist unless the individual is made aware of the effects of their behaviour. The group must express its concerns to the individual and move the issue into the public arena. We will look at this 'feedback' process in more detail shortly.

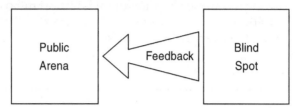

Fig. 8.3

The last box, **hidden**, represents a situation in which an individual has concerns or needs about the team or its work that they do not express – they are kept 'hidden' from others. The rest of the group are unaware of these needs or concerns and carry on regardless. A team example to illustrate this might be that of an individual who feels that their ideas are not listened to or seriously considered by the rest of the team. Because the team are unaware of these feelings they will not consider changing their behaviour – while the individual will go on suffering in silence, perhaps giving up any attempt to express ideas as being a waste of effort.

Again the way forward is clear: the individual must make their feelings and concerns known to the team – moving them from 'hidden' to the public arena through disclosure (Figure 8.4).

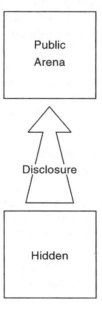

Fig 8.4

The Johari window provides a useful tool that managers can use to explore with the team the need to be more open and explicit about the issues that prevent team development. As with all models it is a simplification, but it provides the opportunity to discuss just what sort of behaviours the team could move into the 'public arena' and about the need for a trusting environment in which to do so.

While working through this model can lead to acceptance and commitment to being more open in principle, it is important to understand that there are very real and complex reasons why people feel that being open in practice is a difficult or even 'risky' business.

Learning activity

Developing open communication

Think about your own work team or learning group situation:

- What might prevent an individual from openly sharing their concerns, ideas, needs, feelings or views?

There are many barriers to openness between team members, but some of the common ones that you may have noted might include:

- Our tendency to hide thoughts and feelings through fear of appearing ignorant or incompetent
- A wish to avoid at all costs possible conflict or confrontation
- A fear of 'punishment' in some way or that our feelings or views will be 'held against us', particularly by those 'senior' to ourselves
- A personal lack of confidence that our ideas or feelings will be taken seriously
- The view that sharing these thoughts and feelings is not a 'normal' part of working life
- A strong 'task' culture can also present a block to exploring more fully the contributions of team members' needs and concerns
- The view that showing concerns or feelings is 'a sign of weakness'.

Many of these are rooted strongly in our natural desire to protect ourselves from difficult situations, threats or embarrassment. As such they are as valuable to us as the ability to run away from physical danger. The difference here is that it is possible to create an environment where the open discussion of team issues and personal concerns no longer constitute a threat to ourselves or other team members. Concerns and feelings are more likely to be raised in an atmosphere which is based on trust and a constructive and joint approach to resolving workplace difficulties.

In general, the development of an atmosphere of trust and support will go a long way towards encouraging people to 'put their cards on the table'. Some of the following practical actions may help to provide your team with opportunities to express their needs and ideas:

- **Checking understanding**: by summarizing contributions made by individuals to ensure clarity and provide an opportunity to add comments, or by reflecting back feelings you have picked up.

- **Disclosure:** share your own concerns, thoughts and feelings with the team. This models the sort of behaviour you are trying to encourage, and demonstrates your willingness to take risks, to trust others, and to be human!

- **Asking questions:** using open questions to give others time and space to disclose their views to the team. You may sometimes need to do more than add 'Is everyone happy with this?' at the end of a discussion because of the strength of the barriers noted above.

- **Using feedback:** a powerful tool (if used sensitively) for increasing people's awareness of the effects of their behaviour on others. (We will discuss this more fully in the next section.)

- **Challenging:** try playing devil's advocate sometimes, particularly with quick decisions taken without full participation or pushed through without full debate – you may be voicing hidden concerns or opinions. It is also a useful way of checking out the validity of arguments put forward or of raising interesting alternatives.

The manager will need to accept that it is not a simple task to encourage openness quickly in a team, the drive for this must come from within the team where people understand and commit to the value of open communication, and are willing to learn together about how to move their team forward. It is also important to be realistic about removing misunderstanding, hidden agendas and so forth – efforts in this area will reduce these things but are unlikely to eradicate them completely.

This is yet another complex area of management where it is relatively easy to see the value of openness in theory and agree to it in principle. In practice, developing open and honest relationships at work is a difficult but immensely rewarding experience and ultimately the only way forward. After all, if you envisage a future where working relationships are based on manipulation, game-playing and competition, then all you have to do is nothing!

Using feedback

If we return for a moment to the Johari window model and the 'blind spot' box, we talked about the need to express concerns about the behaviour of others through the use of feedback (Figure 8.5). It is only when individuals become aware of the difficulties their behaviour may be causing – when it becomes 'public' – that they are then able to consider adapting their behaviour in some way.

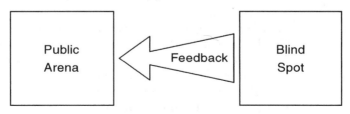

Fig 8.5

Feedback is a way of sharing with individuals or groups the effects of their behaviour on others. Again, the emphasis here is on the need to bring difficulties out into the open in order to both understand and accept them, and to take action to change or accommodate the behaviour in question.

In a team situation feedback should be encouraged between all members of the team, though initially it may be a useful starting point if the manager invites feedback on his or her working style to 'get the ball rolling'. This shows a willingness and commitment to increased understanding and improved performance. Remember too that giving feedback on successes and good performance (i.e. praise) is just as important as commenting on areas for development.

For feedback to be productive (and not destructive) we need to consider two important factors – the atmosphere in which it happens, and the practical skills involved in delivering and receiving feedback.

Learning activity

Feedback guidelines

Reflect on a situation in which someone gives you feedback about your behaviour. What sort of guidelines, or 'do's and don'ts', would you suggest should apply to this process?

Feedback skills

Feedback is more likely to be effective if it is delivered in a positive and constructive style, where an effort is made to reduce the level of defensiveness of the receiver. Listed below are some of the feedback guidelines that we think are important – you may be able to add some of your own. It is worth noting the range of situations that these ideas can be applied to include appraisal or supervision sessions, and discussing learning or development opportunities.

Feedback should be:

- Focused on **behaviour**, not on the person
- About **specific** behaviour/situations, not generalizations
- **Objective** and not judgmental
- **Wanted** or asked for
- **Positive** (praise) as well as **developmental** (negative)
- **Timely** – as soon as possible
- **Constructive** and helpful – concerned with the future
- **Achievable** – focused on the realistic
- **Shared information** – not advice or solutions
- In an appropriate **environment**

- In **handleable** chunks – not too much at once
- An opportunity for **clarification**
- Not **hidden** or dressed up in waffle, flattery or sarcasm
- Not via **other people**.

As with skilled appraisal, it is often possible to use questioning techniques to help individuals think through the effects of their behaviour on others, to suggest ways of accommodating or adapting their behaviour, and to discuss any support they might feel is appropriate. The focus with feedback should always be on what we do and how we do it, and not venture too far into discussions about 'why'.

Of course giving feedback is not as simple as following a set of guidelines might suggest. People can react defensively to many forms of criticism however well-intentioned or skillfully delivered. Even where the feedback is requested and accepted there can often be an emotional response to having our short-comings pointed out to us. It is important to recognize that this is why we find using feedback somewhat daunting – we are concerned about the reaction it generates and any damage it might cause to our relationships. The difficulty is that this 'caring' approach to others actually becomes a way of avoiding pushing for change or improvement, and a frequently used reason for not confronting personal issues in a team. There is always a balance to strike here, but the message is that in avoiding giving feedback on difficult issues you will need to be aware that this is often for your own 'safety' rather than a real concern for others.

On a practical level within the team, it is useful initially to precede the actual feedback by reminding people what you are doing and why – let them know that you are 'trying it out'. This is not to water down the value of the feedback or to apologize for it, but rather to put it into the context of the commitments you have made to team development and process work.

Argyris, C. (1990) *Overcoming Organisational Defences*, Prentice Hall.

The caring and easing-in approach

Chris Argyris suggests that the caring approach to difficult issues is ultimately counter-productive and a product of our own 'defence mechanisms'. To illustrate this let's work through a situation in which we see the need to deliver some difficult feedback to a colleague, feedback that we perceive might be threatening or embarrassing to them. In thinking this we re-frame our comments in soft and caring language. The colleague, however, senses we are doing this and interprets the criticism as serious **and** that we are ducking the issue and not being honest. Their reaction is understandably defensive, which in turn confirms to ourselves that the 'easing-in strategy' is necessary and useful. The result of this 'caring' approach is that the issue is never confronted – the situation does not change – our defence mechanisms are reinforced – negative views are watered down or smoothed over – and the fact that all this has happened becomes undiscussable.

Feedback – atmosphere

The list of guidelines above can appear quite daunting – 'I'll never remember to do all of those things correctly' would be a reasonable reaction. But of more importance than these 'rules' is the atmosphere in which we try to give feedback to each other.

In this respect we come back again to the crucial areas of trust and honesty that underpin the development of positive working relationships. Some of the factors that provide a foundation for the successful use of feedback (and many other aspects of management) are illustrated in Figure 8.6.

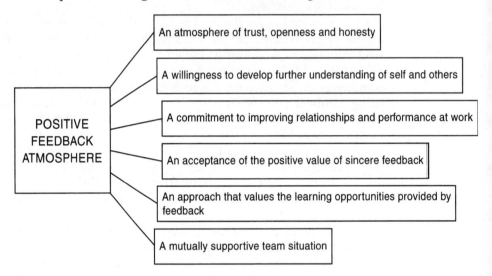

Fig. 8.6

The point about operating in this sort of environment is that the approach to giving feedback becomes less critical as the purpose and intent behind it are clear and accepted. Equally, the use and acceptance of feedback in a team is likely to vary significantly between individuals depending upon their own personal approach and attitude towards this form of development – it is worth beginning with less threatening topics to establish the positive use of feedback.

Building support mechanisms

Support provides people with the opportunity to tackle sometimes difficult or personal team issues in the knowledge that others understand and back up these efforts to move forward and are there to help if required. In addition to the challenges of team development, the need for the team to cope with rising work demands, the mounting pace of change and moves towards shared responsibility all add to what is expected of people at work. It is far from possible for individuals to handle these scenarios effectively on their own; indeed team effectiveness depends firmly on the ability of members to provide each other with support on a continuous basis.

In this section we will look at the need for support in enhancing team effectiveness and performance, some of the barriers to the practice of supporting each other, and practical ways in which support mechanisms can be developed in your team.

To create a situation where people are motivated and positive about the challenges facing the team, the level of support provided by its members becomes crucial. The model in Table 8.1 illustrates the feelings and effects of this interplay between support and challenge. Above all this model suggests the value of support not only in tackling the complex demands of today's workplaces, but in meeting the challenges of increased productivity and rapid change with excitement rather than anxiety.

Table 8.1 Support and challenge

High challenge *and* high support: (HIGH PERFORMANCE)

Feelings:	Excitement and enthusiasm
Effects:	People want to be involved; cooperation
	High motivation for moving forward

High challenge *but* low support: (STRESSFUL)

Feeling:	Fear, anxiety, sometimes anger
Effects:	People avoid involvement/stressful climate
	Change attempts likely to be damaging and fail
	Eventual 'burn-out'

Low challenge *with* high support: (COSY)

Feelings:	Complacency, relaxation and warmth
Effects:	People seek out and resist changes to this cosy environment
	No motivation to move forward

Low challenge *and* low support: (APATHETIC)

Feelings:	Boredom and depression
Effects:	People become apathetic

So how do you encourage a supportive atmosphere at work? Again this cannot be seen in isolation from the other processes and actions discussed in this chapter and others such as tackling blame, social and teambuilding events, improved communication and valuing differences. This is as it should be, for developing support mechanisms is inherent in many of these areas. You will also find that we return to the value of support when we look at delegation, the management of change and, crucially, learning and development in later chapters.

But what type of support do people in the team need and how do we know the difference between support and interference? Clearly the first thing to remember is that the answers to these questions will be different for each person and for differing situations, and so managing this process requires flexibility and an individual approach. The crux of this issue is the need to get know your team well as individuals, reinforcing the 'developing relationships' theme that underlies effective management. More specifically, think through some practical suggestions for managing support in the workplace in the following activity.

Learning activity

Managing support

What sort of actions could you take to effectively manage support in your own workplace or learning situation?

The crucial ideas behind managing support come from sharing an understanding of its value and recognizing the need to manage it openly. The following suggestions may reflect some of your own ideas.

- **Discuss support overtly**. As part of the development of effective team processes, gain commitment to the value of support in pursuing team objectives. In terms of raising awareness and developing understanding, it is also worth discussing some of the personal issues that make providing and asking for support difficult for some of us.

- **Negotiate it.** We are sure that you are aware that some individuals need lots of support and encouragement on a continuous basis, while others need less – even seeing your efforts to be helpful as interfering and distracting. While everyone has developed some skill at picking up what support is needed by individuals (from non-verbal signals for example), it is very useful to negotiate openly about the type and level of support a team member may need. This needn't be a lengthy process. A few simple questions such as 'How can we help you with this' or 'How often shall we review progress on this' together with creating openings such as 'How are you getting along with . . .' may be sufficient once the practice is well established.

- **Your needs**. Another reason to negotiate support is the barrier presented by the manager's needs in this situation. Often it is not easy for a manager to 'let go' and allow staff the room to tackle new problems or developments. This can come from a wish to retain control, the need to ensure your own high standards, or the expectations of the organization about what are 'effective' ways to manage. The effect of this may lead to a desire to over-support and monitor your staff. This tendency is particularly evident in times of high pressure or when things go wrong, when both manager and team may feel the need to revert to the 'safety' of an order and control approach to management in which the team relapses into dependency.

Tackle this by being open about the difficulty you have in 'letting go', and enlist their help in changing the way you support each other. Encourage the team to challenge your 'interference' and respond positively to such challenges.

- **Ask for it yourself**. It's easy to see the provision of support to your team members as a crucial part of the role of a manager, but less easy to accept that this is part of a two-way relationship in which the manager is frequently supported by the team. Not only will you need the team's support in many ways, but by making your need for support known it gives you the opportunity to 'model' the open behaviours you are trying to encourage. Look after yourself by building networks of colleagues who can provide you with support from outside the team or even the organization.

- **Encourage it internally**. Find and use opportunities to encourage team members to support each other rather than rely solely on the manager. There are plenty of opportunities to formalize this when, for example, you are away on holiday or business. As the team will develop its own support networks through social interaction and friendship, stressing the value of mutual support builds on an existing and understood social process.

- **Value support from outside work**. There are numerous sources of support from outside the working environment that will be vital to individuals in your team, the obvious ones being spouses or partners and friends. Do not underestimate the value of these relationships or downplay the importance of maintaining a balance between work demands and 'life outside'.

The principle of valuing support in the workplace is unlikely to meet with a great deal of resistance, providing that it takes place in a positive and trusting atmosphere. We all recognize that everyone needs support and we all have some experience and skills in giving support to others both in and away from work, so you will be building on inherently understood needs and already developed interpersonal skills. In practice though, some people find it very difficult to give or ask for help in a work situation. It is one of those areas where we may believe in the value of support but find it hard to put into practice.

One of the reasons for this has to do with our images of what represents a confident and competent member of staff – an image we somehow think is shattered if we ask for help or say that we are finding a situation difficult to cope with. This may be reinforced by our perception that the organization, or at least some of the people in it, would view asking for support as a sign of weakness. (An extension of this image barrier is the 'macho culture' in some working environments that many individuals find difficult to combat.) Of course the fact is that failing to ask for support and carrying on 'bravely' often compounds a problem and results in added stress for the individual and less effective performance all round.

It is a vital part of teambuilding, then, not only to develop effective support mechanisms within the team, but also to encourage a culture where support is valued for its contribution. Providing or requesting support must be seen as a sign of maturity and competence and not one of weakness.

Celebration, stories and fun!

The informal or social relationships which abound in any working environment play a very significant but often underrated role in shaping the way people work together. While some will argue that 'the grapevine', for example, is a barrier to effective working, informal processes have a very positive contribution to make to organizational culture, and also to 'getting the job done'. In this chapter we would like to encourage the manager to work with the social and informal aspects of their workplace. There are a number of ideas here that provide useful support for your team development efforts and an opportunity to see informal social situations as valuable allies in developing working relationships.

Celebrating success

With apologies to the RSPCA, 'Celebrations are not just for Christmas, they are for life.' Every organization has something to celebrate: individual or team successes, staff changes or projects completed, for example. Celebrations can range from formal events to a half hour after work with a bottle of wine, but the purpose is to recognize achievements and thank those involved (usually everybody) publicly. It is important that such celebrations are both appropriate and genuine, as lavish 'dos' with long speeches by out-of-touch senior people can be counterproductive. Celebrating successes with your team sends a clear message to team members and to others in the organization that their individual contributions are valued and that the team are capable of achieving their goals.

Social events

Of course it is not necessary to restrict social gatherings of work colleagues to celebratory events, they have value in their own right. Uncluttered by immediate work tasks, social events give people the opportunity to get to know each other and, often, to talk about how things are at work in a broader sense, with time to 'catch up' with issues left behind under the daily pressures of getting the job done. This 'getting away from the workplace' has long been a recognized factor in teambuilding events, and is why many seek to hold these at conference centres or hotels away from work.

Social events of various kinds probably already happen at most workplaces, and are not something the manager should 'organize' necessarily. Rather, the manager can support (and hopefully attend) these events with the understanding that they can promote teamworking directly through strengthening relationships.

Social time

Time spent by staff chatting socially to one another is often seen by managers as 'unproductive' – the very word 'gossip' has come to imply worthlessness or time-wasting. (We might ask what this 'us and them' view tells us about the level of trust and commitment and the manager's need for control in such a situation.)

It is possible, however, to view this very differently if we look at the value of such social time in helping to develop relationships at work. Social time gives people the opportunity to share concerns, discuss decisions and get to know each other as individuals. Useful work can also be done in these situations if no other avenues are available – examples might be sharing more efficient ways of doing tasks or bending the rules to meet customer needs. Here the emphasis is on 'getting the job done' effectively, in some cases despite established methods or procedures. A classic example of this effect concerns the way in which air traffic controllers in San Francisco developed informal ways of dealing with real situations that enhanced air safety. In their position, the accuracy of verbal communication with incoming pilots in crowded skies is crucial. In situations where pilots found communication in English very difficult, controllers by-passed the risks of any misunderstanding by allowing these pilots to land straight away while stacking the aircraft of those whose command of English was good. The shared but informal understanding of this strategy between experienced controllers actually improved their ability to operate safely and effectively.

Weick, K.E. (1994) 'Organisational culture as a source of high reliability' in Tsoukas, H., *New Thinking in Organisational Behaviour*, Butterworth-Heinemann, Oxford.

Many organizations today are concerned to provide the time and physical space to facilitate just this type of informal activity, recognizing its value in promoting communication and relationships. One creative company in London has even designed its office space around the largest room in the building – the coffee lounge – recognizing that this is so often where the really valuable communication of ideas and information takes place. In this case even formal meetings are held here, allowing people to drop in and out as need demands, and sending clear signals about openness.

Myths and stories

It is in the social or informal situations noted above that the myths and stories about the organization and its people circulate and 'develop'. It is here that shared perceptions and beliefs about the organization or about individuals are expressed and reinforced – free from the need to 'say the right thing' inherent in formal work situations.

On one level, the stories that circulate in your own organization may be exaggerated tales from social events or notable situations from work – something unusual, creative or even classic bungles. They serve a useful purpose in providing the organization with a sort of collective 'history', which helps people identify with the organization through people they know and events they can remember. They can add to the fun and 'banter' shared by work colleagues, and can also serve as reference points to remind staff of situations they have shared and in some cases survived together. As well as facilitating a sense of identity, stories serve a valuable purpose in reducing the complexity of organizational life – people remember incidents or stories more readily than policy documents or long speeches.

This shared experience, particularly of things like teambuilding events, can become a reminder for ways of working that the team have agreed to adopt, allowing people to refer back to things that were committed to at the event.

Reference to events or situations in this way can be a valuable way of sharing learning throughout the organization – they become 'case studies' passed around in the form of stories with important lessons attached.

Case note

Symbolic reminders

Here is one simple example from our own work with teams from a major retail company on a teambuilding event. Returning to work, they bought dinosaur key-rings for all team members – a reference to one of the more amusing activities they undertook. These served as a reminder of the event and more importantly of the actions they had committed to together. It is also possible to suggest some symbolic significance in their choice of 'reminder' – perhaps an oblique reference to the 'extinct' behaviours of the past, or of 'slaying dragons and defending the faith'? Other examples of 'reminders' that could be used in this way are key words, saying or slogans, or designed screen-savers and logos for those using computers.

On a deeper level these stories and shared perceptions may disclose more about 'the way we work around here' than any number of values or mission statements can do. They form part of the collective understanding of the organization's culture, and heavily influence the way in which people respond to new initiatives or attempts to introduce change.

In our work facilitating team development events with many companies we have the opportunity to listen to these stories and learn a great deal about the organization in the process. The interesting thing to observe, though, is that along with the exaggerated tales of disaster and the usual moans are a great many stories of good practice, sound and innovative management, and real improvements in the way a company operates. It is these 'good news' stories that provide the opportunity to influence and change perceptions about the way you work both within the team and in a wider context. It suggests that your efforts to develop, for example, open and honest relationships will be discussed and circulated through informal or social channels, which become powerful ways of communicating new ways of working together. These channels provide an important opportunity for you and your team to influence others in the organization by demonstrating and sharing effective working practice.

Fun at work

Perhaps the idea of celebrations, socials, storytelling and having fun make work sound a little too frivolous. The image of work as a sombre and serious place to be, where people work in Dickensian silence, may seem equally extreme. But the idea of enjoyment, of having 'fun' in the workplace, can add real value to your team's productivity and teambuilding efforts.

The obvious benefits for all concerned are the motivational ones – people are significantly more productive in a fun environment than one dominated by seriousness and anxiety. Working in an atmosphere that is playful and enjoyable creates a mood that is picked up by clients and customers; it can help with creativity and ideas, and sharing 'the fun' with colleagues helps to build the team and relationships in informal ways.

The use of humour in the workplace can also add value as a means of relieving tensions and anxiety – laughter in particular is a great antidote when things get too chaotic or very serious. This must be qualified of course because the humour needs to be appropriate and acceptable to the team. There are times when it can get out of hand or 'go too far', and staff should be sensitive to the possibility that others can be offended, or may use humour in the form of sarcasm to make veiled attacks on others.

The physical environment

It may well be worth asking your team to think about ways in which the environment at work affects both communication and the general atmosphere it supports. While most of us do not have access to unlimited budgets to improve our surroundings, there are many cost-effective and simple improvements that can make a difference – plants, comfortable chairs or better facilities for lunch-breaks, for example.

In particular, attention needs to be paid to any barriers to communication that can be addressed. Think about the layout of meeting rooms, the space set aside for informal gatherings at break times, and physical barriers such as screens or filing cabinets that prevent a continuous flow of information and ideas.

Peters, T. (1992)
Liberation Management,
BCA/Pan
Macmillan,
London.

> *Case note*
>
> *Oticon*
>
> Oticon, a Danish manufacturer, have taken this one step further and introduced mobile workstations and lots of open space – allowing employees to move around and work with colleagues wherever they see the need to. They have also attacked the use of paper for communications – encouraging real conversation to replace memos and reports. Symbolically, they have a transparent chute running through the canteen down which oceans of shredded paper cascade as a reminder of this search for better communication.

There is also, of course, the need for access to private space, especially for interviews or meetings with clients and customers – you may need a clear system for notifying people that such a space is in use to avoid disturbances. As an example, one company has a stock of red baseball caps that people in an open-plan office wear when they need this personal time. It is also worth considering the impact of any changes on visitors to your workplace.

Finally, looking at the physical environment at work provides a very useful way for both managers and teams unused to working with consensus and empowerment to try out handing over full responsibility for improving the surroundings to staff and clients. Having an input or control over the working environment is a positive step that most managers should not find too threatening.

Being positive

There's an old song that provides a useful motto here:

You've got to accentuate the positive,
Eliminate the negative,
Latch on to the affirmative,
And don't mess with mister in-between.

And a quote you might like to remember:

Whether you believe you can,
Or you believe you can't,
You'll be right!

Alder

Adopting a positive approach to problems, issues, people and the future needs little justification here. Believing that your team can influence events, overcome difficulties and create its own future is an important part of the group atmosphere that the team needs to work towards. Often though, particularly in times of rapid change, it is natural for team members to respond to any situation in a negative way, blaming the circumstances or moaning about workloads, and generally feeling down about the possibility of moving forward.

The manager needs to accept, of course, that such negative reactions are normal and understandable for all but the most optimistic of us. However, to build a more positive atmosphere, there are ways that managers can challenge negativity in the team. Try the activity below.

Learning activity

Positive approaches

List the strategies you might adopt to promote a positive approach to challenging or difficult situations in your team, with colleagues or in a learning group (e.g. problems, difficult decisions, unacceptable behaviour).

Once more there are no simple answers in developing a positive approach within the team. Some of the more practical ideas you might have generated could include:

- Behave positively yourself. It goes without saying that appearing to be negative will undermine all your other efforts. Use your positive behaviour and that of others as a model. Lead your team with enthusiasm and inspiration.

- Challenge 'can't do' statements with 'What prevents us from . . .' or 'How can we deal with . . .' Move on to discuss what you can do together.

- Develop an understanding of the way people react to change. Learn to accept the feelings this arouses – anger or confusion for example – and develop strategies for supporting people through change. Share these ideas with your team and accept that these feelings are a necessary step in the change process. Give people space and time to adapt.

- Make a start. Some progress, however small, demonstrates the possibility of completing the task and moving forward. 'All journeys begin with a small step.'

- Take a fresh look at any written rules or procedures – replace lists of 'Can't do' rules with expressions of what people can do!

- Split up major projects into smaller more handleable chunks and take them one at a time. Be positive about your success after each 'chunk'.

- Work together on building a positive vision of the future – a realistic view of how you would like to work as a team.

- Establish a 'norm' that people not only identify problems but offer solutions to them as well if possible.

- Avoid 'labelling' people as negative – they will quickly learn to live up to the label.

- Keep work in perspective – we all have other more important things to consider in our lives outside of work.

- Accept that work will be difficult and confusing for everyone at times but remind yourself of the possibilities and the excitement.

In addition to these, the progress a team makes in developing, for example, support mechanisms, a commitment to learning, shared responsibility and the acceptance of a changing work environment will all help to reinforce a positive approach to challenges faced by the team.

Lastly, it is important to ensure that a positive approach does not blind the team to real issues or become an excuse to ignore difficulties on the grounds that discussing them is 'negative'. Developing a strong 'can-do' culture has its value perhaps in the form of being positive, helpful and constructive in the face of a realistic appraisal of difficulties and change. Again the development of effective team processes should reduce the possibility of the team allowing a positive approach to become an excuse for ignoring issues in this way.

How do we make decisions?

The way in which the team makes decisions is one of the areas where mistrust, hidden agendas and other destructive behaviours often show themselves. This is sometimes because time has not been set aside to agree on how the team should take decisions or to set boundaries about the degree of consultation and involvement expected by staff and manager.

This 'gap' between what people want or expect and what actually happens in practice can be narrowed by openly discussing decision-making processes with the team. It is an interesting area to explore with your team as hopefully it will challenge people's understanding of your role and give you feedback about the impact of your management style.

In discussing the way in which your team makes decisions it might be useful to consider how this might vary in response to a number of important factors:

- **The type of decision to be made**. It needs to be acknowledged that decision-making methods may change according to the situation and the type of decision to be made. It is not necessary to engage in lengthy consultation, for example, over trivial matters, and an autocratic 'get out' is appropriate when the fire alarm goes off.

- **Your management style**. Be prepared to accept that the team may have a different perception from your own and to learn from it by sharing these views. A more detailed appraisal of the style issue follows in Chapter 9 on creating direction and inspiration.

- **The expectations of the team regarding involvement and participation in decision-making**. Be aware here that expectations may be closely tied to previous practice. A team that has always suffered the manager taking all the decisions will need some help moving towards involvement and away from dependency.

- **Sharing responsibility.** This cannot be divorced from the issue of decision-making and again will make an interesting topic for discussion. The danger here is that the team may initially demand lots of participation and involvement, but will still see the manager as being solely responsible for the outcomes, at least when things go wrong.

Particularly in the case of sharing responsibility, these factors can provide a starting point for developing open discussion with the team on a range of issues embracing subjects like delegation, empowerment and control.

In exploring decision-making with the team we need to say a word or two about 'consensus' and 'voting' as methods of reaching a decision. When teams move away from a situation in which the manager makes all the key decisions (with or without consultation) towards a more participative approach, the decision-making process becomes more complex. Voting and searching for consensus are commonly used as ways of dealing with this new complexity.

Voting

With everyone encouraged to express opinions and ideas openly, the decision-making situation can appear to become confusing and lengthy, with a wider range of viewpoints to be considered. It is tempting to end this, sometimes uncomfortable, scene and get the decision made by 'moving to a vote'. Voting on issues is of course an accepted part of our traditional view of 'democracy' and is readily sanctioned by most people as a 'fair' way to take decisions, in that at least the majority will be satisfied with the outcome.

However, there are a number of concerns here that qualify the usefulness of voting in the workplace. Firstly, voting can readily be used to avoid confronting difficult decision-making situations head-on – with comments like 'We're not getting anywhere', 'We need a decision' or 'This is taking too long', voting provides a quick way out. People may opt for a vote for a variety of reasons – because they find the lack of a quick decision frustrating, because they are not interested or because the discussion is not productive or focused. There are no prizes for guessing what happens to the difficult issues or differences when this escape route is taken. Voting can become a common way of dealing with complex issues where the variables are not easily quantifiable and the relationships between them difficult to assess. In this case taking a vote is a double-edged sword. On the one hand it facilitates a decision being made and therefore prompts action of some sort, but on the other it avoids the team exploring the complexities of the issue and developing their understanding.

Another feature of 'voting' is the adversarial quality it brings to decision-making – a sense of 'for and against'. Voting presents the team with a 'win/lose' situation, where those who are out-voted may feel they have 'lost' and seek to undermine the decision or work for their own option in other, less overt ways. It is worth reflecting on how you feel personally when out-voted in this way – does the vote change your view? How do you feel about taking a course of action you disagree with?

This is important from a team building perspective as you will need to be able to deal with the divisive effects of the possible split between 'winners' and 'losers'. If voting becomes your only method of making decisions then proponents of particular ideas or agendas will know that they only have to convince half of the team to ensure they 'get their way'. In this scenario minority viewpoints such as radical or challenging ideas may not get the crucial attention that they deserve – a great loss to the team seeking to be creative and innovative.

This is not to suggest that voting does not have a useful role to play in team decision-making, but to remind managers of some of the pitfalls of relying on the vote. To quote Socrates: 'The trouble with democracy is that the majority is always wrong.'

Working towards consensus

An alternative may be to try to reach a decision without recourse to voting. Consensus means that in an open and free exchange of ideas and views, each member of the team feels that they have been listened to and understood. In this situation the team is looking for a decision that is accepted by everyone as the way forward, even though it may not be what some individuals feel entirely happy with. It is this acceptance which is crucial, as individuals will not feel they have been ignored or 'out-voted' in an inconsiderate way. They must 'buy in' to the decision for it to be fully supported, accepting the team view and committing to any required action.

The difficulty here is in avoiding what could be called 'false consensus'. Here the same pressures to make a decision or avoid conflict can lead to public acknowledgment by everyone that a particular way forward is acceptable when in fact it is not. In terms of avoiding false consensus the manager will need to become an acute observer of the silent language of posture and expression within the team, and be concerned to check out people's acceptance if in doubt. You will also find that as the team develops confidence in handling disagreement and voicing their concerns there should be less pressure to appear to agree with colleagues simply for 'a quiet life'.

Finally, it is important to remember that it requires an investment in time to get the benefits of participative decision-making, and the manager should allow for this especially when working towards establishing new ways of reaching decisions through the team. It is worth also noting that decision-making is not a precise science, particularly in dealing with difficult issues or complex decisions. Remember that:

- There is rarely only one 'right' answer – there are usually many
- Decisions are not 'wrong' – they may be less effective than others
- You cannot know all the consequences of decisions when you make them
- Hindsight is for learning, not for attributing blame
- Occasionally doing nothing may be more useful than taking action
- Conversely, doing almost anything may be more useful than endless reviews and avoidance.

Where are we going – clear goals and objectives

It seems an obvious point that team members need to be clear about their objectives and goals – those that relate to the organization, the team and to themselves as individuals. It is difficult to build a team if there is no shared sense of direction or purpose, yet this is an all too common feature of the way many teams function. Let's look firstly at the implications for a team of not being clear about objectives.

Learning activity

Own goals

What might be the effects on a team of having no clear objectives and goals?

The key problem arising from having no clear agreed objectives is the lack of a focus for the work being undertaken. This might result in:

- Effort and enthusiasm wasted on less important or conflicting/duplicated areas of work

- Work responding 'reactively' to situations and dissolving into fire fighting mode (being proactive needs a direction)
- Increased confusion and conflict within the team over decisions and policy
- Frustration of efforts to share responsibility and encourage empowerment
- Individuals pursuing their own objectives which may not be open or agreed
- Difficulty in acknowledging achievements or progress, or identifying areas for development
- Confusion resulting from having nothing concrete to commit to or become involved in developing
- Increased levels of frustration 'What are we trying to do and why?'

A common scenario is that managers assume that all of the team are aware of objectives, goals and direction. But is this always the case? It is worthwhile taking the time to review this with the team on a regular basis rather than rely on last year's appraisal or your assumptions. This is an exercise that can be part of a teambuilding event or handled in-house by the team itself.

A useful way to begin is to ask everyone to jot down, without consulting each other at this stage, what they think are their personal objectives, what the team is aiming to do and what the organization wishes to achieve. Sharing these thoughts can be interesting and enlightening. It will provide a starting point to discussing and agreeing openly what the team's objectives are. Involving the team in setting its own objectives is a valuable way to encourage ownership and commitment and ensure clarity. This may involve the manager giving input to the team about objectives from an organizational point of view, but is a move away from the traditional approach of the manager setting these objectives for the team remotely.

There are of course other aspects to managing the team's objectives that need to be considered in order that the setting and meeting of objectives does not exclude other ways of moving forward. Firstly it is important to recognize the sense of security that having a clear direction and recognizable objectives provides for many of us. This is of great value but can also work against challenge and change. It is possible, for example, that they provide a false sense of security, a case of pursuing objectives that have ceased to mean anything because it is more comfortable to do so than change the objectives.

Secondly, in a rapidly changing environment, objectives can become redundant almost from the moment they are written down. It is vital that they do not become tablets of stone but are open to continual challenge and free to be adapted or thrown out as appropriate. The message here is to use objectives as helpful and productive tools and not as a prop to replace a dynamic approach to effective management.

Setting objectives

The standard advice concerning setting objectives is that they should be SMART, standing for:

Specific
Measurable

Achievable
Relevant
Time framed

This is a useful starting point and has some practical value in clarifying team or individual objectives. For example, being specific helps to avoid vague statements of intent that are hard to relate to – people have something tangible to aim for. Setting unachievable goals sets everyone up for failure and needs to be avoided – large goals for example can be broken down into more achievable targets. Time frames too are important in indicating when particular objectives need to be met – many of us respond well (if stressfully) to deadlines which may help us to 'stop the drift'. SMART is very useful for setting objectives in the short term for tasks which are straightforward or not subject to too much human interference.

It is important, however, to be aware of its limitations and be flexible about its use. The most contentious area is the pervasiveness of the idea that only that which is 'measurable' is worthy of commitment when in fact the most significant areas of achievement, such as building productive relationships with other staff and with clients, are difficult if not impossible to 'measure' in any meaningful way. To test this out you might like to consider if it is possible to measure or set deadlines for crucial business areas such as promoting change, seizing opportunities, creativity, intuition, feelings, perceptions, complexity, engagement, commitment . . . add some of your own – the list is endless!

This is perhaps something that most of us 'believe' in, but which is difficult to sustain in a world driven by performance targets, league tables and anything with a number attached. Perhaps we have to understand that an obsessive reliance on 'measurement' is a fearful retreat from the difficulties of understanding complex and subtle relationships and systems, and an unsophisticated way of avoiding having to trust other people. As a manager you will need to be cautious about using measurement in this way.

Here's an interesting quotation to pin above your desk, entitled 'A Corporate Tragedy':

Mitroff, I. and Kilmann, R. (1984) *Corporate Tragedies*, Praeger, New York.

The first step is to measure what can easily be measured.
This is OK as far as it goes.
The second step is to disregard that which can't be measured or give it arbitrary quantitative value.
This is artificial and misleading.
The third step is to presume that what can't be measured easily really isn't very important.
This is blindness.
The fourth step is to say that what can't easily be measured really doesn't exist.
This is suicide!

Managing through objectives

There are abundant references in management literature about the application of management by objectives; indeed, for some organizations it has become an integral part of their approach to managing their 'business'. From what we have said above, the benefits of knowing 'where we are going' for the individual, the team and organization are clear.

The important thing about using objectives in a management setting is that they must be put into context. Frequently targets are set with deadlines and quantifiable indicators and so on but without information that enables us to answer some important questions. Objectives often tell us nothing about how we might go about achieving them or what resources are available. In a supportive environment that values initiative and a flexible approach this is an advantage, but it can cause stress to others who wonder who dreamed up the targets and how on earth are they going to be met.

Similarly it is important for people to understand why they are being asked to achieve certain objectives – how do they fit into the 'bigger picture?' To ask people to meet objectives when they do not know why they are important or how to go about it is unlikely to generate genuine enthusiasm or commitment.

These comments about the need to support objectives with information about their context apply largely to situations where the objectives are set by others, particularly by distant senior staff. Understanding of and commitment to objectives will be greatest, however, when they are set by those who will be doing the work.

Interestingly the approach to setting business objectives based on targets and numbers is rapidly being supplemented by less specific 'visions'. These visions still focus on direction, but say much more about values, purpose and meaning.

The issue of responsibility

In this chapter we have explored a number of practical actions and approaches that might help to 'build the team'. As manager or team leader you may be wondering if you have the skills to drive all of these initiatives through and create a worthwhile and effective teamworking situation. Even if you feel you have the skills, is it possible (and desirable) to control and direct a group of people towards a teamworking approach?

Learning activity

Build that team!

Think about the following questions:

- Can I ensure that positive relationships are developed between other members of the team besides myself?

- Can I force people to participate?
- Can I demand a certain level of commitment?
- Am I responsible for everyone's motivation and involvement?
- Is it my job to manage all of the conflict in my team?
- If 'my' team has hidden agendas, am I doing something wrong?

Hopefully you will not have answered 'yes' to too many of these questions. The issue of responsibility is crucial to teambuilding and many·other aspects of management, and we would strongly advise that this responsibility in a team setting must be a shared one.

Let's take the 'managing conflict' question as an example. Certainly you can encourage a positive view of conflict, promote the need to resolve or accommodate it, mediate if it is helpful or even arbitrate, but the individuals concerned must accept responsibility for their behaviour and its effects. Similarly with participation, you can support an environment that promotes participation, demonstrate your willingness to involve everyone and take seriously individual efforts, but in the end you cannot 'make' people participate, they have got to want to.

It is clearly important then to get across this message about shared responsibility at an early stage in your teambuilding journey. This form of personal responsibility in the workplace is more fundamental than that attached to positions of 'authority' or statements in a manager's job description. You will need to create the fertile ground in which this sense of shared responsibility can grow and prosper. Make it abundantly clear that equating 'responsibility' with 'the person to blame or sack' is history. Responsibility means people contributing to work as adults not slaves, creating purpose and direction through their own efforts and involvement, and having a real sense of ownership that comes from the excitement of working in a genuinely successful team.

Going forward

In this chapter we have explored some of the strategies you might consider using to build an effective team at work. It is important that you recognize that this is a continuous management process rather than something to do once and then forget about. The strategies suggested do not fall comfortably into a linear plan, but can be seen as a web of activities and approaches that mesh together through actions taken in the workplace. The complex and interactive nature of team development makes this a fascinating and rewarding area for managers to work on. Interestingly, it is one where seemingly trivial events or small-scale interventions can have significant impact. This invites the manager to explore with enthusiasm a wide range of techniques and ideas, enjoying the interactions and the experiments, and continually learning about the richness of working closely with others.

Summary

In this chapter we have explored some of the practical actions that you may like to consider in your efforts to 'build the team'. The emphasis has been on developing an understanding of the complex factors that may support or divert your efforts to build effective relationships within your team. Whilst practical suggestions have been made throughout, it is important to grasp that teams do not respond in simple ways to a 'ten-easy-steps' approach to teambuilding, and that team development is a continuous and not a one-off process.

We have focused heavily on the need to develop open and effective communication in your team – both in terms of improving performance, and crucially as this provides the environment to enable progress on team development issues. The sections on being explicit and on feedback in particular are vital in this respect.

The often undervalued importance of social or informal interaction has also been stressed in the section on stories and myths as this provides vital opportunities for the sharing of positive moves to improve the way we work together, and a somewhat different view of organizational culture.

Finally we have noted the importance of encouraging the sharing of responsibility for the teambuilding process with every member of the team. Developing effective teamwork relies on the commitment of people to finding more rewarding and productive ways of working together.

Further reading

In many respects the subjects covered in this chapter do not easily fall under a single heading or topic, and so recommending reading that covers the whole chapter is a little difficult.

Many of the ideas presented here are the result of exploring teamwork issues with managers and students we have worked with for which we thank them sincerely.

Give yourself a break from reading and go out and experiment with your own ideas – **put teambuilding into action!**

References

Argyris. C. (1990) *Overcoming Organisational Defences*, Prentice Hall.

Bennis, W., Parikh, J. and Lessem, R. (1994) *Beyond Leadership*, Blackwell Business, Oxford.

Chaudhy-Lawton, R., Lawton, R., Murphy, K. and Terry, A. (1993) *Quality: Change Through Teamwork*, Century Business.

Harris, T.A. (1967) *I'm OK, You're OK*, Pan Books, London.

Hirschhorn, L. (1993) *The Workplace Within*, MIT Press, Cambridge, Mass.

Makin, P., Cooper, C. and Cox, C. (1993) *Managing People at Work*, BPS/Routledge, London.

Peters, T. (1992) *Liberation Management*, BCA/Pan Macmillan, London.

Philips, N. (1993) *Innovative Management*, Pitman, London.

Stacey, R. (1992) *Managing Chaos*, Kogan Page, London.

Tsoukas, H. (1994) *New Thinking in Organisational Behaviour*, Butterworth-Heinemann, Oxford.

9

Creating direction and inspiration

People wanted The Truth – and I was giving opinions.

Warren Bennis

Objectives

By the end of this chapter you will be able to

➤ Describe the key issues that contribute to your understanding of leadership
➤ Use this understanding to evaluate your own leadership practice
➤ Apply the concepts from some practical and contemporary approaches to leadership to your own management situation

Introduction

This chapter is about that thorny subject – Leadership. The quotation above was chosen to reflect the difficulty of exploring a topic that is both emotive and complex – one for which there is no real agreement and plenty of lively opinion. It is one of those terms we often accept and use freely in talking about management, but where a reluctance to discuss and question differing perceptions and understanding can create real problems in the workplace.

We are aware that in some cases the very word 'leadership' arouses images that some people find uncomfortable. For instance, a traditional view of leadership may have associations with authoritarian behaviour, with notions of control and directing, and with 'giving orders'. In this case maybe coordinator or facilitator would be a more acceptable term to use, and that's fine. Whatever word we use though has drawbacks, and it must be recognized that neither facilitator nor coordinator convey the full range of activities that a 'leader' might engage in. Perhaps manager would be the most useful title, though as we will see below, it can be argued that leadership is about something more than management. In the end it is what you do as a leader or manager or coordinator that is far more significant than the choice of terms.

Interesting issues are raised when we begin explore what we mean by leadership and challenge some of our assumptions about it. What exactly do 'leaders' do and does this differ from a manager's role in any way? Do we really need leaders at all and if so why? Neither can we dismiss the political aspects of the leader's role, the relationship between leaders and the expectations of the 'led', or the use and abuse of power, for example. These questions relate to the core of our understanding of management, in particular to the relationship you develop between yourself and your staff or team. As such, your view of leadership becomes a reflection of your beliefs about your own role and about other people.

The aim in this chapter is to encourage you to reflect upon and develop your own understanding of the 'leadership' role, using ideas and approaches that are useful to you and appropriate for your own situation. This will require being aware that others, including your staff, may well have very different views and needs to your own.

Rather than simply list and discuss the many different approaches to leadership that are available in management literature, we have chosen to begin by exploring images of leadership. We then go on to develop this by discussing some of the crucial issues that are common to any understanding of leadership, and indeed management – such as the challenge of change, a focus on the future and our beliefs about people. In the second half of this chapter, we look at some useful practical approaches and some contemporary views that led us to title this chapter 'creating direction and inspiration'.

What do we mean by 'leadership'?

As we noted in the introduction, leadership is one of those complex ideas we all have opinions about or think we understand, but in practice find very difficult to pin down. Why is this? It is partly because we have all built up pictures about leadership throughout our lives from a variety of sources – from work, the family and our general knowledge of history, politics and war, for example. In this way we pick up ideas about leadership from our parents, teachers or managers and from political or military leaders and other 'famous' people. A useful starting point in developing your own awareness of leadership is to try thinking through your own images of leadership in the activity below.

Learning activity

Images of leadership

Think about the sort of images that 'leadership' conjures up for you and note down as many key words or ideas that come to mind. You can use the subjects below to focus on some of the areas that might give you additional ideas:

Politics   Leaders in history   A 'military' approach   The family

The workplace   Films/TV   Survivors on a desert island   The community

---

It is worthwhile spending some time looking through your ideas and images and thinking about what they tell you. Is there a consistent view of 'the leader', or are there many different and often contradictory ideas? The purpose of this activity is to encourage you to think about the complex and varied views of leadership that different people hold, and to see if this helps us to define what leadership means in practice.

You may also have found that your list of 'images' includes:

- The thing that leaders **do** – the 'functions' that they carry out, e.g. plan, motivate, give direction, take decisions
- Some **personal characteristics** – examples might be that they are: charismatic, aggressive, strong, supportive, ruthless, caring and so on
- Ideas about their **situation**, the circumstances in which they lead and the people that 'follow' them.

The range of situational factors are enormous. Figure 9.1 suggests some of these variables as they impact on the 'leader', ranging from the expectations of the team through to the culture of the society in which he or she operates. We will be returning to some of these aspects of leadership later but they serve to illustrate the difficulty in establishing an agreed understanding of what leadership means.

The issue is further complicated when we try to include something about the

Fig. 9.1 Some of the situational factors affecting the leader.

outcomes or consequences of a leader's actions – in effect to make judgments about what 'good' or 'bad' leadership means. A good recent example of this debate is Margaret Thatcher's time as Prime Minister. Depending upon your perspective she either provided the kind of strong leadership that the UK desperately needed, or led a policy revolution that had dire social and cultural consequences that are still being felt today. This demonstrates that we cannot look at leadership separately from its context in any meaningful way.

It also suggests that leadership means different things to different people, as this will depend upon their individual background and experiences which have led them to construct their own meaning for the term. This has important implications for the manager, who must be aware that staff will have very varied expectations regarding the sort of leadership that their managers provide. It must also cast doubt on the practical value of pursuing a comprehensive definition of 'leadership', as unless this definition is clearly understood, shared and agreed by everyone, individual interpretations will always vary and lead to misunderstanding and confusion.

It is not enough, then, to look at leadership simply in terms of skills or personal characteristics – we must consider the situation in which people 'lead' and the effects of their actions on others, particularly the relationship between the leader and their staff. This 'situational' factor needs to be widely defined to include not only this relationship, but also the culture of both the organization and the wider society in which it operates. We need to consider, too, that all of these factors will interact dynamically. They will all be changing and influencing each other in a continuous and complex way, requiring us to constantly update and review our leadership approach.

It is important, therefore, to create and develop your own understanding of leadership rather than search for an off-the-shelf answer. In helping you to do this the next section focuses on some of the key issues you will need to think about that are common to most if not all approaches to leadership.

Key leadership issues

In the introduction we briefly identified some of the factors that we need to consider in developing our understanding of leadership, including personal characteristics, the functions that leaders carry out and a wide range of factors that influence the situation in which you might lead. Before looking at some of the practical and more contemporary approaches to leadership, this section sets out to discuss some of these key leadership issues. You will need to think through these issues in developing your own approach, and you may wish to use them to evaluate the various approaches we look at towards the end of this chapter or as a basis for discussing leadership with your team or colleagues.

We discuss here the relationship between the leader and 'the led', including the varied expectations we all have about the leader's role. The crucial issue of our beliefs about people is also explored, followed by the need to consider the way leadership tackles both change and the future. But we begin by looking in more detail at the idea that leadership ability springs from the characteristics and qualities of an individual.

Leadership as 'personality'

Handy, C.B. (1985) *Understanding Organisations*, Penguin Books, London.

One of the ideas that may have come out of the activity on images of leaders is a discussion of the sorts of characteristics that you might associate with a good 'leader'. Some of the earliest attempts to get to grips with the concept of leadership took this approach which became known as 'trait' theory. It is still a common view for many people that 'leaders' have some mysterious special qualities that single them out from the rest of humanity, a myth reinforced by the media and Hollywood. There are clearly a number of problems with this approach – try thinking them through in the activity below.

Learning activity

Exploring characteristics

- Think about and suggest some of the personal characteristics you regard as necessary for 'leadership'.
- What issues does this 'leadership as a personality' approach raise for you?

One of the major difficulties with a 'trait' view is the lack of agreement about what characteristics are necessary for leadership – which traits are important. Some of the traits that have gained broad acceptance include a reasonable level of intelligence, the ability to use initiative and take action, self-confidence and a feel for the broader picture or context. Even if agreement could be reached on the traits needed for leadership, however, several problems arise. Firstly there will be plenty of examples of leaders who do not display these characteristics at all, and secondly this may suggest that leaders are 'born' rather than 'made'. The idea that there are 'born leaders' is both depressing and unhelpful for the majority of us who might not consider ourselves as 'natural' leaders. Fortunately most of the traits associated with leadership can be learned or developed, and as we shall see when we look at some contemporary views of leadership, the skills and approaches that are most effective are within everyone's reach.

Perhaps the most powerful argument against the 'personality' approach to leadership is that it focuses entirely on the individual and ignores the effect of the situation or the needs of those being led. In a business setting, leadership cannot be separated from its context. The effects of the organization's culture, for example, the people who work there, the type of work being done and the broader economic and social environment in which it operates, all have a major impact on 'leadership' in practice. A simple example of where the context can be crucial might be the impact of an authoritarian manager trying to operate in an empowered environment, and the real difficulties this might cause.

Focusing on leadership 'traits' provides an interesting debate, but in practical terms it is a little difficult to see how it might help managers to develop their own approach to leadership in the wide variety of situations in which they manage. One of the most influential of these 'situational' aspects is the relationship between the people the leader seeks to lead, and the leader him or herself.

Leaders and 'followers'

It's an obvious but important point that leaders cannot operate in isolation: there's a two-way process to consider here which is at the heart of the debate about leadership. The team has hopefully a great deal of opportunity to influence the 'leader' (or indeed to 'lead' themselves), and their expectations of what a 'leader' should do and take responsibility for are critical. Similarly the team's willingness and ability to take on responsibility and new tasks (known as the group's 'maturity') can have a significant impact on the way in which you might behave as a leader.

In developing your own approach to leadership, it is worth looking at some important aspects of the leader–team relationship that you will need to apply in your own situation.

People's expectations

If we assume that your staff will have different expectations about your role as a leader and manager, it becomes very important to understand what these expectations are. We can all come up with examples of people who 'need to be told exactly what to do all of the time', and yet others who like the freedom to do things their own way and use their initiative. This is not to suggest that you adopt wholly different styles for different people – to do so would increase confusion – rather that you may need to vary the way in which you communicate your approach and build understanding with your staff. It's worth remembering too that these expectations can change as people learn and develop, or as the culture changes for example. This suggests that your own approach to leadership will need to be dynamic and responsive to new situations too.

Dependency

People at work often develop a pattern of dependency on the leader to take decisions and solve problems for them. There are many complex reasons for this and some that are worth mentioning are previous experience of managers or leaders, a lack of confidence or a fear of responsibility (usually meaning 'fear of blame'). In this situation staff will habitually take problems to the manager, refer decisions 'upwards' and seek approval for even the most trivial actions. This situation can often be reinforced by the organization and by managers either explicitly through rules, rigid procedures and detailed monitoring, or implicitly via the organization's culture – the use of blame and punishment, low levels of trust or risk-taking for example.

While this pattern of dependency is understandable and even flattering for some managers, it is inherently unhealthy for both the individuals and the organization. It provides real barriers to learning and development, and directly challenges efforts to empower individuals or to adopt more flexible and dynamic processes at work.

It is important therefore that the manager challenges dependency on a consistent basis through his or her responses to staff. A manager needs to reflect on the way in which their own behaviour (keeping tight control through checking and approval for example) actually suggests a dependent response from staff. In this situation staff quickly 'learn' to rely on the manager for decisions and approval, and accept the 'comfortable' position of taking no responsibility whatsoever. It becomes a cycle that is hard to break and may be one of the reasons behind the seeming unwillingness of some people to accept increased responsibility at work.

This can be particularly noticeable when the going gets tough – the tendency then is to retreat from responsibility behind the broad shoulders of their 'leader'. The term 'magic helper' has been coined to denote this aspect of a leader's role. It is interesting to speculate that in times of rapid change and insecurity, the 'leader' may actually come under increasing pressure to shield staff from uncertainty and to resolve ambiguity – a growth in reliance on the 'magic helper'. Clearly there is a fine balance to be struck for the leader, between providing sufficient genuine support for the team to move forward and at the same time tackling the dependency issue.

Bion, W. (1961)
*Experiences in
Groups and Other
Papers,* Tavistock
Publications,
London.

Base assumption behaviour

A useful idea that helps us to understand group behaviour in times of stress is Bion's ideas about 'base assumption'. This suggests that groups have underlying forms of behaviour to which they retreat, or which become dominant, when things are difficult. A good example might be a team which is busy developing participative and empowering working practices, which finds itself under serious threat or faced with a major change situation. Their 'base assumption' might be one of dependency on the 'leader', in which case they might abandon the sharing of responsibility they have been developing and return to the comfort of letting the leader deal with the situation, at least while it remains difficult.

The leader as a model

Whether we like it or not people will take their cues not from what a manager says he or she will do, but from what actually happens. The behaviour the leader displays in dealings with the team becomes an influential and unavoidable part of the leader–team relationship. This 'role model' position reinforces the need for managers to reflect upon the effects of their own behaviour, and to consider what values and attitudes underpin their actions. This becomes crucial when dealing with issues such as developing trust and acting with integrity, which are important aspects of contemporary views of leadership. A classic example is one where a leader seeks to inspire people and generate enthusiasm – clearly the key way of 'transmitting' this message is to act positively and enthusiastically yourself, in other words to model the behaviour. There are surely few people who are inspired by the pessimist and the moaner!

A web of influences

To begin to understand the relationship between leaders and 'followers', we need to also consider a wide range of factors that we will look at in detail elsewhere in this book. Those of particular relevance to the leadership issue might include managing teams or groups, dealing with conflict, learning and development, managing change, and empowerment.

   The emphasis here then is on integration – the leadership role and the impact of the staff or team is a complex business revolving essentially around their relationships and the situation in which these develop.

 Learning activity

Thinking about expectations

You will need to consider, then, the expectations of your own team in this respect, perhaps in discussion with your staff.

- What do you feel your staff or colleagues think of you 'as a leader'?
- What implications does this have for your approach to leadership?

If you are working or studying in an environment where you do not manage a team, try to reflect on or discuss with others how you might deal with staff who have a very dependent view of their relationship with you as a team leader or manager. What strategies might you adopt to tackle this situation?

Our beliefs about people

This perhaps deserves a chapter to itself as in many ways it is the starting point of all approaches to management. Underpinning your view of management is an understanding of your own values and ethics regarding other people. An awareness of these values is fundamental in guiding your actions as a manager. For the purposes of discussion we might begin by considering two opposing views about people at work that impact on approaches to leadership.

One view might be an optimistic one, that people are generally motivated to perform well at work and, given the opportunity and support, will seek responsibility, enjoy control over their work, and generate their own commitment through involvement and enthusiasm. This perspective sees the need to provide opportunities for everyone to realize their potential, and views learning and change as an opportunity.

An alternative view would be to see people as inherently incompetent or lazy, dependent and requiring control to ensure they work satisfactorily. This view might see people as basically resistant to challenge and change, and little interested in learning. It is easy to see that these two admittedly polarized views would support very different ideas concerning leadership and management.

It becomes increasingly complex when we consider that it is quite possible to hold both views simultaneously, depending upon the context and the people concerned. This 'inconsistency' is much more common than we might at first think. An example frequently cited by managers is the perceived gap between the approach an organization promotes through training, values statements or policy, and the actual behaviours of senior management which may reflect a more autocratic or traditional style. In other words these managers may not practise or reward the more open and empowering style of management that the organization says it wishes to support. In practice their words may reflect a positive view of people while their behaviour may suggest a rather more negative one.

It is important to accept in this situation that expecting other people's behaviour to be entirely consistent with their stated values and to be standardized across an organization is unrealistic and unhelpful. Further, it is interesting to consider the consistency question as it applies to ourselves – just how often do we find ourselves in a position that creates conflict or tension between what we believe is the right thing to do and what we think is required of us as managers? Perhaps our own behaviour can sometimes be seen by others as inconsistent, acting as a barrier to change and learning.

Learning activity

What you say and what you do

Think about your own beliefs about other people, and about the two views noted above. How do they relate to the way you 'lead' or manage? How can you identify your own 'inconsistencies'?

Returning for a moment to the optimistic/pessimistic views about others noted above, it is worth looking at these alongside trends in the way in which organizations are managed. The move away from autocratic towards real participative or empowering forms of management is rooted in optimistic views about people. The rhetoric about realization of potential and 'people as our most valuable asset' sits comfortably here but creates tension for those who see the need to control and direct. This indicates that not only do we need to think about our own beliefs and values but also about the prevailing values of our organization.

In shaping your approach to leadership, then, you will need to reflect upon your own views about the value of other people, and about how these views are demonstrated through managerial action. This is a complex area with few clear pathways and ultimately no right and wrong answers. We are suggesting here that understanding our own values can help to close the gap between our beliefs and our actions. An acceptance, too, that the sort of inconsistencies discussed above are inevitable can help us to engage positively in the whirlpool of politics and influence that surrounds management in organizations.

A focus on the future

Common to all views of the role of leader is a concern for the future. We are all familiar with the need for leaders or managers to plan ahead and focus on goals, objectives and targets, and this is widely accepted as a key managerial concern. But on its own is this sufficient to cope with a rapidly changing business environment or increasing levels of uncertainty and insecurity?

Contemporary views on leadership place a greater emphasis on the need for direction and on providing a 'vision' for their team – a realistic but inspiring view of the future for their organization. Interestingly these 'visions' move away from being purely projections and forecasts of, say, turnover or profit or new markets, and instead look at the sort of organization they envisage. This might include stating values and beliefs, the way in which people would like to work together and the purpose of the organization, among others. Crucially it does not commit to inflexible plans or targets, but seeks to inspire people and provide a focus around which all employees can share a common sense of direction.

A useful way of imagining the leadership role in these turbulent times is the analogy of a guide, helping the team or company on a journey. In this sense a vision provides a 'destination' (a future desired state), while the leader acts as a navigator, helping people to stay broadly on course. Day-to-day plans and

Philips, N. (1993)
*Innovative
Management,*
Pitman, London.

objectives can then be seen as a map which is changed, adapted and even created by people as they go along. The 'map' provides useful structure in the short-term and the vision provides a clear sense of direction for the organization as a whole without being prescriptive.

De Pree, M. (1989) *Leadership is an Art*, Arrow Business Books, London.

It is perhaps at this point, in looking to the future, that for some the term 'leader' becomes more appropriate than 'manager'. Again this view looks at images and language. Manager can suggest an ability to 'cope', to handle a situation, even to control – while 'leadership' implies above all movement, momentum and energy. Despite the problems with the word, 'leader' can be a useful term in its emphasis on moving forward.

In developing your leadership approach it will be important to consider your role in terms of taking your team or organization forward. You will need to think about whether you are managing in a static environment, simply reacting to new demands, or whether there is a need to look ahead, support their 'map-making' skills, and help people to create their own future.

The challenge of change

Linked to the future-focus of leadership is the growing need to be adept at managing situations involving rapid and continuous change. Some of the more obvious changes people are experiencing at the moment could include, for example, reorganization/restructuring, initiatives focusing on customers or quality, or flexible working. These are not just 'minor adjustments' or incremental improvements but major changes that impact on everyone in an organization.

This raises serious questions about traditional approaches to management, rooted as they are in authority and control, and operating in a largely static environment – will they be adaptable enough to cope with current and future ways of working? Not only can we question the effectiveness of this approach but we also need to ask whether it is acceptable to employees and managers now or for the future.

The challenge of change then presents us with the need to promote an approach to leadership that will include the ability to be flexible, innovative, adaptive, responsive and empowering, not only for survival, but also as a way of understanding and using changing situations positively. Contemporary ideas about leadership incorporate these themes with a real emphasis on creativity and learning. As the example below demonstrates, it is also not simply a matter of adding new skills to the manager's repertoire – there is a real feeling of excitement here about the possibility of generating energy and enthusiasm at work!

Read through the ideas below and see what you think.

- The leader masters the context, the manager surrenders to it.
- The manager administers, the leader innovates.
- The manager maintains, the leader develops.
- The manager focuses on systems and structure, the leader on people.
- The manager relies on control, the leader inspires trust.
- The manager asks how and when, the leader asks what and why.

- The manager accepts the status quo, the leader challenges it.
- The manager does things right, the leader does the right thing!

Bennis, W. (1989)
*On Becoming a
Leader*, Century
Business.

These suggestions come from Warren Bennis, a writer on leadership. They usefully highlight the flavour and excitement of new approaches to leadership by contrasting them with somewhat outmoded management methods. This is not King Canute trying to use his authority to stop the tide from his sand-stuck throne, but a call to grab the surfboard and enjoy the waves!

Of course, it would be equally useful to rewrite the above using 'the traditional manager' and 'the new manager'. The important thing is not the choice of terms, which in any case are open to widely differing interpretations, but the ideas, actions and energy that flow from them.

Some thoughts on power

Power is another of those ideas that has become a 'dirty word', summoning up images, for some people, of manipulation and corruption. But power is simply the ability to influence the behaviour of others, and as such is an integral part of working relationships (and others of course). In any form of management or leadership role, the use of your power through your ability to influence others is unavoidable. More than this, since management is an active and complex art with no 'right answers', it is all the more crucial for managers to engage in the process of influencing through their relationships with others in the workplace.

The way in which you use power and influence others is always a personal choice. It is not helpful to see power in traditionally destructive terms, but rather to look at influencing others in positive and productive ways. Neither is power solely the preserve of those in senior positions in organizations – as we shall see below, everyone has the opportunity to influence events in some way or another. Some of the sources of personal power you may have access to in your own situation are as follows.

- Power based on your **'social and political skills'**. This is your ability to use a range of interpersonal skills – such as persuading, providing solutions, looking for compromise, putting your case, negotiating, active listening – to influence people and events. All of us have access to this one.

- Power based on 'position'. Also known as legitimate power, this is based on the perception people have of the power attached to a particular job or position. This includes their 'authority' – the 'right' to control resources and make decisions within certain boundaries. Despite current moves towards more open and empowered organizational structures, this is still a very important, though perhaps over-emphasized, source of power in the modern workplace.

- Power based on **'fear'**. Also known as coercive power, this comes from the threat (real or perceived) of physical violence, or more commonly through psychological threats of withdrawal of benefits (e.g. promotion, redundancy, exclusion or getting told off/shouted at/blamed).

- Power based on **'knowledge'**. Also known as expert power, this relies on having skills or knowledge, or sometimes experience, that others perceive as valuable. Most useful when shared, not withheld.

- Power based on **'rewards'**. This includes obvious rewards such as control over salaries, promotion, resources, perks, etc. (not always available to the manager/leader), but more usefully it includes the value of praise and giving recognition for achievements.

- Power based on **'who you know'**. Sometimes called referent power, this includes the typical use of references to senior or influential people to add weight to your argument, and also references to outside sources, for example 'At a recent conference on . . .' or 'Studies show . . .' The ability to influence simply because you know the other person well or you like each other can also be added in here.

In developing your approach to leadership, it is interesting to explore how you feel about each of these 'sources of personal power', and how you might understand and use some of them yourself.

Learning activity

Using personal power

Think about the sources of personal power above and about how you might use them in your place of work or study group, then consider:

- Which of these sources do you use currently (with examples)?
- How do you feel about each type of power when used to influence you?
- Which are likely to be most effective in influencing other people in a positive and open way?

This activity should have raised some interesting questions about sources of power for you to consider, and helped you to understand something about their effective use. In relating this to leadership you may have thought about, for example, whether power based on coercion or position provides a sustainable base from which to influence and manage your staff.

Another challenging idea relates to knowledge as a power source. The oft-heard comment here is 'I wouldn't ask someone to do something I couldn't do myself', suggesting that you can't lead a team of people who have more knowledge about their jobs than you do. There are a number of obvious reasons why this piece of management folklore needs to be put to rest. Firstly, it simply is not possible – you cannot continue to know the details and practice of each team member's job, especially as the volume of information and the range of skills required grows. Secondly, it is undesirable; for both yourself (you have your own key role to develop) and for the team (they need to contribute their own strengths and expertise to team discussions and for that to be valued). Lastly, being a team leader or manager requires real management skills that are not specific to particular industries or services – things like facilitation, co-ordination or providing support are not dependent on detailed job knowledge.

Hopefully you can see that the use of power, your capacity to influence people, has a very positive and valuable side as well as the destructive and divisive aspects we often associate with 'power'. To focus on the positive side of the use of power it is essential that it is open, acknowledged and challengeable. If, however, you seek to influence 'behind the scenes', where the use of power is hidden, where 'games are being played', then this will get labelled as manipulation – the association being that this is an 'unfair' use of power. Of course there is no clear dividing line to help us here, and what is an acceptable use of influence for some will not be so for others. But if in the end you are seeking to build trusting relationships with colleagues you will need to think seriously about the effects of being manipulative (withholding information for instance), and consider influencing more openly.

Finally, don't run away from 'power' in thinking about leadership or management – it is an integral part of your relationship with your staff or colleagues and is as important (and hopefully less destructive) here as in the boardroom or Westminster. Remember its place in 'empowerment' – and the needs of your team in having an influence and impact on their work.

We have looked at some of the key issues you will need to consider in thinking through your role as a 'leader'. These provide a particularly useful focus for looking at some approaches to leadership that we will explore in the second half of this chapter. Hopefully you will have begun to clarify your own views on these issues, and to appreciate the complexity of the idea and practice of 'leadership'. It will also be important to consider your views in the light of current trends in approaches to management, in particular the move towards managing people as responsible, competent and committed adults.

Lastly we hope that you will use your own perspectives on these key issues to evaluate the usefulness of the selection of practical and more inspirational models which follow.

Approaches to leadership

Up to this point we have been considering and discussing some key issues surrounding leadership without offering any practical ideas, tangible theories, lists or models. This is partly because it's a complex topic that benefits in practice from reflection and an awareness of your own views before plunging into the theory. There is also a danger with simply presenting off-the-shelf leadership theories in that it might encourage a simple 'here are the answers – go and apply them' approach. Primarily, though, we have sought to stress the value of thinking things through for yourself. You may find the key issues we have just looked at useful in evaluating different approaches to leadership, both here and from other sources.

There are many textbook theories on the subject; some are too complex to be used easily in practice, and others go in and out of fashion as the leadership debate ebbs and flows. Almost all of them have something useful and often important to say. We have resisted simply cataloguing all the available theories as this could lead to confusion and in any case many of them overlap. The further reading listed at the end of the chapter enables you to check out other approaches should you be interested.

In this section we look firstly at a couple of approaches to leadership that provide practical tips for day-to-day team leadership/management which focus on the functions a leader undertakes, and the leader-team relationship as displayed through decision-making processes.

In working through these views on leadership we would encourage you to build an approach that you are comfortable with and that can be related to your own situation. Take what makes sense to you from each of these models – it must be stressed that these approaches are not mutually exclusive – it is more than possible to use all of them at once.

Adair, J. (1988) *Effective Leadership*, Pan Books, London.

The first is a model used extensively in 'leadership training'. Developed by John Adair, it is called 'action centered leadership' and provides a very practical tool for the manager seeking to develop their approach to team leadership and the management of teams.

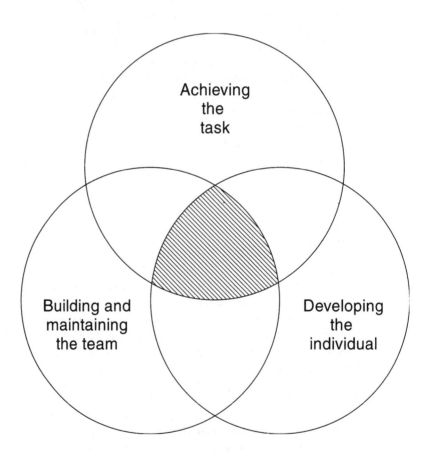

Fig. 9.2 Action-centred leadership.

Action-centred leadership

Thinking back to the chapters on teambuilding you might recall looking at group processes in terms of 'task' and 'maintenance', and also remember the importance of 'individual needs' to the way in which groups function. Action-centred leadership uses a very similar model to look at the role of a leader, and as such is easy to relate to a team situation and to use on a day-by-day basis. It is essentially a 'functional' approach in that it concentrates on what the leader needs **to do**, rather than looking for particular characteristics.

Adair suggests that leaders need to focus on the three 'core responsibilities' illustrated as overlapping circles in Figure 9.2 – achieving the task, building and maintaining the team, and developing the individual. In this model the leader needs to operate as far as possible at the heart of the three circles (the shaded area in the diagram), ensuring a balance of effort between the three areas. You will remember that we have already discussed in the chapters on teams some of the problems arising from an imbalance, particularly between getting the task done and maintaining the team. It will rarely be possible to balance the three areas at all times; rather the leader will need to manage the tension between potentially conflicting needs.

The role of leader in managing these core responsibilities involves, in Adair's model, eight key **functions**:

- Defining the task
- Planning
- Motivating
- Modelling
- Evaluating
- Briefing
- Organizing
- Controlling.

These functions will already be familiar to most managers, mixing some traditional managerial roles with some newer ones like modelling and briefing. It is the 'leader's' responsibility to ensure that these are carried out, but the approach is quite flexible in that any team member can take on these functions as the situation and skills of team members allow – it is very much a team approach.

The value of this model is that it provides a straightforward framework for the manager to look at their leadership of a team or group. It is easy to remember (and therefore more likely to be used!) and on the whole fairly people focused. Its strength lies in reminding leaders that the success of the team relies not simply on getting their tasks done at whatever cost, but in spending time and energy on the processes used and the needs of team members. This is a vital balance to maintain, particularly in a climate of demands for raising productivity and the achievement of ever higher targets, where all too often the team and individual are forgotten in a dash to 'get the job done'.

Action-centred leadership is a very useful tool in practice for the reasons given above – but if you refer to some of the issues we discussed at the beginning of this chapter there are clearly important areas that it does not fully address.

We need to look elsewhere for some more ideas about change, the future (creating direction) and about the relationship between leaders and the team.

One way to examine this relationship is to look at the way in which leaders involve (or not) their team in the key process of decision-making. The model outlined below considers this level of involvement by centering on the leader's decision-making 'style'.

Leadership 'style'

While there are many different varieties of 'style' theory, most concentrate on comparing an autocratic with a democratic style of management. This one looks at a 'continuum' of styles that runs from no team involvement (autocratic) through to full team participation or delegation (a democratic style). Figure 9.3 shows this as a play-off between the degree of influence of the leader and the influence of the team.

The decision-making styles displayed along the bottom of the figure can be described as follows:

A simplification of a variety of models, e.g. Tannenbaum, R. and Schmidt, W. (1958) 'How to choose a leadership pattern' in *Harvard Business Review*, March–April.

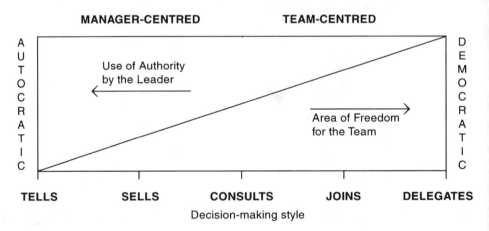

Fig. 9.3   The management/leadership continuum.

Tells	The leader resolves problem or makes decision and then announces it to the team.
Sells	The leader makes the decision or solves the problem and 'sells' the benefits of it to the team.
Consults	The leader asks the team for opinions, weighs up all of the evidence then makes the decision him or herself.
Joins	The leader and team discuss the matter and decide according to a consensus or majority opinion.
Delegates	The leader gives the team equal freedom to define the problem or decision and to decide upon action to be taken.

This model provides us with a simplified way of thinking about a range of management styles that many people will have observed in their workplace. The image of the 'autocratic boss', the one who just 'tells', is easy to relate to in the experience of many managers, and it gives us an opportunity to think about where our own style might fit in to this 'continuum'.

Of course one of the strengths of this model is that it suggests managers can adapt their approach depending upon the situation, i.e. the type of decision required, the people being managed or the prevailing company culture. The classic example here is the one where the fire alarm goes off. It is easy to defend an autocratic style as appropriate in this situation – there is no time for lengthy participative decision-making here!

It is also crucial that managers are aware that they can learn to manage in more effective ways by adapting their own preferred style, in some cases changing it altogether – it is not necessary to be locked into behaviours of the past. An example of this is Ricardo Semler, the owner/director of Semco, a manufacturer of domestic and industrial goods. On taking over the business he adopted the techniques of monitoring and control, and made decisions from the centre. This proved a less than effective strategy, and subsequently, over many years, he has developed an extremely 'democratic' approach to decision- making at Semco, delegating almost all decisions to workers on the shop floor in a very empowering environment. This has resulted in Semco becoming a very successful business, and required a major change in Semler's approach to leadership.

Perhaps the most valuable contribution this model makes to the leadership debate is the questions that arise in discussing the merits or otherwise of the various 'styles' it displays. It is a useful exercise to think through some of the following as you work towards your understanding of leadership:

- Do you have a preferred 'style'? Does it vary, and if so, in what circumstances?
- Observing other managers in your workplace, can you relate this model to their style as you see it?
- What do the autocratic and democratic styles suggest to you about:
  — The relationship between leaders and the team?
  — The leader's values and beliefs about people?
  — The impact each style has on the team – their reactions to it?
  — The culture of your organization – perhaps the 'accepted' management style?
- What might be the implications of each style on ideas like:
  — Empowerment and sharing responsibility?
  — Creativity and innovation?
  — Excitement, enthusiasm and fun!
  — Effectiveness and productivity?

These are crucial issues and it is well worth taking time to think through these questions with your team or debating them with colleagues. This provides an opportunity to explore the complexities of the leadership issue, particularly the distribution of power and responsibility between a team and its 'leader'. Taking the last of the above issues as an example, we might explore which style of leadership supports the most effective and productive workplace. Of course there are many variables at work here but a move towards a more democratic and participative style is more likely to enable an organization to unlock the immense potential of its most valuable 'resource' – its people.

The management style model does not in itself provide all of the answers, but it makes a helpful contribution to our understanding of the leader–team relationship nonetheless. On its own, though, it clearly does not tell us enough about leadership. In particular it doesn't suggest what skills or qualities a leader might need to develop, and there is little help here in creating a sense of direction, inspiring people or with dealing with change.

The next section on empowering leadership takes a very different approach, challenging assumptions about the leader–team relationship and suggesting a new emphasis on a different range of management skills that provide a supportive environment in which the team can operate flexibly and responsively.

Empowering leadership

There is a common understanding in leadership, and management, that is reflected in the assumptions behind hierarchies, organizational charts, 'levels' of authority and the language we use – leaders/followers, subordinates/bosses, the 'top'/'bottom', control 'over', etc. The implication is that somehow the leader is 'senior', 'superior', 'more knowledgeable' or more 'valuable', a perspective that is reflected in most reward systems and in the status attached to managerial roles. This institutionalized view is so ingrained that it blinds us from taking a wider perspective, or at least makes it difficult to consider different ways forward.

What we shall consider here is an alternative way of seeing leadership that in some respects turns this hierarchical view on its head. This is an approach that offers an opportunity for you to consider a form of leadership that focuses on enabling and supporting, almost 'leading from behind'.

The background
If we take the traditional view of the leader and team and depict it as a pyramid (albeit a somewhat flatter one these days), with the leader at the 'top' and staff at the 'bottom' as in Figure 9.4(a), this gives us a visual picture that fits well with the concepts of leaders providing control, direction, coordination or defining the task, for example.

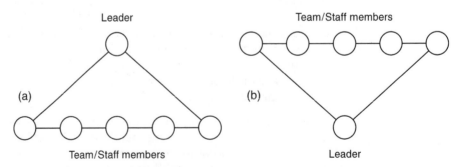

Fig 9.4 Leader–team perspectives.

For the purposes of exploring a different view, we might try turning this pyramid up the other way, with front-line staff at the top, and the leader at the 'bottom' as in Figure 9.4(b). This gives us a very different angle on the role of the leader: In this picture the leader supplies a supporting role to the team, providing staff with the resources and opportunities to deliver high quality services to clients or customers.

This model challenges us to create new ways of expressing control and authority in the team. It suggests a change of focus, a different way of defining the relationship between leader and team. Nor is this at all a 'radical' picture, as it fits well with the ideas about empowering front-line staff, flexibility and responsiveness, and devolving responsibility for action to those nearest the customer.

Learning activity

Inverting the pyramid

Think about your own team, or consider a typical team situation, in terms of an 'inverted pyramid'.

- What issues does this view raise for your approach to leadership?
- What sort of skills would be particularly valuable in considering 'leading from behind'?

The supportive role suggested in this view of leadership places emphasis on a different range of management skills than those traditionally associated with leadership. Crucially these are approaches that are all about providing opportunities – about leading the team towards the realization of their potential. There is a real sense here that valuing people's contribution, a belief in their capacity to learn and develop, and a commitment to trusting relationships is the only way forward.

The focus of this way of viewing team leadership puts the emphasis on a range of 'supporting' skills. Consider the importance of the following to your view of leadership:

Enabling
This refers not simply to ensuring that your staff have adequate resources to maintain and develop the service being offered, but also encouraging an atmosphere where staff feel confident about taking on new tasks and following up opportunities. It ties in closely with empowerment, facilitation and development, and underlines strongly a positive view of the contribution people are able to make given the right environment.

Empowering
Going beyond simply looking for ideas and opinions, or token consultation, this means full recognition of the unique knowledge and experience people hold,

particularly in respect of their close relationships with the customer. It also includes involving the team in wider aspects of decision-making such as the process of creating and sustaining a vision for the future, since they will have a key role in 'making this happen'. In any case there is no good reason why the team leader should take this on in isolation. The process of empowerment itself also has value in building commitment and supporting growth and development. The move towards involvement in strategic responsibilities ties in with the need to develop a sense of direction and vision – a real concern for a better future.

Developing

For staff to feel confident and able to act independently, the leader will need to provide opportunities for staff to enhance their technical and interpersonal skills. This is far removed from simply arranging training courses. A whole range of opportunities for development are available in the normal course of working, including new tasks and responsibilities, rotating job roles, or projects for instance. We look at the options for developing staff in Chapter 11 on developing a learning culture.

Facilitating

This is about working on barriers that exist between people and helping to build relationships. Within the team the leader can use facilitation to help navigate through day-to-day difficulties. It is a useful approach to adopt for staff development or training and team development, and also in consensual decision-making. Again the focus is on assisting others to understand and work through their own issues rather than 'sorting it out' for them.

Advocating

Advocating here means supporting, even defending, your team and its relationships with others in the workplace. Some practical examples might be promoting cross-functional approaches, handling 'head-office visits', and making sure your team influences rather than just responds to changes in policy, strategy and direction. It also includes defending your staff, partners and customers against the rules, procedures, systems and paperwork that organizations (both your own and outside ones) develop to check and control, but which end up defeating initiative and get in the way of effective performance. These can prevent or slow down the positive response staff can provide to clients and customers.

Collaborating

Collaboration in this sense is about seeing staff as effective partners in the running of your business. In time collaboration can extend well beyond day-to-day decisions and initiatives to include looking at strategic issues such as creating vision, what new products or services should be developed and policy issues. This partnership approach extends to sharing both responsibility, control and rewards.

Process consulting

A further aspect of this role is the ability to operate as a 'process consultant' within your own team or organization. This requires new skills in being able to 'step back' and help the team look at its own processes and agree its own solutions or ways of working together. This might focus on issues such as team development, handling conflict, providing structure or valuing diversity, for example.

Managing outside the team

We are concerned here about the role of the leader or manager as a link between his or her team and people outside the team whether they be 'senior' people, colleagues, other organizations or customers/clients. This role includes liaison, procuring resources, bringing in information and ideas, as well as negotiating and representing or protecting the team in a wide variety of situations. This is using influencing skills outside of the team for its benefit, and has been labelled the 'ambassador' role. There is of course no reason why this role cannot be undertaken by members of the team, providing a valuable development opportunity for them.

Coaching and mentoring

These are ways of supporting your staff in the development of personal and technical skills that they have identified that will improve individual and team performance. Encouraging staff to take on responsibilities and make decisions for themselves needs to be backed up with opportunities to learn and grow, so that they will feel confident and able to move forward. This support need not mean expensive training courses – the team leader encourages the sharing of skills and experience throughout the team using coaching and mentoring.

This is not a definitive list, but it gives a flavour of the sorts of skills that you may wish to develop or emphasize as you explore the leader's role. What all of the above have in common is their commitment to a supportive style of leadership, to 'leading from behind'.

While we have listed some of the management skills that form the core of this approach to leadership, it is not at all a matter of throwing all of the traditional ones out of the window. The need for the manager to motivate and coordinate fits comfortably here, and tackling functions like planning simply means redefining the way in which this happens – planning 'with' people instead of 'for' them. The issue of 'control' is perhaps more challenging and is often a difficult one for managers to consider redefining. It is not a matter of 'losing' control, but of sharing it out by developing the sense of mutual responsibility that leads to self-control. Ultimately self-control – an understanding and commitment to responsible action – is far more effective and constructive than the 'policing' approach so often considered a key management role.

Also it cannot be stressed too strongly that empowering leadership is not an excuse to sit back and do nothing, nor to abdicate any of your managerial responsibilities! It is a highly demanding way to manage a team, and an extremely rewarding one. It requires the personal commitment to embark on a journey that explores, with the team, a wide range of crucial management issues like learning, change, trust and building relationships.

Looking back to the key leadership issues raised at the beginning of this chapter, it can be seen that the empowering approach to leadership tackles head-on the relationship between leader and team, and grows out of a very positive view about people's abilities and potential. It also seeks to encourage an atmosphere that is responsive to change, placing emphasis on learning and development, and supporting challenge and involvement. What it perhaps lacks, though, is a strong focus on the future and a sense of energy and enthusiasm that can inspire others. The last approach we consider seeks to provide both direction and inspiration through 'visionary leadership'.

The visionary approach

There is a growing interest in the need for a vision of the future that gives direction and inspires commitment. While much of the writing in management literature deals with the need for visionary leadership by individuals as guiding lights in large corporations, the approach is just as valuable to teams and smaller organizations, and indeed to individuals.

These ideas form part of a search for new ways of managing in an increasingly complex and rapidly changing world, an environment where change makes a clear sense of purpose and direction all the more important. Of course 'visions' don't provide us with a detailed map for our journey any more than strategic plans do. Their real value comes from meeting our needs for an idea of a better future, and having something meaningful we can commit to. In this respect it is the process of creating a vision and the fact that one exists at all that is more important than what it might actually contain or how 'accurate' it might turn out to be.

So what do we mean by a 'vision'? Where does it come from, and how does it relate to leadership? Perhaps it might be appropriate to try and 'conjure up' an image of what a vision is by looking at its two key ingredients – a focus on direction and the future, and its inspirational quality.

Creating direction:

- A shared view of an 'achievable and desirable future state'
- It deals with 'aspirations as well as its intentions'
- An emphasis on 'how' people will work together rather than 'what' they will be doing
- Pictures, images and ideas, not about targets or objectives
- The idea of a journey – guiding and navigating, creating maps together
- The longer term – sustainability – a belief in the future.

Inspiring people:

- Generating enthusiasm and excitement
- Reflects and develops the authentic values and beliefs of an organization/ team
- Supports commitment and ownership

- Inspires creativity, imagination and innovation
- Adds meaning and purpose to our lives.

The statements above not only help to generate an understanding of 'vision' but reflect some of the value that a shared vision can have for a team or organization. Creating a direction and positive view of the future gives people something tangible to strive towards and motivates through meeting people's needs for achievement and belonging. It adds a sense of purpose and meaning to work beyond that of simply 'earning a living', particularly if the 'vision' is created, and therefore owned, jointly by everyone in the team/organization. It also tries to provide a new focus for our need for security, following the demise of the career and 'job for life' expectations of the recent past that have led to so much uncertainty about future job prospects and income.

In this respect, the value of a 'vision' in helping to meet these needs becomes more important than the detail or accuracy of the vision – in fact one of the strengths of the vision idea is that it is deliberately fuzzy round the edges and designed to be dynamic and flexible. This is a major step away from the detailed 'five-year plan' approach with all its attendant projections and forecasts, facts and figures, objectives and targets.

Lastly the visionary view, as the name suggests, is focused firmly on the future. It encourages a forward-looking (exciting) rather than problem-solving/crisis management (frustrating) approach to work. This concern with generating energy and enthusiasm is not a case of 'getting on a soap-box and rousing the masses' but of building a shared sense of excitement about possible futures for individuals as well as organizations. It is about inspiring others through your relationships, beliefs and actions.

The visionary leader

It would be tempting to see the leader's role here as something like a charismatic evangelist, a peddler of dreams who wanders the workplace preaching to anyone who will listen – now that would be interesting! Many of us might need a more accessible starting point, one that can be developed and applied by all managers.

Bennis, W. (1989) *On Becoming a Leader*, Century Business.

Warren Bennis suggests six basic 'ingredients' that are a useful and uplifting way of describing visionary leadership. It is worth noting, as you look down the list, your own reaction to the terms he has chosen to use. A leader should develop:

- **A guiding vision** – a clear understanding and commitment to a 'vision' which outlines where you are going (direction) and why (purpose/meaning)
- **Passion** – a real enthusiasm for the job, profession or course of action, a sense of hope and excitement about the future, and a sense of fun in getting there
- **Integrity** – understanding yourself, and being honest in thought and action, being driven by ideas of principle and conscience
- **Trust** – earning and maintaining the trust of colleagues

- **Curiosity** – learning all the time, especially from mistakes and adversity – exploration
- **Daring** – a willingness to try things, take risks and experiment.

You may not be used to describing managing in terms of 'passion' or 'daring', but these ideas are very accessible, and have been deliberately chosen to be more powerful and emotive than commonly used terms such as enthusiasm or risk-taking. They reflect strongly many of the recurring themes of this book: the need to understand yourself and others, a belief in learning and a total commitment to trust and integrity as key values.

The interesting thing about the list above is that it operates well beyond the traditional emphasis on control, planning, monitoring and directing, and enters the 'messy' realms of feelings, beliefs and values. There is no 'science' here, no step-by-step processes, no certainty and no 'facts'. Its strength is that it reflects the reality of human interactions and states a belief that:

Leadership is more tribal than scientific, more a weaving of relationships than an amassing of information.

Whose vision?

We have looked at the value of having a positive 'vision' for the individual, team and organization in terms of direction and inspiration, but a key question is – who creates this vision? Where does it come from? Does this imply that the role of creating and maintaining a vision lies in the lap of the 'leader' or manager? Let's look at some of the difficulties a leader might face in 'going it alone'.

Learning activity

Creating a vision

Think about the role of 'team leader/manager'.

- What difficulties might you face in trying to create and communicate a vision for your team?
- How might you tackle these difficulties?

What we are looking at here is whether a vision is more usefully created by a leader individually, or by all of those with an interest in the organization – its staff, management, partners and customers. In many ways a leader is in a unique position to create such a vision – he or she should have a more strategic and longer-term view, and perhaps a better grasp of the wider business environment in which you operate.

But this creates a number of difficulties. Firstly it places very high expectations on the leader's ability to come up with an inspirational vision, and to 'sell' it or communicate it to the staff. Secondly it leaves the organization vulnerable if the leader leaves, to be replaced by another whose 'vision' may be very different (this is a common occurrence in organizations that rely on charismatic management). Most importantly, though, this approach fits ill with efforts to promote involvement and empowerment – it appears to confine such initiatives to day-to-day work leaving leaders to defend their control over areas such as policy and strategy. Ultimately, relying on a leader's vision retains the dependent 'I lead – you follow' relationship that is unhealthy and undermining for all involved.

The leader or manager will also need to be aware of the potential in some workplaces for a gap to appear between their vision and the views of their staff, who may not have given the future of the organization too much thought, or be well informed about initiatives and trends in their business sector generally. That staff are not committed to the vision of senior managers is hardly surprising – it's not their vision after all. It is of course possible to encourage staff to become involved and develop partial commitment to, or compliance with, the company vision, but perhaps there is an another way forward.

A shared vision

A real alternative must be to create your vision with your staff and even other 'stakeholders' (e.g. customers, suppliers), sharing the role of developing and maintaining it with others. This helps to deal with some of the problems raised above regarding a leader's vision. The key advantage, though, is that a vision is only valuable when everyone can identify and relate to it, so that they are motivated to 'make it happen'. Clearly if everyone is involved in its creation, and they 'own' it, the battle to gain commitment is already half won.

It is worth challenging another myth at this point – that people are not capable of creating a vision of a brighter future for themselves and their organization. Try asking people what they want from their work or how they would like to work together. Of course everyone wants to earn a living, but people will also talk about friendship, doing satisfying work or a 'good job', taking up challenges, trying something new, being supported and treated with respect. The language used may not be in terms of 'empowerment' or 'learning', but the message is the same. People do care about many aspects of their working lives beyond the wage packet, often in spite of the way in which they have been 'managed' in the past.

Crucially the very process of involving everyone will ensure that staff are keenly aware of and agree to both the team's direction and how they would like to work together. This supports and models efforts to share responsibility, for example by helping staff to make decisions which reflect what is 'good' or 'bad' for the organization and its customers. It provides a real opportunity to experience empowerment, develop working relationships and experiment with ways of influencing others. Building the vision in an open and exploratory atmosphere also helps to counter notions of self-interest that are at the heart of organizational politics and mistrust.

In developing your approach to 'leadership', then, you will need to consider your own contribution to the creation of a vision for your team or organization.

The visionary approach provides us with a future-focus that is stronger and more dynamic than the other models we have discussed. This commitment to providing a sense of direction is supported by the need to inspire others and act with 'passion'. With a shared and negotiated vision, you will need to play a key role in maintaining momentum and in generating the enthusiasm and energy necessary to see it through. Above all it acknowledges the desire to 'create your own future' as an antidote to behaving reactively, becoming victims of ever-changing circumstance, and dancing to the tunes that others play.

Putting it all together

We have discussed some of the difficulties of providing a clear understanding of the emotive subject of leadership and suggested that you think through your own position on this issue. This process helps to develop a view that reflects your beliefs about people, the situation in which you manage and the people you work with.

This chapter has illustrated a number of ideas that contribute to the leadership debate which we feel are valuable starting points in this process, though there are many others that have useful comments to make on the subject. The obvious question is – do they all fit together, or is it a matter of 'choosing' one approach?

An integrated view

Handy, C.B. (1985) *Understanding Organisations,* Penguin Books, London.

The role of the leader is a complex one, riddled with ambiguity, incompatibility and conflict.

Charles Handy

You may have found that the more you try to 'nail down' the idea of leadership, the more unresolved issues come to light. It is a crucial part of developing your understanding of management that you begin to accept this complexity, and move on from seeing management as a science that has an answer for every problem and a theory for every eventuality.

An example of this complexity can be taken from two of the approaches to leadership we have looked at here – leading from behind and the visionary leader. At first glance they may seem incompatible, almost opposite views of a leader's role – one supportive, the other leading from the front with vision and passion. But this is only a problem if you view it as an 'either/or' situation; we would suggest that you consider using both approaches in developing your leadership style. Certainly there is a tension between the two views, but it is a tension that is inescapable and will need to be managed on a day-to-day basis.

It is not difficult to see the value in all of the approaches shown here (and many others), and use them together however you feel is appropriate. Though each has merits, they all have weaknesses also – that is the nature of models that seek to aid understanding by simplifying the real world. In addition to merging useful views from a range of leadership ideas, you will need to be aware of all the other aspects of management that are inescapably linked to the practice of leadership. These include understanding yourself and others, trust and openness, valuing differences and empowerment, amongst others.

It is also important to see leadership as a continuously developing process that will change with the situation, the people you work alongside, and as your own experience and understanding grows. Above all leadership is not a static 'skill' that can be learned and then applied without recourse to constant review and development. It is this dynamic element that ensures that leadership will remain intimately bound up with change, learning and challenge.

Becoming an effective 'leader' is a lifelong journey, it is an art, not a science, and an approach, not a 'competence'. Over and above the range of management skills needed to be effective in today's organization, it requires the manager to develop a climate based on positive relationships, openness, trust and sharing, and managed with integrity. You will need to support your team in creating meaning and purpose through a shared vision and sense of direction. Above all, you will need to inspire others with energy, passion, and commitment.

Adapted from Senge, P. (1990) *The Fifth Discipline*, Century Business.

The bad leader is one whom the people despise.
The good leader is one whom the people praise.
The great leader is one where the people say 'we did it ourselves'.

Adapted from Lao-Tzu

Summary

This chapter approaches the issue of leadership through creating direction and inspiration. It advises that this complex and emotive subject does not lend itself to proposing definitive ideas of leadership, and suggests that managers create their own personal view of leadership. This will be dependent on an understanding of themselves, their team or colleagues, the situation and type of task being undertaken, and the culture of the organization for which they work.

The chapter begins by exploring our images of leadership and follows with a discussion of some key leadership issues that are crucial to our understanding:

➤ Our beliefs about people
➤ Leadership as personality
➤ Leaders and 'followers'
➤ A focus on the future
➤ The challenge of change.

The second half of this chapter looks at some 'models' of leadership and assesses their usefulness in dealing with the issues above. These include action-centered leadership and a leadership style model. Moving on from these more traditional views, we look at a supportive view under the title 'empowering leadership', in effect leading from behind.

Lastly we explore the role of the visionary approach in helping to focus direction and inject passion into our actions as leaders. The intention is that managers should build their own concept of leadership from these (and many other) views.

Further reading

Some of the other most commonly used traditional 'theories' about leadership not covered here are outlined effectively in Lita de Alberdi's *People, Psychology and Business* (Cambridge University Press, 1990). These are written up in a light and accessible style in a useful book which also deals with group processes, motivation, perception and communication.

Warren Bennis' book *On Becoming a Leader* (Century Business, 1989) gives a really inspirational view of leadership in practice. It is full of stories, quotations, ideas and observations delivered in an enthusiastic style. In a similar vein Max de Pree's *Leadership is an Art* (Arrow Business Books, 1989) gives a vibrant personal view of the art – as opposed to science – of leadership, with a very human, almost spiritual, focus.

If you are interested in exploring some exciting new ideas about leadership, management and organizations that offer a new way of thinking about how we work together then you will enjoy Margaret Wheatley's *Leadership and the New Science* (Berrett-Koehler, 1992). As the title suggests this explores some of the radical ideas emerging from science that are now being applied to organizations and which challenge current ways of thinking about the world.

Taking on the crucial issues of power, control and politics as they relate to organizations and 'leaders', Peter Block's work *Stewardship* (Berrett-Koehler, 1993) is a wonderfully hopeful book. In it he challenges people to choose service over self-interest, and invest in partnership instead of the dependent relationship we usually have with organizations.

References

Adair, J. (1988) *Effective Leadership*, Pan Books (revised), London.
Bennis, W. (1989) *On Becoming a Leader*, Century Business.
Bennis, W., Parikh, J. and Lessem, R. (1994) *Beyond Leadership*, Blackwell Business, Oxford.
Block, P. (1993) *Stewardship*, Berrett-Koehler, San Francisco.
De Pree, M. (1989) *Leadership is an Art*, Arrow Business Books, London.
Makin, P., Cooper, C. and Cox, C. (1993) *Managing People at Work*, BPS/Routledge, London.
Stewart, A.M. (1994) *Empowering People*, Pitman, London.
Wheatley, M. (1994) *Leadership and the New Science*, Berrett-Koehler, San Francisco.

10

Empowerment

If organizations are machines, control makes sense. If organizations are process structures, then seeking to impose control through permanent structure is suicide.

Margaret J. Wheatley

No one should make a living simply planning, watching, controlling or evaluating the actions of others.

Peter Block

Objectives

By the end of this chapter you will be able to:

➤ Describe empowerment as a positive step beyond consultation and participation
➤ Evaluate the benefits and difficulties of an empowering approach to management
➤ Explore your own views, concerns and feelings about empowerment

Introduction

Empowerment is very much an 'in vogue' topic at the moment and is sometimes regarded as just the latest in a long line of management fads. But empowerment is more than another 'technique' to be flung at the complex problem of managing effectively, it is an approach that focuses on the heart of the way we choose to manage people in our organizations.

In this chapter we look at what empowerment means in terms of an approach to managing people and businesses, focusing on its benefits and some of the difficulties it raises both for staff and managers. Because 'empowerment' is an approach rooted in our beliefs about people – rather than a system, initiative or programme – the chapter aims to encourage managers to examine empowerment in the light of their own particular style and situation and decide for themselves about its value and development.

It is worth noting from the outset that exploring empowerment cannot be divorced from our own view of areas such as leadership, your management style or your approach to teamwork and staff development, among others. In this respect it is useful to refer to your own thoughts and conclusions from previous chapters as you work through this one.

What is empowerment?

Empowerment in an organizational setting means devolving responsibility for taking decisions and action to those who need to be able act quickly and flexibly to meet the needs of clients or customers. It is very much about removing unnecessary restrictions from staff at all levels so that they are free to act in the interests of the organization and its clients – it is an enabling process. A useful definition describes empowerment as 'the humanistic process of adopting the values and practising the behaviours of enlightened self-interest so that personal and organizational goals may be aligned in a way that promotes growth, learning and fulfillment'. This reflects some of the key aspects of empowerment – its foundation in values and our beliefs about personal development linked to the more effective achievement of organizational aims.

Luechauer, D.L. and Shulman, G.M. (1993) 'Empowerment at work – separating folklore from fact' in *At Work*, November – December.

Moving towards an empowering environment is crucially about changing the culture, 'the way we work together', and as such reflects the very beliefs we hold about the role and contribution of people in the workplace. It seeks to move the oft-quoted idea that 'our people are our most valuable resource' out of the mission statement and into action. In some respects it also seeks to address the gap between what we believe about people and how we act in our role as managers.

In terms of control, empowerment does not involve the loss of control or a descent into anarchy in the workplace; rather it seeks to move the responsibility for control from the manager to the team. This shift is reflected in the move from reliance on control through systems and bureaucracy towards control through trusting the competence and integrity of your staff. We will look at the issue of control separately as this is both the crux of what empowerment means in practice and one of the most challenging aspects for a manager to deal with.

It is also important to distinguish empowerment from participation or consultation, and the difference is most easily seen if we look at how decisions are taken. In a consultative situation, a manager may 'consult' staff to get their views and ideas which he or she may or may not use in coming to a decision. With participation, staff are involved in this process to a greater extent, perhaps through finding consensus or voting, but the decision-making focus still lies with the manager. In a situation where staff are 'empowered' they will be free to make decisions themselves, without continual reference to their manager or even their team for approval.

Nor is empowerment just a new word for delegation. Delegation shifts the actual work or task from manager to staff but does not usually include transferring either responsibility for or control of the task away from the manager. Empowerment devolves not only the task but also the responsibility to make decisions and changes as and when necessary.

This is broadly what empowerment means in an organization. Since it deals with a shift in the focus of power, control and responsibility, it is difficult to divorce empowerment from discussions about the culture of an organization and indeed from politics. In the next section we need to look at the benefits of empowerment for an organization, its clients and its people, as unusually empowerment is an approach that has justifications on a number of levels. Finally it is important to stress that empowerment is not something you can 'do' to other people, it is about creating the space for others to think and act by themselves.

Why empowerment?

At first glance the impetus for empowerment appears to come from two different directions. On the one hand there is the recognition of the purely business benefits that can accrue from the best use of its 'human resources' – the bottom-line improvements to performance and productivity held out by empowerment. On the other hand the impetus comes from the desire to create working environments that are meaningful and liberating for individuals – where learning and mutual respect replace obedience and blame. One of the strengths of empowerment of course is that it embeds the search for a fulfilling work experience firmly alongside 'hard' business strategy – it is not an either/or situation, but a case of each reinforcing the other, as demonstrated in Figure 10.1.

Empowerment has the potential to provide benefits across the board in an organization, not only in terms of its effectiveness but also for the workforce and, crucially, its clients and customers.

Benefits for the organization

One of the primary purposes of empowerment is to improve the quality of service you provide to customers. The impetus for continually improving products and services comes not only from your personal commitment to do

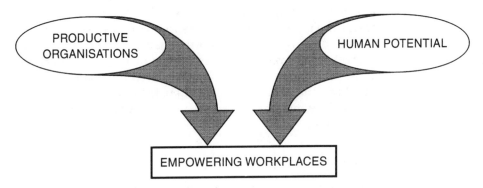

Fig. 10.1 The impetus for empowerment.

so, but also from the need to ensure that your organization remains viable and effective in an increasingly competitive environment. Empowerment encourages staff to seek approval for their actions not from management, but from customers.

Decisions affecting customers are taken by or with those who work most closely to them and who are best placed to develop positive relationships with customers and therefore to gain awareness of their needs. Requests or questions are dealt with faster if staff are empowered to respond without always referring to management for approval, or being held back by procedure and bureaucracy. There is also no doubt that customers are aware of, and react to, the atmosphere in which staff work. The benefits in terms of increased staff motivation and positive commitment to getting things done is likely to help to support relationships with their customers.

Case note

Staff empowerment

An example of this would be in a supermarket where sales staff are trained and empowered to accept cheques and credit cards at the till. Not so long ago, they would have been required to summon the manager to approve the transaction. This procedure had real impact on the manager, the staff and the customer. The manager wastes valuable time on a relatively routine job, while the customer also has to wait for this performance to run its course. The effects on the staff can be numerous, including maintaining low skill levels, displaying messages of mistrust and dependency, and dealing with customer reactions to waiting.

In removing the constant need for the manager to make operational decisions or give approval to staff actions, managerial time is freed up to be invested in more productive and fulfilling ways. This reflects the changing role of the manager in an empowered environment who, freed from the need to constantly control and monitor, can invest effort in providing support and learning opportunities, driving through improvements or reflecting on direction and the future, for example. The potential for managerial contribution to the future success of a business in this respect is greatly enhanced.

Perhaps the greatest business benefits of empowerment stem directly from the way in which it encourages a new level of involvement and commitment from people.

Benefits for people

Empowerment has the potential to dramatically change the nature of the relationship between people and 'the organization'. It is here that values and beliefs about people are portrayed most starkly. In a fully empowered situation:

- They are trusted and treated as adults
- People feel significant, involved and valued
- People have control over their own work
- They can use their initiative, and be creative
- They are encouraged to value learning and development
- They are supported fully by colleagues and management
- They are able to access their full range of skills and abilities
- People are freed from petty rules and restrictive policies
- They contribute to the development and future of the organization.

These conditions are extremely powerful in terms of individual growth and human potential. Equally, though, they point towards an organization driven by learning, energy and initiative, and away from top-down strategy and rigid control. Empowerment focuses on working towards a new relationship between people and organizations with the aim of sharing a more productive and fulfilling view of work for the future.

Empowerment in context

The benefits of empowerment, alongside other complimentary approaches to management, support and reflect current trends in the way organizations are managed and beliefs about the value and role of individuals within an organization. To emphasize the links to be made we have noted some of these trends below. It is important to understand that empowerment both supports and is supported by these moves – the relationship is complex and two-way.

The changing focus of management

This may be seen in the move away from autocratic management towards more democratic styles which involve people and value participation, and in the rise in the importance of management skills such as coaching, supporting and enthusing – away from the traditional emphasis on control and command. This is also reflected in contemporary approaches to leadership (empowering/

visionary leadership for example), and can include experiments with self-managed teams in organizations such as the Body Shop, among others.

Changing organizational structures

The trend towards 'flatter' organizations with fewer levels of management requires the devolution and sharing of responsibility, while the move towards a teamworking culture means responsibility and control are shared rather than defined by a strict hierarchy. Allied to these changes are moves to decentralize and split-down large-scale business operations into smaller business units. One oft-quoted example of where this has been successful is Asea Brown Boveri, an international engineering and manufacturing company. They have organized their workforce of over 200 000 people into smaller autonomous companies, business units or profit centres, each with an average of around 200 people. On top of this they dramatically reduced the size of their 'head office', and manage the whole process with only two layers of management between the Executive Committee and the people on the shop floor.

Various: Peters, T. (1992) Liberation Management, BCA/Pan Macmillan, London.

The learning culture

Following this trend involves moving beyond 'training for the job' towards a culture that supports continual learning and development in its broadest sense. This creates the need to support personal development and so focus on the realization of potential. There is a need to support risk-taking, the pushing out of boundaries and the positive use of mistakes and experience, as well as the need to create and innovate, and to fend off inertia. There are myriads of examples of the new interest organizations are taking in learning and development. These range from traditional 'training' initiatives to developments such as Unipart's establishment of an on-site 'university' to facilitate continual learning, or Chapparral Steel who send people off on sabbaticals to trawl the world for new ideas and technologies.

Garvin, D.A.(1993) 'Building a learning organization' in Harvard Business Review, July–August.

Valuing people

There is a growing understanding and awareness of the skills and qualities people bring to the workplace and the need to provide for their expression and development. The value of difference and diversity is becoming appreciated, and the values and beliefs that underpin empowerment are gaining widespread acceptance (if not yet practice) amongst those who manage and lead organizations.

Social responsibility

Awareness is growing of the impact and contribution organizations have on their community, and the larger (even global) society in which they operate. In particular, concern for environmental issues such as pollution and recycling is slowly beginning to mean more than simply a reaction to changing consumer sensibilities. There are many well known examples of companies taking these concerns seriously. Clothing manufacturer Patagonia now produces a range of outdoor clothing made from recycled plastic – they are more expensive to produce, but consumers are recognizing the value of Patagonia's commitment to sustainable and environmentally aware production. Other examples are the car manufacturer Volvo, which is seeking to introduce environmental responsibility into both its products and processes, and the success of the Co-operative Bank in attracting custom with its ethical investment portfolios.

'Sustainability, not growth, at Patagonia' in *At Work*, May–June 1993.

Seeing empowerment in the context of other changes and trends in the way organizations are managed helps to support and justify your efforts to develop this approach to managing people in the workplace. The benefits to organizations in 'bottom-line' terms are also becoming increasingly clear, even to the most sceptical. A recent DTI/CBI survey of successful and innovative UK business's, for example, suggests that these 'winning' companies put 'unlocking the potential of their people' as one of the five key ingredients for success. Defining this further they found that the three important characteristics under this banner were:

DTI/CBI Report (1994) *Competitiveness – How the best UK Companies are Winning.*

- 'Creating a culture in which employees are genuinely empowered'
- 'Flattening and inverting the organizational pyramid'
- 'Investing in people through good communications, teaming and training'

The DTI and CBI are not renowned purveyors of radical theory or wacky management ideas – these statements resulted from researching current good practice in a real business environment. Above all, though, the impetus for empowerment in the workplace must lie with a genuine belief in the potential contribution people can make to a successful and vibrant organization.

Barriers and problems

While the benefits held out by empowerment are very attractive, there are nevertheless real difficulties in promoting this approach to management within an organization. In this section we will look at some of these issues as they present themselves to managers, beginning with the problems of 'control'.

The issue of control

There are really two linked issues here, one a personal one for the manager, and the other a broader one for the organization as a whole. We have already noted that empowerment does not dispense with control but shares it within the work team. But it is this sharing of control and direction that poses the key difficulty for the manager.

Control and the manager

For the manager to learn to 'let go,' to pass on responsibility to his or her staff with confidence, is fine in theory but not as easy in practice as it sounds. It involves a reappraisal of your own feelings about your role as manager and the calibre of your staff. Try thinking through this issue in the activity below.

Learning activity

Losing control?

- Reflecting on your own management style for a moment, try to identify your concerns/fears about the empowerment process, about passing on responsibility and control to your workforce.
- Try to think about where these concerns might come from, and what you might do to put these concerns into perspective.

It would be unusual for managers not to have some concerns about empowered staff as the idea runs contrary to some of the traditional views about the key roles of a manager – controlling and directing for example. Let's explore some of the common concerns that you may have expressed about empowerment, in the form of a question and answer session.

How will I know what's happening?

Part of the empowerment process includes understanding each other's need for quality communication and more effective ways of providing mutual support. People communicate best when they want to, and because they understand why it is important. On a more challenging note, can you be certain that you know what is happening at the moment? To what extent do people tell you what they think you want to hear, or what's actually happening? Lastly, if your staff are competent, empowered and trusted – do you really need to know everything anyway?

Will I look weak and unable to manage?

On the contrary, managing in an empowered environment should be more demanding – and more rewarding – than in a traditional command and control situation. Empowerment is not an 'easy option' nor a recipe for abdication or lower standards – it requires a high level of understanding and personal commitment.

Can I trust them?

The choice is between moving forward by developing trusting and open relationships with your staff or spending your time trying to control and monitor everything that they do. The approach is to trust that people want to do a good job unless they prove otherwise, and not to assume the worst about people from the outset.

'Will they match my standards?'

Given the opportunity they may well match or hopefully exceed the standards you expect. It is part of your role as manager to help people develop the skills and confidence to attain the highest standards of performance.

'Surely more mistakes will be made?'

There is no reason why more mistakes will happen; in fact the converse can occur as commitment and involvement focus people on achievement and quality. More than this the emphasis on learning from errors provides real opportunity to ensure that mistakes are not repeated.

'Will they do things the way I have done them?'

They may do so at first, but hopefully not in the long run. It is one of the real benefits of empowerment that people will freely explore more effective and innovative ways of doing things. Remember that individuals should know more about the detail of their jobs than you do, and are often better placed to make these improvements.

Part of the problem here is the dependent nature of the manager/staff relationship, which provides a perception of safety in that managers feel in control and responsible, while staff feel 'managed' and ultimately 'not responsible'.

The first step in dealing with these concerns is to develop your own awareness of the areas that cause you difficulty, and then try to look at these in a more positive light. For example, worries about the capabilities of staff to cope with new responsibilities can be viewed as an opportunity for you to develop your skills at coaching and supporting which is part of the process of redefining your management role. A crucial element of empowerment of course is to provide the necessary support and training to ensure that staff are equipped to handle an empowered approach. The chapters on teams also stressed the need for people to share concerns in order to deal with them, and difficulties in 'letting go' need to be shared with your staff in this way.

Lastly, the manager will need to accept that in adopting an empowering approach it is likely, indeed desirable, that your staff will do things differently and arrive at alternative decisions or solutions. These must be supported and the temptation to step in and impose your own ideas or way of working needs resisting; rather you might use more open ways of influencing people. Here the manager needs to appreciate the benefits to the staff and the organization of the process of allowing staff to take responsibility over the occasional cost of a less than ideal solution or decision. It requires a longer-term view, one focused on people and their development, rather than one focused solely on the immediate task.

Control – the wider issues

Most of us will be familiar with the 'headless chicken' image of managers running around frantically trying to give orders, monitor everything and do the job themselves. It is easy to laugh at the thought and conclude that being so 'out of control' is simply bad management.

Think for a moment about how difficult it is for us to control our own behaviour at times – add to this a team of, say, half a dozen other people, all with unique personalities and behaving as differently as individuals will always do. Put this team in a normal work situation where tasks and demands change quickly, customer requirements fluctuate, new processes are introduced or the technology goes on the blink. Think about how all these individuals react to one another and to the rapidly evolving situations in which they find themselves – can you really 'control' this situation? Is it really possible to be aware of all the interactions and relationships that are going on here, let alone hope to predict the outcome of your own interventions with any certainty?

This scenario illustrates the complexity of even a 'simple' work environment – it suggests that the idea of being 'in control' is just an illusion. This illusion has a serious impact on our ability to function effectively as managers. To start with we learn that control is a key management skill and spend our managerial careers trying to exert control over situations that appear to sabotage our best efforts. We worry that we can't 'manage' properly, and react to out-of-control events by struggling to apply yet more controls. In the end this is both un-productive and unhealthy.

This is not to say that some form of control is not necessary, but to suggest that recognizing its limitations in complex work settings, and banishing the myth of always 'being in control', helps us to put chaotic and confusing situations into perspective. It helps us to see that this is a normal and inevitable facet of working life, and reduces the need for us to 'punish ourselves' over our inability to control everything that happens at work. It also helps us to see the value of sharing the task of influencing (rather than controlling) events with your staff.

The second major difficulty with the control issue is the paradoxical idea that an organization can somehow control the way empowerment is introduced and the exact extent to which it develops using traditional mechanisms of authority and power. This is not just an academic or philosophical question. In practice initial efforts by staff to act in an empowered way can easily be frustrated by negative and inflexible responses from senior people who may be tempted to see empowerment as a good thing only if actions are in line with their thinking and if no mistakes are made. This lack of real commitment to empowerment is quickly picked up by staff and seen as a barrier to real progress and a continua-tion of 'the old ways of working'. It is no surprise then that in this environment staff respond half-heartedly to the opportunity to take on new responsibilities and make decisions for themselves – the risks involved are perceived as too great. Individuals will act cautiously for their own safety when they are faced with mixed messages about empowerment – only when 'what they say' is matched consistently with 'what they do' (referring to their managers) will employees perceive that it is safe to experiment with new responsibility and initiative.

For the manager, then, the challenge is to be consistent and positive in promoting and supporting an empowered approach with their staff, developing their skills and confidence and resisting the temptation to fall back on traditional control mechanisms when the going gets tough.

But who is responsible?

A key issue that surfaces very quickly when empowerment is discussed is that of who is 'responsible'. In a traditional hierarchical organization the need to pinpoint individuals who are responsible for each task or role is seen as of utmost importance, but in reality this is a shorthand for 'we need to know who to blame when things go wrong' – it is less often used to praise individual achievements in this respect. This need to know who should be 'held responsible', who should 'take the blame', is one of the reasons why people are concerned, even frightened, of taking on wider responsibilities in the workplace. It follows then that passing responsibility 'down the line' to members of staff is unlikely to be successful in an environment that allows blame and even punishment to hang over the newly responsible like the Sword of Damocles – staff may be reluctant to take the perceived risk of accepting additional responsibility.

A further challenge to this narrow notion of responsibility arises in considering the complexity of contemporary organizations. As with the control issue, it is just not possible to single out simple cause and effect links. To say that the actions of 'X' caused the problem 'Y' and therefore 'X' is responsible is naive and defensive. It ignores the important effects of the situation, people's perception and many other factors, let alone the improbability of knowing all the relevant facts.

In an empowering environment the responsibility for delivering the kind of service to customers that you would wish is a shared one, and needs to operate in an environment that is free of blame. We have talked about seeing success as a result of team effort – here it is also necessary to see responsibility as something accepted by the team too. In this scenario, individuals will know that they will be supported by both the manager and the rest of the team should things get difficult, and that everyone is concerned to meet the needs of clients directly. An empowered environment seeks to create a positive vision of 'organization' which is free of unnecessary control, full of hope, and where responsibility is shared.

Bureaucracy

One of the purposes of empowerment is to free people to act in the best interests of the client/customer and the organization. In this respect it is important to have a very critical look at your organization's systems and procedures to see if they present a real or perceived barrier to such actions. The issue of bureaucracy has strong links with the 'need' to control and the lack of trust.

Some simple examples of rules becoming barriers might be rules about staff spending petty cash only with permission or gaining access to materials by asking for a key every time from the manager. But it can be more serious than that. There are the once-a-month computing cycles that leave invoices unpaid – can you imagine suppliers or partners taking this excuse seriously? Or perhaps 'I can't send you a quote/proposal as my boss is away for a fortnight' – a great way to lose business.

Apart from the obvious wasted time and slow responses to situations, what message do these control systems send to staff and clients? That's right, there's no trust here. The answer is simple, treat people as the responsible adults they are.

Many outmoded timekeeping systems also demonstrate this lack of trust. Committed and responsible staff know the problems caused by poor time-keeping, they are aware of the need for their presence in terms of meeting production or service demands. Most people will do everything they can to arrive on time, they don't need the threat of disciplinary action or wage stoppages. Get rid of timekeeping systems – they insult and demotivate people, and do not in any case solve problems of persistent lateness. Look elsewhere for the solution. It might be worth posing the legitimate question: 'Why do we have rules and procedures anyway?' In some cases the answer may be accept-able – to protect people (e.g. health and safety or equal opportunities), to meet with legal requirements, or to provide structured ways of undertaking routine or technically complex tasks. There will be other rules and procedures, however, that exist for more dubious reasons – these might include:

- Because we have always done it this way
- Because the last manager wanted it done like this
- Well, no one can remember quite why we do this
- They are a product of a manager's need to control through rules, guidelines, procedures, signatures, numbers, reports, 'put it in writing', and so on
- Because structures and rules give us the illusion of safety
- Because I can just follow the rules and don't need to think
- Because we have to (but we haven't challenged this and don't know why)
- And worst of all – 'To cover my back.'

Semler, R. (1994) 'Why my former employees still work for me' in *Harvard Business Review*, January–February.

Case note

Semco

Semco, a manufacturing company in Brazil, has practised empowered forms of organization that challenge the need for many of the rules and systems in place in most organizations.

Workers monitor their personal timekeeping on a flexible basis, collect-ively set their own and each others' salaries, and do the hiring and firing. Semco rarely bothers with an 'organizational chart', has only three 'layers' in their hierarchy, and questions the value of strategic planning or endless monitoring. As 'owner' Ricardo Semler says: 'We treat our employees like responsible adults. We never assume that they will take advantage of us or our rules (or our lack of rules); we always assume they will do their level best to achieve results beneficial to the company, the customer, their colleagues and themselves.'

You might like to challenge your bureaucracy by seriously asking of each procedure or rule some simple questions like:

- How does it contribute to meeting our objectives or improving performance?
- Who benefits?
- What happens if we get rid of it? (Try it and see.)
- What does it tell us about the way we work together?

Empowerment does not mean getting rid of systems and procedures, it involves making sure that they work for you and not against. If your staff think that it is useful to introduce new procedures or to change existing ones, then let them create ones that add value and are user-friendly.

A quote from Max De Pree is worth keeping in mind. He described bureaucracy as:

De Pree, M. (1989) *Leadership is an Art*, Arrow Business Books, London.

The most superficial and fatuous of all relationships.

Handling resistance

In thinking in general terms about people at work, perhaps from your own perspective, it is easy to assume that others see the benefits of taking on new responsibilities and being involved in shaping the working environment, and will jump at the opportunity. Of course many people will do so, but this is not always the case. Resistance to empowerment and a reluctance to accept responsibility can be an understandable response from many individuals. As a manager, you will need to try to understand why people respond in this way and work through their concerns with them.

Learning activity

It's not my job

Can you think of some of the reasons why individuals may not wish to accept more responsibility, or be anxious about moves towards empowerment?

There are many reasons for such resistance, and you will need to bear in mind that these may vary significantly between individuals and in different situations. However, there are some common concerns that are worth noting that will help in understanding these barriers to empowerment.

- **Fear of responsibility**. A desire to avoid taking responsibility is often linked to the perceived risks involved and a fear of failure, blame or punishment. Though there may be some very personal aspects to this view, it can be eased by tackling the blame culture, providing support unconditionally, and by developing a positive, learning-together view of mistakes. People may well need to experience and observe this new environment before they are willing to experiment with responsibility and be given the opportunity for early successes.

- **Beliefs about the employee/manager relationship**. This is the 'managers are paid to manage – I'm paid to do as I'm told' view. People may feel that it is not their job to make decisions, become involved or take responsibility. These feelings betray the narrow concern and self-interest inherent in traditionally managed hierarchical organizations usually reflected in their pay and reward systems. It will be important therefore to get across through dialogue the changing nature of relationships at work, the personal benefits of working in a new and exciting environment, and perhaps a vision of an 'us and them–free' future. In many respects empowerment presents a challenge to the security of traditional hierarchies and views about responsibility.

- **Dependency**. This is the need in individuals for the security of a manager who will take the difficult decisions (and the blame) for them, look after them, and tell them what to do. They become dependent upon managers (parent figures?), and thus avoid taking responsibility for their own actions. Dependency also props up the game of blaming managers for everything while accepting no responsibility, which can be a comfortable position that is hard to give up.

- **Lack of confidence**. This is an idea that must be equally familiar to staff and managers. Even when the benefits of empowerment are accepted and desired by employees, a lack of confidence may prevent individuals from taking up opportunities available to them. As with other situations where confidence needs to be developed, providing real support and the encouragement of early successes are vital ingredients.

- **The need for structure and order**. It is important to recognize that an individual's need for the security of established procedure, rules and order is both valid and will vary from one person to another. As empowerment seeks to establish more flexible approaches to work and some of the traditional boundaries are redefined, some individuals can become unsettled or even angry. Think about their needs, and the anxiety caused by any change process, and seek ways of replacing the 'security' of systems with the mutual support of the team and more positive working relationships. Further, reassure them that empowerment does not eradicate procedures or systems, but gives them the opportunity to keep or create the systems they feel they need to do their job well, and get rid of those that prevent them from doing so – a 'win–win' situation!

With all of these understandable concerns, the manager must recognize that he or she will need to spend time with their staff working through the issues alongside promoting an atmosphere which supports and encourages staff to experiment with an empowered way of working. A positive response to their early efforts is particularly important here – empowered behaviour should be reinforced and modelled by the manager consistently.

Supporting empowerment

We have looked at empowerment very much as an approach to working together in an organization rather than as another in a long line of management initiatives that come and go. Real empowerment is putting positive beliefs about the value and potential of people into action. As such the idea that it can be systematically implemented through detailed planning and preparation, followed by training programmes and evaluation, is less than helpful. This is not to say, however, that supporting empowerment does not require thought, discussion and reflection – these indeed are the starting points if empowerment is a worthwhile step forward in your organization.

Developing understanding

Perhaps an early step in considering an empowered approach is to reflect upon your own views about management in an empowered situation – in particular how you feel about the issues of control and responsibility discussed earlier in this chapter. This should help you to consider what barriers your own style produces to empowerment, and to what extent 'letting go' will be difficult for you in practice. It should be possible to share this awareness with your team and enlist their support in working through practical examples with them.

Secondly, it will be crucial to develop an understanding of your team's view of empowerment, both as an idea and in practical situations, through dialogue and discussion. Bear in mind here the concerns that they may have that lead to resistance, and that individual responses may vary significantly from enthusiasm to outright hostility. In this respect those who can embrace this approach quickly may prove to be valuable 'allies' who can help to model empowered behaviour and demonstrate positive responses.

Discussing what empowerment means in practice can also help to dispel some of the myths about this way of working and calm fears about workplace anarchy or being loaded down with responsibility resulting in stress and being blamed. This understanding is crucial because empowerment is driven by values and not a set of managerial practices.

An empowering climate

Empowerment encourages and is supported through the development of effective management actions in a whole range of areas we have discussed in other chapters. It is also underpinned by the emphasis we have given to the need to understand yourself and others, and the building of positive relationships with your colleagues.

Learning activity

Empowerment in context

Think about your own perspective on the following topics and give some time to reflect upon the links between these topics and your understanding of empowerment.

- Leadership – what it means to you
- Learning and development in your organization
- The further development of teamworking in your own situation.

As well as the three topics – leadership, teamworking and learning – in the activity above, it is worth thinking through the links between empowerment and the following themes:

- High quality communication
- Understanding self and others, particularly motivation
- Removing blame as a response to mistakes
- Using conflict positively
- Valuing differences
- Trust, openness and honesty.

Perhaps the last one about trust is the most crucial as far as empowerment is concerned as genuine trust provides the basis for the sharing of control and responsibility. These themes are crucial in underpinning empowerment and should form the foundation of any strategies for action.

Taking action

Thinking about, reflecting on and discussing empowerment are useful ways of setting the scene and beginning to understand each other's position in relation to empowerment. For this approach to become a reality, however, action needs to be taken. Putting empowerment into practice is very much a case of **'just do it!'** It's rather like the trust issue – people may agree with the approach but will only really accept it if it is demonstrated repeatedly and supported by positive responses, even when things go wrong.

The 'just do it' strategy also recognizes that empowerment is a learning process for everyone, including the manager. In many ways the problems and opportunities that arise from this way of working together cannot be accurately predicted or planned for in detail, but need to be dealt with and developed as they arise.

There are some suggestions, however, that might help to avoid some of the difficulties in adapting to an empowered way of working:

- **Reinforcing empowered behaviour**. It is vital that empowered actions are rewarded with praise and positive responses and never with blame. The manager must support initiative and creative action, and accept that staff may choose to do things differently. When things go wrong it is still possible to be positive about the taking of action (valuing 'having a go') and to use the experience for shared learning.

- **Go for successes**. Try to ensure that early efforts at empowered behaviour lead to successful outcomes, as this will help with confidence and encourage staff to experiment further.

- **Model the behaviour**. Your role as manager in demonstrating, with integrity and openness, the value and practice of empowerment is vital. It is particularly important as it is easy to undermine your case by sliding back into a 'controlled' way of dealing with situations, especially when things get difficult or mistakes are made. Make it clear to staff that they should challenge your behaviour on this and value their challenge as a sign of progress and learning.

- **Setting new boundaries**. It is necessary to maintain continuous dialogue with the team about new boundaries and responsibilities, and how these change over time as people get more confident about taking action on their own initiative. The potential for misunderstandings to occur can increase if not enough attention is paid to good communication and a shared awareness of each other's decisions and work areas. The manager may have to quite overtly 'give permission,' or 'allow', staff to take actions on their own that are perceived as being beyond traditional boundaries. In any case it is useful to discuss with the team the issues of new boundaries, taking risks and the consequences of making mistakes so that feelings and concerns can be worked through and understood.

- **Cutting bureaucracy**. One of the practical actions you can take is to work through current procedures and 'rules' with your staff with the aim of removing barriers to swift and effective responses to client needs. Be sure to allow your staff the space to critically appraise these systems and to suggest alternatives if appropriate, without recourse to defensiveness.

- **Tread lightly**. In a situation where there is a high level of concern about empowerment, it might be useful to start off with smaller, less critical issues that give staff the opportunity to get used to this way of working while keeping the perceived level of 'risk' manageable. Examples might be decisions about their working environment, or drawing up staff rotas where the outcome in terms of service cover is clear but choices about how this is met can be left to the team. While it is important to pace the introduction of empowerment so as not to over-stress individuals, it is equally vital not to use this as a justification for retaining control on key issues but sharing it on unimportant ones.

- **Providing the tools**. Of course your staff are already equipped to work in an empowered way, though they may not have the confidence to do so at first. Even the most 'junior' member of the team will have taken responsibility for major 'life-decisions' about work, families, relationships, education, housing, etc. and coped with the changes and complexities these situations bring. Apart from creating an environment that supports this way of working, confidence can be built by ensuring the provision of effective skills training and a range of development opportunities. Devolving responsibility without giving staff the opportunity to gain new skills or awareness sets them up for stress and failure which, apart from the obvious human consequences, will scupper future attempts at supporting empowered behaviour.

- **Stress the learning**. Empowerment is a way of working that has to be experienced for people to really learn what it means in practice. Stress that it is something that you learn about together, continually, and that as a manager you do not have all the answers and have much to learn yourself.

These then are some of the things that you can do to support the development of an empowered way of working in your organization. They flow from beliefs about the potential contribution each individual could make to your organization given a positive and supportive environment.

Going forward

Empowerment is much more than a theory about management, it is an approach that underpins the way we view our role in the management of people and organizations. It combines the hopeful message about developing people's potential with that of building successful and dynamic organizations.

The practical suggestions that we have looked at in the chapters on, for example, teambuilding or managing change benefit from a real commitment to adopt an empowered way of putting these actions into practice. Crucially, empowerment is not a movement that can be isolated from day-to-day management practice – it must be introduced largely through managerial action and behaviour.

Lastly, empowerment offers unique opportunities for everyone to learn and develop, having the potential to be a truly liberating experience of real meaning for people, and particularly for managers with the imagination to 'just do it'.

Summary

In this chapter we have tried to convey an understanding of empowerment as a way of working based on positive values about people, linked to the more productive achievement of business goals. In this respect we have not described empowerment as an 'initiative' to be introduced in the usual 'top-down' manner, but as something to be understood intuitively and implemented with commitment.

We have discussed some of the potential benefits of empowerment for individuals and the effects of an empowered staff on the organization as a whole and its customers. In the process we have looked at some of the barriers to the acceptance and practice of empowerment, including the fears managers have about changing the way in which they manage people.

The crucial issues of control and responsibility are particularly important here as empowerment challenges traditional notions of the role of managers as 'controllers' and advocates sharing responsibility with all members of staff. We also pay attention to the understanding of employee resistance to empowerment, particularly in a situation where responsibility equates to who takes the blame.

Lastly the chapter covers some practical ways in which you might consider moving towards an empowered way of working together, suggesting that a 'just do it' approach may be the most productive. This section has stressed the links to putting empowerment into practice through our approaches to leadership, teams, communication and motivation.

Further reading

Maverick by Ricardo Semler (Arrow Business Books, 1993) is a highly inspirational account of Semler's personal 'management journey', discovering the real value of empowerment through his experience of running Semco, a manufacturing business in Brazil. Far from being a textbook, it provides some wonderful examples of the amazing achievements of an empowered workforce and pulls no punches about the difficulties encountered along the way.

Empowering People by Aileen Mitchell Stewart (Pitman, 1994) provides a practical and very readable introduction to the management and implementation of an empowered approach. There are some useful practical ideas here for those who prefer a more structured approach to empowerment in the workplace.

References

Block, P. (1987) *The Empowered Manager*, Josey-Bass, San Francisco.

Clutterbuck, D. (1994) *The Power of Empowerment*, BCA, London.

DTI/CBI Report (1994) *Competitiveness – How the Best UK Companies are Winning*

McLagan, P. and Nel, C. (1995) *The Age of Participation*, Berrett-Koehler, San Francisco.

Peters, T. (1992) *Liberation Management*, BCA/Pan Macmillan, London.

Phillips, N. (1993) *Innovative Management*, Pitman, London.

Semler, R. (1994) *Maverick*, Arrow Business Press, London.

Stewart, A.M. (1994) *Empowering People*, Pitmans, London.

Thomas, A.B. (19) *Controversies in Management*,

Whetten, D.A., Cameron, K.S. and Woods, M. (1994) *Developing Management Skills for Europe*, HarperCollins.

11

Developing a learning culture

A mistake is an event, the full benefit of which has not yet been turned to your advantage.

Peter Senge

Objectives

By the end of this chapter you will be able to:

➤ Apply an understanding of the value of a continuous and integrated approach to development to your own workplace
➤ Describe the practical applications of the learning cycle to continuous learning and development
➤ Identify and use the wide range of learning opportunities that are inherent in the work of your organization
➤ Describe ways in which you can facilitate the development of a learning culture in your own organization

Introduction

It is not so long ago that learning in organizations was treated as a marginal activity, relegated to the provision of training courses to improve skills, and always the first budget area to be savaged in any move to cut costs. Today, learning is moving to centre stage in discussions about how to create and maintain flexible and competetive companies in a rapidly changing environment. Learning is fast becoming the key to survival not only for organizations but for the individuals who work in them. It is no longer feasible to wait for the lessons of experience to filter slowly down the organization in an adhoc manner – it is now more urgent than ever to put learning and development at the core of the way we work together.

This chapter looks at the value of working towards a state where learning and development become an integral part of the culture of your organization, and some of the approaches to development that can help to facilitate this move. It emphasizes the wide range of learning opportunities to be found in everyday working situations, and the need to encourage people to take responsibility for, and a critical interest in, their own development.

While we do look at a number of ways in which you can facilitate learning in the workplace, we have not set out to provide comprehensive coverage of 'training techniques' as such. To place too much importance on 'how to run a training session' would only serve to reinforce the narrow view of development as something that takes place away from the normal working environment. It is also vital to promote the idea that 'training and development' is a key managerial responsibility, not something that can be left to personnel or training professionals. Managers have perhaps the most crucial role to play in creating a climate of continual learning and development.

As far as terminology is concerned we have used both 'learning' and 'development' almost interchangeably, as for practical purposes this is how they are used by most people on a day-to-day basis. 'Training', on the other hand, refers here to the more specific process whereby people acquire skills or knowledge of particular relevance to their current job. Learning and development imply a great deal more than simply improving skills – they reflect ideas about discovery, realization of potential, growth, change and maturity. It is this broader vision of the benefits of a learning culture that provides the momentum for learning as a critical factor in developing effective management and in meeting human potential.

Development is important

Before exploring some of the issues and methods relating to development and learning in the workplace, we need to clarify briefly why it is important. All too often learning is relegated to an adhoc reliance on 'learning from experience', something which is regularly sidelined in the face of operational pressures. Whilst this is to some extent understandable, it is also short-term thinking and potentially very destructive for both the organization and its stakeholders.

Most people would accept (though might not always demonstrate in practice) the value of basic training provision in their organization, particularly for new employees. This might cover, for example, areas like: induction; health and safety/first aid; vocational qualifications/NVQs/professional development; specific job-training. Many of these will meet basic requirements for an individual to perform their job adequately, or satisfy minimum standards laid down by the organization or statutory authorities. While these are obviously essential, promoting development in an organization beyond this basic level can have profound benefits.

Learning activity

The value of learning

What might be the benefits of a real commitment to development and learning, in its widest sense, throughout an organization for:

- Individual members of staff and managers?
- The organization as a whole?

For individual members of staff one key benefit of being involved in continual development is a motivational one. Where learning is encouraged and valued they will see opportunities to enhance their skills (both technical and interpersonal), learn new ones, and progress beyond basic competence and narrow job roles. Not only will they then be able to make a more valuable contribution to your organization, but the opportunity to develop and grow in itself satisfies personal needs. The opportunity to develop broader, more marketable skills of benefit for future jobs has been called enhancing 'employability'.

This is further supported by the belief in the value of individuals and their 'right' to self-development – to work towards the realization of their full potential, both in terms of 'work' and in its widest sense as a human being. In supporting this process through work, the organization becomes a place where people can achieve growth and meet some of their personal needs for development. Given the large proportion of time we invest in work, it is arguably immoral to subject people to a working life that denies them opportunities for personal and social development. Work is far more significant than a contracted exchange of labour for money – and our approach to management needs to embrace this wider responsibility.

Encouraging individuals to make an active commitment to learning, however, is not simply a philanthropic activity, it is crucial to the success and survival of organizations today and into the future. Creating a learning culture is not at the expense of productivity and profit but a key to ensuring these outcomes. Some of the specific benefits you might have thought of in the activity above could include:

- Improving performance and competence in current job or role
- Increasing levels of confidence
- Supporting increased commitment and participation through motivation
- Facilitating professional development/promotion
- Broadening the individual's range of skills (multi-skilling) and flexibility
- Developing relationships/teamwork through shared learning
- Using mistakes positively and taking risks.

In more general terms, learning needs to become a key part of the culture of the organization to enable it to tackle change and challenge with enthusiasm and energy – to move from a static state where change is forced upon people (reactive), to one where continuous development drives the process of change in a positive and exciting way (proactive). Think about some of the current issues and developments in managing organizations, things like continuous improvement, flatter structures, empowerment, the impact of technology, greater flexibility and responding more rapidly to customer needs. They all require new approaches, new ideas and new behaviours, they all demand the ability to adapt and change – in short, they require the ability to learn.

This is the hub of the idea of the 'learning organization', one where the commitment to development in all respects allows a rapid and flexible response to changes in the way we work together and manage our organizations.

Some common themes

This section introduces a number of broad themes that underpin development and learning in the workplace in all its forms. The underlying assumption here is that learning and development is an integral and crucial part of a manager's role rather than something to be delegated to training or personnel functions inside or external to an organization. While specialists can provide invaluable support and input to the development process, managers are uniquely placed to ensure that learning becomes a continuous and prominent feature of an organization's culture. They are able to integrate learning and growth with real day-to-day work with clients and colleagues.

Learning relationships and ownership

One of the key ideas that you will need to explore and understand with your staff is that only individuals can learn and develop – they cannot be made to do so by managers or tutors. It is a vital first step that people take responsibility for, and 'own', their own development – they must want to learn. Though individuals should retain responsibility for their own learning, this does not mean that an organization can leave development to individuals to sort out – it also has a crucial role to play in providing the resources, time and support for learning in all its forms. The manager has a major responsibility here too, not only for her or his own learning, but for providing a positive environment and a range of opportunities which facilitate staff development.

Helping people to move from a situation of learning 'dependency' to one of being responsible for their own learning is a process of developing awareness and understanding, and is a crucial feature of developing a learning culture. This process can be shown diagrammatically as in Figure 11.1.

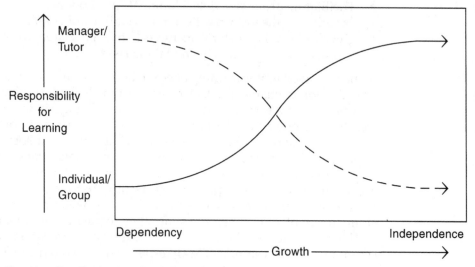

Fig. 11.1 Developing responsibility for learning.

This illustrates, in general terms, the process of the growth of a positive learning culture. It begins with people being fairly dependent on tutors or managers to provide information, ideas and skills in a traditional passive 'training' situation. As confidence and understanding grow, individuals or groups 'learn how to learn', and take increasing responsibility for their own learning. The end result is independent learners who are able to define the direction, content and style in which they wish to learn, as well as support each other in the learning process. Note that there is still an important role for the manager or tutor here in providing facilitation, support and challenge, and in introducing ideas and knowledge.

An understanding of this 'ownership' issue raises important questions concerning the relationship between the learner and those facilitating or 'helping' the process along. Careful consideration should be given to this relationship in planning learning events or using experiences retrospectively. It should be possible to ensure that this relationship is overt and understood by both the 'learners' and those facilitating, allowing issues such as control over pace, direction and content, the role of the facilitator or the right to 'opt out' to be discussed and agreed.

While most people will readily accept the idea of personal responsibility in principle, for some this idea runs contrary to many years of experience of formal education and training which focused responsibility for learning on the teacher or trainer. This experience results in the perceived need for a teacher or expert to somehow 'provide' or 'deliver' learning, and that these people have responsibility for 'making me learn'. This subtle but dependent relationship must be challenged as it provides a major barrier to real learning and reflects a need to avoid responsibility for personal development with its inherent risks and challenges.

A discussion with staff and colleagues about the issue of responsibility for learning is a good starting point, but by itself this will not be enough. It will need to be constantly reinforced at every opportunity through the way in which you support learning in the workplace. A simple example might be the common case of a manager being asked to solve a problem for a member of staff. The expected response – and on the surface the helpful one – is to provide the solution as requested. But the member of staff has not learned much from this exchange, they have not learned how to solve the problem for themselves, and the manager has not explored his or her coaching skills at all. A response that focuses on learning in this situation, by asking constructive questions and promoting discovery for example, illustrates the need to put learning firmly on the agenda. Both of the individuals and also the organization benefit from a learning approach here – they are better equipped to deal with similar problems next time around.

In the case above, the member of staff retains ownership of the problem and solution, and more importantly the learning process. They have not shifted their responsibility to the 'teacher' (manager) who might traditionally have provided the expert answer. This approach demands that managers change their role from that of 'the expert', to that of facilitator and coach – refusing to deny others the responsibility for their own learning and supporting them in this process.

Creating diversity of opportunity

Another assumption upon which this chapter is founded is that people learn and develop in different ways. We have already looked in an earlier chapter at the value that diversity brings to the workplace and learning style is another factor that varies widely from person to person. At an obvious level this means that managers will need to explore with their staff the methods and styles of learning that are most appropriate to each individual, and work towards providing learning opportunities based upon this understanding. Since everyone can learn via a range of different situations, this does not commit the manager or organization to exclusively individual 'learning opportunities'; rather he or she must be aware that relying solely on training events, for example, might favour some staff members but be inappropriate for others.

Taking this further, it is important to think widely about what opportunities are available to managers and staff for development, learning and training in the workplace.

 ### *Learning activity*

Creating opportunities

List as many 'opportunities for learning and development' that you can think of relating to your own situation. Think about the informal ones as well as the structured ones like training courses or open learning.

A common response to this question is often to begin with structured situations we usually associate with 'training', such as:

Courses	Workshops	Open learning
Going to college	In-house sessions	'Induction'
Conferences	Reading	

In fact it is still common to find many organizations still seeing learning and development entirely in terms of training courses. But if you think more widely about it, hopefully you will have included many valuable opportunities arising from work itself, and many other life experiences. Here are just a few examples:

- **Trying things out – experimenting**. You don't learn much from doing things the same old way. Value taking risks, try new ideas, support creativity and innovation.
- **Learning from each other**. Sharing understanding, observations, examples and skills. Actually seeing good practice put into action with successful outcomes. So many good ideas are wasted through not being shared.
- **Through decision-making and problem-solving**. A great opportunity to explore alternatives, and to look at each other's way of approaching problems.
- **From feedback and disclosure**. Learning about yourself and others and the way you work together. Actively seek out feedback, including that from customers, and learn from it.
- **From mistakes** (your own or others). Mistakes focus attention on the need to do things differently next time – use this as a learning opportunity. Think about not only what went wrong, but what it is about the way you do things that led to the error.
- **Taking on new roles, or responsibilities**. A chance to develop new skills and confidence in real working situations.
- **Working on a project/initiative**. Develop management skills, confidence and a wider range of skills for each project member.
- **Through discussion**. Thinking things through, sharing ideas and observations, working on processes and relationships.
- **From reviews and asking questions**. Use dialogue to challenge assumptions and ways of thinking as well as actions and behaviours.

There are very many others. In fact apart from the most routine of tasks, work consists largely of opportunities to learn in one way or another. We will be looking at some of these options later in the chapter. The point here is that learning is an integral part of work itself. Almost everything that happens, every experience, is an opportunity to change and improve what you do providing you choose to take advantage of it. Interestingly many of the well-quoted quality initiatives and continuous improvement programmes adopt just such an approach, and have learning actively from experience as their key process. So don't wait for experience to seep through, nor training to provide you with pearls of wisdom – learn from everything.

A continuous process

In tandem with development as an everyday part of working life is the view that development and learning is a continuous process. All of us already learn, through our experiences, on a continuous basis and it is important not to underestimate our ability to grow and adapt in this respect. However, learning based on our experiences of everyday life can benefit substantially from giving this learning a focus, particularly in the workplace, structuring it towards clear development objectives. Development here needs to be a conscious and active process, rather than relying on the issues that just happen to come up on a day-to-day basis. The concept of 'life-long' learning has long been accepted and has almost reached the status of a cliché; nevertheless, this is an approach that needs reinforcing at every opportunity.

Learning is for everyone

There would hopefully be few people who would not agree with this view. This is just a reminder though that 'everyone' means anyone in an organization whatever their position or role, including staff who are very competent and comfortable with their current job. They may wish to be involved in new areas of work, have useful hidden talents, or wish to pursue learning that is not immediately applicable to work but which will have indirect benefits (e.g. promoting confidence, or transferable skills like interpersonal ones).

Be particularly wary of people who feel they have nothing to learn because they know their job inside out. This view is not simply complacent, it is highly unlikely to hold up in the face of rapidly changing working practices or technology. More important than these changes is the implication that competence is simply a matter of technical proficiency. Being effective at work, as the focus of this book suggests, is about developing positive relationships, understanding yourself and others, and of course learning. The idea that a person can have nothing to learn in these areas is nonsensical.

Lastly, remember to look after your own development needs. It is all too easy to put this aside in your efforts to provide development opportunities for your staff. To promote learning in your organization you will need to emphasize its importance by taking development seriously yourself and 'modelling' a positive approach.

Moving on from these underlying ideas about the opportunity and responsibility for learning, the next section explores some key approaches and ideas about learning that can readily be applied by managers in real working situations. An understanding of these ideas is valuable to the individual manager, in helping him or her make the most of opportunities to learn and to see more clearly the value of risk-taking and challenge. It is also important that a manager is able to pass on this understanding to others in promoting real learning in the workplace.

Approaches to learning

For many of us learning is something that takes place in a classroom with a teacher and a textbook; it is an idea deeply ingrained through our education system and reinforced by many approaches to training in the workplace. In this model, learning is divorced from what we do, and relies heavily on the expert or teacher to deliver to us the knowledge and skills we need. The problem with this narrow view is that it does not encourage people to take responsibility for their own learning, and it separates learning from what we actually do in the workplace. If learning and development are to be an integral part of work culture then we need to explore ways of ensuring that learning becomes an active process, part of our daily working lives for which we retain responsibility.

This section looks at some ideas that you may wish to share with your colleagues in order to help you to develop a positive view of learning in the workplace. It focuses on the idea of the learning cycle as a way of learning from experience for both individual and team, and goes on to explore the role of risk-taking in development.

Learning from experience – the learning cycle

Of course we all 'learn from experience' – without doubt most of what we have learned throughout our lives has not been the result of training courses or even formal education. Experienced managers talk of 'learning on the job' or of being 'flung in at the deep end', giving credence to the lessons this has provided. This type of 'informal' learning obviously has great value, but it is also often slow, ad hoc and unintentional. For learning to become a driving force for organizational and individual development, however, we need to use experiences more purposefully – to learn more overtly from them.

The 'learning cycle' provides a valuable tool to help us understand the process of learning from experience. In developing this understanding we are better placed to structure the provision of learning opportunities, and to take real advantage of everyday work situations. Importantly, it focuses on more than just 'experiencing' something – it requires the learner to actively learn from the situation through a process which begins with review and reflection.

Kolb, D. (1983) *Experimental Learning*, Prentice Hall, Englewood Cliffs, New Jersey.

The learning cycle can be drawn as a four-stage process as in Figure 11.2. There are many versions of this cycle, most of them originating from the work of David Kolb (whose original terms are included in brackets).

The learning cycle follows a pattern of reviewing an experience through reflection and observation, resulting in the generation of concepts or guidelines that we then plan to test out in new situations. It emphasizes the importance of using experience positively through 'reflection-in-action' – taking the time to think through the implications of actions and behaviour and their effects on others.

It is perhaps easiest to see how this works by running through a practical example, say coaching a colleague. The **experience** in this case would be the coaching itself. This would be **reviewed** by yourself and the colleague, looking

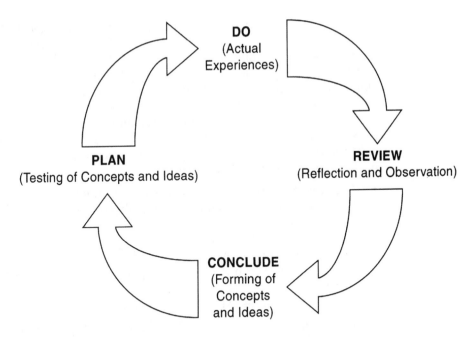

Fig. 11.2 The learning cycle.

at what went well or badly for each of you. This should lead, through discussion and questioning, to you drawing some **conclusions** – identifying the lessons to be learned from the coaching experience. Finally it is important to **plan** out how you would actually approach coaching next time around. In this way coaching can be purposefully and overtly used as a learning opportunity, rather than relying on the vague idea that the experience alone has taught us something.

In many respects the cycle represents a process that everyone goes through continuously, as we test and modify our own views and behaviours in the light of experience. It becomes more valuable in learning terms, however, if we consciously seek to 'complete the cycle' to make positive use of our experiences. This is a particularly important discipline in a working environment dominated by a need to 'do' things, to complete tasks to deadlines and to meet targets, for example. In this situation it is all too easy to 'do', but miss the opportunity to learn by reviewing, concluding and planning. In the long run this failure to learn can lead to repeated mistakes, low productivity and quality gains, and a slide into crisis-based management.

In applying the learning cycle in a more conscious way to workplace development, the manager can take advantage of everyday experiences as they happen, and seek out or create opportunities for learning by planning ahead.

Retrospective learning

Perhaps the first step in capitalizing on our daily experiences is to apply the learning cycle 'retrospectively' to events that happen in the normal course of work. Here the events are not identified as learning opportunities in advance, but rather are used as such afterwards, when the process of review and reflection – conceptualization – testing can be applied.

This is an opportunistic view of development and needs to be fostered alongside more planned and formal approaches as it uses situations that cannot be planned-in or anticipated. The manager needs to be aware of situations from which 'lessons can be learnt' and apply the learning cycle appropriately. The reflection and review can be done individually or as a process in which the team or group of individuals work together. There are two areas where a retrospective approach is particularly useful:

- **Learning from mistakes**. Almost by definition these should not be planned, but they provide one of the most valuable opportunities to learn. Partly this is because the realization that a mistake has been made focuses attention on the need to learn to do things differently, and hopefully to share this learning with others. Mistakes provide a good practical way of introducing the value of learning in your organization, and of starting to build a 'learning culture'. Seeing mistakes as learning opportunities demands a positive and 'blame-free' response to mistakes from yourself and your team.

- **Learning about processes**. While there are many ways of formally learning about 'the way we work together', the manager should look out for interesting situations that can be used to illustrate process issues. A meeting that ends with bad feeling, for example, can be used to open a discussion (review) with colleagues about how you might have worked towards a more constructive outcome, and how you might agree to tackle similar situations in the future.

Learning activity

Exploring opportunities for learning

- In your own situation, think back over the last month or so and try to identify opportunities where you might have learned from mistakes. Did you use those opportunities? How might you have used them more effectively?
- Think about situations where you might have learned about 'how we work together', like the one above – bad feelings at a meeting. Why do you think people tend to avoid using these opportunities to learn?

This active use of day-to-day experiences, though unplanned, can be a valuable addition to your efforts to encourage continuous development in the workplace. One advantage that it has over 'off-the-job' training is that it provides learning opportunities that are always in context, being about actual work-based experience. The issue of 'relevance' and 'transferring to work' that plagues many training courses just does not apply here.

Planned learning

If development were to be restricted to using 'whatever comes up' in a retrospective way, it would be very difficult to target development to meet clear objectives, either those of the individual or those of the organization. To do this we need to think again about the first step in the cycle – the 'experience' – and try to plan or anticipate the learning opportunities that might arise. Planned learning in the workplace seeks to create opportunities or identify situations where specific learning can be generated. As such it firmly embeds the development process within normal working activity, with all the advantages this brings in terms of relevance, context and improved performance.

Some typical examples of the sort of situations that can provide valuable learning opportunities might be:

- Changes to an individual's job – new responsibilities/roles
- Delegating particular tasks
- Working on a special project or initiative, development work
- Broadening skills to allow for cover/back-up for absence or holidays
- Meetings – problem-solving or decision-making situations.

In these examples, a manager will need to actively consider the learning potential of the situation in advance and discuss this with the individuals concerned. For instance, delegating a task to an individual who has not done it before should have a clear development focus. The manager will need to ensure not only that they understand what needs to be done and how, but also that they are clear about why they have been delegated the task (its development objective). It also requires an understanding of the support mechanisms available to facilitate learning – who can help, and how they might do so.

Learning activity

Planning 'experience'

In your own situation, try and identify as many current or future events as you can that might present opportunities for development. How will you ensure that you can 'complete the cycle'?

Lastly, this approach to learning through normal working activity should be integrated with the development needs of both the individuals concerned and the organization. The manager should endeavour to link these objectives (however identified) with the opportunities that exist currently or in the near future within the organization. This can be tackled from two angles, either by taking a particular development need and asking how this can be met through work-based opportunities, or by anticipating an opportunity and asking which development needs does this address. Keeping open both these channels allows events in the workplace to influence and broaden the scope of development beyond the boundaries of formally identified training needs.

The problem of complexity

In order to reflect upon and review an 'experience' effectively, it is obviously necessary to be aware of the consequences and outcomes of that experience. One of the weaknesses of relying on learning from experience is that we can rarely be aware of all of the effects or consequences of our actions when we review. In simple cause and effect situations this may be possible – an archer, for example, can be given accurate information about the effects of his or her shot in terms of where the arrow landed. In the complex and dynamic systems of the workplace this is just not possible. We can never know the real effects because this information may be withheld from us, or the effects may be felt in another part of the organization or at some point in the distant future. We need to recognize that our reviewing and reflecting will always take place without this knowledge – that in complex situations the idea of a 'perfect solution', based on all the facts and with knowledge of all the effects, is a fantasy.

These are two practical ways of applying the learning cycle to continuous development in your organization. (You will also find that many training or development courses 'off the job' use this cycle, often using exercises or activities as the 'experience'.) Both focus on actual workplace experiences that staff and managers regard as real and relevant, and it is here that the value of making learning and development an integral part of your organization lies. As with many other facets of management, the potential benefits of learning for the organization can only be transformed into reality through the action of people. Basing development on work experiences reflects this approach and overcomes some of the difficulties people have in transferring 'training course' learning back to the workplace.

Formal learning

At the beginning of this section we suggested the need to break away from a reliance on the classroom and the teacher–pupil relationship that characterizes many training situations. Looking again at the learning cycle we can see how off-the-job training events can become a catalyst for workplace learning rather than a substitute for it.

Formal training events can be regarded as the 'experience' in this respect, and like any other experience they should be reviewed, with conclusions drawn and plans for action drawn up. Whereas the weakness of work-based learning can be that people get locked into the 'doing' phase, training events should provide ample opportunity to reflect, conceptualize and plan. They then often rely on individuals to continue the cycle back at work by putting their ideas and plans into practice – the next round of 'doing'. It is here that a climate that supports continuous learning and development provides opportunities for people to act on their plans and ideas formed at training events. If people are not given the opportunity and encouragement to put their plans into practice, or at least to experiment, then the value of off-the-job training can be lost.

A further and crucial reason for retaining formal training events is the need to introduce fresh perspectives into the working environment. When learning revolves solely around workplace experience there is a danger that the same ideas and ways of thinking take precedence. Ask yourself whether you can potentially learn more from someone with similar views, or from someone who is very different and will challenge your perspectives. There is real value to be gained from exposing people to new ideas, different perspectives, and to what is happening in other companies. Likewise it is often possible that tutors or consultants are able to challenge current practice and suggest alternatives in a way which is difficult for 'insiders' to do. They have an important role in reversing the focus of responsibility, so that learners control the pace and content of the learning, and the tutors become facilitators and challengers rather than 'instructors'.

Taking it further – double-loop learning

Argyris, C. (1990) *Overcoming Organizational Defences*, Prentice Hall, Englewood Cliffs, New Jersey.

This need to challenge the way we think about our experiences leads on to Chris Argyris's notion of 'double-loop learning'. (The 'double-loop' refers to a second 'learning cycle' attached to the one we have been using above.) This idea displays our original learning cycle in simpler terms by looking at how it is used at work to solve problems or to deal with mistakes or issues, as in Figure 11.3.

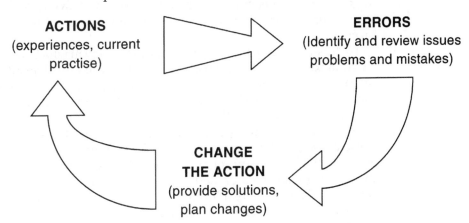

Fig. 11.3 Single-loop learning.

The value of this approach is that it produces solutions – it modifies the 'actions' or current practice in an effort to avoid repeating 'errors'. The difficulty is that in providing solutions, there is no incentive to look at why these problems or 'errors' existed in the first place. Argyris notes that this single-loop approach simply adds to current systems and seeks to achieve progress by doing 'the same things better'. He suggests the need to add a second loop to explore what he calls 'governing values', as in Figure 11.4 overleaf.

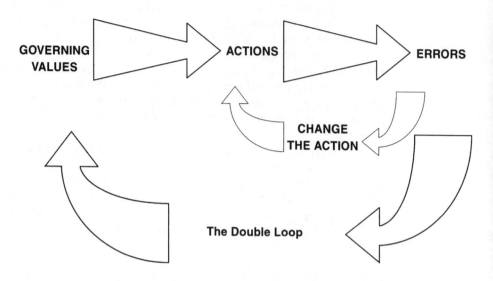

Fig. 11.4 Double-loop learning.

Looking at governing values means exploring the established ways we think and behave at work, and the values that lie behind our behaviour. This can be done by raising and questioning assumptions and perspectives, and challenging some of the defence mechanisms that prevent us from asking why we adhere to ways of working that are not effective and do not address the root cause of problems.

To illustrate this in practice think about the way in which many organizations try to tackle high rates of absenteeism (the problem). The attendance figures reveal the problem, and numerous solutions can be proposed and tested, ranging from increased control and tough discipline to supportive discussions with individuals about their particular circumstances. While some of these solutions may well 'work', the really important questions about the underlying cause of the problem have not been asked – there is no 'double loop'. To take this situation further, an organization might seek to explore what it is about their management style or their culture, for example, that produces the problem with attendance. The real 'double-loop' question then is: 'What is it that prevents us from addressing or even discussing these underlying issues?' Of course these are very difficult and threatening issues to raise for most people, but they are crucial to stepping beyond the superficial gains to be had from a single-loop approach to producing quick solutions. It requires a shared understanding of the value of exploring issues of this sort, a high level of trust and the interpersonal skills to handle them positively.

Team learning

While the learning cycle can be applied to individuals, groups and even organizations, there is great potential for teams to use the learning process collectively. In some respects there is the possibility for synergistic learning in a team – a situation where the members of a team learn more together than they could do working as individuals. To illustrate this we might rewrite the learning cycle in 'team' terms as in Figure 11.5.

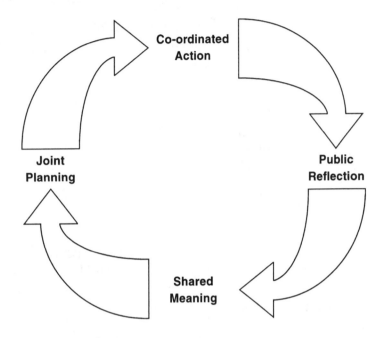

Fig. 11.5   Team learning cycle.

Developed by Spear, S. in Senge, P. (1994) *The Fifth Discipline Fieldbook*, Nicholas Brealey, London.

In this team model, public reflection implies more than simple reviewing, adding the need for discussion of team processes and the questioning of assumptions and approaches. The shared meaning stage provides an opportunity to clarify insights and refine vision, generating mutual understanding amongst the team. It is these two initial stages that often get skipped in the rush to plan and implement joint action. Conversely, it is possible for a team to get locked in the 'inactive' reflecting and discussing mode and fail to take advantage of the learning opportunities presented by actual experimentation. It is important therefore, that the team seeks to balance out these tendencies and move around the cycle.

About learning styles

Lastly, one of the useful things about the learning cycle is that it offers a framework for looking at different learning styles. That people learn in different ways is readily observable, not just in their response to different 'methods' such as reading, projects or training courses, but in the way they like to be involved in various work activities. This might show up as, for example, people who prefer to experiment and 'do', or those who prefer to think things through in detail. The different ways in which individuals prefer to learn can be described in terms of four 'learning styles' which originate from the learning cycle, as illustrated in Figure 11.6.

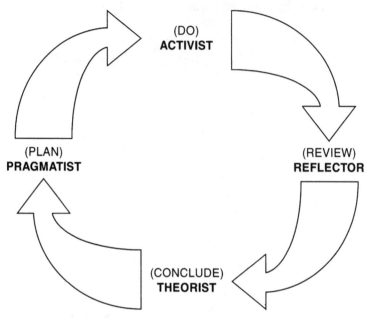

Fig. 11.6 Learning styles.

This model suggests that individuals have a preference to learn in one or more of the ways noted above, though each person has the capacity to learn through all four styles.

- **Activists** prefer to try things out and have a go, particularly in exciting environments. They learn best from experiences, and may have more difficulty in learning from reading or theoretical discussions. They are enthusiastic and reasonably open-minded, but may not always think before they act.

- **Reflectors** like to think things through before acting, and tend to act with more caution. They prefer to observe, analyse and evaluate data carefully. They may appear to be indecisive.

- **Theorists** prefer to put their observations into clear patterns and like models, principles and a rational approach. They may like to create conceptual frameworks that help them make sense of their experiences and are keen on understanding situations fully, including how and why things happened the way they did. They may have difficulty with emotional or hasty responses.

- **Pragmatists** are keen on trying out new ideas and experimenting, and like to apply new approaches in practical situations. While ideas and theories are of interest to pragmatists, they need the opportunity to test these out in practice. They may be sidetracked by 'flavour of the month' ideas.

Individuals will be able to learn in all of these modes to some degree, but this analysis can show a person's preference for a particular way of learning. This has important implications for learning in the workplace – in particular in supporting a manager's efforts to ensure that all parts of the learning cycle are covered. A knowledge of personal learning styles can help to redress an imbalance in a work group. For example, a team dominated by activists may benefit from focused reviewing and planning sessions, or one dominated by reflectors may be helped by setting deadlines for decisions and action.

Using change and challenge

All learning is about change – whether it be about changing behaviour, acquiring knowledge/skills, or even developing different attitudes and ways of thinking. It implies moving forward, approaching something new and perhaps unfamiliar, and with this change comes a whole range of feelings and reactions from boredom through to excitement, anxiety and even fear. For the manager looking to provide staff with opportunities for development this has important implications, particularly once learning is established as valuable in a team or organization. The activity below will help to illustrate this.

Learning activity

Learning situations

What effect might the following situations have on your own ability to learn, and how might you react to them?

- You have been sent on a training course and are lectured all day on subjects you are already familiar with – the food was good though!
- You have been set a seemingly impossible task, involving expertise you do not have, a short timescale and no obvious support.

Here, undemanding situations that induce boredom, cover old ground, are not perceived as 'relevant' or are just uninteresting will not facilitate learning and may have the effect of reducing commitment to development generally ('I can't be bothered with another course'). At best they simply fail to change or progress anything. At the other extreme, it is equally possible to push people into situations that are too demanding, where the only learning that takes place is learning how to avoid such situations in the future and where the stress levels prevent a positive approach to learning.

Clearly the manager will need to pursue opportunities that fall somewhere in between, avoiding both inertia and 'flight' so that learning can take place. Responses to these extremes are essentially emotional ones, and produce a situation in which the the tensions between them will need careful management.

There is a simple model that may be useful in illustrating this balance – one which you can use with your staff or colleagues when discussing development in general or specifically when looking at new tasks or delegation or are with new employees. It looks at three 'zones' in which an individual can operate: the comfort, risk and danger zones, which can be shown diagrammatically as in Figure 11.7.

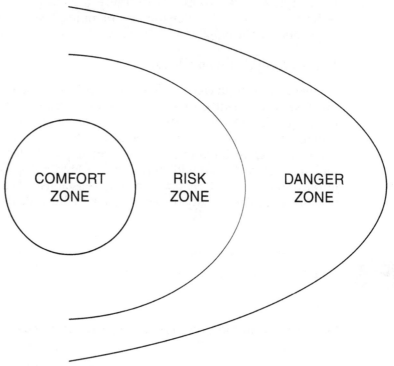

Fig. 11.7 Zones of operation.

This model can be used to explore reactions to learning situations in terms of responses to change and challenge. In looking at development, the zones can be interpreted as follows.

- **Comfort zone.** This is the area without change or challenge, where an individual is 'comfortable' with a familiar environment, work and relationships that remain relatively static. Though some learning will take place here it tends to be incremental. In a teamwork situation this might be described as 'better the devil you know' – an unwillingness to confront issues or to change the way you work together.

- **Risk zone.** This is the area where change is desired or imposed. Associated with some anxiety, challenge and often excitement, this zone provides opportunities to learn and grow, using change positively. Examples here might be the opportunities presented by embarking on a new job or project where the outcome is uncertain but the prospects exciting.

- **Danger zone.** This is where anxiety or fear becomes dominant, reducing the opportunity to learn. The desire to hurry back to the 'comfort zone' to avoid this level of stress is overriding. Often feelings of insecurity during restructuring exercises can produce a very understandable desire to return to 'the good old days' rather than a need to learn and adapt.

For the manager taking responsibility for creating development opportunities this simple model shows the need to think carefully about the type of challenges and changes created for each individual or the team. A good metaphor is learning to swim – at the shallow end, with water a few centimetres deep, there is no risk, and also no chance of learning to swim; being chucked in at the deep end, however, is very risky and may put people off swimming for life or at least give them a frightening experience. Somewhere in the middle of the pool is a 'zone' where risks can be taken and learning can occur, but always with the option of being able to put your feet on the bottom if you need to.

The 'zones' provide a useful tool to aid thinking about workplace learning in terms of moving the boundaries. The boundary between comfort and risk relates to an individual's perceptions of the situation, and will vary from one person to another. People will grow and develop when what they once perceived as being risky becomes routine and comfortable. Learning in the workplace then becomes a process of encouraging people to act in their risk zones so that these actions can be perceived over time to be comfortable. In other words the boundary has moved for the individual through experience and action.

This is of course a highly individual process, since what is dangerous for some may well be routine for others. In managing development at work it is irresponsible to simply push people into their risk zones without support, and arguably unethical to do so without their consent. In the next section we will look at the value of providing the support required to help people to operate in their 'risk' zone and learn.

Supporting learning

The swimming pool analogy can also be used to illustrate the need for support to enable learning to take place. Clearly the level and kind of support required will vary enormously depending upon the person and the situation. In the pool, some of us can get by with a little encouragement and a lot of experimentation resulting in gallons of water being swallowed. Others though may need to start in pretty shallow water, where hands and feet can touch the bottom or a friend can physically support them until enough skill and confidence is acquired.

We have already looked at the value of support in the chapters on teams, and at the need to negotiate the appropriate type and degree of support required. But how can learning be supported in the workplace and who can 'help' here?

Learning activity

Supporting learning

Consider your own working or learning situation and note down your ideas on the following:

- In what ways can your organization or colleagues provide support for your learning and development?
- Who else might help and support your staff or colleagues in their efforts to learn?

Perhaps the most critical thing supporting development is the creation of a climate that values highly people's efforts to learn and grow in every respect. It is important that the right signals are sent out about learning opportunities, demonstrating a positive commitment across the organization. There are a number of things a manager can do in this respect:

- Encourage staff to share their learning (i.e. from courses, projects, etc.) with each other, or the whole team if appropriate, and thank them for doing so.
- 'Model' this commitment by actively pursuing a broad range of learning opportunities yourself.
- Use in-house, in-work opportunities such as reviewing and discussion. Make 'What have we learned today?' part of every review and meeting. Don't relegate development to the odd 'course' outside the workplace.
- Encourage a positive view of the need for challenge and questioning, and respond positively to it yourself.

In terms of the people who might support learning, you might have included yourself, tutors, trainers and advisors of various kinds. These would traditionally have some kind of 'responsibility' for development in an organization, but in addition some of the most significant support can come from:

- Spouse/partners/family
- Friends
- Colleagues at work/peers/managers
- Clients and customers.

Support through friends, family and partners can help us to put workplace concerns into perspective, helping to achieve a balanced approach that does not allow commitment to the job to be at the expense of social or domestic life. These people may or may not have the technical experience to help, but can provide extremely valuable support in terms of working through anxieties, fears and issues of confidence on a very personal level. It is important to recognize that there are no clear boundaries between our work and home life in this respect. You carry with you from work to home and back again all the emotional responses you may feel about changes and risks.

Thinking back to the comfort/risk/danger model, support becomes the key to encouraging people to operate further into the risk zone, or indeed entering it at all. Their fear of failure, ridicule or punishment can be reduced through a supportive environment, freeing them to 'risk' and therefore learn. Again, creating the right climate at work will lead to colleagues 'naturally' providing support to each other without formal structures or systems.

Development in action

This section looks at some practical ways in which managers can facilitate learning in their workplace on a continuous basis, and provide support in line with their responsibility to encourage staff development. This covers reviewing, coaching and mentoring, and the value of networking in seeking opportunities to learn outside of the organization. Lastly, we have taken a brief look at the value of training events, and suggested ways in which you might get the best out of formal, off-the-job training situations.

Since the focus of this material is on management and not on specialist training and development roles, this section does not include detailed discussion of the vast range of techniques used in the running of more formal learning opportunities. There is a huge range of learning material on the management of training, including training needs analysis, design and delivery, 'up-front' dos and don'ts, and evaluation for those of you who wish to become more familiar with the training world.

Review and reflection

One of the recurring themes of this material has been the importance attached to the need for a manager to see reflection as an integral part of the management process – the purpose being to promote an understanding of the complexity of 'managing people', and above all to actively learn from their experience. In terms of personal learning, the need to reflect on your own behaviour and its effects on others needs to become second nature if you are to make the most of the experiences you have at work and elsewhere.

In terms of development, the purpose of reflection and reviewing is to add value to the experience and ensure that learning is explicit. Reviewing is an activity that encourages people to discuss, analyse and learn from recent experience. As a crucial element in the learning cycle, reviewing seeks to ensure that useful actions or behaviours are reinforced through praise and recognition, while unhelpful ones are identified and challenged with a view to doing things differently next time around.

Greenaway, R. (1993) *Playback: A Guide to Reviewing Activities*, The Duke of Edinburgh's Award, Scotland.

There are many different ways of approaching reviewing experience, but it is worth thinking through some of the skills that you will find useful and working towards a constructive way of handling the review itself.

Learning activity

Reviewing skills

In considering running reviews in your own situation, what skills can you bring to this process from other areas of management?

Useful skills such as those noted below can be transferred to the reviewing situation from many other management areas:

- Counselling
- Feedback and disclosure
- Questioning, discussion and dialogue
- Being positive and forward looking
- Handling conflict and differences
- Performance management or appraisal
- Chairing or coordinating.

Approaches to reviewing may vary greatly with the situation, subject and the people involved, but in seeking to use reviews for learning as well as improving performance, it would be worth considering some of the following suggestions or questions:

- Try to ensure that 'learning' is a clearly understood objective of review sessions – reviewing is a learning opportunity in itself

- Who is facilitating the review? Offer others the opportunity to learn from this

- Be clear about what the facilitator's role is, and agree this with the team/colleagues

- Think about the time available – think about the consequences of tackling an issue you can't end constructively

- Consider focusing on a small number of issues and moving these forward rather than creating demoralizingly long lists of things to be addressed

- Remember to review successes too – don't concentrate solely on 'areas for development' or what went wrong

- Don't restrict yourselves to reviewing actions – review processes, and challenge assumptions and perspectives as well

- Summarize learning points, as well as actions, at the end of the review.

Clearly a way of developing your own reviewing skills might be to allow time to reflect upon each review session you have taken part in, perhaps by considering some of the points listed above – in effect 'reviewing the review'. While this seems a little formal to start with, the aim is for reviewing to become a regular and 'natural' process, so that you will be able to take advantage of learning opportunities as and when they arise, without the need for it to be preplanned or formally organized.

Lastly, be aware that it is possible to learn the wrong things from experience. As Peter Cook once said: 'I have learned my lessons, I am certain I could repeat them again exactly!'

Coaching

Coaching staff should be an integral part of a manager's role in providing development opportunities 'on-the-job'. It is more than simple 'instruction', but includes helping a member of staff to maintain or improve their job performance through encouragement, guiding, reflection and experimentation.

Coaching is not about prescribing solutions or direct instruction, it is based firmly on the need to foster a learning approach, owned by the person receiving support. There are many situations at work that can be used as a focus for coaching, some beyond basic skills coaching, which might include everyday events, for example:

- Handling conflict situations
- Delegating
- Taking on new projects or responsibilities
- Rotating roles during meetings (e.g. 'chair' etc.)
- Problem-solving/decision-making
- Making presentations.

Of course coaching should not be confined to the manager–staff relationship, but can be encouraged between staff members as a way of sharing skills and information. This can be built into situations such as supporting new members of staff, or briefing the team after attending a training course.

Interestingly, regulations governing the selling of financial services covering the banking industry, for example, stress the need for managers of sellers to be competent in coaching and feedback skills as a method of ensuring quality and compliance with regulations.

Though there are formal 'models' that seek to structure the coaching experience, we believe that it is more valuable to adopt an approach to coaching based on helping others to learn from a wide range of workplace situations. It is important to take advantage of opportunities as they arise as well as those that can be agreed and planned in advance. Above all, to provide coaching effectively requires a supportive approach to helping others learn, and benefits from skilled listening, questioning, checking and giving feedback or promoting self-review.

One of the vital skills in this respect is the ability to use questioning instead of supplying information or solutions. This seeks to keep the ownership of the learning with the learner and reduce dependancy. Some generalized examples might help to clarify the difference here.

- Instead of telling a staff member how they should do a particular task, ask: 'What do you think is an effective way to handle this?', 'What are your options here?' or 'How would you like to approach this?' You could follow up with suggestions by asking 'Have you considered this option?' or better 'Here are some other ideas – could they be of use?'

- In place of stating your view of the likely effects of an action or decision on others at work, try asking: 'What do you think would be the effects of this on . . . ?' 'What might be the consequences of this for . . . ?' or 'How do you think . . . will react/feel about this?' In these examples you are encouraging the individual to think things through more widely, developing their ability to reflect on the outcomes of their decision or actions.

Adopting this 'coaching' approach can be used just as effectively with groups as it can with individuals, during meetings for example. It values every workplace experience as an opportunity to learn, and reinforces a supportive role for the managers. The coach's role here is primarily to encourage learning through discovery, by moving away from the traditional role of coach as teacher. It builds on the existing relationship between manager and staff, benefits from a mutual understanding of workplace roles and performance, and provides a real opportunity to develop positive approaches to giving and receiving feedback.

Mentoring

Though it usually includes a coaching role, mentoring is somewhat different in that it involves building a one-to-one relationship between a member of staff (or yourself) and a mentor. The mentor is often a more experienced person who has the time and commitment to provide an additional source of guidance and support concerning an individual's development.

The mentor needs ideally to have no direct involvement with the individual concerned (i.e. is not a 'line manager') so that they can provide:

- A different and 'uninvolved' viewpoint
- An opportunity to try out/share ideas or thoughts
- Someone to express concerns or share problems with
- Another role model
- Help with putting things in perspective.

Confidentiality and trust is a crucial aspect of this relationship as sometimes the mentor will be approached with issues that the individual is uncertain about dealing openly with in a team context or with their manager. It is important that the relationship is therefore established along agreed guidelines, outlining things like the type of help and support the mentor can or cannot give, what time is available, and the issue of confidentiality.

Mentoring is a useful addition to the array of development tools, but should not be seen as a substitute for continuous learning in the workplace. It may also be difficult to arrange within smaller organizations, though it may be possible to work with other similar organizations locally with managers mentoring individuals almost on an 'exchange' basis. Given the demands on time and skill that mentoring requires, it may be an option that you can consider for occasional use, or perhaps as a way of providing a focus for your own development. It may also be helpful for supporting individuals through longer formal development such as professional or managerial courses.

Mentoring is now an established management development tool for many organizations. Trafalgar House Construction and British Alcan, for example, use mentoring to support graduate entrants or those undertaking MBAs, while Brent Council uses mentoring to help women managers break 'the glass ceiling' barriers that deter women's progress to senior management posts.

Networking

Just as it is important to share learning within a group or team, there is every reason to cast the net wider than this and look for opportunities to learn by establishing and developing networks within and outside the organization. The purpose here is to tap into a rich source of information and experience that enables you and your colleagues to learn from others. It is worth actively searching out and sharing internally such information as:

- New ideas and thinking
- Schemes and initiatives that have been tested elsewhere
- Policies and systems that can be adapted
- 'Intelligence' about current trends in the field
- Training and development opportunities
- Resources/support/'sponsorship'
- Clues and perspectives on the future.

Using networks to collect this sort of information can assist in avoiding mistakes that others have made, though you will need to be aware that no two situations are the same – you might succeed where others have not. More importantly, this type of information may help to cut down on some of the work you need to do in terms of not having to 'reinvent the wheel'.

Lastly, bringing back information about your particular sector or business (e.g. what's going on, new developments and changes, how we are doing compared to other organizations) will help your team put their own work into context and develop a broader understanding of the 'industry' as a whole. In this respect there are opportunities here to explore the value of belonging to professional bodies or network organizations to develop contacts and keep 'up to date'.

Training events

The emphasis in this chapter has been firmly on grasping opportunities for learning from a wide variety of sources within your organization by establishing a 'learning culture' approach. The aim here has been to confront the often held view that training and development is all about off-the-job courses, an activity somehow separate from management. But training events do provide a valuable additional opportunity to further development in your organization, and this section looks at some of the benefits they can bring, together with some of the questions you will need to consider in evaluating opportunities for yourself and your staff.

The benefits

Though there are some very obvious benefits to taking advantage of off-the-job training events, it is worth being clear about what these are, particularly because such events provide a wider range of opportunities than might be at first be expected. Try the activity below.

Learning activity

Using training

Note down some of the benefits that using training events can bring to individuals and to an organization. Try to think beyond the evident ones of directly acquiring new skills and knowledge.

In addition to acquiring skills and developing understanding which can help to improve performance at work, there are other benefits and other ways in which attending a training course can be used to enhance development. Some of those you have listed might include an opportunity to:

- Network with people from other organizations
- Experiment and challenge in a 'safe' environment
- Share experiences with outsiders in similar or different fields
- Access the views and experience of specialist tutors/trainers
- Focus on learning away from operational distractions
- Have your views and practices challenged by others
- Learn about facilitating learning by observation of tutor/trainer
- To share information and ideas with colleagues upon return to work, and to learn about the process of doing so
- Put your situation into perspective through sharing experiences with others.

The emphasis here is on seeing training events as more than just sending staff away for the day to learn about a particular topic – it is an attempt to broaden the range of learning opportunities available to the organization. Being aware of these opportunities is one way of getting more from the training you engage in, but there are others that are worth exploring.

In particular, off-site management development events can be extremely valuable in providing an arena for the development of 'soft' management skills in a safe environment. In our work with managers in this situation, we find that being able to take risks and experiment with new behaviours or strategies without fear of the 'costs' that might arise from mistakes in the workplace greatly helps progress.

Getting the best from training events

Apart from the obvious investment in time and money made in using training events, it is crucial that staff are not exposed to poor quality or inappropriate training which may sabotage your efforts to raise the profile of learning in your organization. Focusing on open events that you or your staff are considering attending, two of the key things to think about are what to do prior to the event and how to follow it up afterwards in the workplace.

Perhaps the first thing you need to be clear about is what is on offer, and is it likely to be useful or stimulating. Though you can never guarantee this, of course, it is amazing how often people turn up to workshops not having any idea quite why they are there or what they want from the event. Here are some suggestions that might help to ensure that the training is appropriate.

- Check through the programme information – does it tell you enough about what is being covered? If not, then find out from the providers or the trainer concerned. Ask too about how basic/advanced the event might be.
- Find out about the style of delivery. It could be a 'lecture' or highly

participative/discussion based. Think about how this relates to preferred learning styles of potential delegates – is it appropriate?

- Give some thought to what you or your staff want from the event. What do you want to learn or explore? What do you already know in this area? Taking your own expectations along will enable good trainers to incorporate your needs into the agenda. You could always check this out beforehand, of course.

- Try to get a feel for the approach to be taken. Will the event try to model things like flexibility, welcoming questioning, promoting discussion, etc. Are the ideas presented up to date and challenging, or rehashed from old textbooks? Talk to the providers about their approach to both the subject and to learning.

- Don't confine people solely to topics that are listed on their training plans, nor restrict access to management courses, for example, to those with manager in their job title.

It is also worth giving some thought beforehand on how you might follow up the event back at the workplace. One of the criticisms of off-the-job training is the perceived difficulty of transferring learning back to the 'real' world of work; being clear about how you might support this transfer and apply the learning becomes very important in getting the best out of these development opportunities. We have suggested the following actions that you could take in supporting the training event.

- Provide learners with opportunities to reinforce their learning through taking on appropriate tasks or responsibilities.
- Try to identify specific actions that attendees can take to implement their learning.
- Encourage delegates to share their learning experience with colleagues upon return, either formally or informally.
- Support their efforts to apply learning through feedback and encouragement.
- Review their success in applying learning in the not too distant future.

What these points are illustrating is the importance of a manager's role in supporting development even when the actual training is delivered outside the organization. It is not sufficient to simply book staff onto a course and assume that their 'development' has taken place – work done before and after an event is crucial and probably as important as the event itself.

A last important point about training events takes us back to the issue of responsibility, not only for learning itself, but with applying it in the workplace. This is particularly noted in events which look at developing awareness or interpersonal skills, where a training event can raise and discuss issues, look at some theories or explanations to develop understanding, and suggest actions or approaches that may be useful. What they are unlikely to be able to do in a short space of time is to fundamentally change people's behaviour. The responsibility for transferring understanding into long-term changes in the way we behave back at work remains with the individual concerned and must be supported through actions taken in the workplace.

Barriers to development

While there are numerous opportunities to foster development in an organization, it is also worth being aware of some of the obstacles to learning that can hinder development at both a personal level and a team or organizational one. An awareness of these obstacles can assist in the planning and selection of appropriate development opportunities, and help you to understand what has happened if your efforts fall on stony ground.

Learning and the individual

There are two important aspects here – the different ways in which people prefer to learn, and their perception of current views about learning, development and training.

An individual's attitude to development, as well as their feelings, opinions and expectations, can provide major barriers to effective learning in the workplace. An oft-quoted example is their own experience of learning while at school (a positive or negative one), which may influence their level of commitment to development in general, or at least colour their view of certain training methods.

 ## Learning activity

Barriers to learning

Apart from experience of school, what other personal experiences, feelings or attitudes might present a barrier to learning?

People bring a whole history of contact with education and training with them that may affect their view of development, ranging from previous experience of training courses through to negative attitudes about self-improvement, or 'I'm too old or too thick to learn'. Some of the most common ones relate to people's understanding of the student–tutor relationship, one in which, traditionally, the responsibility for ensuring learning takes place has resided with the tutor/teacher. This is a passive model in which the student expects to somehow 'receive' knowledge and wisdom from the tutor – it is widely held and needs to be challenged if continuous learning is to flourish in the workplace. Linked to this narrow understanding of learning is the difficulty some people experience in adjusting to more interactive styles of training and development. Ideas such as exploration, discussion and challenge as learning vehicles can be unsettling for people who expect to be 'given' something directly in a training session. In many respects the view that focuses responsibility for learning on the trainer or teacher provides a 'comfortable' and disengaged situation for some learners. They will always have the trainer to blame if they do not learn or if their suggestions cause problems. This is a defence mechanism that protects individuals from exposing their thinking and actions to challenge or risk.

The manager will need to treat these attitudes sensitively on an individual basis, offering encouragement where appropriate, but ultimately an individual must retain the responsibility for their own development, and reserve the right to say no to opportunities if that is the way they feel. In this respect, individuals will need to decide 'how far they want to go', i.e. they may accept the need for skills training but decide not to approach personal development issues or get involved in exploring interpersonal relationships.

The different ways in which individuals prefer to learn is also significant – we have mentioned earlier in this chapter those that relate to the learning cycle, for example. There are many theories of learning to refer to here, but it is possible to make some general statements about learning that you can apply when considering development opportunities, based on the premise that people own and are responsible for their own development.

Learning is generally more effective when:

- People want to learn
- People are involved and participate, rather than behave as passive 'recipients'
- It is perceived as relevant and useful
- It can be seen to serve a purpose/meet an objective
- It involves challenge and discovery
- It uses and values the participant's experience
- It takes place within a context – people understand why and how it fits in
- When people understand and commit to the learning process
- When the organization provides a positive learning environment.

It is worth noting that many people may find difficulty at first with some of these ideas as they will have expectations about dependence and 'being taught' – the novice/expert relationship. Consider these statements in relation to your own situation in the activity below.

Learning activity

Learning conditions

- Look through the statements listed above. Are there any that you would challenge and why? What would you like to add to the list?
- Are these 'conditions' applicable to your own current development efforts?
- How might you use these statements in your creation of development opportunities for others?

Learning and organizations

The last statement on the list above refers to the organization providing a positive learning environment. It is crucial that the organization creates a climate where learning is valued, encouraged and supported, as it is an essential ingredient in improving performance and meeting objectives/realizing the 'vision'. This commitment to development should:

- **Be communicated.** There must be a clear understanding, communicated regularly to all staff, of the role and value of learning and development in, for example, the achievement of personal and organizational goals, or in responding to change.

- **Be demonstrated.** Stated views on the importance of learning and development will need to be backed up by actions. Learning opportunities cannot be seen to consistently take second place to operational issues – they must be integrated with day-to-day working.

- **Be modelled.** The manager will need to reinforce this message by showing their own commitment to personal learning, particularly by ensuring that every opportunity to learn from normal work situations is taken up enthusiastically.

- **Have broad boundaries.** Where possible try not to limit support for development to that which relates only to specific job skills. Broader learning opportunities are likely to have transferable elements that will be useful at work (e.g. interpersonal skills) and in any case it is worthwhile fostering the learning habit as this will spill over into development at work. If possible look for the opportunity to set objectives that benefit both the individual and the organization.

Organizations are already signalling their commitment to promoting learning in the workplace in this way. Unipart, the automotive parts suppliers for example, is one of a number of organizations that have opened their own 'university' on site. This development, which, incidently, trains managers to be trainers of their own staff, has led to an increase from two to ten days training per staff member per year, and sends a clear message to staff about the importance of training and learning.

Unlearning

There is a story of a university professor from Tokyo who visited a Zen master to attain wisdom. The Zen master invited him to a tea ceremony. He poured the professor a cup of tea until it overflowed onto the table. The Zen master continued to pour more tea until the professor stopped him. He explained that in order to have your cup filled, it needs first to be empty.

Of course this story is not strictly 'accurate', the human brain has an immense and largely untapped capacity, but its message is clear – that a significant barrier to learning for individuals and organizations are the things we already 'know', the way we currently do things. The suggestion here is that in order to facilitate learning something new or accept new approaches and ideas, we may have to 'unlearn' some old ones. Teaching old dogs new tricks is hard because old tricks have worked to some extent in the past – they are reliable, 'comfortable'. The question is are the old tricks as effective as they could be, and will they be useful in the future?

In practice we can't actively 'unlearn' something, but it is crucial to constantly challenge and question accepted ideas and concepts, and our current way of doing things. The challenge needs to go beyond 'what' we do and 'how' we do it, and ask. 'Why are we doing this? Is there another way? Do we want to do this? Does it add value to what we do?' It is this move to challenge our thinking and our actions at a more fundamental level, moving away from a restricted view of an issue or problem, that allows the possibility of radical change, innovation and creative responses to problems (it may of course confirm the value of current practice).

It is also valuable to constantly confront complacency in respect of learning and development. There is always something to learn that will add to your understanding of a subject, or different ways of approaching it. We would hope, for example, that you regard this book as just a small contribution to your understanding of management, and that you will not finish it and assume that you can 'tick off' management training on your personal training plan. There are a lot of ideas in this material that need challenging, and many more that are not here at all – learning is indeed a continuous process.

The learning organization

We have focused in this chapter on the importance of continual development and learning primarily in terms of realizing potential and growth for individuals within an organization, with its attendant benefits to the delivery of improving services to clients and customers. The above definition, though, suggests taking this one step further, transposing this approach onto the organization as a whole.

A learning organization has been described as an organization which facilitates the learning of all its members and thus continually transforms itself. The key word here is 'transforms', implying a process of continual and fundamental change, the idea of continual reinvention if you like. This may sound a bit dramatic, and even unrealistic in a practical world where change is often incremental and small scale. Nevertheless the idea of a learning organization recognizes the need to:

- Respond quickly in a rapidly changing environment
- Be adaptive and flexible in its operations, culture and structure
- Be proactive and innovative
- Experiment, question, explore and challenge
- Actively promote and support learning and development in all its forms.

This is basically applying an approach that could be applied to individuals to an organization as an entity. In practice this means encouraging every individual to adopt the learning strategies listed above, but in addition it incorporates these into an organization's culture and vision in an attempt to ensure that learning is not only desirable, but essential to its future and survival. If the idea of a learning organization helps to promote effectiveness and productivity in this way, it must be supported by a clear and overt message that time taken out for reflection, thinking and review is productive time and to be valued highly for the contribution it can make. It requires a cultural change where learning together moves up the list of priorities in terms of personal skills and effectiveness, and in terms of teams, project groups and whole organizations. This move can be facilitated not only by clear messages 'from the top', but by staff training in some of the techniques and concepts that will enable them to understand the learning process and harness its energy for continual growth and development. In a very real sense, there is potential for a learning culture to transform organizations and provide a working environment for individuals that is full of the opportunity for personal development.

Summary

This chapter set out to explore the importance of learning for both individuals and organizations. The emphasis throughout is on seeing learning as an integral part of workplace culture, rather than the objective of specialist provision off the job. It views the facilitation of learning as a key management skill – one that is becoming increasingly recognized as vital for the survival of organizations in an era of rapid change and increasing competitiveness.

We began with some underlying ideas concerning the 'ownership' of learning and the need to create diverse opportunities to learn on a continuous basis.

A great deal of emphasis is placed on learning from experience, looked at through discussion of the learning cycle and developments arising from it. We also explored the role of risk-taking and the need for support in developing a learning-focused approach to everyday management.

Rather than covering a range of standard 'training techniques', this chapter looks at some practical in-work skills such as coaching, mentoring and networking as valuable ways for the manager to encourage continuous development. We also discussed some of the key issues to pursue when arranging training away from the workplace to complement these efforts and ensure its effectiveness.

Lastly we have explored some of the real barriers to developing a positive approach to workplace learning, including the way in which traditional tutor–learner relationships can deny individuals the possibility of taking responsibility for their own learning.

Further reading

Peter Honey's *101 Ways to Develop Your People* presents an easy reference to the many ways in which managers can use day-to-day working situations as a platform for learning and development. None of the '101 ways' are more than a few pages long, making this a very accessible and practical book to dip into for ideas and reminders.

On a more inspirational note, perhaps one of the all-time classics about learning in organizations is Peter Senge's *The Fifth Discipline*. It is not necessarily an 'easy' read as it draws on diverse fields of interest and hinges on a 'systems thinking' approach to understanding organizations. The ideas and links presented here provide a powerful way to develop your thinking about learning in organizations. It goes into greater detail on a number of the issues raised in this chapter for those of you who wish to pursue this subject in more depth.

References

Garratt, B. (1994) *The Learning Organisation*, HarperCollins, London.

Garvin, D.A. (1993) Building a learning organization in *Harvard Business Review*, July–August.

Greenaway, R. (1993) *Playback: A Guide to Reviewing Activities*, The Duke of Edinburgh's Award, Scotland.

Harrison, R. (1988) *Training and Development*, Institute of Personnel Management.

Honey, P. (1994) *101 Ways to Develop your People*, P. Honey.

Mabey, C. and Iles, P. (1994) *Managing Learning*, Routledge, London.

Mumford, A. (1989) *Management Development*, Institute of Personnel Management.

Senge, P.M. (1990) *The Fifth Discipline*, Century Business, London.

Senge, P.M. (1994) *The Fifth Discipline Fieldbook*, Nicholas Brealey Publishing Ltd.

12

Change and opportunity

Change – Change – Who wants change? Things are bad enough as they are.
Attributed to Lord Salisbury speaking to Queen Victoria

Objectives

By the end of this chapter you will be able to:

➤ Describe the change process and the behaviours to be observed at each 'stage'
➤ Understand the effects of change as uniquely personal and often emotional
➤ Identify some common responses to change situations
➤ Describe ways in which you can effectively manage change in your own workplace

Introduction

It is very difficult not to be aware of the growing impact that change is having on the workplace and in the wider spheres of our personal lives and society as a whole. While change has been a continuous and natural process throughout history, the pace and frequency with which change challenges us, particularly in the workplace, appears to be growing rapidly. It is not easy to pinpoint exactly what is driving this complex process, but new technologies, the globalization of markets and communications and the restructuring of many organizations in search of competitiveness provide some contemporary examples.

Within organizations, managing change has become a major issue. The proliferation of books, courses and consultancy assignments around the subject of 'managing change' bear witness to the need for an understanding of the process of change and the tools to facilitate it. It is clear that the move from relatively stable working environments to one of almost continuous change requires a fundamentally different approach to managing and working together in the responsive, flexible and agile organizations of the future.

In this chapter we focus primarily on the need to understand the process of change as it affects individuals. It is not enough to see change as a simple process of planning and implementing new ways of working, new structures and improved processes. Individual responses to change vary enormously, and range from outright aggression and flight, through to excitement and high achievement. Crucially, change is a very personal process that invokes a highly individual and essentially emotional response in all of us. It is an understanding of the process of change that is vital in enabling the manager to recognize the behaviours it generates, and to support people through what can often be very difficult and confusing times.

More than this, looking at change from a personal perspective reinforces the work we have already done in the chapter on learning and development. To learn requires a change, whether it be acquiring new skills or knowledge, or adopting different approaches and behaviours. Many of the difficulties and opportunities presented by change situations reflect identical issues in the learning process – change and learning are in many ways the same thing.

It is an understanding and acceptance of the complexities of the change process that enables us to manage change more effectively. We can begin to see it as an opportunity to learn and grow, to understand each other more fully, and to move people and organizations forward. Cultivating a positive approach to change holds the promise of real learning and development becoming a focus of excitement and achievement for both the individual and the organization.

Change – a threat or an opportunity?

One of the crucial points about change is that it can be viewed as both threatening and liberating at one and the same time. Stating that all change is an opportunity glibly sidelines the real pressures it can bring to bear on organizations and individuals – the loss of job security, feelings of incompetence and helplessness, for example. Focusing solely on change as a threat, though, is also unhelpful. Change is at the heart of ideas about learning, development and growth – holding out the prospect of improving the way we work and live together. At an organizational level, too, the ability to change and adapt rapidly in a competitive and ever-changing environment has become a key survival mechanism.

Managing change becomes the ability to manage this tension between threat and opportunity effectively. The challenge is to tilt the balance more strongly in favour of the opportunities change brings and away from its disruptive and demoralizing effects. In shifting the balance in this way we must recognize that it is rarely possible to remove the 'threat' implied by change completely.

An example of this might be where you have just got an exciting new job with a progressive organization, where the opportunities for learning and adventure in a supportive environment abound. Even here, though the opportunities are clear and attractive, the change involved presents you with a source of anxiety. 'Will I meet their expectations?' and 'How will I get on with my new colleagues' are just some of the many questions such an opportunity raises.

At the other extreme, major restructuring exercises, with redundancies, greater workloads and changing job roles, vividly illustrate the threats posed to individuals by change. In this situation there is also opportunity, though it may be hard to see at first. Job loss can sometimes mean new beginnings, new careers or interests, while those remaining may have enhanced opportunities to develop new skills or move to new positions.

Change then is a complex process both to understand and to manage. There are no effective 'easy solutions' and no simple 'right ways' to manage change. Figure 12.1 shows change as producing both threats and opportunities. In seeking to shift the balance towards change as a positive process, a range of strategies are suggested, some of which will be discussed later in this chapter.

The **change** referred to above can result from, for example, strategic decisions about an organization, new technologies, culture change programmes, new products, services or working methods, and changes in legislation. On a more personal level change can also mean working with new people, new roles or tasks, and of course a wide range of events that happen outside of work in our domestic and social lives.

The **threat** in this model may be both actual and perceived, and looks at responses individuals display towards significant change. Change provokes fears and concerns about what will happen to familiar ways of working and current relationships that are compounded by the ineffective management of the change situation. The reactions this situation generates, such as defensiveness and resistance, become issues that those managing the change process must work through. These reactions are present in any change situation and cannot be avoided entirely.

The **strategies** listed in Figure 12.1 provide some examples of the way effective change management can reduce the 'threat' of change and help to focus people on the opportunity that change presents. The latter part of this chapter looks in more detail at some of these strategies, particularly those that relate to the understanding of the change process, and the management of some common responses to the threats posed by change.

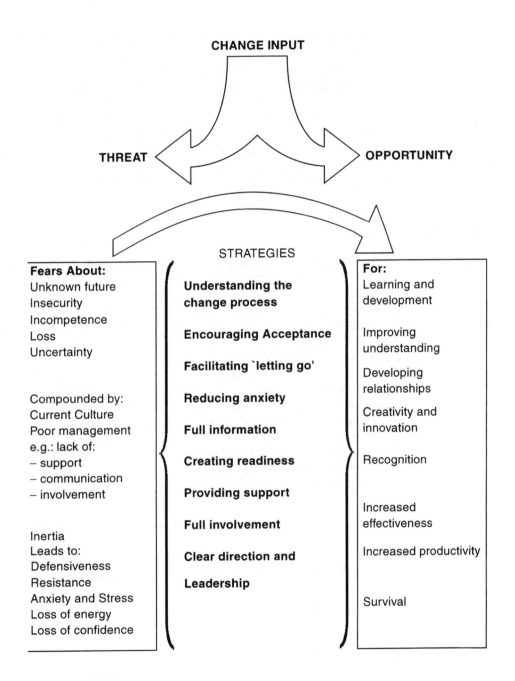

CHANGE INPUT

THREAT **OPPORTUNITY**

STRATEGIES

Fears About:
Unknown future
Insecurity
Incompetence
Loss
Uncertainty

Compounded by:
Current Culture
Poor management
e.g.: lack of:
– support
– communication
– involvement

Inertia
Leads to:
Defensiveness
Resistance
Anxiety and Stress
Loss of energy
Loss of confidence

**Understanding the
change process**

Encouraging Acceptance

Facilitating `letting go'

Reducing anxiety

Full information

Creating readiness

Providing support

Full involvement

Clear direction and

Leadership

For:
Learning and
development

Improving
understanding

Developing
relationships

Creativity and
innovation

Recognition

Increased
effectiveness

Increased productivity

Survival

Fig. 12.1 Threats AND opportunities.

Lastly, the **opportunity** column on the right side of Figure 12.1 suggests a selection of positive ways to view change. These acknowledge that there is a need to embrace change in order that both individuals and organizations can survive, as well as grow and develop.

The key to finding effective ways to manage change, and experimenting with some of the strategies we have listed, lies in an understanding of the change process and the responses it induces in individuals. If a manager is unaware of the effects change has on people, he or she is unlikely to be able to deal sensitively with their responses or to find productive ways of helping people to see the opportunities it provides. The first half of this chapter seeks to explore the change process and to develop an understanding of some of the responses people will inevitably make to the threats posed by significant change. We then go on to look at some of the strategies that can be used to help managers shift the balance in favour of a constructive view of change.

The change process

An understanding of the process of change – the way in which people react to and move through it – provides us with the basis for exploring the management of change situations at work. Though there are many change process models, we have chosen to use a simple one called 'the change apartment', which helps us to recognize our own reactions to change, and those of others, in the form of a journey through the 'rooms' of an imaginary apartment, shown diagrammatically in Figure 12.2.

Weisbord, M. (1987) *Productive Workplaces*, Jossey-Bass, San Francisco.

In this 'apartment', a static, unchanging situation is represented by the contentment room. Any significant change will see people set off on a journey through the rooms, starting with denial, then confusion and renewal, finally returning to the contentment room. As change becomes a common, if not continuous, feature of work in many organizations, people 'rotate around the rooms' – it becomes a cycle. To build up a picture of this cycle, let's look at each of the rooms in turn, firstly giving a general description, and then discussing the sort of **behaviours** you are likely to observe at each stage, and the

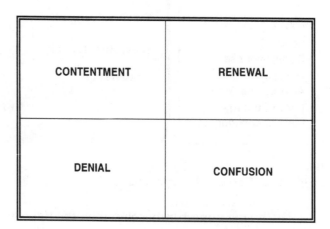

CONTENTMENT	RENEWAL
DENIAL	CONFUSION

Fig. 12.2 The change apartment.

approaches that are helpful in supporting staff in their efforts to **move on** through the rooms.

The contentment room

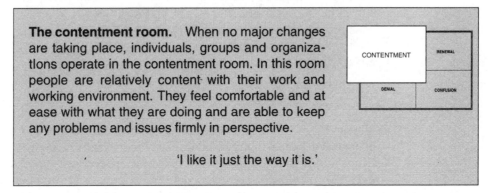

The contentment room. When no major changes are taking place, individuals, groups and organizations operate in the contentment room. In this room people are relatively content with their work and working environment. They feel comfortable and at ease with what they are doing and are able to keep any problems and issues firmly in perspective.

'I like it just the way it is.'

This room provides people with a period of stability and consolidation, where any previous changes have been accepted and incorporated into a normal work routine. The atmosphere here is often one of security and confidence, and there is a clear parallel here with the 'comfort zone' mentioned in the previous chapter on learning. The full range of 'normal' behaviours will continue to be shown in this room, but of particular interest may be signs of boredom or apathy from individuals who thrive in a changing environment.

Moving on

It is tempting to assume that people should be left to reside here as long as possible. Certainly the anxiety and stress of major changes is not something to inflict on people for the sake of it – most people do not subscribe to the 'if it ain't broke, break it' school of thought. But this stage still requires active management for a number of reasons. Firstly, it provides an opportunity to prepare people for change by developing relationships, processes and support mechanisms that will be invaluable when the next major change comes along. It is also useful to share at this stage an understanding of the change process, and the opportunity change presents for learning and development. Developing an awareness of the changing nature of work and exploring current trends in your business sector can help people to accept the necessity for change more readily too.

The contentment phase also presents the opportunity to develop and initiate change yourselves, thus promoting change that is understood and which carries commitment. This further helps to combat complacency, and meet the needs of those who find that change and challenge are essential to their working lives.

Any significant change, particularly that perceived as a threat such as a change of job or a reorganization, is likely to send people into the denial room.

The denial room

The denial room.   In this room the change required is not ackowledged or accepted – people 'deny' that anything is happening and carry on 'business as usual'. They are effectively pretending that nothing has changed, and in doing so free themselves from the need to do anything about it.

'I'm too busy to worry about it.'

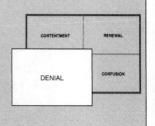

In the denial room, people will have been informed of the change required but will not have 'heard' or accepted it. They are basically refusing to deal with their feelings about something new by resisting or ignoring for as long as possible the changes proposed. Commonly observed behaviours at this stage can include a renewed enthusiasm for the past (the good old days stories), failure to get involved in any planning for the future, being too busy 'getting the job done' to discuss change, or putting down any changes or initiatives as simply passing fads. On the surface this may appear as 'business as usual' as their anger and fear about the change are not yet being expressed.

The length of time an individual will spend in this room can vary greatly from a few seconds for minor incidents – 'I don't believe it . . . Oh well then' – to many years in the case of dramatic personal changes such as bereavement. In fact seeing change as a loss of some kind is a useful way to understand the effects it has on people, and we shall be looking at this aspect later in this chapter.

Before looking at the actions a manager can take to help people move out of the denial room it is worth stressing a number of points. Firstly, denial is a natural and emotional response to the threat posed by change – it is not irrational or stupid. It hardly needs saying that labelling people as dinosaurs or ostriches is not a helpful strategy here. Change directly challenges the way things are at the moment and seeks to replace this with an unknown and perhaps challenging future. It can invoke a wide range of fears and anxieties that many people will find hard to express, or even to acknowledge to themselves. There can be real fears about the confusion and upheaval caused by change; in particular it can threaten an individual's sense of identity and security which are innately bound up with their current view of themselves and their work.

Moving on

To move out of the denial room people need to be able to express their anxieties and fears about the change in question, to 'let go' of the comfort of the past and the familiar. People need support at this stage, not advice. It is useful to encourage individuals to express their feelings no matter how negative, and to reassure them that these feelings are a normal reaction to the change situation. Attempts to 'force' people through denial will be met with resistance and at best a superficial form of compliance. It is worth remembering that people may fear not only the change itself but also the next stage of the process, the confusion room.

The confusion room

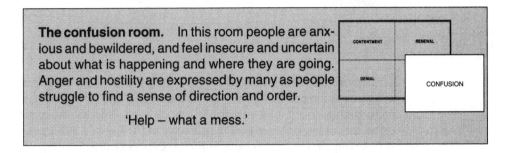

The confusion room.   In this room people are anxious and bewildered, and feel insecure and uncertain about what is happening and where they are going. Anger and hostility are expressed by many as people struggle to find a sense of direction and order.

'Help – what a mess.'

CONTENTMENT | RENEWAL
DENIAL | CONFUSION

The anxieties inherent in the confusion room can show up in many ways. Often a great deal of anger is expressed towards those introducing or making difficult decisions about the change. There can also be a rise in conflict between members of a team as people struggle to preserve status or territory and protect their position and relationships. This defensive behaviour is a natural response to confusion and chaos – after all, we have been brought up in a world that values order and certainty. Passing through this confusion room, however, is a necessary and useful step, for it is here that the energy and drive can be found for creating something new.

Moving on

The critical factor in moving people through the confusion room is to generate an understanding of the key role confusion has in the change process. It is vital to get across the need to accept confusion, not only as 'normal', but as a positive contribution to change. People will need to be reassured that such confusion is inevitable and healthy. They should continue to be encouraged to express concerns and feelings through discussion and sharing. Gaining acceptance requires a great deal of support, backed up by the full disclosure of all current information about the changes to come. Failure to keep people fully informed will add to fears that 'something' is being planned behind their backs – that the full horror of the change is being kept from them. Only open disclosure can help to combat this mistrust. Again, people need time and space to accept and understand this situation. Offering advice and solutions too early in the change process can add to people's fears and send them back into denial.

With sufficient time and support, people begin to accept the change and to focus on the opportunity to move forward to the renewal room.

The renewal room

The renewal room. A room full of energy and excitement about the future. People rush around making plans and generating lots of ideas, and may need help with implementation and clarifying direction.

'We've got too many ideas – where are we going?'

CONTENTMENT	RENEWAL
DENIAL	CONFUSION

This is the exciting phase where plans are made and implemented and real progress is possible. People will need help here with a variety of processes including decision-making, planning and agreeing a new sense of direction. It is the part of the process where motivation for the new is high and this will need supporting. In particular people will be experimenting with new ideas and ways of working, and it is likely that some of these experiments will not be successful. It is very important that early attempts to move forward are not reversed through adverse reactions or blame which would send people back to the confusion room. A positive view of mistakes as learning opportunities can be invaluable in this respect. The renewal room provides a good opportunity for development events, particularly teambuilding and looking at process and awareness issues.

Gradually, what is new and exciting becomes accepted as routine and people enter the contentment room again – the cycle is complete.

The change apartment – key lessons

Summarizing the understanding to be gained from the change model, we can say that:

- Change invokes responses that are primarily personal and emotive
- These responses vary widely from one individual to the next
- Personal and emotional responses are natural and to be expected
- It is not effective to try to 'force' people to change. You need to provide a climate that facilitates change by promoting understanding of the process and providing support and information.
- People change and 'let go' in their own time and at their own pace.

The apartment model presents a useful overview to enable managers and staff understand what happens to them during a period of change. We need to look now in more detail at the sort of responses people make when confronted with change. Clearly these responses vary enormously from one person to the next, but nevertheless behaviours such as defensiveness and resisting change are familiar enough features of workplace change to warrant greater understanding.

Learning activity

Reaction to major change

In your own work or social lives, consider a time of major change. This might be a change in your job, a reorganization, or a new process or system being introduced, for example. Think about how people, including yourself, reacted to this change, and record your observations in terms of what happened in:

- The denial 'room'
- The confusion 'room'
- The renewal 'room'

Personal responses to significant change

We have looked at the process of change in general terms using the change apartment model. This included exploring some of the behaviours associated with each stage of the process and the ways in which a manager can support people along the way. In this section we set out to develop further understanding of some of the responses a manager is likely to encounter from individuals and groups when faced with major change. We discuss the value of seeing change as a 'loss', the idea of resistance to change, and explore the notion of 'self-concept' as a way of understanding the anxieties created by change.

Changes as a loss

Perhaps one of the most accessible ways for a manager to understand the impact of change on individuals is to see all change as involving some kind of loss. It is an approach we can usually identify with from our personal and working lives. The change process in this respect has many parallels with that of bereavement – change triggers an emotional response resembling grief, though generally the effects are far less traumatic. Some examples serve to illustrate the scope of this idea.

On a small scale, a change involving a colleague moving away to another job can be regarded as a loss. What is 'lost' here for remaining staff members is the relationship with the colleague, with all the friendship, support and networks this may provide. There may be a further loss to the group or team in terms of the skills and knowledge they take with them, and perhaps their useful role in some of the group's processes.

On a larger scale, let's look at the 'loss' involved in a major restructuring exercise – a common scenario and one which usually has an enormous effect on people. For this example we can imagine that the organization's restructuring efforts are introduced 'from the top', and that it involves redundancies and a major reorganization of work teams and job roles. Think through the effects of this change in the activity below.

Learning activity

Losses through change

Think through the situation described above. The effects of such a major change can be dramatic, but what is it that those people who still have a job might feel they have 'lost' in this situation?

Scott, C.D. and Jaffe, D.T. (1989) *Managing Organisational Change*, Kogan Page, London.

There are many types of 'loss' in such a scenario. In general terms we can categorize these as the loss of:

- **Security.** People will experience a loss in security, particularly if there has been redundancy – people will wonder 'who's next?' Overlaying this is a wider concern about the future based on uncertainty and confusion. There may also be a loss of control, a feeling of powerlessness, and a view that an individual's contribution to the organization may no longer be valued.

- **Relationships.** This includes the loss of relationships with colleagues, but also links with others in the organization, managers and customers. The loss of these relationships is significant enough in itself, but added to this is the sense of belonging, identity and purpose that comes with working in established groups or a stable organization.

- **Direction.** With major change people loose a clear sense of direction. They may not be sure about where the organization is going or what it is trying to achieve. They may not understand why the change has taken place and find it difficult to create new meaning for their work. This loss of direction and purpose has major effects on commitment and productivity. The links here with leadership are important.

- **Territory.** People may lose or feel uncertain about work areas that have traditionally been perceived as 'theirs'. This can be both a range of tasks and job roles, and also the physical workspace they regard as a sort of 'home'.

- **Competence.** Following a major change staff may feel unable to cope competently with new responsibilities and demands. In particular managers left to deal with the consequences of the change may find their self-image as a competent manager under attack from a barrage of new requirements and the confusion and disruption caused by change. This may also include deskilling resulting from new technologies or centralization of decision-making functions, for example.

Again the 'loss' here is essentially a personal one. Understanding change as involving a loss is important, as it is all too easy for managers to misjudge the intensity of the loss and its impact on individuals. This is especially likely as the manager will also be experiencing loss of some kind, and has therefore to deal with his or her own feelings about change as well as seek to manage and support other people. It is valuable to recognize that the effect of major change in an organization also destroys part of the informal network of communications, with a resultant loss of information about the culture, shared stories and understanding of where to go for help and expertise.

King, N. and Anderson, N. (1995) *Innovation and Change in Organisations*, Routledge, London.

Managing this situation involves the approaches discussed for helping people in the denial and confusion rooms of the change apartment, particularly the expression of feelings and concerns. It may be useful to encourage this expression by indulging in some form of ritual goodbye ceremony, such as a party to wish those leaving well, or the disposal of something symbolic about the past – old paperwork or machinery for example. Such a celebration gives people a chance to tell stories and share memories about the past – a ritual that provides for a release and expression of feelings that is essential in coming to terms with a loss of any kind.

A failure to take into account the 'loss' that change brings, with all its emotional responses, can lead to a manager spending time trying to push change through by concentrating on the new tasks to be done, and by exhorting staff to 'get their act together'. Such an approach is likely to meet with resistance and defensiveness if people have not been given the time and support to work through the change at a personal level. The next section looks at the nature of resistance, not in terms of 'overcoming' it, but by way of raising awareness of the reasons for resistance and the way in which it manifests itself.

Resistance to change

Resistance to change is commonly recognized as a major barrier to introducing change in a team or organization. Yet seeing resistance purely as an obstacle often leads to discussions about ways of 'overcoming' or bypassing the 'problem of resistance' that can miss the opportunity to understand where it comes from and why people 'resist'. An understanding of these aspects of resistance encourages the manager to adopt more effective approaches to managing change based on gaining commitment to the change rather than forcing people to comply with it.

So why do people resist change? Though individual responses will vary greatly, there are three main concerns that lead people to resist change.

- Change is **'the unknown'**. It is virtually inevitable that change will be resisted in some way simply because it represents the 'unknown' and is therefore perceived as being threatening. All of us are to some extent creatures of habit, needing some structures and certainty to give order to our lives. Change can be seen as challenging these routines and invites us to defend them – in other words to resist the change. The fear of change, of the unknown, is the anxiety of entering the 'risk' or 'danger' zones described in the chapter on learning.

- Change **challenges the status quo**. Whatever our position in an organization, we usually have some vested interests in maintaining things as they are. Change threatens to disrupt this comfortable situation and may result in people 'losing out' – the 'loss' we discussed above. For example, in an organization that plans to restructure itself, people may fear the loss of control and authority, resources may be cut, or they may be moved around and lose their social relationships. Where current conditions are far from ideal, the 'better the devil you know' viewpoint may prevail over the risk of ending up with something worse.

- Change **means extra work**. Change necessitates learning something new, whether it involves new systems, technologies or behaviours. This learning means an investment of time and energy while people 'get up to speed'. On a more practical level, change can often mean that workloads are 'redistributed', which usually means more work for each person. The perception that additional and unfamiliar work will lead to overload and stress provides a very rational justification for resistance to change.

These reasons for resisting change need to be accepted as justifiable, both as emotional responses and often as rational ones in specific situations. It is important to see that resistance can provide a constructive balancing mechanism in countering poorly devised plans and ill-conceived changes, sometimes proposed by those who are unaware of the effects of the change or about how to manage change situations humanely. In these situations resistance becomes an ally rather than an enemy – fighting the destructive consequences of unjustified changes.

Some forms of resistance are easily recognized, particularly if it involves industrial action of some type, work-to-rule or non-cooperation being examples of this. Generally, though, resistance manifests itself in more covert ways. Try to identify some of these in the activity below.

 Learning activity

Resistance to change

In your own work or personal situation, think about what happens when major changes occur. Try to identify some of the ways in which people resist change – how does resistance show itself?

We have already mentioned overt forms of resistance such as industrial action, but perhaps the following are both more common and less easy to identify as forms of resistance:

- A decrease in commitment and energy levels
- A rise in expressions of anger, hostility, frustration and verbal abuse
- Reverting to a blame culture, 'setting people up' for failure
- Increase in lateness, absenteeism, errors and accidents
- Acts of sabotage – ensuring new initiatives fail
- Withdrawal and non-cooperation, lost messages, non-attendance at meetings
- Spillover conflicts to and from other issues and people
- Reinforcement of group identity and conformist behaviours
- Development of informal groupings and networks to engage in resistance:

Of course resistance to change may not be the only reason behind the actions listed above as change will always be happening alongside many other complex issues and processes. But being aware that resistance can take many forms can help the manager to gauge reactions to proposals and developments, and to alert him or her to the need to take action in supporting people through the change process. In terms of the apartment model, resistance is commonly found in the denial room (i.e. withdrawal and sabotage) and confusion room (i.e. anger, conflict and blame).

The purpose of looking at resistance is to gain an awareness of the behaviours that this inevitably generates in times of change. In the second half of this chapter we will be looking at some of the things a manager can do to promote a positive approach to change and reduce the destructive effects of resistance.

The art of self-defence

When challenged by change, or perhaps the need to do things differently, one of the most common reactions is for people to become 'defensive'. Defensiveness lies at the heart of responses to change and provides us with a tool to appreciate why change can be so painful or difficult for some people. To understand defensiveness, we need firstly to look at the idea of 'self-concept', and why this is so crucial to managing change.

Self-concept refers to the collection of ideas we have about ourselves that have been built up from many years of experiences and interactions with others. It is essentially the image we have of ourselves that holds us together, and provides us with a sense of identity and confidence about who we are. It serves us with a view of ourselves as we act out various roles, be it parent, friend or a work role such as a manager.

In a workplace situation there will be some aspects of this self-concept that are easily shared with colleagues, things like 'I like to work on my own' or 'I'm not too good at figure work, can I have some help?' There are many other areas, though, that we do not share readily with others. These include very personal views and feelings such as insecurities, fears, desires, a lack of confidence or hopes for the future. An important part of this self-concept is made up of our sense of identity, of who we are. In a workplace situation this is structured around a whole range of ideas we have about our status and worth, our skills and confidence, and in the relationships we have established with those we work with.

As part of a work 'community', we accommodate ourselves to current circumstances, norms and routines. What we do and how we behave at work becomes vital in maintaining our self-concept. When change is proposed or enforced, new ways of working, new relationships or new technologies challenge more than just current practice, they challenge our own self-concept. Change therefore threatens not simply what we do at work, but can often be perceived as a threat to the very idea of 'ourselves.'

People react to this threat by resisting, and by **defending themselves** – by seeking to protect the self-concept. Clearly there are some aspects of our self-concept that are defended more vigorously than others. Figure 12.3 illustrates the 'safe' subjects that we are willing to share openly with others, even strangers. Though these subjects may have an important role to play in

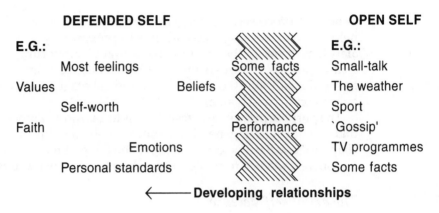

Fig. 12.3 The defended-self.

our social relationships, we are not likely to defend our ideas here too seriously. The areas to the left in the diagram are much more central to our ideas about ourselves. Change that threatens these areas is likely to provoke a person's defences.

The crucial point about this idea is that to help people through the change process it is important not to induce a defensive reaction from others if at all possible, as they will concentrate their efforts in defending themselves rather than learning or moving on. Telling people to change, or pleading with them to 'see sense', will generally provoke defensiveness, whereas encouraging expression of feelings in a non-judgmental way and fostering open discussion is less likely to do so. It also emphasizes the value in spending time developing positive working relationships with staff. These enable you to more easily access some of the difficult areas, like those on the left of the diagram, which are essential to the change process and require trust to disclose.

Listed below are some common defence strategies that will no doubt be familiar, and which provide practical examples of defensiveness and resistance to change. When 'threatened', people understandably sometimes respond by:

- Blaming others or circumstances 'beyond our control'
- Rejecting the threat – arguing, denying
- Running away – withdrawal, avoidance, non-attendance
- Lying or covering up
- Looking hurt or devastated, crying
- Overreacting – going to opposite extreme
- Acknowledging the threat then quickly changing the subject.

These defense mechanisms work because they succeed in keeping interactions superficial. In doing so they support people in both denial and confusion by preventing expression of feelings and anxieties that are viewed as threatening to share with others. It is important to understand that such defenses are an essential part of our make-up, and as valuable and instinctive to us as raising an arm to protect us from a blow.

In managing change in the workplace, you will need to be aware of this defence system and be able to recognize its value in protecting people from threat. Remember that the fact that the change is planned or in progress also implies that the way things are currently being done is to some extent 'not good enough'. It implies, basically, a criticism of established ways of working that are important for our self-concept.

To promote change it will be necessary to try to get around these defences by developing relationships, providing time and support, and giving feedback and information about the change situation. Provoking defensiveness does not help others to change, and may reinforce their efforts to deny and resist.

The lesson from this section is to use your understanding of defensiveness, resistance and loss to think through effective ways of approaching and supporting others through the change process. Not applying an awareness of these very natural responses to the way change is managed will inevitably damage relationships and possibly prolong both denial and confusion. It helps us to understand why change management that focuses solely on planning, coordination and task allocation, while ignoring the human side of the change process, can run into 'unexpected' difficulties and barriers.

Having explored some of the complex reactions change produces, particularly those that come from perceptions of threat, we need to move on to think about ways in which this understanding can be used to manage change situations more effectively. The next section explores some of the strategies you might consider adopting in order to approach change positively – building up the real chance to see the opportunities present in all change events

Strategies for supporting change

Managing any major change demands a broad range of strategies rather than applying a simple step-by-step linear approach. Change situations are, as we have seen, inevitably complex in nature, particularly where people's emotional reactions are concerned. Crucially, ways of supporting change cannot be divorced from management issues such as style of leadership and attitudes to empowerment and learning, among others.

In this section we look in more detail at some of the approaches to managing change that you might consider adopting in promoting a positive view of the opportunities change presents.

Reducing anxiety

It is simply not possible to remove all anxiety from the change process. We have looked at the roots of this anxiety or fear from a personal perspective, and tried to convey the importance of the emotional responses that change invokes. While recognizing this as a key point in understanding change, the actions of managers and others impacts significantly on the level of anxiety that people experience. In other words, our awareness of the effects of change provides the opportunity to act to reduce anxiety, and in doing so to productively support the change process.

A simple example of taking action to reduce anxiety comes from the need to provide information about planned changes. As we have seen, one cause of anxiety is the fear of the unknown: What will happen to me? What will 'work' look like in the future? Withholding information about planned changes on the grounds of 'protecting people,' or because the details are 'not fully worked out yet,' only serves to increase worry amongst those desperate for an idea of what will happen to them. Worse than this, if information is not forthcoming, the grapevine and rumour will inevitably fill this information gap with exaggerated horror stories which simply increase anxiety and make the whole business of change more painful. Managerial action, in the form of full and honest disclosure of information at all stages, gives individuals the opportunity to begin working through the change process towards acceptance, and to become involved in shaping their own future.

From what we have discussed about people's reaction to change and the anxiety change can generate, there is a great deal that managers can do to reduce the pressure on people at times of major change. Think through some options in the activity below.

Learning activity

Reducing anxiety

Think about your own or other's experience of major change. In what ways could those managing the change process have helped to reduce anxiety?

As a manager, you can help to reduce anxiety by providing:

- **Information.** Full disclosure of information about change is required, including:
  (a) why – the reasons for the change;
  (b) how – the change will affect people and the organization;
  (c) when – the change will take place.

- **Support.** Understand and accept people's reactions to change in order to provide support through listening, raising awareness of the change process, and reassurance that their personal reactions are 'normal.' Provide an environment that helps people through denial and confusion. At a later stage, support may involve helping to set direction, make decisions and plans and encourage experimentation.

- **Time and space.** Give people the opportunity to come to terms with the change. Allow time for expression of feelings and concerns, and space for exchange of information and discussion.

- **Learning and development opportunities.** Give people the possibility of learning new skills or ways of working together to help build competence and confidence. It also demonstrates the organization's commitment to the individual and to their future.

- **Opportunity for involvement.** Finding ways in which people can partici-pate and even drive the change process reduces anxiety by developing commitment and ownership. It also helps to combat the loss of control that many people experience during the change process.

Anxiety generated by change also promotes the tendency among many people to work harder, often using existing methods and processes. One of the import-ant lessons about change is that moving toward new ways of working may require a real change in approach from both staff and managers. Working harder and faster using established methods has obvious limits and very human costs. As change becomes a continuous feature of the working environment, pressure can be reduced by refocusing on flexible and innovative approaches, encouraging shared learning and ensuring that goals are established which are both short-term and achievable. Efforts to reduce anxiety may benefit from:

Moving away from:	'Solve the problem'
	'Give it to an expert'
	'Set up a task force'
	'Find the right technique'
	'Do it all now'
Towards:	'Do what's do-able at the moment'
	'Involve everybody'
	'Help each other learn'
	'Create the future together'.

The emphasis here is to develop new approaches to working together that adopt a more realistic and hopeful response to the demands of change rather than to simply do 'more of the same'.

Providing leadership

Leadership provides the opportunity to support the management of change in two key areas. Firstly, in the discussion of change as a loss, we noted that loss of a sense of direction and purpose can be a significant feature in change situations. This is the feeling expressed as 'I don't know where we're going' and 'What are we trying to achieve?' Leadership provides a valuable role in giving focus to the need for clear goals and real meaning – the opportunity to create and agree an exciting vision of how the organization or your work will look after the change. This leadership approach, with its emphasis on creating direction and inspiring others, also gives space for people to work together to produce ideas and plans that 'map out' a constructive way through the change situation.

The second contribution leadership can make to the management of change lies in the approach of the 'empowering' leader. This view sees the manager as providing high levels of support and coaching, and in sharing responsibility. We have already seen the value of these skills in helping people through the change process and preparing them for new roles and relationships. The thrust of this approach is a supportive and developmental one, and as such is in tune with the skills of helping others effect change. It questions the effectiveness of a more directive and controlling leadership style which may inflate defensive reactions to change and strengthen resistance.

Preparing for change

There are perhaps two aspects that a manager will need to consider when preparing themselves and others for change. Firstly there is the need to develop a positive view of change in general, not only as an inevitable process, but as a source of real opportunity. Secondly there is the need to prepare for specific changes so that people understand and commit to the need for the change being proposed.

Viewing change positively

This refers to a general process of 'education' about change, about both the process and its effects and the opportunities it presents. The aim is to develop an awareness amongst staff about the importance of change in contemporary work situations with a view to helping people to understand what is happening to them and why change is necessary. It is useful for managers to explore the process and effects of change with staff in an effort to advance not only their understanding but ways of supporting each other during change. Developing awareness also helps people to put the anxieties produced by change into perspective and to focus on the benefits of being involved in shaping the future.

Part of this education process is to raise awareness, through discussion and sharing information, about trends and changes in the way organizations are managed and structured, and about what is happening in your specific industry, business or sector. Getting across a more 'global' picture helps people to put any major changes into a wider context by understanding the pressures your organization faces from 'outside'.

Supporting readiness

Achilles *et al.* (1993) 'Creating readiness for organisational change' in *Human Relations*, 46 (6).

The idea of 'readiness' is one that applies to situations where people are faced with the prospect of proposed or specific changes that are about to be introduced. It describes the extent to which individuals or groups are aware of and believe that the change is both necessary and can be successful. This belief provides the motivation to work through the difficulties that change will bring, and the impetus to let go or 'unlearn' established ways of working. In terms of the apartment model, readiness suggests that people have moved beyond the denial phase, and have accepted the need for change.

It is important for the manager to seek ways of helping people to 'get ready' for change, to engage in the change process rather than deny it. The key to this is to work to generate an understanding that change is necessary. This can be supported by looking at whether current goals, aspirations and missions are being met. If, for example, targets and deadlines are being missed, or workplace issues and problems are not being resolved, the message is that current work methods and processes are no longer effective and need to be changed. At the organizational level, an awareness of the operating environment, changes in markets or what competitors are doing, coupled with an assessment of current performance, can help to establish this need to do something different. Developing this awareness of the need to change has been called 'unfreezing' – in effect, helping people to move out from a situation in which they are comfortable with the way things are by demonstrating the need for change.

Schein, E.H. (1987)
*Process
Consultation*,
Vol. 2.
Addison-Wesley.

In practical terms this requires the provision of a great deal of information about current performance and about aims, objectives and longer-term goals. It is important to allow time to discuss and interpret this information to allow people to conclude for themselves that changes are necessary. It is here that the value of full disclosure of information and a high degree of involvement in planning changes bears fruit.

The second thing to note from the idea of readiness is the belief that the changes proposed have a good chance of being successful. This suggests that people will find it difficult to commit to or even comply with changes that are seen as sure failures, bad plans or poor strategies. Again, while 'selling' the benefits of any change may work here to some extent, involving people in designing and creating new ways of working, in planning and implementing change, will be more effective in ensuring a belief in its success.

Taking this further, we need to explore the value of adopting not only positive responses to change, but a proactive one where change is generated 'from the inside' rather than something that just happens to people.

Creating change

Grosnick, P. (1992)
'Empowerment at
work' in *At Work*,
November–
December.

People in general commit to what they create, and at best comply with what is created for them. This 'strategy' moves beyond ideas of preparing to use an understanding of the change process and its effects to improve change management, and looks at the value of generating change internally – change that is demanded and driven by everyone in a team or organization. So far we have looked at managing change that is imposed on us, either from 'higher up' the organization or by other external factors. In this sense people can always perceive themselves as being 'victims' of circumstances beyond their control. While this may often the case, it is possible for people to get stuck in this victim role, waiting fearfully for the next change and then reacting to it, often defensively.

Turning the tables on this process and being proactive about making changes is not easy: after all, being a victim of change can be comfortable – it at least means that we do not need to accept responsibility for what happens, for example. The approach revolves around not waiting for change to happen to you, but to search continuously for improvements, new ideas and creative solutions, and to implement these because you want to, rather than because you have to. The advantage here lies in the difference between generating commitment and ensuring compliance.

- **Commitment.** People want change, will make it happen, and will do whatever it takes to make their ideas a reality – they 'own' the change. There is full involvement and real participation.

Senge, P.M. (1992)
The Fifth Discipline,
Century Business,
London.

- **Compliance.** This ranges from acceptance and agreement of the need to change and the direction chosen, through to high levels of resistance or grudging acceptance of 'fate'.

The distinction is important in many aspects of management, not least of all in change situations. Change being imposed 'from the top', for example, is only ever likely to induce some form of compliance, with all the attendant reactions of resistance we have noted previously. Managing change here is often seen as a process of 'selling' the benefits of a proposed change, which people are expected to 'buy into' at some level. There are advantages to this approach, of course – it can be a 'quick' way of making drastic changes, and may in many cases be seen to be the legitimate role of those entrusted with strategic leadership.

However, perhaps the real difficulties and pain of dealing with change can be reduced if we look at the value of change born from commitment. In this case, individuals, people within a team or an organization, use their understanding of the opportunities brought by change to recognize the need, generate ways forward, and plan and implement change themselves. Change is not imposed: it is sought after, it is not someone else's idea – it is their own.

In practical terms, this approach will not prevent all change being imposed from 'outside', but it will attune people to a positive approach to change and provide commitment to drive internal change before it is 'imposed' by crises. To manage change in this proactive way asks managers to commit to developing:

- Full involvement and participation – sharing of responsibility
- Disclosure and sharing of information, feelings and ideas
- Creating agreed new direction and purpose (vision).

The links between change management and the ideas we have discussed about empowerment and leadership are clear from the list above. This emphasizes the need to develop an approach to management that recognizes the interrelated nature of the different topics we have explored. It is in managing difficult and dynamic situations like that of change that the value of developing a real understanding of others and positive working relationships comes sharply into focus.

Looking after yourself

In managing complex change situations, with all the hard work supporting people through difficult times and the stress that comes with it, it is easy for managers to forget the toll this can take on them personally. There are two main reasons for looking after yourself in a change situation – or at any other time for that matter. Firstly the obvious one – no one owes an organization their health and well-being, so don't confuse commitment with running yourself into the ground. The second reason is that if you are not functioning fully because of stress, you will be less effective as a manager and, ultimately, less able to support others through the change process.

The following strategies may help you to look after yourself during periods of major change:

- **Accept that change is a normal part of life at work** and elsewhere.
- **Understand the change process** and its effects on people, including yourself.
- **Reduce uncertainty** by finding out about the change – why, how and when.
- **Be positive** – recognize the benefits and possibilities for achievement.
- **Be flexible** – be prepared to let go of old ways and experiment with the new.
- **Be confident** about your ability to cope – use experience from the past to reassure yourself that you will cope well. Focus on your strengths, and use change as an opportunity to develop new skills and awareness.
- **Go for improvement** – perfection is simply not possible. Don't beat yourself about the head with any failures, they are a normal feature of doing anything new. If you are supporting others through their mistakes in a positive way, then apply the same 'rules' to yourself.
- **Develop support networks** – who looks after you? Find support from your team, manager or peers. Don't neglect the valuable emotional support provided by friends and family.
- **Get involved in planning change** – counter the sense of 'loss of control' by getting involved and influencing what happens.
- **Break change down** into manageable, short-term targets.
- **Stay healthy** – avoid the temptation to drop your social life or stop having fun. Try to maintain a healthy lifestyle including diet and exercise. Be aware of how you like to relax and use these methods deliberately.

While we have discussed many of these strategies elsewhere in this chapter, and some reflect familiar approaches to managing stress, there are two important aspects of looking after yourself that need to be explored.

Keeping perspective

The first is the need to step back and put the effects of any major change into perspective. This is about the need to maintain a balanced and realistic view of what is happening at work. It is all too easy to slip into viewing the management of significant change as the most important and demanding part of your life at the moment. The danger here is that you get wrapped up in these demands and neglect the balance between work and other aspects of your life such as relationships with family or friends, or simply having fun. Keeping this balance is vital – most people, on reflection, would value their relationships outside of work very highly, often much more highly than a particular job for example. Seeing current work demands in the light of other more important parts of your life helps to keep work in perspective. Another view of the 'perspective' idea is to look back at other major changes you have experienced in the past and try to recall how you felt at the time. However difficult the change may have been, you will have 'come through it', learned something, and perhaps seen the benefits once the process was all over. Knowing that you have worked through changes in the past helps you to see the current situation more realistically, and to look forward to a time when this change is also a memory.

The perfection trap

The second idea that we would like to stress deals with the extra burden we impose on ourselves in our efforts to be 'perfect'. In a change situation there is often a fair degree of turmoil and confusion. There are pressures to plan and implement, new skills to be learned, and feelings are running high. In these circumstances it is easy to feel out of control, unable to cope and overloaded with work and others' reactions to change. In understanding the change process and its effects we can begin to accept that this is to be expected. But nevertheless, it is hard sometimes to escape feelings of inadequacy and incompetence, which may be verbalized in statements such as:

> 'I'm working so hard, taking work home – why can't I get a grip of this situation?'
> 'Why can't I manage this change properly, there must be a better way?'
> 'Things aren't going according to plan, why can't I organize it?'
> 'I can't handle this – I must be a lousy manager.'

To a large extent it is our own expectations that put pressure on ourselves. We expect to be able to handle anything, to keep control of complex situations, to predict what will happen and cope with the responses of others. It is part of our image of an effective and competent manager, and we wonder why we can't live up to it.

It is very important to recognize that we cannot hope to match this idea of perfection; it is unrealistic and destructive, particularly in the confusing world of change.

It might be worth considering some of the statements below, and thinking about firstly whether they are realistic expressions about the work environment, and then, if that is the case, whether they offer reassurance when things appear chaotic and confused:

- You cannot expect to control every event, person, or interaction
- You cannot plan every detail and expect things to happen that way – they won't
- You cannot predict the future, you can only make informed guesses
- You cannot fully understand each person's responses to change
- It is difficult to fully understand your own response to change
- You cannot fully understand the complex social systems of a workplace – the unexpected will often happen.

This is not a bleak picture, it's a reassuring one. It helps to explain why change can be so confusing and complex to manage, why plans need to be flexible, and why efforts to rigidly control the process are sometimes unhelpful. Confusion and chaos are normal, not a sign, necessarily, of 'poor' management. It is an acceptance of this 'reality' that is potentially so liberating in generating a healthy approach to change situations. It helps us to see that our experience of change as confusing, as well as energizing, is both very understandable as well as inevitable.

Change and opportunity

We have spent some time in this chapter in looking at the effects change has on individuals, their reactions and responses, both to perceived threat and to opportunity. The focus on the individual is crucial if a manager is to begin to feel comfortable with the wide range of behaviours a change situation can trigger amongst colleagues and those being 'managed'. Without this under-standing, efforts to simply plan and implement change in a mechanistic and unthinking way are likely to cause more pain and anxiety than is necessary. More than this, such efforts may fail completely in the face of resistance, or leave a legacy of anger and grievance that return to undermine future efforts.

We have stressed that change inevitably causes anxiety as well as excitement. That it is unrealistic in today's working environments to avoid this anxiety by trying to avoid change will be clear to most of us. But change needs to be embraced not just because it is a 'fact of life', but because of the opportunities it creates.

Change is essential if we are to move forward, to make progress towards more productive and satisfying ways of working. We all have dreams about a 'better' life, though we may define it in different ways. It might mean work with a more human face, personal achievements or fulfilling potential, for example. Whatever we aim for will require a change, a move from how things are to how we would like them to be. This desire for improvement, for better ways of working together and for success provides the energy, our actions are the vehicle, and change is the process we use to make it all happen.

Summary

This chapter has sought to explore the management of change. The key focus has been on the need to develop a real understanding of the way people react to change situations, and how this understanding leads to strategies that present change as an opportunity to move forward and to learn.

We began by seeing change situations as producers of both threats and opportunities. It is how individuals perceive the change that determines their reactions to a particular situation. In managing change we have suggested the need to adopt strategies that reduce the perception or impact of the 'threats', while encouraging a positive view about change.

Developing an understanding of change management began with looking at the change process itself, focusing on the behaviours observed at different 'stages' and the approaches that managers can use to help people 'move on'. This was followed by a more detailed discussion of personal responses to change, including defensiveness, resistance and change as a loss.

Following on from this need to understand the effects of change from a personal perspective, we went on to explore some of the strategies that can make use of this understanding in approaching more constructively the management of change. This covered techniques for reducing anxiety and creating readiness, and the need for managers to look after themselves if they are to be effective in stressful situations such as change.

Finally, we looked at the need to develop a proactive stance on change – to be the implementors of change and seekers of opportunity, rather than waiting silently for the next round of change to be imposed.

Further reading

There is a proliferation of books about managing change, mostly from a strategic organizational perspective, but one of the most useful for managers is *Managing Organizational Change* by C.D. Scott and D.T. Jaffe, part of Kogan Page's 'Better Management Skills' series. This 'booklet' is short, accessible and practical in its approach, and provides learning activities to enable readers to evaluate their own change situations. Though it takes a more structured approach than our work, it stresses the need to look at personal responses to change such as resistance. It also makes brief but valuable links to other topics such as leadership and teams.

Nicola Phillip's book *Innovative Management* provides some useful chapters on the subject of change. In particular, it discusses the change process model used here, and looks at change as a motivator and change in relation to stress. The writing is clear and easy to read, and well supported by contemporary case studies.

References

Hirschhorn, L. (1993) *The Workplace Within – Psychodynamics of Organizational Life*, MIT Press.
Hunt, J.W. (1986) *Managing People at Work*, McGraw-Hill International, London.
Kanter, R.M. (1983) *The Change Masters*, Simon & Schuster, New York.
King, N. and Anderson, N. (1995) *Innovation and Change in Organizations*, Routledge, London.
Mabey, C. and Mayon-White, B. (eds) *Managing Change*, PCP, Paul Chapman Publishing Ltd.
Phillips, N. (1993) *Innovative Management*, Pitman, London.
Schein, E.H. (1987) *Process Consultation*, Vol. 2, Addison-Wesley.
Scott, C.D. and Jaffe, D.T. (1989) *Managing Organizational Change*, Kogan Page, London.
Vickers, C. (1988) *All Change: The Management of Change*, Video Arts Booklet.
Weisbord, M. (1987) *Productive Workplaces*, Jossey-Bass, San Francisco.

13

Making conflict useful

Dealing with conflicts lies at the heart of managing any business. As a result, confrontation of issues about which there is disagreement can be avoided only at the manager's peril. Workplace politicking grows quietly in the dark, like mushrooms; neither can stand the light of day.

Andrew Grove, President of INTEL

Objectives

By the end of this chapter you will be able to:

➤ Understand the basis of conflict in organizations
➤ Value the potential contribution of conflict to organizational dynamics
➤ Help manage conflict to develop positive outcomes for people and the organization
➤ Give and receive criticism positively

Introduction

Wherever there are differences between people, there is a potential for conflict. We can see this through the daily reports on seemingly intractable conflicts across the globe, and in the sometimes bitter disputes and polarized views that politics parades in the soundbite exchanges of the media. On a more personal level, conflict can be a more or less serious feature of our work and home relationships, a normal element of the day-by-day problem of making our way in the world. Differences between people are bound to surface sometimes, as opposing views, approaches or feelings become evident, making some degree of conflict or contention inevitable. On occasion, these conflicts can become significant, developing levels of interpersonal tension and stress that can lead to serious dysfunctions in working relationships. When this happens, in-fighting, avoidance and political behaviour can predominate, leaving organizational objectives to become lost in the business of battle.

While the negative consequences of unresolved differences are part of most people's experience, conflict also provides a positive opportunity to explore basic differences in perspectives. Such exploration is a rich source of organizational learning, and a foundation for innovation, creativity and personal change. The aim of this section is to explore how conflict can become an agent of organizational vibrancy, a progressive pathway to individual and organizational learning.

Approaching conflict as an opportunity

In some respects, it is easy to see the potential problems that conflict can bring to a workplace. Disagreements among staff can easily become divisive, particularly when people feel that their own security is threatened by new ideas or perspectives. A conflicting point of view, perhaps advocated by someone with a passionate commitment to new approaches, can undermine the very perspective on which people have built their whole approach to working life. The potential value of a new approach can be lost, simply because it arouses understandable feelings of defensiveness in others and gives rise to conflict between opposing points of view. Such situations can quickly become characterized by political manoeuvring, with people being drawn into making personal attacks as a means of defending their position. Yet hostile responses do not help reasoned consideration of the issues, and lead to entrenched and polarized positions being adopted, with a considerable degree of personal animosity clouding the debate. Managing conflict therefore places great emphasis on the skills of the team if positive outcomes are to be achieved. The negative potential outcomes of conflict are an understandable consequence of differences between people, and the sense of threat or insecurity that arises when our own values, beliefs or approaches are called into question.

Differences between people ensure that there will always be some degree of contention concerning workplace issues or approaches. Exploring this contention should be an opportunity to build understanding of others and learn from the alternative perspectives that they hold. Nevertheless, it is difficult to assess what effect conflicting ideas will have on people, and one strategy to avoid 'opening up a can of worms' is to attempt to keep the lid tightly shut. Once conflict is out into the open, the effect on working relationships is unpredictable, and full of potential embarrassment and threat. While a great deal can be done to prepare people to take on challenging and contentious issues, conflict is a complex situation to grasp. Managers need to rely on intuition, interpretative skills and their ability to maintain a connection with people in difficult circumstances, if they are to help support positive outcomes from the process. The situation taxes interpersonal skills to the limits, and the fundamental nature of the differences that conflict reveals can make it a very committing process to encourage. Perhaps at the outset, it is important to be clear about the potential benefits of allowing contention and conflict to take the floor in workteam discussions.

 Learning activity

Conflicting ideas

Think about situations of conflict that you have experienced.

- What are the potential benefits that conflict can bring to individuals and groups?
- What happens to these potential benefits if conflict is suppressed?

For the organization, conflict has the potential to:

- Encourage review, reflection and learning through people having to explore their own position and understand that of others
- Encourage the exchange of good practice and provide challenges to that which is less effective
- Encourage an appreciation of the strengths of other people through a better awareness of the basis of their approach
- Develop a creative and dynamic work environment that looks to solve problems through an open exchange of ideas
- Help provide a wide range of solutions by encouraging people to give their points of view
- Bring underlying issues or concerns into the public forum for resolution
- Increase the depth and quality of communication through the exploration of values, attitudes and beliefs.

Although these potential benefits do depend on the ability of people to manage conflict effectively, the list does provide an indication of the gains that organizations may obtain through approaching conflict constructively.

In addition to these organizational benefits, for the individual, conflict has the potential to:

- Help establish an individual role, by allowing a position to be clearly expressed and discussed
- Allow an opportunity for feelings to be expressed
- Encourage the development of influencing skills
- Help shape perspectives through the exploring of complex issues
- Help define informal networks and power relationships
- Provide an opportunity to be involved in the process of solving problems and defining organizational direction
- Help develop a fuller understanding of other people's values, attitudes and beliefs
- Establish an understanding of the strengths of other approaches.

The potential benefits of allowing conflict to surface are many, and keeping these in mind may help people to approach difficult and stressful situations more positively. It is common for people to view conflict as a situation that can only be negative and which therefore should be avoided. Yet, conflict is a doorway of opportunity to learning, and by adopting a positive view of the benefits, people can use the situation to help them fulfil both individual and organizational potential. Conflict is a normal consequence of the differences between people, and while it contains the possibility for embarrassment and threat, these need not be an insurmountable barrier to the positive progress of people at work.

Exploring the political aspects of conflict

In situations where the differences between people are exposed, resolving those differences will involve influence and persuasion. This is particularly true of situations where there are no single, correct outcomes, but where the process of conflict is attempting to define a way forward through a variety of options. In these situations, where all of the options have possible advantages and disadvantages, finding a solution will not necessarily depend on rational, objective criteria. Instead, subjective feelings, interpretations and values are likely to help define outcomes, making the process much more dependent on people using political behaviours, such as building alliances and exercising persuasion. Of course, there will be differences between people that are simply due to a lack of factual knowledge and these can easily be resolved, but most situations are more complex and open to differing interpretations. Defining a way forward under these conditions depends on political behaviour if results are to be achieved. Somehow, agreement needs to be reached by exploring options and resolving differences, and this cannot happen by simply depending on objective facts.

The idea of political behaviour in organizations can produce uncomfortable images of people manipulating and manoeuvring others as they scramble single-mindedly towards the pinnacles of organizational success. Yet, organizations are social systems as well as profit centres, and they retain the characteristic that at some level people will engage in shaping a society that reflects their needs and values. This process must involve political behaviour of varying sorts. In some organizations, with a clearly defined hierarchy and rigid control procedures, ordinary workers may feel disenfranchised. This can lead to the development of informal, covert sub-systems or formal unionization in an attempt to build a base for political influence and satisfaction of needs. In other organizations, where the approach involves all people, political behaviour leads to diversity, as people build alliances and approaches that meet organizational goals yet satisfy their own preferences. Political behaviour is an inevitable and irreducible feature of any social system. While it has a negative image that is happily supported by the 'losers' of any political debate, it is worth trying to assess how this behaviour can be made an acceptable and valuable part of the organizational culture.

Learning activity

Accepting politics

How can working groups and organizations learn to use political behaviour productively?

An important part of what happens in a conflict situation is to do with the society of work. Debating and resolving the differences in approach may appear to be the point of conflict, but it can only be got at through a process that impacts on relationships within groups. Sorting out our differences gives us opportunities to satisfy some of our psychological and social needs – holding the floor in debate allows us to feel the recognition of our peers, swaying the opinions of others allows us to feel influence while building agreements reaffirms a sense of belonging to a group. However, the paradox here is that the very situations that allow this to happen also contain potential threat and embarrassment – expressing differences can be isolating, losing a debate can make us feel devalued and expressing our feelings can make us feel vulnerable and weak. In addition, the very things that help some people to satisfy their needs – exploring potential learning through expression of inner values – might make others who need higher levels of security feel very uncomfortable and threatened. Conflict therefore contains opportunities for people, but it also hides a variety of risks, making it a demanding and sensitive situation to manage effectively.

So, conflict provides one outlet for the natural political behaviour that characterizes any social system. People need to meet their psychological needs, and will become anxious when the situation prevents this from happening. In situations where people's work keeps them apart, any gathering can easily be characterized by social jostling rather than by productive work. Staff meetings are a common place to observe this kind of behaviour happening, with minor conflict being a way of restating social values rather than moving business forward. Suppressing this conflict is unproductive, as it can drive the social behaviour further into the informal networks of the organization, where it can develop a hidden and sometimes destructive agenda. If people are unable to address their needs in some way, then they may build alliances informally and create issues to organize around that are not necessarily helpful or productive – for example, the conventional management–worker divide. Alternatively, the lack of opportunity to engage in this necessary social behaviour can lead to people making their political point more extremely, with an open lack of cooperation between people as a result. These circumstances lead to entrenched positions and to the spread of conflict, as unresolved tension over one issue is expressed through a willingness to do battle over others. Obstructive and destructive behaviours can easily escalate and polarize opinions between camps, making the situation increasingly difficult to challenge and resolved productively.

While the potential advantages of allowing conflict to emerge in the workplace are perhaps clear, conflict that is handled poorly can develop a destructive capacity. Having differing points of view, approaches and understanding can be seen as a healthy reflection of diversity in a workplace, but differences can attack our own position. This is particularly true if we also feel threatened or insecure at the same time, as might happen during a major upheaval or time of change. Poorly handled conflict can build up aggressive behaviour in an attempt to weaken the position of others, or defensive behaviour in situations where openness would develop more complete solutions. It is conflict that can sometimes reveal the symptoms of a disintegrating workplace, with poor communication, entrenched opinion and petty point-scoring taking hold. People in conflict soon bring in others to help support their position, often involving any identifiable or symbolic 'big guns' in the situation. This kind of pointless escalation illustrates the potential dark side of conflict that goes on unexpressed or unresolved. Failing to deal with conflict productively can force organizations to rely on rules and procedure as a way of making some progress in a situation where the social system is failing; paradoxically it is exactly that effort to exorcize the conflict that can make it more likely to happen.

Learning activity

Conflict watching

When the opportunity arises take time to watch conflict taking place. What things seem to provide a source for conflict? Try to observe and record the behaviours of people involved in the conflict (body language to other combatants, responses to others). Try also to analyse the reactions of others in the group. What kinds of behaviours do they display? Do they encourage or discourage the action? How do they attempt to cope?

Sources of conflict

It can be tempting to look at conflict as something that hinges upon personalities, as if the differences bring expressed merely related to basic flaws in the characters of the people involved. While this approach helps managers justify a 'hands-off' approach, it is hardly productive management of a difficult situation. Nor is it a fair reflection of the complex pressures and strains that can affect us all. The particular shades of people's characters are bound to have an impact on the nature of conflict, but it is simplistic and misleading to think that most disputes relate to personality. Instead, most conflict appears to be rooted in four main sources, as illustrated in Figure 13.1.

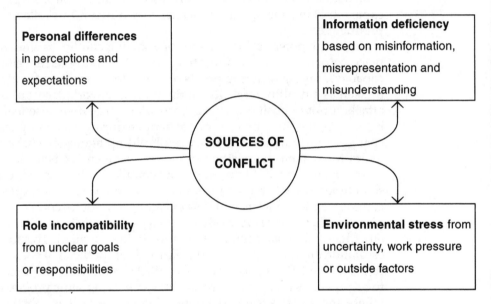

Fig. 13.1 Sources of conflict (adapted from Whetton, Cameron and Woods (1994: 343)).

Conflict and group dynamics

Taking time to observe workplace conflict happening can be useful, if sometimes stressful, exercise. Very often, a close study of the conversation and behaviours taking place reveals how little emphasis people place upon reasoned analysis or careful debate to build their position and allegiances. Much more likely is that people will base their position on perceptions of power and a sense of authority in the situation, particularly when the situation becomes at all heated. Conflict sparks off defence mechanisms in individuals and groups associated with developing uncertainty and anxiety as polarized views are revealed. This may be observable in the body language of people, who will start to display avoiding behaviours, such as failing to make eye contact and physically closing themselves to the conflicting individuals. More significantly, as potential threats in the situation continue to develop, anxiety rises and the decision-making process is driven further away from a rational basis as people resort to primitive psychological behaviour.

This effect is based on our infantile psychological development, whereby we all bring to work groups an emotional assumption about what groups can provide for us. As a consequence, when we join groups we do so to achieve task goals, but at the same time we also have a basic emotional expectation about how groups work that operates on a primitive level. This normally assumes a background role as the group proceeds with its task objectives. However, it is this 'base assumption' that we fall back onto when the going gets tough, and this develops several possible characteristics for groups in conflict, none of which are necessarily helpful.

The first base assumption is that groups should depend on a particular leader, drawing groups that are experiencing anxiety to actively seek charismatic leadership upon which they can depend. In resorting to this basic behaviour, the group is abandoning independent or critical thinking in the single-minded pursuit of dependency as a means of reducing anxiety. Note that this strategy is a result of group dynamics rather than a response to the particular qualities of the individual chosen as leader. Anxiety-reducing decisions tend to be made without rational foundation; in these circumstances almost anyone will do, and the group are likely to develop an idealized view of the 'leader' to support their need to reduce anxiety.

The unrealistic assumptions about the leader make this a difficult situation for groups to maintain. Having selected a leader without much concern for either the appropriateness of the person or the real needs of the situation, groups are often frustrated by the results. The person selected for the group to depend on rarely has the answers to situations as complex as conflict, and a common outcome is that rising frustration and anxiety lead the group into a second base behaviour.

The second base assumption is that the group will begin to behave as if they are together for the purpose of fighting or fleeing from some outside enemy. In an organizational setting these 'enemies' are readily found in other departments or bosses, and the effort of the group is quickly absorbed in the dynamics of competing. Groups continue to project leadership onto a figurehead to lead the fight or flight, which can be a dangerous position for the individual involved to maintain. The group support for the leader is ill-founded, transient and likely to dissolve at the first sign of real trouble! Indeed, in a difficult situation, the group would be quite likely to push the leader outside of the group – the figurehead can easily become the thing that needs to be attacked.

A third base assumption is that the group will behave as if they can depend on two of their number for solutions to the problems. This is similar to the dependence on the leader discussed earlier, except that it reflects our infantile dependence on parents to resolve our difficulties. Again, it involves the other members of the group losing their independent and critical thinking as an atmosphere of unrealistic security and hope descends on the situation.

A fourth base assumption is that the group will display oneness. This is where an overriding sense of unity surfaces, with little attempt to explore problems or

Case note

Outdoor management development

Using outdoor management development to aid a variety of organizational objectives provides a useful insight into this process in action. The nature of outdoor 'adventure' tasks is that they have an impact on levels of anxiety which tutors running such events need to manage carefully. Groups may be planning an approach to a complex and unfamiliar project involving outdoor activities, and this has a natural effect on levels of anxiety that might not necessarily surface in a familiar, workplace setting. It is very common to observe a collapse in a rational approach to the problems, as basic assumptions surface about what group behaviour should provide. People have leadership foisted upon them, often at a stage where the basic problems in the exercise have not yet been identified or resolved. Leading complex situations, where there are unresolved objectives and issues overlaid with basic anxiety about the project as a whole, taxes even the best of people and usually leads to group ineffectiveness.

Reviewing such situations is also instructive, as groups will initially focus on the behaviours of the leader and the actions that they could have taken that would have been more successful. Given the complexity of the task and the group processes, it is soon realized that there are no magic steps that would have led to to an organized and efficient response. Indeed, groups begin to identify that the dependence on a leader was an unrealistic way of addressing complexity and anxiety. What is needed is for the group to recognize situations that trigger a build-up of anxiety, and to seek to address this in ways that do not compromise effectiveness in achieving task objectives. This means that groups have to be open with issues, and prepared to reach a level of understanding that allows progress to be made through exploring fears and anxieties as they arise, rather than leaving them to exert a fundamentally destructive influence.

issues that caused anxiety to build in the first place. Conflict, for example, would be absorbed by an overwhelming sense of unity and togetherness in the group. Problems, anxiety and threat all become subsumed by a passive dependence on the union of the group. Group energies tend to be directed towards reaffirming the strength of their oneness, rather than productive behaviours relating to the task or other issues that surface.

These base behaviours that are adopted by groups experiencing anxiety can typically be surfaced by the stresses of conflict within the group. The conditions that cause groups to descend into the base behaviours are impossible to define precisely, as there are no clear relationships of causality that link specific actions to emerging anxiety in a group. All that can be observed is that under conditions of increasing anxiety, group dynamics become extremely unpredictable, with the group changing focus from task objectives to base assumption behaviours of one form or another. Pressures that would cause one group to flip from an effective group to one dominated by dependence behaviours might not have any impact on another group that dealt with anxieties through open discussion or some other means.

This analysis of group dynamics illustrates some of the difficulties of managing conflict situations. A group that is normally effective in pursuing task objectives may respond to a situation of conflict by adopting one or more of the base assumption behaviours. Paradoxically, on the surface the behaviours on display may appear to be positive team behaviours; strong leadership may seem to be providing a useful sense of direction, or a powerful sense of cohesiveness may seem to demonstrate team togetherness. However, where these symptoms are evidence of a group responding to anxiety by invoking defence mechanisms, it is unlikely to lead to successful resolution of the issues facing the group. Indeed, the build up of frustration as leaders fail to fulfill expectations is likely to lead to a further breakdown in group relations. One strategy that can help the manager and the team identify the problems is to develop a systematic approach to analysing conflict situations through review.

Analysing group behaviour in conflict situations

One way to help groups look at these aspects of their behaviour is to conduct a review of the dialogue that takes place in conflict situations. Each person uses a sheet of paper that has been divided in half vertically. The left-hand side is used to record the actual conversation, while the right-hand side is used to provide a commentary on the thought processes and assumptions that helped to feed the discussion. This is a powerful way for a group to explore the way in which conflict links into different agendas and power relationships, and also helps to identify the things that trigger anxiety and the patterns of responses that this develops.

Defining the basic approaches to conflict

Approaches to conflict can be defined in terms of two basic characteristics. The first is the degree of cooperation being brought to the situation, and loosely reflects the willingness of the parties to try to meet the needs of other people. The second is the degree of assertiveness that people bring to the situation, which reflects their willingness to engage in satisfying their own needs. These two characteristics help define five potential responses to conflict situations which are illustrated in Figure 13.2 overleaf and discussed below.

1 Avoiding the issue

Where the parties to conflict are unwilling to assert their own needs and are not prepared to cooperate with others, then conflict will be ignored or avoided. This approach is ultimately unproductive as it means that issues will not be resolved. Problems will tend to persist and even develop under the surface,

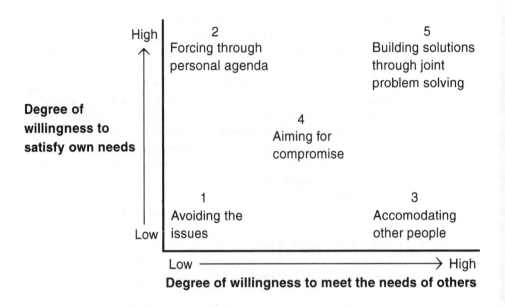

Fig. 13.2 Five approaches to conflict situations (adapted from Whetton, Cameron and Woods (1994)).

meaning that potential conflict is always in the background as a hidden feature of workplace relationships. The avoiding strategy implies a certain 'covering up' or hiding from the truth, and this adds behaviours to the situation that limit openness and honesty. This erodes confidence and lends a sense of confusion and mistrust to the work environment, leading to further misunderstanding and tension over time. This approach characterizes teams that do not have high levels of trust, or lack the collective strength to confront issues with confidence or purpose.

2 Forcing through an agenda

If parties to conflict are prepared to assert their own needs and concerns but unwilling to cooperate in meeting the needs of others, then the approach is characterized by forcing behaviour. For this strategy to be effective depends on having the authority or personal power to push through a personal agenda, despite the position of others. Adopting the forcing approach to conflict does enable results to be achieved, at least in the short run, and the strategy may appear effective in obtaining progress. However, this approach ultimately has damaging consequences for teams in that other people become less cooperative in the face of their needs being continually ignored or squashed.

3 Accommodating other people

Where people are willing to address the needs of others at the expense of their own, the approach is characterized by accommodating behaviour. This tends to arise when people are anxious to protect the quality of relationships, and believe that open discussion of difficult issues may cause damage. While the approach has the advantage of showing concern for other people, it does prevent issues from receiving critical analysis and productive options are less likely to be explored. Further, a person employing this approach is doing so at the expense of their personal needs and interests, and these losses will eventually undermine the individual's confidence and self-respect.

4 Aiming for compromise

If parties are willing to give up some of their own needs in an effort to meet the needs of others, then the approach will be characterized by behaviours aimed at achieving compromise. As an approach this has immediate appeal as it appears to reflect fairness in the search for agreement, as well as allowing all parties to protect some of their position. However, compromise is based on sacrifice and exchange, breeding an approach based on the mechanics of trading rather than investigating the quality of ideas. Further, if the approach becomes common, it leads people to ratchet up their 'needs' in the recognition that they can then trade downwards to a comfortable position. This type of game-playing does not allow the issues of conflict to be explored productively, but merely allows them to be traded away. The danger is that the real issues persist and continue to surface, despite the compromises that are reached. An approach that is based on fairness and harmony ultimately leaves behind continuing tension and unhelpful behaviours.

5 Building solutions through joint problem-solving

Where people involved in conflict bring their own needs and concerns to the situation, but are willing to try to meet the needs of others, then the approach is characterized by joint problem-solving. By seeking to find solutions, possibly through inventing new options, that satisfy the needs and concerns of all, this approach provides win–win outcomes. By accepting the potential value of all positions, it encourages an exploratory approach based on the issues involved, rather that based on exercising power or bartering for a result. As a result, the approach is more likely to develop positive feelings of value in participants, and leads to rewarding feelings of success when issues are faced and resolved openly.

The approach that gets used in particular conflict situations depends on a number of factors, not least the personalities of the people involved. How people approach conflict depends to some extent on their need for recognition, power and relationships, and these things change according to life stages and other circumstances. However, while the problem-solving approach has appeal in terms of providing win–win outcomes, it may not be the only appropriate approach to resolving conflict. Organizational pressures, such as time, resources and competition may make it difficult to use a problem-solving approach, making it likely that a manager will adopt one of the alternatives. As long as the potential problems of expediency are recognized, a short-term solution may be effective, particularly if the people involved are given the opportunity to review the issues at a later stage.

Handling conflict

Managing the process of conflict presents many challenges. It offers a range of valuable opportunities for exploring issues and developing understanding of other people, but it also presents a dark side that holds destructive potential. Achieving the potential gains while avoiding some of the pitfalls provides one of the great challenges facing managers. This section aims to develop strategies and skills that can help people to cope with conflict situations positively.

Learning activity

Exploring positive and negative behaviours

Consider some of the conflict situations you have been involved in or observed closely. List the behaviours by the people involved that have appeared to make the situation worse, or more difficult to resolve.

- What behaviours or actions have helped to make the conflict an easier process to work through and resolve?
- What effects have you observed when the conflict is not dealt with?

This exercise may well have illustrated the wide range of possible responses, reflecting the different experience and contexts of anyone approaching the problem. Actions that may have worsened one conflict situation are sometimes exactly what was needed to put other situations right. This effect parallels the conflict resolution efforts that we see the United Nations or NATO engaged in; sometimes diplomacy appears to be effective, whereas at other times it appears that force achieves results more readily. Conflicts often go through phases during which the people involved have time to think and reassess their position. Bringing in an outsider to provide an objective overview might be an unhelpful intrusion in the early stages of conflict, providing nothing more than an excuse to vent anger, whereas later on it may be exactly the right step towards achieving a collaborative solution. Handling conflict depends crucially on sensitivity and interpretation skill, rather than the application of a well-worn formula. That said, the ten guidelines that follow provide some positive strategies which, used in the appropriate context, may help to provide steps towards solutions.

Guidelines for dealing with conflict

1 Encourage openness

Conflict situations are more easily worked through in an atmosphere of openness. It is difficult to make any progress if people in conflict cannot explore real objectives, facts, views and the assumptions that surround the issues. Keeping these things hidden builds a layer of confusion around the issues that makes getting to the solution difficult. Further, it raises the level of suspicion and mistrust, leading people to attack any perceived weaknesses as a means of undermining opposing points of view. The more the discussion hides issues, the more likely the attacks will be directed at the person instead of the point.

Openness can be encouraged by restating the potential benefits for individuals and the organization of bringing conflict out into the open. It is worth emphasizing that issues cannot be resolved while they remain hidden, and that ongoing issues can lead to a great deal of damage in teams. However, while it is relatively easy to get people to make an overt commitment to openness, it is not a behaviour that is easily maintained in conditions of potential embarrassment or threat. This is because social conditioning has led to people having well developed 'caring' responses, which make genuine openness difficult when it may cause embarrassment in the group.

Argyris, C. and Schon, D. (1974) *Theory in Practice*, Jossey-Bass, San Francisco.

Argyris and Schon: Human theories of control

The problems created by the caring aspect of our behaviour have been extensively explored by Chris Argyris and Donald Schon, and form the basis of their analysis of organizational defence routines. One important aspect of their study is that it highlights a significant paradox that lies at the heart of the way in which people exercise control over difficult, threatening or embarrassing situations. This paradox can lead to ineffective behaviour in a whole range of group situations, including conflict and contention. Understanding the way in which this works provides useful insights for managers and teams, and is fundamental to successfully challenging their own defence routines.

People hold widely different values and beliefs and espouse radically different approaches about life. Nevertheless, underlying the variety of actions and behaviours that people make are simple, basic rules built up through our social upbringing. In contrast to the variety in our behaviours, these basic rules are consistent across people, no matter what their background or circumstances. In a sense, they are rather like master programs that govern our basic approach to life and enable people to maintain some direction and control. These basic rules are known as the model one theory-in-use, as it operates all the while and governs the way in which we put our values and beliefs into practice. The rules are simple, guiding people to do three basic things.

Firstly, model one theory-in-use instructs people to try to maintain control over themselves and the situations that they meet. As a rule this is fairly straightforward as losing control has consequences in terms of physical and psychological safety. People who lose control face a situation that is uncertain and unpredictable, which raises the level of risk. As the perception of danger grows from within the group, it makes efforts to organize the group more difficult. People become preoccupied with avoiding the risks rather than finding solutions to the original problem. As situations become difficult, leading people to respond with strong emotions, control is more difficult to maintain than usual. Conflict, by highlighting uncertainty, differences and interpersonal tensions, is therefore a situation where our basic rules about maintaining control are put under pressure.

Second, the model instructs people to win. Again, this is relatively straight-forward, guiding people to achieve personal gain rather than personal loss from the situations that they enter. This may be achieved through cooperative behaviour as in many situations we face it is possible to identify and pursue win–win outcomes. However, if this fails, the rules dictate that we may compete, as continual losses are an unsustainable route through life. The competition may take many forms, as can the definitions of what constitutes a 'win', according to individual preferences. Conflict is one situation that can throw up differences and opposites, leading to the possibility that losers will emerge. This again puts our basic template for behaving under stress.

Thirdly, the model instructs people to avoid upsetting people. This leads us to adopt a caring approach that tries to support other people wherever possible. It also means that we generally attempt to implement our strategies through persuasion, negotiating or by selling in an attempt to create win–win scenarios that avoid upsetting others while also maintaining control of the situation. Again, situations of conflict can lead to threat or embarrassment, raising the possibility that people may get upset. This violates our basic rules and leads to strategies of avoidance or face saving; in general we do anything to prevent us from causing unnecessary upset to other people, unless it becomes necessary to win. These face-saving strategies are common enough to be recognized as an important component of high-level negotiations.

The paradox emerges when the theory-in-use is put to work. For an individual to be in control of the situation, win and avoid upsetting people ultimately requires that everyone else suspends their use of the rules. Instead, others have to be submissive, dependent and willing to lose for model one to be effectively pursued by an individual. Yet others will not behave in this way because their own behaviour is governed by the same basic template. Our theory-in-use that gives us a model for effective behaviour also gets in the way of the effective behaviour of other people. Furthermore, the situations that tax us and force us to depend on our basic rules are exactly the situations that need us to raise our effectiveness in the search for a positive outcome. Yet model one is built on social virtues such as providing care and support for others, respecting others and behaving with basic honesty, strength and integrity. In short, pursuing our needs with a basic care for the needs of others is paradoxical and leads us to be less effective. It leads us to strategies that attempt to develop solutions but which focus on avoiding embarrassment, threat and upset. Furthermore, face-saving and avoiding strategies must be covert otherwise they lose their potential to save face and bypass difficulties. Model one therefore engages people in well-intended but subversive strategies that disguise real feelings and intent, despite being rooted in caring for others.

2　Model appropriate responses

It helps people to explore conflicting points of view if some people are prepared to take the step of making positive responses to contention. This might be as simple as carefully acknowledging contrasting points of view rather than being defensive or dismissive. Similarly, taking the time to encourage and support people who are trying to express differences also helps people to become more comfortable with perspectives being explored. By seeing that these responses can be made by some people, even in situations of potential threat, others can be inspired to take a more positive approach. Group confidence can be developed by seeing appropriate responses being enacted and the consequences that arise.

3 Provide summaries and restatements of the position

Taking time to recap on points of view and the key points of the debate helps keep conflict productive. As a technique it helps to keep communication effective in a situation where it may otherwise begin to break down. This ensures that people have the best possible chance of coming up with new insights and making useful contributions. Also, the process of conflict can easily become heated, allowing little time to absorb points or reflect on their value. By slowing the process down and clearly restating the position, it allows people the time and space to think and lowers the risk of the temperature of the debate spiralling out of control.

4 Bring in people who are not directly involved

Using other people from outside of the immediate team can often help provide additional facts to help the search for a solution. Sometimes facts will have a direct bearing on the issues, though as we have already noted, conflict often revolves around different interpretations, views or values. Perhaps more valuably, other people can bring in alternative viewpoints and balance to the debate, helping the process of summarizing and restating arguments. Having some detachment from the root causes of the conflict can allow others to identify core issues cleanly, without the obscuring effects of defending a position. Other people can also be used to provide support to people in conflict, not in the sense of taking sides, but by a process of developing and exploring the issues productively. These strategies all help bring balance and dynamism to the business of finding solutions, creating levels of support and encouragement that give the process genuine opportunity and learning.

This strategy has two potential dangers that need to be addressed. The first danger is that people from outside the team can be exactly the kind of external figure that the group may choose as a threat, causing a defensive closing of ranks. Any outsider needs to be aware of this possibility, and should take care to negotiate their role with the group. This process of seeking consent helps the group to manage their inclination to project anxieties onto the outsider, and helps to maintain their control over the situation. It is also important for anyone in this role to continue to make their actions overt, providing clear reasons for any intervention that they make.

The second danger is that the group can also seek an outside visionary, or 'magic helper', as a means of delivering them from their conflict. It is therefore important for the outsider to avoid providing answers, especially those based on an 'objective' view. If the real issues of conflict are to be productively explored, the group needs to find the solutions within itself. Having a facilitator in to help provide clarity and provoke investigation is valuable, whereas having a 'consultant' come along to provide the answers is not.

5 Encourage people to take time to think and reassess

Sometimes all that people need to resolve conflict is time to think through issues more clearly. Space apart can help people develop understanding of the position of others, and recognize the value of their contribution. Given better understanding of the issues, a common position is more likely to be found that makes the most of both positions. The heat of debate, and the reactions that opposing points of view provoke, make it difficult to value the positive aspects of other people's position. Time and space can help this process onwards.

6 Use the strengths of the group

It can be valuable to use the strength of the group to help the process of exploring conflict. It is often productive to use non-combatants, perhaps working in small groups, to develop the strengths and weaknesses in each point of view. This has the advantage of bringing other members of the group into the conflict with a positive and creative role to play. This helps to provide a wider range of solutions. Further, it removes the initial conflict away from the original personalities and works to cool the situation down.

7 Focus on shared goals

It can be productive to highlight the shared goals at the heart of the conflict as a means of encouraging people to look beyond the differences that exist. This can help to get people involved in moving towards the solution, rather than defending or attacking the current positions. This encourages a problem-solving style and helps people to look for the potential gains to be had from joint effort. It helps too if work is aimed at developing possible directions and aspirations rather than consolidating existing positions at the outset. This emphasis creates room for possibilities to be expressed, allowing people to explore the options positively rather than retreat to a position they can defend.

8 Use directions and interests to develop areas of new gain

Actively listening to people provides ideas for areas of potential gains. It can be difficult to hear anything other than the differences in situations of conflict, particularly as the debate becomes heated, but identifying aims are a step towards finding mutual benefits. It also helps people to broaden their approach to conflict; rather than stating a position, it allows people to express the reasons behind the position and the wider interests that they are trying to serve. This helps to build understanding and develop areas where joint gains can be identified.

9 Try to build objectivity into the process

The nature of conflict means that positions will depend partly on individual perspectives and values. These are ultimately subjective and occasionally incompatible with other views, and can present a dead end in terms of resolving the issues. However, while it is essential to allow these personal perspectives to be expresses and valued, it can be useful to try to develop an objective view of the positions being expressed. The people involved in conflict can be used to help this process along, by encouraging them to express both the strengths and the weaknesses of their position. Other people can be used to help expand the process, and can also be involved in evaluating and testing the arguments that are presented.

The role of objectivity in conflict can be misleading and needs some consideration. It can be tempting to assume that situations of conflict are best resolved by relying on the balanced overview of an objective person. However, this can be a dangerous and misguided strategy, particularly when the issues are complex or related to differences in values. Even those who try to reach a balanced conclusion based on a careful, fair weighing of the issues can only do so with recourse to their own value system. Ultimately, there are no objective people, only those whose position convinces people that their view is more objective than others. The danger here is clear that some people, finding that the objective view does not match their own values, will not accept the solution and will continue to fight the issues. It is better to use the positions expressed to design a solution that has the subjective approval of all.

10 Adopt an enquiring approach to managing

The success of conflict resolution is hinged on understanding the root causes of the conflict. Conflict can flare up over one issue but actually hide a more fundamental cause. In these situations, solving the presenting problem does not necessarily solve the conflict. Reaching the core issues requires sensitive analysis of the situation and careful probing into people's perspectives. Fundamentally, this depends on an ability to maintain connections with people, even in adversity, that allow effective ongoing communication. Techniques that help include:

- Practise managing through enquiry – always look for opportunities to ask what people think and how they feel. This demonstrates your interest, involvement and care for people.

- Using active listening to improve understanding and demonstrate support and empathy.

- Keep talking going in an effort to build understanding through dialogue. Be sensitive to the different needs of individuals in terms of approach.

- Show an impartial approach to the people involved. If people in conflict sense that you will take sides, then they are less likely to reveal their position.

- Be prepared to work on your own openness. Inevitably, as situations arise you will form your own opinions as to causes, based on your own judgments and preconceptions. Model appropriate behaviours by sharing these and testing the assumptions on which they are founded.

The points above all help the process of getting to the root causes of conflict and exploring the issues. While the manager may be placed to give these points special attention, it should be accepted that all people involved in a conflict situation can contribute positively to finding a solution. Sometimes the expectations that go with the territory of management get in the way of action, and other group members are better placed to explore the issues without the complications of other agendas. Resolving conflict is one area where the group has many advantages over the individual in working towards a learning solution of mutual gain.

Aiming for success with conflict is easiest if teams learn to operate with such levels of candour and trust that all differences are explored in a positive and productive manner. In the process of discussion people will develop understanding of each other, and learn about alternative approaches to the business of work. The situation will never become overloaded with negative feelings or behaviours because of a shared commitment to valuing individuals. Achieving this state might be straightforward if conflict only ever concerned technical and work-related issues, as these succumb to a calm and reasoned approach. However, once we recognize that conflict is also a means by which people explore personality and establish their place in an ever-changing social network, it becomes clear that conflict is a difficult thing to leave behind. Indeed, seen from this point of view, it is a positive sign of vigour and health that issues are being brought to the surface and dealt with openly in the workplace.

Nevertheless, it is rarely productive to leave conflict to resolve itself. While expressing differences may well be a healthy sign, people need to take on the responsibility for using the differences as a platform for progress. The world is full of examples of groups of people who cannot see beyond their differences, and who try to impose their views with violent actions. The risk of ignoring conflict is that it opens up a spiral of despair, with ever more vigorous defence of a position being met by ever more persistent attacks. Yet, in work as in the wider world, such situations can be helped and supported to become a vital source of positive change and gains for all involved.

The interpersonal angle

Conflict that has its roots in personal differences is especially difficult to resolve, partly because it is closely tied to values, attitudes and perceptions. As a result, the problems tend to be based on subjective feelings and interpretations rather than on misinformation or misunderstanding. While discussion helps to throw light on the issues, these differences cannot necessarily be resolved by drawing on facts or explanations. These situations are therefore difficult for teams to approach, even though achieving some kind of resolution is essential for long-term team stability. The model in Figure 13.3 below draws together ideas to provide a basic approach to resolving the difficult area of interpersonal conflict.

Coping with criticism

Situations where conflict has arisen can also involve a certain amount of criticism, even if only through implication. When criticism occurs it is difficult for people to remain calm and continue a process of joint problem-solving. More likely, criticism can lead to a build-up of tension, hostility or defensiveness in the recipient. This can lead to more or less veiled attacks on other people, often with little relation to the issues under discussion. Dealing with criticism positively, allowing it to become a valid and useful part of the process of conflict, is one of the most difficult skills to develop. This section looks at ways of coping with criticism productively.

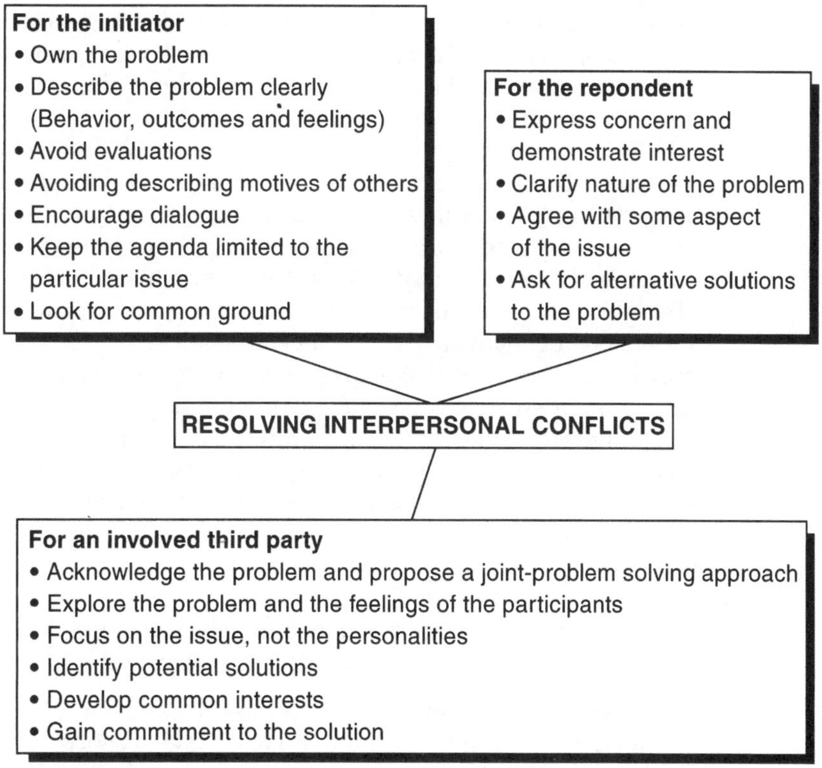

For the initiator
- Own the problem
- Describe the problem clearly
  (Behavior, outcomes and feelings)
- Avoid evaluations
- Avoiding describing motives of others
- Encourage dialogue
- Keep the agenda limited to the
  particular issue
- Look for common ground

For the repondent
- Express concern and
  demonstrate interest
- Clarify nature of the problem
- Agree with some aspect
  of the issue
- Ask for alternative solutions
  to the problem

RESOLVING INTERPERSONAL CONFLICTS

For an involved third party
- Acknowledge the problem and propose a joint-problem solving approach
- Explore the problem and the feelings of the participants
- Focus on the issue, not the personalities
- Identify potential solutions
- Develop common interests
- Gain commitment to the solution

Fig. 13.3 Approaches to interpersonal conflict (adapted from Whetton, Cameron and Woods (1994)).

Learning activity

Feeling criticized

Try to recall any situation where you have been openly and insensitively criticized.

- What feelings do you develop in such a situation? How do you react to such a situation?
- What things make criticism more difficult to accept?
- What things would make criticism easier to accept?

Criticism that is given without any thought for people's feelings can be hurtful. When it is loaded with anger, based on supposition and aimed at personal failings, it can be very threatening indeed, undermining confidence and self-esteem. An insensitive critical comment can be a powerful trigger for our very basic instinct to engage in 'fight or flight'. Most of us will have experienced the perfectly natural reactions, unthinking and very fast, that occur whenever we are threatened or frightened. An immediate, hair-raising alertness develops, highly focused and aware, with a considerable degree of muscle tension as the body prepares for action. When this kind of threat happens on our crowded roads it leads to the common symptoms of road rage. Heart rate and breathing increases, there is a tightened grip on the steering wheel, driving style becomes more aggressive and there is often an overwhelming inclination to wind down the window for some choice abuse!

These natural responses are part of our defence mechanisms, providing a useful state of readiness to respond to danger. However, while the brain is busy responding to the threats by gearing up the body for action, it blocks higher brain activity, preventing conscious thought processes from taking place. The effect is that things that get said in moments of threat are rarely carefully thought out responses but are instead triggered by our primitive aggressive-defensive mechanisms. This is a useful skill when faced with situations of real threat, but does not necessarily help us deal constructively with well-meant criticisms. Instead, our heat of the moment responses can begin a spiral of attack and counter-attack leading to continued conflict. Worse still, the aggressive or defensive responses can easily sidetrack the discussion, leading it away from the basic issues that caused the conflict and which need to be resolved.

Accepting the value of criticism

For criticism to be valuable, it needs to lead to some kind of resolution of the problem that is at its core. This can only occur if three basic steps occur:

- **First, the problem needs to be communicated**. Many people are uncomfortable giving criticism for two basic reasons. Our social upbringing teaches us to avoid hurting people with embarrassing information and the situation itself involves the threat of an unpredictable response. This usually means that criticism occurs only after a considerable build-up of tension.

Inevitably, the communication is poor, as it comes loaded with anger, upset and anxiety. This is more likely to spark off aggressive–defensive responses.

- **Second, the problem needs to be clearly explained** if the criticism is to be effective. This is because it is difficult to respond to a problem unless it is stated in specific terms. For example, a critical statement such as 'you really make me cross!' is not helpful unless the reasons why this is happening are made clear. Criticism is difficult enough to handle without adding confusion to the situation as well. Unfortunately, the communication problems developed by the build-up of tension make clarification difficult, particularly if any initial outburst is met with an aggressive or defensive response.

- **Third, the people involved must develop commitment to some sort of solution**, otherwise the situation will persist. The solution needs to be something that provides a way forward and meets the needs of both parties. Completing this third step means that the original criticism has been effective in beginning a process that has led through to the problem being solved. Achieving basic communication, clarification of the problem and commitment to a solution can only happen if the person receiving the criticism manages to avoid an aggressive or defensive response. These reactions block the considered responses that will allow the problem to be surfaced and explored constructively. An initial step towards handling criticism is to look at ways in which the initial reaction can be made more productive.

Learning activity

Controlling our responses

The primitive responses to threat are very quick, happening in the first few seconds. If we can prevent these initial responses from taking hold we can allow the higher brain time to develop a more considered response. What techniques can you suggest to help block the primitive responses?

Several things can help block our primitive responses and help us improve our ability to get to the core of the problem. These can be difficult to employ, especially if it is felt that the criticism is unjustified or wrong, but controlling our responses gives the best possible chance for resolving the issue. It is important to note that even in a situation where the criticism is 'wrong,' a problem exists – even if it is only one of misunderstanding. Responding aggressively or defensively does not help to put right simple problems of misrepresentation; it simply makes them worse. The following techniques can help:

- Use physical anchors to help keep a firm grip on responses. Some of these are well known – taking a deep breath helps to overcome the initial seconds of response. Others include making a conscious effort to hold your wrist, mental humming of a familiar tune, counting mentally to ten or any other simple and distracting thoughts.

- Avoid denying the criticism, however misguided it seems. Assume that it hides some kind of problem and that it is best to resolve it out in the open. Denying the criticism prevents it from reaching through and is a defensive response.

- Natural though it may seem, do not start to defend yourself by giving excuses. These responses are defensive and prevent people getting to grips with the problem. A few moments spent exploring the issue may help you to realize that the critic has a point.

- For similar reasons, avoid a response that seeks to justify your position. This is based on attacking the critic's position as untenable, and again does not allow the problem to be developed.

- Avoid descending into argument. It may be fun, but it is a long-winded and destructive route to the cause of the problem. In any case, it is a dynamic form of attack and defence that makes people less comfortable with raising problems in the first place.

- However much it feels like an attractive response, do not run away. It does nothing to help advance the situation or put right the problem.

- Perhaps most difficult of all, avoid wholesale agreement with the critic. This sometimes seems like an effective mechanism for defusing criticism and taking the sting out of it, but again it is a defensive response designed to minimize the impact of what is being said. This prevents the issue being developed and the problem being solved. Further, such a passive response can be damaging to self-esteem – it can allow the feelings of being criticized to build up, without any attempt to deal with the effects.

- Whatever else, avoid the well-worn 'Hang on a minute . . .' 'Yes, but . . .' or 'I hear what you're saying, but . . .'

The aim with employing these blocking strategies is to encourage a more considered discussion of the problem to develop. Our objective when being criticized should be to recognize that a basic problem exists, even if it relates to misunderstanding. By listening to the issue, and being prepared to value the point of view of other people, it is possible to work together to solve the problem. Our natural reactions can tend to worsen the situation, making it more difficult to resolve differences. By controlling these responses, we can move to a situation where the core problems are confronted and dealt with in a framework of cooperative problem-solving and mutual support. Being able to work productively and positively in the midst of tension, stress and interpersonal conflict is a rewarding skill, demanding an ability to come to terms with the impact of our behaviour on those around us.

Making progress with criticism

The first step in making productive use of criticism is to ensure that the initial responses do not create a barrier to dealing with the problems. However, despite designing a response that does not worsen the situation, we have to recognize that criticism can hurt. Making further progress can depend on the ability to manage the points being made that accepts them as useful, but protects from the potential damage that may be done. Such a response is assertive, based on using the higher brain to make a considered contribution, rather than relying on our more primitive responses to threats. By blocking our initial responses, then going on to respond constructively, it allows the situation to be managed without provoking unnecessary aggression or allowing the critic to manipulate events for personal gains.

A constructive response is best made by calm recognition of the possibility that the critic has a valid point of view that may contain some truths. This is different from wholesale agreement with the criticism, as it maintains the receiver's ability to exercise judgment and control. Rather than just saying 'you're right, I am hopeless', it is saying 'I can see that you have highlighted a problem, let's work together to put it right'. The strength of this is that it allows the process to proceed between equals, giving the critic a proactive role to play beyond taking the initial plunge. The following suggestions give some responses that replace the aggressive–defensive with assertive responses, allowing recognition of the points being made yet retaining control over the discussion.

Making these assertive responses helps to develop an atmosphere of acceptance, yet protects the recipient from the potential excesses of misplaced criticism or manipulation. Having laid the foundations of a constructive approach, the real issue needs to be fully explored and clarified to allow progress to the last stage of designing a joint solution. Difficult though it may be, this stage of the process simply involves prompting and encouraging the criticism to continue. This ensures that all useful information is obtained about the problem. The possibility exists that the criticism is merely intended to score political points or achieve some other personal gain. In this case, prompting further open exploration of the problem has the effect of exhausting the point, and encourages the critic to come to terms with their own agenda.

The following techniques help to explore the criticism and encourage an objective approach.

Some assertive responses

- One option is to agree with the truth that is being presented: 'You're right, **I was late again today**.'
- A second option is to acknowledge the possibility that the critic's point is correct: 'You **may be** right about that.'
- A third option is to acknowledge that the critic's points have internal logic. For example, in response to 'I said we needed more people on this project. If we had the admin. support, we would not be running around following up loose ends', the receiver might say: 'You're right. If the department did have additional staff it would solve those problems.' This is a response to what they actually say, rather than the implied criticism contained in the statement of the critic.
- A fourth option is to recognize the potential for improvement: 'I'm sure we could find an alternative way of managing the meeting.'
- A fifth option is simply to show empathy: 'I can see why you feel that things are not going well.'

Going forward

Exploring the points

- Resist the continued temptation to strike back by developing questions that focus on your own behaviours and actions.
- Adopt communication techniques that encourage the critic to give more information.
- Encourage the critic to move from the general to the specific. It is easier to correct specific problems.
- Encourage analysis of all aspects of the problem by questioning.
- Keep going until all points have been exhausted.

Conflict comes with risks of despair and disillusionment in an atmosphere of backbiting and criticism. Yet it also offers up riches and hope. Managed effectively, exploring conflict gives an opportunity for progress and enlightenment, an unbounded source of learning for people and organizations. Conflict provides a tumultuous sea of differences, ideas, emotions and prejudices. Travelling out onto the waters holds the promise of discovery, but takes acts of great managerial vision, inspiration and boldness.

Whatever you can do or dream, you can begin. Boldness has genius, power and magic in it.

Goethe

We cannot choose adventure and then promise safety.

Peter Block

Summary

This chapter has made the following key points:

➤ That conflict provides a source of personal and organizational opportunities.
➤ That conflict is an essentially political process.
➤ That conflict has effects on group dynamics through raising levels of uncertainty and anxiety that may block solutions.
➤ That conflict is best approached using a joint problem-solving process.
➤ That handling conflict is facilitated using ten guidelines:
  - Encouraging openness
  - Modelling appropriate responses
  - Providing regular summaries and restatements of the position
  - Bringing in people who are not directly involved
  - Encouraging people to think and reassess their position openly
  - Using the strengths of the group to support the process

- Focusing on shared goals
- Using interests to develop shared gains
- Trying to bring objectivity into the process
- Adopting an enquiring approach to managing.

➤ That dealing with criticism productively can benefit from techniques to limit our initial reaction.

➤ That handling criticism is improved through assertive behaviour.

Further reading

Chris Argyris' *Overcoming Organizational Defences* (Prentice-Hall, Englewood Cliffs, New Jersey, 1990) provides a fascinating and challenging look at how human defence mechanisms inhibit organizational learning. The book is full of clear examples and illustrates how positive intent can turn into organizational failure because of our reactions to embarrassment and threat.

Tom Peter's *Liberation Management* (BCA, New York, 1992) is a long read in an endlessly enthusiastic style. Many of the cases explore the creative aspects of differences and contention, inspiring a belief in the value of allowing conflict to become an open feature of organizational life.

References

Argyris, C. (1982) *Reasoning, Learning and Action*, Jossey-Bass, San Francisco.

Argyris, C. (1990) *Overcoming Organizational Defences*, Prentice-Hall, Englewood Cliffs, New Jersey.

Argyris, C. and Schon, D. (1974) *Theory in Practice*, Jossey-Bass, San Francisco.

Bion, W. R. (1961) *Experiences in Groups and Other Papers*, Tavistock Publications, London.

Bion, W. R. (1992), *Handling Conflict and Negotiation*, Kogan Page, Manchester.

Fisher, R. and Ury, W. (1991) *Getting to Yes*, Century Business, London.

Robbins, S. P. (1974) *Managing Organizational Conflict: A non-traditional approach*, Prentice-Hall, Englewood Cliffs, New Jersey.

Thomas, K. W. (1976) *Conflict and Conflict Management* in Dunnette, M. D. (ed), *Handbook of Industrial and Organizational Psychology*, Routledge & Kegan Paul, London.

Whetton, D. Cameron, K. and Woods, M. (1994) *Developing Management Skills for Europe*, Harper Collins, London.

14

Managing to counsel

I am on the left, which is the side of the heart, as opposed to the right, which is the side of the liver.

Oscar Wilde

Objectives

By the end of this chapter you will be able to:

➤ explain how counselling can be used to help manage people
➤ recognize situations where counselling may be an appropriate management approach
➤ recognize situations where expert help is necessary
➤ undertake counselling of staff with a range of personal problems
➤ assess the causes of stress in the workplace
➤ describe the disadvantages of unmanaged stress
➤ use techniques to help people to cope with stress productively
➤ give support and help where necessary
➤ protect yourself from the damaging impact of others' stress

Introduction

Counselling is often regarded as an activity that is highly specialized and dependent upon considerable expert skills, a view that is reinforced by media images of the analyst's couch and the penetrating gaze of the psychologist. There are situations where this level of expertise is appropriate, though perhaps the stereotypical images presented by the media are aimed at creating good drama and are somewhat removed from reality. Of course, people can develop personal problems that are of considerable depth and effect. These might perhaps be as the result of rejection in relationships, loss of a family member or feelings of inadequacy at work. In cases where the problems are deep-seated and persistent, expert knowledge of how our psychology works is useful to help people learn to manage their problems. As a result, it is common to find professional counselling services in our communities and increasingly in organizations, often targeting particular issues. These include gambling, alcohol, sexual problems and the stresses of family life. The aim of these services is to help people in crisis situations, when problems have developed into intractable and sometimes destructive patterns of behaviour, either for the individual concerned or other people with whom they come into contact.

Against this background it can be hard to imagine that your role as a manager has much to do with counselling of staff. You may not feel that you have the expertise or the time to help people to cope with the kinds of problems described above. However, if counselling is regarded as the process of helping people to solve their problems, then we can see that it is a process that can involve us all at times. Personal problems are something that many of us have experienced in our lives, often without the need to undergo intensive counselling. During our lives, most of us will have experienced a night at the pub or a coffee at work where we have sat down with someone and offered our help with their problems. In many situations of stress, pressure or unhappiness, the support of other people can help them to find their own solutions to the problems.

Learning activity

Helping

Think back over your relationships with friends or colleagues and any difficulties that they may have faced. How have you helped them to cope with their personal problems?

It is likely that at some stage you will have helped someone to think through a personal problem that they were facing. By being prepared to listen and help clarify issues and choices, informal counselling is taking place. Some of these occasions may have happened in the workplace, and been linked to your role as manager. Counselling can occur on an informal level in a variety of settings and forms, in virtually any situation where people are able to talk openly. The objectives of this section are to explore how counselling skills can be developed, so that you will feel better able to contribute to the support of their staff in a positive and productive way.

Understanding limits

Learning activity

Obstructions

In many organizations, there can be a number of barriers to using counselling in the workplace. What obstructions do you think there might be to counselling staff in the workplace?

Case note

The role of the manager

At the start of a management course I once attended the tutor was generating a list of management skills with input from the group. I suggested counselling as an important skill, but the overwhelming reaction was that this was well beyond the remit of the manager. The tutor supported the group view that the skill was too difficult for managers to get involved in at work. The reaction expressed:

• the traditional view that work was somehow separate from people's personal life; and

• the fear of getting involved in such 'messy' personal issues.

Of course, such a reaction would be less likely today, as counselling has become increasingly acceptable as a valuable part of management and organizations.

There may be many answers here, depending on your own particular qualities and on your experience of workplace cultures. Some of the commonly identified obstructions are as follows.

1 The workplace is clearly seen as a place for work, not somewhere where personal problems are a legitimate part of the agenda.
In many workplaces, it is common to hear that 'people should leave their personal problems at home'. While this idea has some appeal, personal

problems are, by their nature, difficult to leave behind. Things that happen to us in life can lead us to become preoccupied at times, until we have had the time and space to think things through to a satisfactory solution. Until then, people will come to work weighed down with issues that arise in their home life. Of course, there are often times when the reverse is true, and situations develop where work pressures are immense and people will take home the stresses and strains of work.

A sensible manager and a supportive workplace allows work to become part of the process of helping to find a solution, not some additional factor that will help to prolong or displace the problem. This helps to ensure that problems do not lead to a downward spiral in work performance and, more importantly, helps to establish and reinforce the message that people are valuable and the core of your concerns.

2 Managers feel that by offering counselling they will be compromising their ability to direct staff, lead the team and exercise discipline

Again, from some perspectives this has a kernel of truth. Certainly, in an organization where management works through structured systems and exercises a high degree of control, counselling will be neither welcome nor effective. Counselling cannot happen in the context of a power relationship, but only through the interaction of two equals. It is effective as one of a range of styles that a manager uses to cope with situations that arise at work and with people. It is based in a belief that people need different things according to different circumstances, and that they cannot be treated as machines that are only capable of responding to one style. From this point of view people are capable of accepting help in some circumstances, while also maintaining their discipline or following directives in others. Counselling enhances, rather than inhibits, the ability to manage.

3 Managers sometimes feel that while counselling is plainly a worthwhile activity, they do not have appropriate skills, or the time, to be effective – this is linked to concerns about the depths of analysis into which it might lead.

Part of this particular obstruction is based on the perception that counselling is a specialist activity that can only be effective when a professional is involved. As discussed earlier, there are instances where this is true, but that does not mean the manager should assume that this is always the case. There are many situations where the manager is ideally placed to offer counselling – after all, some of the problems are likely to be linked to work and the manager is then well placed to help out by offering relevant facts or options. Besides, even if the manager cannot help directly, they should be able to offer the appropriate support by facilitating access to whatever help is needed. However the situation is viewed, ignoring the problem is the least effective management option – indeed, it can scarcely be called management at all.

Workplaces can seem to be short of time, and there are often endless lists of tasks not yet done. Adding in counselling to the list can seem to be impractical and somewhat removed from the purpose of work. However, if we stop to think what would be the consequences of not making the time, we can quickly see that problems can easily develop from the personal to the general. An unhappy employee may leave, leading to time being spent on recruitment and training as well as the problems associated with loss of expertise. Less dramatic but just as damaging is the fact that not making the time to address problems sends signals throughout the workplace, and these often result in loss of motivation, disaffection and dissent. Other people will notice and feel the effect of any problems that exist, and will expect that somehow those problems are addressed. Coupled with the loss of performance brought about by the original problem, failing to spare the time is a potentially expensive excuse.

Counselling is therefore a form of helping people to solve their own personal problems. As such, it has an important role to play in reducing the pressures of life and the impact that stress can have on work performance. Problems that occur in all areas of our life can have an impact on ourselves and on our performance, making us seem preoccupied, moody and overloaded. Part of your role is to try to ensure that work is a place that can contribute to improving people's lives in a meaningful way, and allowing work to be a place where it is possible to get effective help with personal problems is a big step towards such a goal. However, accepting the potential benefits of being able to counsel staff, and being able to translate this into action can often be different things.

The ability to counsel is therefore a useful skill for a manager to develop. As a skill it builds on our ordinary human skill of communicating, and as an activity it has the potential to contribute effectively to the solution of problems that affect people. Helping to solve problems is part of what management is about, and there is no real reason why this help cannot be extended to the kinds of personal problems and issues that life can bring to us all. In offering this support, a manager will be developing a workplace culture that shows empathy for people facing difficulties, whatever their nature, and this makes a clear and valuable statement about the value of people at work.

Identifying the need

The first practical consideration for the manager is that of developing an awareness of the need for counselling. People will often feel reluctant to bring their personal problems along, partly because it needs considerable strength to reveal problems and weaknesses in the work environment. Accordingly, a manager needs to be able to identify that counselling may be appropriate, even though nothing directly has been revealed. This they must do by tuning in to the other signals or signs that people are having problems.

 ### *Learning activity*

Looking for signals and signs

What signs might indicate to you that a member of your team was experiencing personal problems?

There are many possible answers here, some of which will reflect your personal experience and style. Usually problems are associated with some change in behaviour, even from those who attempt to disguise the problem and soldier on regardless. This may be minor, a lack of the usual warmth and cheer in their greetings, to more blatant examples of seemingly irrational and angry outbursts. It is impossible to define or predict how everyone will respond to problems, but there is likely to be some change from their usual behaviour.

Another related indication is a change in performance. People who are preoccupied with problems are unlikely to devote the usual care, attention or time to work, and there will commonly be some signs in their performance. Missed deadlines from those who are usually on time, poor decisions or disaffected and upset staff are all signs that something is wrong.

Another possibility is that the manager will be told of the problem by an affected team member. This may take the form of a complaint about performance or behaviour, or may simply be an observation about apparent personal problems and their effect. Second-hand information like this is a common feature of work, and is often no more than an idle comment about a colleague. However, the things that are said are an indication of changes in behaviour and performance in the same way that your own observations would be, and as such may be a useful signal that someone may need help.

 Learning activity

Second-hand signals

- What problems might there be if the manager acts on second-hand information?
- How do you feel about such comments being a part of a workteam culture?

Information that arrives through the informal network has its problems. No manager wants to encourage an environment of gossip where people trade negative opinions about other people's personal lives in a way that leads to a destructive culture of implied criticism. Nevertheless, other members of the team will be in a position to notice the symptoms of problems, particularly where they work closely with people, and often will have some idea about the reasons behind the problem. Ideally, perhaps, the workplace culture should be one that enables them to offer support in a climate of openness and trust, but many factors can prevent this from happening. In such circumstances, people will often look to the manager for help, and second-hand information will arise. In these circumstances, it is crucial that the information is regarded positively, as a sign of a problem that can be solved rather than a personal fault, and that actions that follow are a positive attempt to help. This ensures that passing on information does not lead to destructive consequences, but instead leads to support and assistance, making it unlikely that acting upon such information will encourage mean-spirited and unhelpful gossip. Second-hand information can be positively viewed as a sign of shared concern.

Creating the right conditions

Once a manager has identified a potential need for counselling, they then have to try to create conditions that will allow a successful counselling session to be conducted. The popular image of the analyst's couch may be impractical in reality, and certainly carries unhelpful messages about power in the doctor–patient relationship, but it does at least offer the person a relaxing, comforting environment in which to work on their problem. The manager's task is to try to produce an environment in which the person can feel relaxed and able to talk openly, and this depends on the physical environment, the behaviours adopted by the manager and the quality of relationships sustained by the organizational culture.

 Learning activity

The right approach

- What can a manager do to ensure that the environment will allow the best possible chance for counselling?
- What actions can a manager adopt that will encourage a person to talk about themselves in a counselling session?

A counselling session implies the revealing of personal problems, and this will only happen in a private environment. For counselling to stand any chance of success, the session must be private, discrete and free of interruptions and time pressure. It also helps if the situation is comfortable and, where possible, removed from a setting that has obvious links to hierarchy or power. Managers can counsel in their office, but it helps the process to stress that the situation is one of equals, and this is difficult to reinforce from behind the physical barrier of a desk.

There are many things that can help to encourage people to talk about issues that are affecting them at work. Firstly, no one will find it easy to talk in a situation where they are worried about the consequences of what they are revealing, and it is important to stress that counselling will not be an effective management technique if information gained through the process is used against people. Rather it must be emphasized that the situation is one that is designed to help people through problems, and the organization is there to support and enhance that process. People therefore need some reassurance that it is normal to have problems and that the organization is supportive. This can be given by being prepared to listen without criticism, disapproval or blame to whatever the person is prepared to reveal. A manager has to accept the problem, regardless of their own views of the position or situation, and comments that attempt to undervalue or dismiss the problem will not help.

It is also important to avoid making assumptions, even about staff that you feel that you know well. Managers are used to thinking and assessing situations, and it can be tempting to apply the same skills to the problems that people are revealing. However, our personal problems are rooted in our own values and responses to the situations of life, and each person may respond very differently to such pressures. It is therefore particularly unhelpful for counsellors to draw their own conclusions or provide their own solutions, as they are very unlikely to match the needs of the person. People must find solutions that suit themselves and their own perspective, and this can only happen if they are allowed the opportunity to fully reveal their situation and their feelings and thoughts.

The behaviours that help this to happen are those that demonstrate openness and an ability to listen with concentration and intent. These have been covered in detail in Chapter 4 and the key points below are a summary of the appropriate actions and behaviours.

A listening approach

Adopt open body language from the outset
- Make friendly eye contact.
- Smile.
- Lean forward.
- Keep arms and legs uncrossed.
- Use palm upward hand gestures.
- Sit at an angle to the person, not opposite to them.

Establish ownership and the manager's role
- Emphasize that the intent and purpose of the session is exploratory, controlled by the other person and without threat.
- 'My role is to help you to clarify things and help you to reach your own conclusions . . .'.
- 'I'm not here to give advice or solve the problem. Perhaps I can help with some ways forward . . .'.

Ask open questions that allow people to express their feelings and thoughts.
- 'How do you feel about that?'
- 'Why do you think that made you angry?'

Encourage the other person to develop their answers through body language
- Nod and encourage with facial expressions.
- Support their answers with listening noises.

Demonstrate listening and check understanding through summarizing and rephrasing their answers
This is a powerful technique that shows your commitment and provides conversational links without taking over the conversation and giving your own

views. It encourages further contribution from the other person, who can then proceed to clarify issues or develop understanding.

Counselling without authority

Counselling depends on being able to get the person to talk about their problems. Without them revealing what problems they have, it is difficult for the manager to help them to work through the issues and develop a solution. The primary skills are in encouraging a person to be open and in listening to them talk. For the manager the situation has added difficulty, for the very nature of organizational hierarchy can place unseen barriers in the way of such a process.

Whether or not an individual manager's behaviour makes it justified, people will sometimes identify managers closely with power and authority, making it possible that they will be reluctant to reveal problems that could be held against them in other circumstances. This view of management, where managers are one side of a power relationship, is one of the enduring legacies of the history of work that still finds expression in many of society's systems. Overcoming this hurdle is a key step in enabling a manager to counsel effectively.

 ## Learning activity

Levelling out

What steps might a manager take to help other people see them as an equal rather than a figure of authority?

Providing reassurance, behaving openly and listening to people without hint of criticism are all behaviours that can help deliver a human relationship rather than a hierarchical one. For counselling to be effective, it helps if the manager is talking as a person to a person, rather than the relationship being based clearly on roles. This relationship can be helped if the manager is prepared to reveal their own human frailties as an aid to showing empathy and human understanding. After all, a critical and unconstructive view is less likely to come from someone who shows that they have also, at times, felt inadequate, overburdened or stressed by life's problems. Revealing some experience of personal problems and stresses helps others to see the manager in human terms, as someone with insights that come from real experience rather than through the requirements and position of their role. This willingness to offer compatibility, to locate your own experiences in other people's frame of reference, will do much to remove the veils of the manager's role and humanize the relationship as one of equals.

Working through the problem

Enabling people to talk about their problems can be helpful in itself, for it allows people the chance to explore their perceptions and understanding of problems in a structured way as they talk. Once a problem has been revealed, it can be tempting for managers to use their problem-solving skills to develop a solution, but this is generally an ineffective approach to personal problems.

Learning activity

Providing a solution

What objections or problems do you think are associated with managers providing a solution to a personal problem brought up by a member their staff?

There are many problems with this approach, not least that your solution as manager may not be one that would suit the person being counselled. Indeed, given that a manager will often have a different viewpoint because of their position and the varying responsibilities of their job, their solution may have very different aims. Just as the problem is owned by the person, any solutions should also be created from the same value base and perspective – other people's solutions are generally only worthwhile in expanding the range of available options open to the person.

More importantly, solving other people's problems may be rewarding where it is effective, leaving the manager feeling satisfied with a job well done, but the approach has significant drawbacks. Ultimately, it is impossible for managers to solve all of the problems that other people might bring to work, because some will be outside of their experience and understanding. Further, managers should be aiming to develop staff in all areas of their work practice, and that principle extends to the development of self-analytical and reflective skills. It is important to encourage people to take responsibility for shaping their own environment, for owning problems and solutions that affect them, especially when those problems are of their own circumstances. Help and support are useful things for a manager to provide, options may even have some value, but ultimately solutions must be created and pursued by the person with the problem.

The manager's role is therefore based on maintaining a position that is empathetic, supportive of the person, yet balanced and neutral. It is useful to supply facts that relate to the situation, as these ensure that the person is dealing with accurate information rather than speculation or supposition. Less helpful are opinions which are based on your own viewpoint and are not neutral. Perhaps least relevant of all to the counselling situation is criticism, which delivers negative feedback based on opinion in a situation where one is trying to help build a positive relationship and a solution to the problem. Far better to maintain empathy by recognizing and revealing occasions where your own weaknesses have emerged.

Building a solution then becomes a matter of encouraging the person to consider and evaluate options and possibilities that they have generated themselves. This can all be achieved through a process of asking relevant open questions aimed at developing ideas:

> 'So what are the possibilities that have emerged?'
> 'How do you think you can contribute to the situation?'
> 'Where would you feel your skills are best used in the circumstances?'

On occasion, perhaps especially when things are desperate, people find it hard to think of any possibilities. Here, it may be helpful to assist in generating options to be considered, but it is especially important to present these neutrally, as people can easily be led to accept ideas that are unsuitable when they come from a person they respect. Neutral presentation is based on appropriate language – 'I've got a great idea!' is not neutral whereas 'one of the possibilities might be . . .' has the correct balance. Ensure that the person is given opportunities to explore and evaluate the options fully, again through the use of open questions that avoid leading the person towards certain choices:

> 'How would you feel about that sort of move?'
> 'What are the strengths and weaknesses of that approach?'
> 'How would other people react to this action?'

Learning activity

Dealing with differences

Counselling may uncover considerable differences, for example, in approach to solving the problem. How would you suggest that a manager copes with ideas that do not reflect their own approach and with which they disagree fundamentally?

This presents considerable difficulties for the manager, who may feel that some of the approaches to solving the problem are unhelpful or inappropriate. It is difficult to resist pointing out the obvious problems, but it is crucial that the manager tries to maintain neutrality and allows the person to develop their own solution. In these circumstances, provide some summaries or rephrasings and continue to use questions as a means of encouraging evaluation of a solution:

> 'So you feel that the situation might be helped by moving Sheila in to support Phil. How can we assess how they might feel about that?'
> 'So one option you suggest is to develop closer monitoring of staff. How else can we achieve similar improvements?'

Dealing with differences provides a real challenge to managers in the counselling situation. It is impossible to listen to someone's problems without forming your own opinions about the best way in which they might be approached. Obviously, our approach is based on our own style and personality, and the manager must remember that this may not be an appropriate way forward for the person with the problem. Encouraging people to look at things from different points of view is useful, but in the end it is important to recognize that people must choose their own solutions. These may not be the solutions that the manager would like, or even approve of, but imposing solutions to other people's personal problems is both an expression of authority and unlikely to be successful.

Supporting solutions

Instead, managers should continue to offer support and help, even of solutions that appear to be inappropriate. This can mean that the manager helps to clarify an action plan for the person to follow, and establishes a date for review of progress. It is useful to offer continued support and the opportunity to talk through any further issues that arise, but beyond that the manager should leave people to get on with implementing their own solution. One other possibility in organizational counselling is that the manager may well need to suggest that the issue is referred onwards. In-company counselling services, provided by trained personnel, are an increasing feature of modern organizations, and there are many excellent services available in the community that a supportive manager can easily access.

Despite the agreed action plan, personal problems must remain in the ownership of the person with the problem, and this should continue throughout the implementation of a solution. It can be tempting to follow up the relationship that has been established in the counselling session with a friendly checking service. Although this may seem helpful, it can prevent the person taking responsibility for solving their own problems, and sends messages about the source of problem-solving and place of authority in your organization. By all means offer an occasional, general word of support or caring enquiry, but do nothing to add pressure or impose stress. A caring and friendly manager is helpful in these circumstances, but an impatient, expectant and authoritative manager will generally lead to problems being hidden in the future.

Dealing with stress

Conflict, difficult relationships and the many problems of life and work are all a source of potential opportunity for the manager, in offering both a chance to build more effective understanding of others and in learning how to help solve problems. By working with others in a framework of supportive problem-solving, managers can join with people in developing skills and self-insight, a process leading to personal growth and organizational rewards. However, while handling the flipside is a rich source of management opportunity, it also provides some considerable challenges, both for the manager and for the people affected by the particular issues. One of the potential outcomes of being confronted with challenges – for all people – is **stress**.

Stress is something we all experience to some degree during our lives. Indeed, in many circumstances, some degree of stress is an aid to reaching an optimum level of productivity – many people feel that they work better under pressure and with some degree of anxiety about the outcomes. The challenge of tight targets or the problem of coping with a new client are things that can move work from the realms of routine to the edge of excitement. However, everyone will have experiences which at some stage are over-taxing, worrying, difficult or dangerous, leading in some cases to the physical and psychological symptoms of overload. These may be apparently minor – tiredness, headaches, loss of concentration or irritability – but with some people the pressure can become overbearing, leading to breakdown, trauma, depression or even suicide. As a problem, stress is estimated to cause the loss of 2% of the gross national product through related illness and absenteeism, and has associated human costs in terms of individual suffering. The object of the rest of the chapter to develop some practical actions that will help to prevent stress from becoming a damaging problem to people in the workplace.

The source of stress

Stress is a response that people have to difficult circumstances or events. This response is partly physical, leading to measurable changes in heart rate, breathing, hormone release and blood-sugar levels as the body prepares itself for defence or aggression to outside threat. It is this state of heightened physical tension that develops some of the related problems of stress such as headaches, muscle tension, fatigue and loss of sleep. The response is also psychological, with a wide variety of emotional responses to the situations that appear to be associated with stress. These responses are less predictable than the physical ones, varying according to the nature of the cause and the characteristics of the person, but they are all fundamentally linked to the level of anxiety that people experience in the situation.

Learning activity

Reactions to anxiety

- Think about people who have been placed in situations of some anxiety while at work. What kinds of responses has this developed?
- In what ways do people differ in their response to anxiety?
- How would you explain these differences?

Reactions to anxiety vary widely, but you will probably have observed that some people respond with angry outbursts, while others display fear or withdrawn nervousness. The range of responses to stressful situations is as varied as people themselves, and a situation that induces apathy and irritability in one person may simply lead to excitement in another. The common feature in response to excess pressure is some element of anxiety associated with the situation, but people differ greatly in the ways in which they deal with anxiety. For some, uncertainty and ambiguity may begin to dominate their thinking, leading to concern and worry about wider issues and a spiral of despair, while others are less likely to succumb to the influence of stress, and indeed will try to build on, or learn from, the experience. However, it is difficult to predict the response of people to particular situations as the factors that can have an effect on our reactions are many and complex. As a result, it is difficult to anticipate what situations or events will cause stress in a given individual, though there are some factors that might be identified as carrying a risk of causing stress for people in general.

Learning activity

Exploring pressure and the causes of stress

Consider the list of factors below in relation to your own workplace and rate each on a scale of 1 to 10 as a potential source of pressure and stress for you (1 for low stress, 10 for high stress). Comment on each score above 5.

Source	Rating for self	Other person
Your working environment		
Your terms and conditions of employment		
Administration and bureaucracy		
Communication at work		
Changes		
Your prospects		
Role clarity		
Aspects of work itself		
Relationships with clients		
Relationships with the team		
Relationships with outside people or agencies		
Levels of responsibility		
Getting results		

When you have finished your own scoring, choose a colleague who you feel has a different approach to work from yourself. Ask them to complete their own rating alongside your own. What differences emerge from this process? How do you explain the differences?

Now consider the factors listed below, which relate to your lifestyle and the environment outside work.

Again rate these factors for potential contribution to levels of stress and comment for those that are 5 or over. Ask the same colleague to provide a comparison as before.

Source	Rating for self	Other person
Self-management skills		
Level of exercise		
Relaxation opportunities		
Your personality		
Relationships		
Levels of support and understanding		
Other factors (provide your own)		

Having taken a careful look at your own stress sources and compared them with those of a colleague, what changes could you make that would help reduce the pressure upon yourself? Thinking about the build-up of pressure – what actually causes anxiety and stress?

It is tempting to think of the pressures of work above as the causes of stress, but in fact stress is only caused by our own reactions to these things. In thinking about other people, and making comparisons between the various sources of stress for different people, it can be seen that none of the factors on our lists will automatically lead to stress. For some people, a minor change in their work routine seems to be a trigger for stress, while others can cope quite happily, and even relish, major upheavals in their working lives. Stress is plainly triggered by external events, but the cause of stress is fundamentally based in our own behavioural and emotional response to various triggers in our environments.

Recognition of this is an important aid to managing the problem, for if we acknowledge that stress happens because of the way that we respond to events, it means that we can begin to manage stress by adapting our own responses, or by helping stressed colleagues to do so. This acknowledges that the problem of stress is best addressed through the person suffering from the symptoms, rather than by simply trying to remove the factors in the environment that are triggering the response. While managers need to recognize when work pressures are overloading staff, and indeed should work to develop feedback systems that allow this to be part of regular discussion, they should not simply respond to signs of stress with a removal of the workload, however caring it might seem. To do so will firstly miss an opportunity for the person to learn to cope with the added pressure or the particularly difficult task, and secondly will reinforce the thought processes, doubts and feelings of inadequacy that have developed anxiety in the first place. Neither of these can be thought of as effective management or support of people, though they might make the manager and the stressed person feel better in the short term.

Placing the focus of stress management on the response that people have to pressure enables a learning process to occur. When situations occur that seem to induce high levels of anxiety, the object becomes helping the person to develop the ability to manage their own responses more productively for themselves. This may still mean that they would negotiate a reduction in workload, or whatever trigger seems to be important, but in the context of a proactive approach to managing themselves, rather than as a response to the declining productivity brought about by a stressed response. It can seem that anxiety is an automatic, or instinctive, reaction to events that occur, happening without our control. However, like many aspects of personality, our emotional reactions are learned through our experience in life.

Learning activity

Thinking about behaviour and emotions

This aspect of stress is worth exploring, for it has lessons for many areas of life at work. Take some time to reflect on the way you respond to the awkward behaviour of a difficult person. What was your response the first time you experienced this awkward behaviour? How did it differ from the response that you would now have?

Think about any of your own emotional reactions. How have these changed over the years?

It is common to discover that our reactions adapt and change as we learn improved methods of coping with situations. In this way people can learn to control their feelings of inadequacy, anger or fear, and a similar process can be applied to situations that trigger stress.

One difficulty is that our reactions are driven by results – we only respond in particular ways because of the positive results that we gain through such behaviour. It is not necessarily immediately obvious that a person responding with anxiety and the physical symptoms of stress, possibly including nausea, is actually gaining very much, but of course such responses usually mean that difficult, challenging situations are avoided. Indeed, in some work environments, such responses are possibly the only way of escaping from the triggers, while in other high-pressure roles symptoms of stress are a valid statement of success. Even in situations where triggers cannot be avoided, a stressed response often gives a plainly visible reason for impaired performance, helping other people to appreciate the level of pressure and anxiety under which the stressed person works. The gain here is again obvious, as other people will learn to understand and appreciate the pressure suffered by the stressed person, and will excuse or make allowances for poorer performance. They will probably adopt a sympathetic stance and avoid loading the person with extra work.

Stress is a response that we have to triggers, and part of that response is in our thought processes. For example, a person who develops stress every time they have to give a presentation to their colleagues is responding because of thoughts about the response of other people to a poor quality presentation, or because they think that they will look stupid to others. It can be helpful to think of stress being triggered in all situations by the **gap** that we think exists between our own performance and that which is expected by other people. If we think other people are expecting miracles, then we can become anxious when we know that we can only deliver card tricks. The thought processes can lead quickly to a self-fulfilling prophecy, as thoughts about the magnitude of the gap intensify feelings of inadequacy and self-doubt. As anxiety levels rise, performance becomes impaired, and a real gap develops between expected performance and that which is delivered. The next time a similar trigger arises, thought processes begin with the poor performance of the last time and so the cycle of stress continues. Alongside this, other people note the impaired performance, and often respond by removing the triggers. This serves to confirm the thought process and validate our original perceptions of a gap – the prophecy is fulfilled.

 Learning activity

Challenging your thoughts

Think about a situation that causes you anxiety and try to slow down and replay the thoughts that you have in these situations. This is often best done by imagining your thoughts as a dialogue with yourself. In what ways do the thoughts that you have affect your response to the situation?

How could you adapt the thoughts to help generate a neutral response to the situation? What actually stops you from thinking the neutral thoughts rather than the negative ones?

Preventing stress

Taking responsibility for stress is an important first step to preventing it occurring. If people can begin to recognize the ways in which they are responding to situations, and accept responsibility for bringing those responses under active control, then the situations are unlikely to cause so much anxiety in the first place. Taking the time and care to think through responses often reveals how the thoughts that people have exaggerate the potential problems in the situation, induce anxiety and do damage through stress.

 Learning activity

Helping people to approach situations

Given the negative thought processes described, how could you help a person reduce anxiety by developing more realistic expectations when faced with pressure situations?

There are several steps that may help in developing a learning response to pressure. It is important that people recognize that stress is something that we can work to bring under control, and a practical process for a manager to facilitate is as follows.

- **Offer reassurance**. This ensures that people can see that the problem is being acknowledged by the manager as a real problem that needs attention rather than some failing of personality for which they are to blame.

- **Explore with the person what situations and feelings are triggering the stress**. This stage looks firstly at the triggers, opening up a dialogue about workload, responsibility, self-management or other aspects. Secondly, it provides the opportunity to provide support to a process of adjusting expectations, allowing people to develop a realistic view of the gap. If the gap between what people feel is expected and their own capability reduces, then they will become less vulnerable to stress.

- **Ask them to suggest ideas**. This opens up the opportunity to learn from such situations. Managing stress is about developing both realistic expectations and improving our capacity to cope positively with situations where gaps do exist. This means being encouraged to focus on situations where we have coped effectively, and using these as a platform for our thought process. Having a positive view of the possibilities may not be necessarily more realistic, but it is less damaging than carrying a negative view into the situation. In any case, having positive expectations is likely to become self-fulfilling through the same feedback mechanisms as operate in the negative cycle.

- **Encourage people to rephrase their negative thoughts in a neutral way**. This helps to counter the spiral of stress, without placing unrealistic demands on the view people have of themselves or the situation. It can be useful to look at the worst possible outcomes, and discuss the likelihood of each element being realistic. In this way people can be encouraged to soften their view of the consequences in a productive way, without them having to try to turn their views around completely. It is helpful to get people to reassess their views, but it can be counter-productive to challenge their perspective completely.

Working towards a stress-free environment

Helping people to manage their stress is linked closely to the manager's willingness to adopt a counselling approach to problems. Understanding the processes by which stress develops will help a manager to approach the issue as an opportunity for learning and development of the stressed person, rather than a problem to be fixed by the manager. However, when faced with a workplace that appears to be creating stress, the wise manager looks to the environment of work to see how pressures can be approached in a different and positive way. There are several things a manager can do that will help to lessen the likelihood of stress.

Learning activity

Preparing staff

Thinking about work environments, and the sources of pressure that exist, what things could be done to help staff to face the pressures with optimism?

Thinking about this activity will throw up some links to material elsewhere in the book. Chapter 12 on change and opportunity is one obvious example of a source of ideas for dealing with some key pressures. Your own experiences may throw up particular issues, but some general guidelines here are as follows.

- Provide opportunities for training and development as these increase people's ability to cope with the demands of their role and help reinforce confidence.

- Encourage dialogue that looks to develop discussion and share the problems of work. This is particularly important where people work in isolation, unable to appreciate that others are experiencing similar issues, as these situations allow perceptions of a gap to grow. Regular dialogue helps people to feel comfortable with raising personality issues where these are a source of pressure.

- Help people to develop their own, realistic goals. Encourage flexibility in the workplace across role boundaries – sticking to your job makes least sense when it is unproductive and the source of stress.

- Encourage people to recognize their strengths, and to adopt goals that will reflect these and give satisfaction.

- Share difficult or unrewarding work across the team, through a process of negotiation. This also helps people to ensure that only valuable work will get done.

- Encourage people to exercise ownership. This develops a sense of value, encourages feelings of competence, enhances coping skills, develops confidence and builds analytical ability.

- Develop effective processes of review that allow people to evaluate and rearrange workloads. Encourage people to build challenge into their work, but to recognize when too much challenge is leading to ineffective behaviour.

- Adopt a counselling approach to managing stress that provides opportunities for it to be revealed, shared and confronted as a learning opportunity.

- Encourage relaxation. Holidays, weekends and even time at work can all contribute to a balanced perspective on workplace pressures. Work is immensely worthwhile as an activity for many people, but narrowing down experience can be a route to boredom and a lack of creativity.

These guidelines, and your own ideas, may help to provide a working environment where stress is less likely. However, it is important to recognize that people are not constant in their responses or their feelings. People who seem solid, dependable and able to cope with anything can change as the result of a single, unexpected failure. In the same way, success in apparently unrelated fields – having a baby, for example – can transform people's confidence and expectations, leading them to seek new heights of challenge and performance. Stress is about people's response to the pressures of life, yet it is through the pressures of life that we learn, grow and develop. Paradoxically, it is the sources of pressure that transform our ability to cope with stress. Managers must always recognize the variety of responses that situations may develop, and allow people the opportunity and support to explore them productively.

The organizational background

In addition to the measures that a manager can try to adopt on a team level, organizations can help to produce a stress-free framework on a wider scale. Primarily, the steps are commonsense measures to ensure that work seems worthwhile, valuable and interesting to people.

- Create enough resource slack to enable people to spend time together on the guidelines above. Without time to think or share problems and ideas, people will eventually reject the pressure that is placed upon them. Efficient use of resources means a different thing for machinery than it does for people.

- Recognize that wholesale change can undermine people's view of the contributions that they used to make. Change processes must encourage people to participate and explore new ideas from a secure base.

- Encourage groups through formal recognition of success in solving problems. This means that organizations must first validate problems through recognition of human issues as part of the workplace agenda.

- Encourage feedback about all aspects of the organization. An organization that is worried about the feedback process has got every reason to worry, because hiding facts and feelings does not reduce their validity or their ability to do damage. It does create a hidden potential for harm.

- Encourage people to contribute to the development of organizational goals and processes. If these reflect people's values and beliefs, then their behaviour will reflect commitment and trust.

Organizations can help by looking at people in human terms. It can be tempting to think of people as human resources, cost centres and in terms of efficiency and productivity gains, and these are all aspects of managing people. However, people are affected by events and situations in ways that other aspects of the organization are not, and the organization needs to recognize this overtly, and take every opportunity to celebrate that it is so.

Summary

This chapter has made the following key points:

On counselling

➤ Counselling is a skill that supports effective management and is built upon the ordinary abilities of people.
➤ The counselling relationship is supported by:
(a) creating the right conditions
(b) developing a listening approach
(c) clarifying the manager's role
(d) using open questions to explore feelings and thoughts
(e) maintaining a relationship of equals
➤ Solutions need to generated and owned by the person with the difficulty, supported by the manager adopting a balanced and neutral stance that encourages evaluation of options and possibilities.

On stress

➤ Stress is something that affects us all, and indeed is healthy up to a point.
➤ Stress can become physically and psychologically harmful.
➤ All aspects of life can have an impact on our ability to cope with pressure. This varies according to our circumstances and experiences.
➤ Stress is triggered by events, but its cause is in our response to those events.
➤ Ultimately, our feelings and reactions are our own responsibility, and only we can make the effort to change them.
➤ Managing stress is about supporting people with a process of working through their problems. Removing triggers without allowing people to face the issues is a waste of a potential opportunity to learn and undervalues the contribution people can make.
➤ Managers and organizations can support an environment where stress is less likely if they encourage and facilitate an approach that fundamentally recognizes the value of people.

References

Back, K. and Back, K. (1990) *Assertiveness at Work*, McGraw-Hill, London.
Pease, A. (1981) *Body Language*, Sheldon Press, London.
Phillips, N. and Sidney, E. (1991) *One to One Management*, Pitman, London.

15

Organizing and planning

A journey of a thousand miles begins with a single step.

Lao-Tzu

Objectives

By the end of this chapter you will be able to:

➤ Describe a basic approach to maximizing personal effectiveness
➤ Use techniques to help manage your time appropriately
➤ Create frameworks and structures to help others achieve results
➤ Manage meetings for productive outcomes
➤ Use planning methods in situations where they are useful

Introduction

Whatever the goals of individual people, ultimately the business of organizations is in facilitating joint action. Through joint action, the organization becomes a framework through which productive outcomes are achieved, and much effort goes into ensuring that the framework includes objectives, plans and monitoring processes. Within this framework, people are given tasks to do and responsibilities to exercise that link into the overall aims and purposes of the particular business. Often, these tasks are broadly stated and encompass a whole range of detailed day-to-day minutiae that make up the manager's work. Responsibilities are similarly broad and often encompass a rich detail of problem-solving, decision-making and conflict resolution that passes under the umbrella of phrases such as 'ensure the smooth running of the department'. Against such a background, managers have to make choices about appropriate actions for themselves and other members of the team; they have to plan and organize a way of doing the organization's work.

The complexity of organizations ensures that the plain statements of any job description hide a bewildering array of possibilities. There are always competing choices in the way particular processes are approached and there is always more and more work to do. Very often, there are new initiatives and projects, some of which will ultimately change the shape of the organization or the nature of work. Whether these seem interesting or threatening, they nevertheless ensure that the pattern of tasks, processes and responsibilities continues to shift under the manager's grip. Even in the simplest of management jobs, organizational processes can seem to throw up a plethora of options and choices. This chapter aims to develop an approach to self-organization and the management of work that can help keep the manager both effective themselves and a positive asset to those working alongside.

Self-organization: approaching your own work

A manager's work can often seem to consist of a chaotic and fragmented melange of loosely related bits and pieces. Interruptions are a frequent occurrence as the ordinary business of maintaining relationships and networks goes on. Problems arise, both technical and interpersonal, that need attention and sometimes override the most careful of plans. Tasks come and go according to changing priorities as the organization moves within its environment. This variety, where managers are engaged in a seemingly endless list of activity, places practical boundaries on the achievement of both organizational and personal goals. Further, it creates fundamental pressures on how we use our time.

Pressure on time is one of the most significant triggers for stress in managers. Many people have direct experience of the stressful feelings that can grow as time overtakes our workload. Important project deadlines approach with too little time left for necessary groundwork; meetings are missed as previous engagements overrun; essential preparation for important presentations is overlooked amongst the growing piles of items on the 'to do' list. Feelings of overwork, loss of control and failure can grow in response to overwhelming time pressures, with the symptoms of stress creeping close behind. The common response to these types of time problems is to develop systems that help managers to become more efficient users of time, mainly through using diaries to ensure careful scheduling and using daily lists to focus on tasks. Coupled together these help managers to take on and complete an appropriate volume of work, and give them the option of turning away interruptions or projects that will not fit into the schedule.

These approaches work well for some people, though there are many who find that long 'to do' lists carry their own stresses. In practice, these methods undoubtedly contribute to improved efficiency, but many managers find that the basic problem of too much work persists, even though their capacity to get through it rises. Further, without careful consideration of personal and organizational priorities, managers can become tremendously efficient, but nevertheless remain feeling frustrated and ineffective. 'To do' lists have a wonderful habit of filling up with the trivial, easy and enjoyable tasks, leading to transient personal rewards and a fair residue of time stress left behind as really important tasks get missed.

Developing basic effectiveness

The flaw in approaching time management with efforts to improve efficiency is that it does not necessarily lead the manager to consider their own personal values and beliefs. It may make us better users of time, allowing us to schedule more tasks into our hectic working life, but this does not necessarily make it any more satisfying or any less stressful. Self-organizing must begin with an examination of the interaction between our personal values and beliefs and those of the organization. This process allows us to fit organizational pressures in alongside our own personal principles, rather than allowing ourselves to succumb to the endless demands of the organization and other people within it. Without taking this step, work will be scheduled that does not reflect personal beliefs, develops no sense of commitment and fosters no real interest. This is unlikely to develop motivated and efficient use of time when pursuing those tasks, and may lead to work being done inadequately or covertly avoided.

A common way of assessing how effective management tasks are is to present them in terms of a grid which categorizes tasks according to their levels of importance and urgency. By using this approach at the outset of self-organizing, the manager is attempting to identify tasks and processes that are of high importance. In making this assessment managers must take into account their personal frame of reference – their own beliefs about the things that are important. This raises the possibility that the manager's personal set of values will be out of step with those of the organization, leading to conflict over appropriate work. This kind of conflict can only be successfully resolved through a process of open dialogue, where people attempt to build shared values and understand other beliefs, strengths and differences. Without this process, organizations and managers run the risk of distributing work that does not reflect people's core principles, and which alienates and disaffects people as a consequence. The work may fit organizational aims, but it does not mean it will be pursued with passion and intensity. Paradoxically, this drives the need for closer monitoring – hardly a positive contribution to value added – which adds further pressures on people, builds stress and contributes to a cultural cycle of bureaucracy, alienation and resistance.

The grid in Figure 15.1 is a starting point to help managers through this process. Jobs that fall into the category of high importance/high urgency obviously deserve attention – indeed these jobs appear in the **critical zone** of a manager's duties. However, in dealing with these 'crisis' tasks, the manager is engaged in reactive management and being driven by events. The combined pressures of urgency and importance can give these jobs a sense of excitement and satisfaction, but can also bring errors and stress. As long as reactive work persists the manager will be unable to pursue their own agenda, as time will be taken up with the urgent and important role of firefighting.

Learning activity

Strategies to reduce the need to react

Part of a manager's responsibility is to respond to organizational or individual crises. How can managers reduce the pressure on them to respond to crisis situations?

One useful strategy is to make the manager less of a focal point for solving problems. If other staff have highly developed skills and are empowered to deal with problems that arise themselves, then things are less likely to reach a crisis. Many of the urgent and important issues that fall into this category can be prevented from happening through the continual development of other people's skills and personal effectiveness. By helping to support a culture of self-direction and responsibility, the number of people able to deal with urgent and important situations will grow. This not only gives the organization more 'troubleshooting' capability, but also reduces the problems at source – better skilled people tend to throw up less difficulties to managerial levels in the first place.

However, this increase in the skill base happens most easily if attention is given to the category where tasks are important yet non-urgent, in the **planning zone**. It is here that things like staff development and team learning can be best supported as a process of preparing for the future. However, time has to be made available to address these issues. A manager has to make a conscious decision to invest time in these activities if they are to make an effective contribution to developing skills of staff across the organization.

Sometimes, making a decision to spend time on team development issues goes very much against the grain of the organizational 'busywork' culture, but it may be an effective way of preventing crises from developing in the

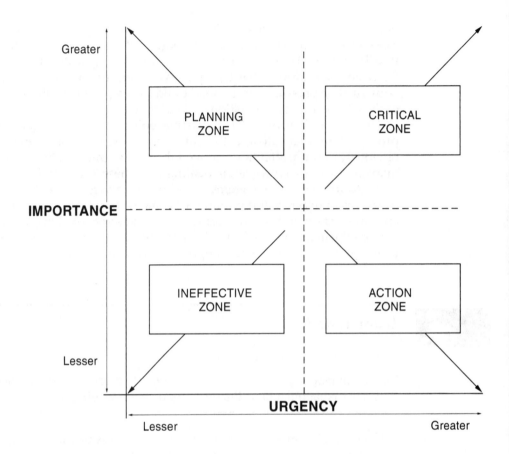

Fig. 15.1 The importance–urgency grid.

future. If tasks are tackled as they appear in the planning zone, before they become urgent, then they can be scheduled into work effectively. By planning, the work can be delegated to the most suitable person or passed to people with a passionate interest in particular areas. The learning and development of individuals can be fully supported in an environment free from the pressure of urgency. Mistakes can be accommodated and used productively rather than become the seeds of catastrophe. Time can be scheduled for any necessary associated work and valuable links made with other people in the network who may be able to help. Targets can be decided and progress reviews agreed. All these strategies, possible in the planning zone, but squeezed out in the critical zone, make it sensible to organize both self and others more effectively.

Tasks that are of low importance yet which carry a high sense of urgency are a third category known as the **action zone**. This zone is characterized by routine, repetitive work that tends to grow in importance as deadlines slip behind. Regular reports and returns – the kind of information that helps monitor the health of the organization – fall into this category. Miss a month and perhaps nothing seems any different, but when six months have been missed the potential for crisis to emerge from calm grows stronger. Producing this type of routine work helps to keep errors manageable and flags up the exceptions that are sometimes the source of problems. These tasks are again best approached while they are in the action zone rather than allowing them to become more critical and grow in importance as time goes by.

The zone also includes tasks in response to interruptions which are necessarily driven by the needs of other people. Responding to the needs of others is a vital part of management, but not if it prevents more important activities from taking place. Managers have to think carefully about how they approach this type of interruptions as they do need to provide staff with support rather than rejection. However, they also need to ensure that they take time to address their own needs, including making progress with their objectives, and are not just a sponge that mops up the problems of others. Of course, undertaking team learning and development will again reduce the need for people to use the manager in this way. Team events also provide an opportunity for others to share and understand the needs of the manager, the constraints that they work under and the conflicting pressures that face us all.

Learning activity

Controlling interruptions

Think about the interruptions that face people in the workplace. What ideas can you suggest to exercise control over the level of interruptions?

One final category is where tasks are neither important nor urgent. This is known as the **ineffective zone**. These tasks can be seen as a means of escape from work and its pressures as they are often low-key and relaxing. Reading unimportant circulars, shuffling paperwork, tidying the desk and even making yet another 'to do' list can all fall into this category. Some people use this category as a reward system, allowing themselves to spend a few minutes doing tasks in this category on condition that they have already spent time on the important but non-urgent tasks described earlier. Others spend a working life indulging themselves in the trivial temptations that lurk in this category; it may be fun and full of successes, but it rarely helps the organization achieve its primary aims. Time spent on tasks in this zone, when other more important work is waiting, is time wasted and potentially builds up pressure. Nevertheless, many people need an outlet or a few moments of mindless activity, and tasks in this zone can have a place on the effective manager's schedule. However, they need to be treated with caution and respect, as there are always plenty more of these jobs to do.

Learning activity

Identifying ineffective tasks

Think about your own approach to tasks and use of time. List all of the activities and tasks you do during the working day that can be classed as ineffective. Try to list ten. When the list is complete work through it to try to identify what you gain personally from doing the task. Then think about how this gain could be achieved while doing tasks that are in the action or planning zones. Now choose five from the list that you can manage without and eliminate these as an initial objective towards becoming more effective. Keep five for rewards.

Using the urgency–importance grid can help a manager to identify tasks that make a genuinely worthwhile contribution to personal and organizational objectives. Part of this assessment will involve the manager in considering their own values and beliefs, and how these fit with organizational aims. This may be an easy fit to make, but it may also lead managers to opening up a dialogue that seeks to challenge the organizational paradigm. This dialogue will be based on values and essentially political in nature. Its conduct will build understanding and open new perspectives. It is a dialogue that will sow the seeds of change and progress.

Developing personal efficiency

The starting point for self-organization is in assessing what tasks are really important to the manager. Sometimes making these decisions will necessarily involve dialogue with others in which goals are redefined and adjusted through a collaborative process (see Chapter 13 on defining the basic approaches to conflict). However, while this process is essential as a basis for self-organizing, managers can also adopt a range of simple strategies that will help them to make more efficient use of the time that they have. As a starting point, it can be valuable to investigate how you organize your own work and use time.

Learning activity

Looking at your work

Use five minutes each day this week to draw up a log of your daily activities. You should use half-hour time slots – anything smaller can become too detailed, whereas larger intervals lose some of the richness of management activity. Some things will occur regularly so using some kind of pro-forma helps to log things efficiently. Use colour-coding to identify activities that were planned as opposed to those that were reactive. Keep some space for explanatory notes so that you can record unexpected interruptions to the plans that you have made.

Once the log is complete, go through the entries to assess them according to their importance and urgency. Also try to assess whether it would have been valuable to involve other people in each task or process, either from the point of view of efficient use of resources and strengths or as a learning opportunity. Careful analysis of the time log will almost always reveal opportunities to develop other people, cut out time-wasting activities, or combine tasks or processes in ways that help use time more efficiently.

Completing the exercise should provide some ideas about the way you organize yourself and use time. Indeed, it may show up some obvious examples of poor organization in relation to your own priorities that could be corrected easily. However, this kind of self-survey may also show up some significant paradoxes of management, and these will be less easily resolved. An example would be where progress with a key project is being held up through delays in someone else's contribution, perhaps because they have given it a different priority. The roots of the problem appear to be simple, pointing to inadequate discussion and goal-setting. Yet the situation may reflect changing management priorities as a complex project grows; the reason for the delay may be a response to genuine crises, personal stress or unforeseen technical problems. Planning, even when it takes into account the personal needs of people involved, cannot hope to anticipate all of the unknown issues of the future. Self-organizing is always inextricably bound up with other people and an indeterminate series of events. In the end, our grip on time is always ephemeral. Managing time is a simple and incomplete response to a complex problem; as such, it is unlikely to provide all of the answers, but it may create the space to allow a more proactive approach to organizational life.

Strategies to improve personal efficiency

The following ideas can all make a useful contribution to your self-organization. However, it is important to recognize that not all of the ideas suit all people, making it important only to select strategies that will work for you. Adopting all of the strategies is impractical, and would probably involve drastic behavioural change for many people. It is better to start with things that will have a significant impact, yet fit quite well with the priorities and preferences that you have. For example, a manager who has creative strengths may value the spark provided by ad hoc interruptions, off-the-wall dialogue and time spent watching the way clouds move. It may not necessarily be effective for such a manager to become a slave to efficiency by introducing rigorous schedules and 'to do' lists. Use the strategies to build onto your strengths, rather than replace them wholesale with adherence to simple rules.

Strategies to build efficiency

Know your own objectives and how these fit with those of the organization
Be clear about areas of tension and make some effort to share them – it is very time-consuming to be continually facing a dilemma caused by the conflict between your own values and those being espoused by the organization.

Work towards your own objectives for some part of every day
It is easy for people to be swept along by the pressures of work and the busy stresses of everyone else's agenda. Make sure your own identified objectives – the things you think are important – get some regular time scheduled in each day. Remember that these are important, and should be done ahead of simple yet ineffective tasks.

Build your own awareness of time use
Keeping a log of your use of time can be revealing. Make an honest record of events and actions over a one-week period in half-hour time slots to help with the initial process of clearly identifying what it is that you actually do. This type of exercise will almost inevitably show up time 'wasted' in conversations and processes that have little apparent connection to value added. Nevertheless, though essentially social in nature, chatting idly with colleagues is one way in which our social needs are satisfied, and serves to allow network links to be developed and maintained.

Manage the way that interruptions can eat up the day
This depends on three basic techniques:

- **Negotiate a time or space that allows you to focus on your own important priorities**. While locking yourself in a broom cupboard is an extreme response that will probably make others feel rejected, it should be possible to negotiate a solution to this problem. Everyone should be able to get some uninterrupted time and space, where they are free from the stresses of responding to everyone else's agenda. In some organizations, people have visual signals, such as brightly coloured baseball hats, to indicate when they are working on an important project. This allows them to maintain focus and concentration by keeping them out of the hustle and bustle of the front line for a while. However, this kind of approach to undisturbed time needs boundaries that everyone shares – people need to understand the reasons and accept the solution. Bright baseball hats are a poor substitute for making others feel that they have been cut adrift and left to handle some particular problem without any support.

- **Encourages self-sufficient problem-solving in others**. This is best developed through continually developing the skills of staff so that they are better equipped to cope. This can easily be encouraged by helping staff to think through the problems and find their own solution whenever an interruption comes along. The temptation is to quickly provide a solution so as to minimize the impact on your time, but adopting an approach that encourages others to own and solve their own problems brings benefits to both efficiency and learning.

- **Be open about your own agenda**. Social exchanges are always attractive and people will always be glad of an opportunity to share your time over inconsequential matters. Indeed, such trivia is quite important as an outlet for concerns and for maintaining organizational health. However, limits do need to be accepted, particularly when deadlines approach or important work waits in the wings. Be prepared to update people regularly on your own position, and assert your own control of time through collaborating with others.

Put important tasks ahead of urgent ones
This is a discipline that effectively puts the planning zone ahead of the action zone, rather than succumbing to the natural inclination to go with the urgent tasks first. Adopting the planning approach has the long-term effect of reducing the action zone tasks through increased staff skills, which enables them to take on the routine elements of this zone. It also reduces the overall need for monitoring and control by supporting enablement and empowerment. Work on important tasks when you feel you are at your best and save your low points for routine work.

Identify something that can be finished each day
Although this can draw people towards the trivial tasks of work, it does enable the rewards of success to be felt regularly. Focusing on important but lengthy projects will bring its rewards eventually, but the sense of not getting anywhere can grow as long periods pass without results. Balance your approach to important tasks and processes with a recognition that regular successes help motivate, by providing symbolic markers on the progress of work.

Establish deadlines
Having targets and deadlines built into work helps to prevent it expanding to fill the time available. The process of identifying key deadlines also helps with the structuring of work by making people think about how to break up larger projects. It is difficult to put deadlines onto big tasks without first going through the process of identifying the various components. This can help large projects become less overwhelming and more manageable.

Use up spare time productively
Some spare time will always arise and indeed many managers will plan in some as a contingency or simply to give themselves time to reflect. Nevertheless, it will also arise unexpectedly – waiting for an important return call, arriving early after a journey or simply finishing a task ten minutes before your next commitment. It can be useful to use this time completing smaller tasks – opening mail, making appointments, small matters of routine or catching up on reading agendas or minutes. These are all things that take very little time, but which can get in the way if left unattended or take up disproportionate time if they are prioritized ahead of important tasks.

Schedule tasks as they arrive
Building tasks into a schedule and fitting them into some kind of plan helps create organization and space. This is easiest to do by having a rolling 'brought forward' file, divided into weeks over the next month, followed by months thereafter. As projects appear, a starting point (based on the target end date) is put into the file. This enables tasks and projects to be put away until they appear

in the brought forward file, avoiding clutter, distractions and stress from arising amongst the piles of paperwork.

Organize the work space

A clean and tidy desk invites action and removes stresses. It also makes it easier to keep focused on the task in hand, as distractions are not spread all around you. Tidiness also makes it easier to find things that you need while you work. This is easier if you have planned the tasks that you will need to work on – it prevents every project being out at the same time because you have a reason for putting things away.

Try to move paperwork efficiently

This is a simple discipline that pays well. By ensuring that paperwork is 'moved' each time that it is handled the trap of lack of progress is avoided. Opening mail should only be done if you have time to deal with the things that arise, even if this merely means updating the brought forward file, responding to the routine action zone matters and using the bin for much of the rest. Items of paperwork that go into the schedule via the brought forward file can then be dealt with at the appropriate time. For some, this will be when you are at your most creative, as they will be tasks that require energy and vision. For others, it will be when energy is at a low ebb, as they are simple pieces of necessary, bureaucratic routine. Beware the ones that offer excitement, as they offer temptations that may get in the way of the plans that you have made, disrupting your approach and developing stress.

Make productive use of routine

Establishing routines to help get through certain tasks can be a useful aid to managing time. The advantage is that it enables a certain amount of your work to be done without having to decide where or when it should be done. It is worth being wary of the way that routines can grow to become the focus of work, blocking progress with more important tasks and processes. Schedule in regular reviews of all of the routine aspects of your work life to ensure that they remain necessary and productive.

Take care to help others manage their time

Be sensitive to the needs of others when making interruptions or phone calls. Prepare yourself by thinking about and noting down what it is you need to find out. Be brief in seeking this information and be prepared to negotiate use of time. If you are making the interruption then check that it is appropriate to continue with the enquiry. Share your objectives openly as a means of gaining the other person's commitment.

All of these strategies have a part to play in the efficient management of time and a productive approach to self-organizing. However, people are unlikely to use the strategies unless they have first taken the time and trouble to think through priorities and identify objectives that fit with their own value system. Taking this initial step, including the potentially difficult process of accommodating personal objectives alongside those of the organization, allows people to develop commitment towards the goal of becoming more efficient. With commitment comes energy, and the self-belief and discipline that will help these strategies become effective.

Organizing others

Engaging in joint action can be difficult when people do not know where they are headed or what they are trying to achieve. Part of a manager's role is in trying to give people a clear idea of what actions might help attain some common objective. Much organizational effort revolves around designing strategies, objectives or targets and making plans to enable the goals to be met. Planning meetings, progress reviews and problem-solving all take place in the context of an organization that is moving towards some shared goal. Without some common direction, people find it hard to give their efforts any meaning and easily become less motivated as a result. Part of the role of organizing others involves creating a real sense of direction (see Chapter 9), and helping to translate this into objectives, structures and plans that help people to be effective. There are several ways in which this process can be developed, and the following sections develop some approaches to creating an environment that helps people to organize.

Developing useful structures

Pascale, R.T. (1990) *Managing on the Edge: How Successful Companies Use Conflict To Stay Ahead*, Viking Penguin, London.

Creating the conditions for effective work provides interesting challenges for managers and teams. Providing carefully framed procedures may be ideal for some people, but can be exactly the kind of bureaucratic barrier that causes others to feel constrained. A real tension exists between helping people to feel organized, yet maintaining their sense of freedom and self-direction. Without some level of organization, people can feel aimless, frustrated and unwilling to participate, but if work is tightly bound by procedure, self-expression, creativity and individual sense of worth can be diminished. There are few easy answers to this organizational paradox, but it is worth noting that the conventional path

Miller, D. (1990) *The Icarus Paradox: How Excellent Organizations Can Bring About Their Own Downfall*, Harper Business, New York.

of providing clear objectives and tight procedures is to some extent the line of least resistance. It may be the easiest solution to the problem of organizing, and helps give staff a strong sense of security and purpose. However, while it certainly makes an important contribution to achieving results, structure can also inhibit the very qualities of innovation and dynamism that organizations need to develop.

Learning activity

Useful structures

Think about work. What kind of structures or systems are often put in place to help fulfil organizational aims? Can you identify any 'costs' to the organization of these structures and systems? In what ways does resistance to bureaucracy surface in organizations?

Structure can be established at a team level in several ways according to the organizational culture and environment. The following ideas can help bring structure and can make an important contribution to a sense of organization in teams.

Develop systems to manage routine work

All organizations will end up with significant parts of work that are relatively routine, where there is little real variety in the task or process taking place. Examples include many financial activities (invoicing, payments and accounting), ordering of supplies to support business activities and many aspects of administrating the daily business. As the tasks do not vary according to the person doing them, it is worth developing an approach that simplifies the process down to the essential elements. This has the advantage of allowing more people to undertake the task, while still achieving set standards dictated by the specified procedure. It also saves time, as people do not have to think about how to approach the particular task, and it can therefore be accomplished with the minimum of fuss.

Learning activity

Valuing procedures and systems

Procedures and systems can simplify many areas of work and produce considerable savings in efficiency. What disadvantages can procedures and systems bring to work?

Schedule essential meetings and inform people of the agenda

When there is a clear purpose to holding meetings they should be scheduled at a time when all of the relevant people can attend. People should receive information in good time to enable them to prepare and plan. This helps limit surprises and ensures that people can be more productive in making contributions to the meeting.

Provide routine briefings

Disseminating important information can be a lengthy process in organizations, and it can also become distorted in passing through a number of links in a communication chain. One approach to this communication issue is to provide briefings that aim to involve all people in sharing information together. The briefings can simply provide a structured way of ensuring that people receive common information, helping overcome feelings of uncertainty or confusion.

However, they can also be used as a forum for discussion and reaction, a means by which the organization stimulates dialogue on issues of substance across everyone who wants to be involved.

Making meetings work

Meetings are an area of work that can easily become unproductive for people. Many managers have left meetings with some feelings of frustration and no clear idea about what has been achieved, on occasion because very few productive outcomes have been secured. Even worse, meetings sometimes generate long lists of actions or ideas giving the appearance of results, yet which no one really feels will actually contribute anything to solving the issue under consideration. As a consequence, implementation is poor and spasmodic, leading to the same issues being revisited time and time again in a cycle of trying to resolve the problem. Meetings can develop into a significant and frustrating user of time, unless careful management is used to ensure that they remain as productive as possible. The following ideas suggest some strategies which can help to keep meetings at optimum effectiveness, where productive work leads to useful results, yet where social needs also can find a much needed outlet.

Identify a clear purpose

Meetings that are held purely because it happens to be time for one are starting off with a handicap. Naturally, the social interaction that this allows can be immensely valuable, but it is hard to get down and make progress with business objectives unless there are clear ideas on what the meeting is trying to achieve. In these circumstances, routine reports can fill the gap, but these may contribute little to organization or individual objectives. Meetings should only be held if there are clear basic purposes that people can understand and share. The following list categorizes how these might arise:

Meeting purpose	For example
To fulfil a clear decision-making aim	To share a decision amongst people and to develop commitment through a process of persuasion and involvement
To fulfil a clear problem-solving aim	To resolve complex issues that need a variety of inputs
To fulfil a clear communication aim	To share information across a group and discuss implications. Also relevant to team development or training objectives

With a clearly identified purpose to meetings, people attending are better equipped to contribute effectively. It also helps people to think about their own perspective on issues, rather than have to react 'on the hoof' to proposals or ideas as they arise in the course of a busy meeting. However, even with clearly identified purposes in mind, it is also clear that meetings should only go ahead when it is possible to achieve those ends. Several factors can prevent the meeting from successfully achieving objectives, all of which can be checked beforehand.

Lack of essential information
When information that will prevent problem-solving, decision-making or information-sharing is not available then the meeting will not be able to achieve its purpose. Rather than go ahead with a meeting that will be limited by the lack of information, be prepared to reschedule.

Lack of preparation
Not having sufficient time to prepare for items on the agenda can naturally impact on the quality of information available. However, it can also have an impact on the many value judgments that arise, making people unwilling to commit to decisions or offer ideas to solve problems until they have had time to think through the issues. People may need to talk through issues in the informal organization to establish perspectives through political dialogue before they feel comfortable and able to discuss them inside the official structures of the organization. Again, there will be little point in pressing ahead with a meeting when people are simply not prepared for the issues.

Lack of the key people
Some problems, decisions or information-sharing need particular people to be present. This may be because of their specialist knowledge or because of their political influence. Either way, meetings can be wasted effort if such key people are not present. One of the critical elements of organizing effective meetings is to ensure that all the right people are able to attend. Meetings that become frustrated by having to refer the decision onwards or waiting until key people return can seem increasingly unproductive and pointless. This devalues the people who have made the effort to attend.

A problem here is that involving the key people does not necessarily make for a productive meeting. On occasion, inviting the people that **need** to be there will also mean bringing in people who have an axe to grind or who have personal difficulties with other members of the group. Personal agendas and political motives may interfere with the most critical of decisions or problems, overriding the clear purpose of any meeting along the way. Contention and conflict between individuals may well provide the sparks for creative processes, but may not help the progress of ordinary business. Interpersonal issues are part of the fabric of organizations, and need to be accommodated somehow in the structures that the organization maintains. It may be far easier to hold productive meetings by assembling a group of people with common values, interests and approaches, but they may not have the political influence or technical authority to achieve the meeting's purpose. Bringing in specialists or influential people may open the doors to dispute, but meetings have to be seen as a crucial forum for making progress on issues of contention. Sometimes the declared purposes of the meeting will have to take a back seat in order to address key issues of conflict along the way.

Provide a basic plan
Establishing the purpose is a good starting point for effective meetings, but does not guarantee that everything will go well. Meetings can still dissolve into aimless and frustrating disorganization unless the people attending are following a basic plan. This is provided by the bare bones of the agenda, which gives people an indication of the topics for reporting or discussion. It should also highlight any necessary preparation that people need to complete, such as reading a report or discussion paper, and should establish time limits for the various items wherever possible.

It is important to strike the right balance with timing – rushing items will leave people with little opportunity to discuss things fully, and may leave problems unresolved or ignored. It can also lead to frustration as people do not get the opportunity to exercise influence or build political allegiances. However, taking too long over items is equally damaging, leading to people withdrawing their involvement as fatigue and boredom arise. A good balance can be found by putting simpler items early on the agenda and encouraging progress by using tight time limits on these items. As the meeting progresses to more difficult issues, time limits can be negotiated as part of the process of approaching the particular item. It is also valuable to choose a time of day that reflects the importance of the items under discussion – routine matters can certainly be dealt with at the end of the day, whereas more complex decisions or problems are worth reserving for times when people are fresh.

Managing the process of the meeting itself
Productive meetings are based on more than basic purpose and an outline agenda. They also need to be managed effectively. This is perhaps the most difficult element of meeting success as it is a live process that happens amongst the complex dynamic interactions of the participants themselves. The business of the meeting can highlight differences between people, causing hidden tensions or historical conflicts to surface. Political agendas can be ruthlessly pursued by people, despite being tangential to the actual business under discussion. Creative impetus can grow on the back of ideas, threatening to carry the group off into interesting, uncharted territory and leaving behind the humdrum business in the meantime. There are many reasons, both positive and negative, why meetings can miss the point, and the job of managing them to achieve productive results needs close attention to many subtle factors. The following section provides some basic guidelines for approaching this task, but many of the themes of this book have focused on developing more productive work relationships. Those ideas will apply in a meeting setting, as in other areas of work.

Provide an update on progress
Often meetings follow patterns, with issues that remain under discussion for several meetings over the lifetime of a project. As the project progresses, various aspects will be discussed, problems resolved and decisions made at key stages. People will also needed to be kept informed about how developments will affect

their own work areas, and the implications that particular projects have for other work in progress. This creates an opportunity for beginning the meeting with an updating process, designed to establish the context and objectives for discussion. This also has the advantage of reminding the meeting of actions taken so far and the outcomes that have arisen. It also allows the opportunity to celebrate successes and touch base with the stories that grow up around any project. These help to develop group identity and sense of cohesion.

This updating process can also be used to lead into the current objectives, using the agenda as a guideline, and confirm the proposed timings for the items under discussion. Gaining commitment to the proposed business is an important part of developing focus and drive towards achieving the objectives.

Jointly agree key aspects of process
There is always a strong temptation to dive straight into the business of the meeting, however complex the issues. This partly reflects the enthusiasm of people to get involved and get things done. However, meetings often lose direction because people have not established **how** certain issues are to be tackled. If people are unaware of how a decision is to be made, they might be waiting for the chair to step in, when in fact the chair is trying to establish group consensus. Time spent agreeing key elements of the process is rarely wasted, particularly where difficult issues might otherwise lead people to be cautious. In these circumstances, allowing people to establish at the outset that openness and honest enquiry are valuable aids to problem-solving helps to build commitment and support for tackling the issues.

Get people involved at an early stage
Encouraging participation helps to build commitment and ensures that people take responsibility for achieving results. This can be easily done where people have taken on particular projects, as they can be involved in the updating process at the outset. Getting people involved helps to maintain everyone's sense of value and provides recognition of the contributions that people have made to work in progress.

Break up the pattern of reporting and discussion by using visual aids
Focusing on discussion throughout long meetings can be tiring and important detail can easily be lost. By changing the pattern of the meeting it is possible to keep interest and energy levels higher. Talking is the heart of meetings, but using flipcharts and overhead slides does support good communication, allowing people to keep pace with complex arguments and ideas. Recording the points raised visually also improves discussion as it prevents people from revisiting issues or making points that have already appeared. It also provides a means of reviewing and recapping on points, helping people to remain fully informed at all times. Flipchart lists created during 'brainstorm' session also provide a starting point for evaluation and prevent good ideas from escaping in the midst of animated debate.

Encourage productive discussion

We have probably all experienced an animated debate that is largely irrelevant to the issue, as people at the meeting pursue their own personal agenda or try to conduct some political battle. To some extent these diversions are an inevitable feature of group settings, as people take the opportunity to explore their place in the social system. Indeed, as people will always have these social needs, the fact that they arise in a meeting setting may be an indication of anxiety and unrest, or a sign that people are not getting an opportunity to meet these needs elsewhere. In any case, the outcome can be a meeting that is dominated by issues and concerns that are not part of the declared business, and this can be frustrating for other people who are seeking practical outcomes.

Learning activity

Managing the social system

Think about a situation where the meeting is being dominated by the re-emergence of historical conflict. What approaches would you suggest to help manage this diversion?

There are few easy answers to these problems. In many respects the fact that these things surface is evidence that for some people the issue is more important than the core business of the meeting. Ignoring the issue, or trying to put it to one side, will only devalue their perspective, which in any case may be valid. However, one approach is to encourage other people to contribute and share their perspectives on the issue, ensuring that some sense of fair contribution and balance is maintained. By opening up the issue, rather than closing it down, people in groups are more likely to feel fairly treated, rather than frustrated. It may also lead the group to collaborate in designing a solution, or to agree to schedule a meeting specifically to look at the issues that people have raised. Either way, productive use is made of issues that surface, even though they may be tangential to the declared purpose of the meeting.

Productive discussion cannot avoid the potential problems created by personal agendas or political actions. However, by developing conditions where people can feel a sense of equal worth, fair contributions can be more easily maintained. This serves as both a source of control and of stimulus. The following simple communication guidelines help to maintain contributions and encourage participation:

- Provide regular summaries of the discussion and the points made to maintain clarity
- Encourage reactions to points raised
- Reflect the words of people that have spoken
- Support people speaking using eye contact and positive body signals

- Encourage people to bring their own values and experiences into the discussion
- Use open questions to encourage contributions and comment
- Bring in your own reactions, feelings and values, but avoid the trap of domination.

Provide a clear summary of progress and actions
Meetings can provide a very productive discussion, yet still not lead to actions and results once the meeting has ended. Also, if the meeting purpose was primarily aimed at exchanging information, updating and discussing possibilities, people may easily end up feeling that there has been little tangible progress or outcome. An important part of the meeting process is to summarize the event.

Learning activity

Summarizing

Think about the end of a meeting. What things should a summary provide to enable people to recognize progress made? How can a summary be used to encourage actions that follow the meeting?

The summary should aim primarily for creating positive feelings about the progress made on the issues under discussion. This helps to reinforce people's sense of value and encourages a positive outlook on the group and subsequent meetings. The following key points can help provide a comprehensive and positive summary:

- Recap on key decisions
- Reaffirm the value of key contributions
- Relocate discussions in their organizational or task context
- Restate alternatives and options generated by the discussion
- Remind people of progress on agenda items
- Review agreed actions or assignments to be completed before the next meeting
- Review plans and check dates, purpose and objectives to help establish the links to the next meeting.

Using these basic strategies helps to keep the process of meetings productive. There will always be occasions when, despite the careful development of purposes and plans, the actual process of the meeting falls down. A natural, though unhelpful, reaction is to blame other people for their failure to stick to the agenda, focus on the business or contribute as agreed. A similar reaction can take place in other people, with the manager or chair of the meeting being the object of blame for failing to control the process. Meetings remain a complex arena, and no amount of planning or preparation will anticipate all of the potential directions, problems and issues that can legitimately arise. Meetings are a place where people can influence policy, shape the organization and bring drama to organizational life. They offer opportunities for enrichment and inspiration alongside the tedious and mundane. Amidst the routine and the ordinary progress of business, they hide hope, reason and meaning. They engage us in making sense, and in doing so we hope to find new questions.

Producing plans

One of the ways to help create an organized approach to work is to make plans. Plans are like maps; they help to define the route from A to B, and enable people to anticipate what hurdles might arise and what changes of direction will be needed along the way. They allow people to determine what resources will be needed to complete the journey, and give markers along the way that can be used to measure progress. Producing plans creates a sense of organization in that it helps to reduce uncertainty and produce common actions that contribute to the achievement of goals. However, plans do have dangers in that it is rarely possible to correctly assess all of the potential variables that will affect outcomes, so that even the best laid plans can end up being unhelpful. Perhaps worse, plans can restrict thinking, leading people to implement the plan even when conditions dictate that other options should be considered. This is particularly relevant to strategic planning, where medium and long-term futures are subject to a number of unpredictable influences and tensions. This is considered in more detail in Chapter 16. Nevertheless, for shorter timescales, producing plans can undoubtedly provide a structure and framework in which people can feel organized, and this contributes to the productive and cooperative pursuit of goals. This section suggests ways in which plans can be constructed and used productively to help achieve the organization's objectives.

Learning activity

Barriers to planning

In some respects, the benefits of an organized approach to tasks seem obvious, yet planning is not necessarily the first step that managers take. What factors in the organization can you identify that get in the way of planning? What reasons can you give for individuals to avoid planning?

Obstacles to planning

While planning is a process that can give benefits, there are many things that prevent people from taking the first step and drawing up plans. One critical barrier is simply lack of time, and the sense of urgency that surrounds people in many work environments. Despite the potential gain of time that planning will allow, the pressure of immediate tasks can work against a planning culture. People are led to respond to the urgent demands of day-to-day activities, rather than get involved in the proactive process of organizing future tasks and processes. The culture in many organizations rewards this, by associating labels such as 'hardworking' with people who always seem to be busy. Against this background it can be hard to take the time to indulge in planning. There are also other factors that work against planning.

In a complex environment, plans may never work out and this can lead organizations to presume that they are therefore obsolete. However, while plans may not translate into reality, they may nonetheless have been crucial in shaping the outcomes that do emerge. A complex environment can be uncertain and confusing, leading to a lack of direction and motivation. Plans may be exactly the thing that helps mobilize people to action, a catalyst for moving onward and resolving the future, even if, with hindsight, they do not provide an accurate map of the route to follow. In this sense, plans can give a reference point with enough detail to enable people to make progress and discover the complications and unknowns as they arise. Plans can make people feel positive about getting involved, even though they may shift and change as time goes on.

Individuals may have a negative attitude to planning, sometimes simply because they have seen plans 'fail' in the past. The advantage of not planning to go anywhere is that it does not matter where you end up – every outcome is equally successful! However, if people can think of plans as part of an approach rather than a simple prescription then they may be more positive about contra-dictory results. Another reason for negative attitudes is that planning can formalize work, pulling people closer to the bureaucratic aspects of the organization. This can reduce people's freedom and flexibility to pursue other objectives, and make them accountable to progress against the plan. This effect can alienate people and stifle genuinely creative actions, both of which damage the organization. Plans therefore need to be put together in ways that involve people, allowing them to bring in their own agenda and share in the design of implementation.

Plans have a way of showing up inflexibility in that people may find themselves being asked to take on work or deliver results in areas where they do not feel comfortable. This concern can lead to stubbornness and an unwill-ingness to face up to the issues or problems that make planning necessary. Some people simply feel that maintaining an optimistic outlook will be suffi-cient defence against the worst that the future holds, smiling through adversity with a belief that nothing more could have been done. Others depend on certainties, resisting any move away from the familiar into uncharted territory and keeping faith with the way it has always been done, even when problems grow and develop. Making plans involves looking into the future and dealing with unknowns; for many people it can feel more secure to avoid the process altogether, relying instead on keeping busy with comfortable and familiar territory.

Learning activity

Planning qualities

What kind of personal qualities would help people to plan?

Useful qualities

Many of the qualities that help planning are closely associated with a learning approach to management. By viewing planning as an opportunity to explore possibilities and resolve uncertainty, people can be supported and encouraged to engage in a process of discovery and learning. Some of the ingredients that help this approach are as follows.

Curiosity

It helps people to undertake planning if they can develop curiosity. A willingness to seek understanding and to try to explore unknowns can stimulate people to plan. Painting problems as opportunities helps people confront the task with optimism and hope.

Creativity

Planning often involves thinking through problems and designing an approach. This process can be more productive if people are encouraged to think beyond the boundaries of current practice and constraints. A culture that resists new ideas also inhibits planning – there is little point if things will only proceed using existing methods. Developing creativity needs openness to new ideas, valuing of differences and a willingness to challenge organizational conventions.

Confidence

Tackling the unknown can require confidence, particularly as there will be people who are critical of the whole concept. People need to be inspired to take on the task, and supported with passion and daring if they are to feel positive about the possibilities. Ideas that they produce need to be valued and supported if they are to develop self-belief and confidence in their purpose.

Persistence

Planning takes commitment and the willingness to persist in the face of difficulty. Any activity that tries to deal with future possibilities is bound to uncover problems that test people's resources, and people need to be encouraged to keep going when things get difficult.

Practicality

Planning takes a keen sense of practicality. Ideas need to be encouraged and valued, yet also assessed for their realism. Strategies and options need to be developed that are within the capability of people to put into action, or are within the reach of influence. Good planners accept the boundaries of the possible, yet work hard to push those boundaries outward.

Wisdom

Planning is enriched by a broad spectrum of ideas and understanding. People who learn well will have more to bring to the process, enabling creative use of ideas from other arenas and confidence that strange possibilities can sometimes work.

These qualities need to be supported and encouraged to help the planning process to be accepted and productive. They are qualities that reside somewhere in us all, and effective management should help to support an environment of learning where they can be released. In an organization bounded by bureaucracy, planning becomes a process of imposing order and control, providing predictable, timetabled solutions to the pursuit of greater efficiency. Yet planning offers the opportunity to tackle problems that go beyond the confines of the existing paradigm, to enter realms of uncertainty and create outcomes that seem impossible. Planning can bring hope, vision and strength, giving people a platform to progress that reaches beyond the ordinary. Planning can not only help people to prepare for the future, but helps to make people's visions and dreams come true.

Developing plans

Good plans sometimes happen through chance and occasionally the most successful even emerge from chaos, and organizations need to be openly accepting of these possibilities. However, working through the key elements of a plan can help people to feel organized and positive, while still allowing spontaneity and opportunism to flourish. The further ahead plans stretch, the more uncertainty is built into the process and the more likely a rigid plan will suffer intolerable tensions. Longer-term planning needs to mirror this tension, by accommodating flexibility, exploring contingencies and encouraging the search for alternative directions. By contrast, short-term plans can have relatively fixed outcomes, as they will be less prone to disruption and divergence. Either way, the following list provides the key elements of a plan; how the organization uses these elements is ultimately dependent on the futures that people encounter.

Clear objectives

People are better placed to develop commitment and pursue plans if they have clear objectives. These are commonly established using the **SMART** criteria, where objectives are stated in terms that are specific, measurable, attainable, relevant and time-bounded (see Chapter 8). While this is usually relatively easy to specify over a short timeframe, it becomes increasingly difficult to do when making plans that try to deal with events some distance into the future. Any number of unforeseen events can have an impact on the organization, causing objectives to be revisited and revised. It can be frustrating for people to be working towards specific objectives, only to find that these have all been altered in response to some event.

Case note

The Department of Employment

In July 1995 the government announced the merger of the Department of Employment with the Department of Education. While the merger had been widely anticipated, the impact on staff was expected to be significant, with many sections and areas of work duplicated across the two organizations. This left staff unclear about their future job security, and uncertain about whether the objectives they were currently pursuing made sense any more. The new department rushed out new organizational objectives, based on a merging of those of the old organizations, which were designed to reassure people that overall goals remained similar. In practice, a high level of uncertainty continued at staff level as the detailed effects of the merger on sections could not be predicted. Despite clear organizational objectives, individual objectives no longer felt valid to many staff, leading to a lack of purpose and declining morale. In the new climate, detailed plans for reshaping the organization became difficult to enact as commitment fell. This demonstrates how significant changes can easily upset both plans and people.

Current position

Plans are difficult to embark upon unless people are clear of the starting point, in the same way that maps are less useful when you do not know where you are. It is important to share a common understanding of the existing position to enable people to feel confident to move on. If people have a different view of circumstances, they may find it harder to develop any real commitment to a particular direction.

Analysis of the gap

It is easier to commit to a plan if you understand the nature of the gap between where you are now and where you want to be. Without a shared understanding of the overall path, the anticipated problems and the implications for resourcing, people may have difficulty understanding the various elements of work. By ensuring that all people involved in the plan have a good understanding of the nature of the terrain that lies between the current position and the objective, people will be better prepared for the pitfalls, more aware of potential options and more creative in designing work to pursue the goal.

Programme of work

Once the gap has been considered as fully as conditions allow, a programme of work can be designed. This should be designed with the input of the people who have to implement the plan, as this helps to build commitment. By participating in the design of work, individual objectives, strengths and preferences will be assimilated into the plan, making it much more likely to be effective. It also allows people to share issues and concerns about the objectives, process and tasks as they arise, helping to develop a cooperative approach to making the plan work. This stage may well take much longer to complete if people are involved, but it is likely to lead to a more thorough airing of the potential issues, with the result that less surprises are likely to occur as the plan is implemented. Time invested here is likely to lead to an approach that recognizes the need for continual review and reshaping, making it more likely that the plan will be robust in the face of complications.

Outline schedule
As the programme of work evolves, the process of scheduling can begin. Again, if the people who will implement the plan participate in this process, it is more likely that realistic timings will emerge that take account of the constraints and practicalities of people's work. It also allows people to share any problems that they would have fitting the work in alongside their existing commitments, enabling solutions to be developed before the problem actually surfaces during implementation. Wide consultation and sharing helps to build a problem-solving approach to planning, helping people to feel both valued and committed to the outcomes and the process.

Review and control points
The same wide participation can be used to develop suitable review and control processes. Targets that are imposed often need to be carefully checked, whereas targets that have been jointly established as part of a process of collaboration stand a better chance of looking after themselves. Nevertheless, even with commitment and energy, things can go wrong and good intentions can easily slip. Using consultation to establish appropriate reviews will help to provide reference points and sub-objectives that people can work towards more easily over shorter timescales. Sharing targets also helps to spread the responsibility for control over more people, giving everyone involved a role in keeping the plan on track and supporting people when problems occur or key areas start to fall behind schedule.

Developing contingency
As part of the process of analysing the gap and designing work, many potential complications are likely to surface. While solutions will emerge, the possibility remains that unforeseen issues will arise or the solutions will fail. Wherever possible, options should be held open, ready to be used according to the circumstances that actually turn up at the various stages of implementation. By thinking through a number of possible scenarios, and developing a range of options or possibilities to deal with each, it is possible to design plans that have a considerable degree of inbuilt flexibility. Planning for a number of scenarios acknowledges the real problems of uncertainty, and helps develop an open-minded commitment to working with the circumstances that eventually emerge.

Ultimately, planning is a process that involves simplification. The rich texture of the future can only be guessed at, and the models that are put together to help organize can only ever approximate the reality to come. Over short timescales, these simplifications will rarely hide much complication, but as plans stretch further ahead the potential for upset grows stronger. Assumptions that underpin the plan – technical, financial or to do with people – are all subject to an unpredictable web of cause and effect. Some things change and some things stay the same, and no one can be sure of which. Plans can help people approach tasks and objectives with confidence and purpose, but it is a poor plan that holds no promise of unintended outcomes.

Going forward

Making plans ultimately has a symbolic value beyond its practical purpose. In a world with unknown futures, planning helps give people a sense of security and control, and helps to narrow down the shape of what is to come through enabling people to act with shared intent. Plans are like maps, they help people to find their place and give them ideas on how to get where they want to go. Just like maps, reality often looks different when you get there, and lots of things appear on the way that are more interesting, detailed and inspiring than might be anticipated. The interesting thing about plans is that they map out something that does not yet exist, giving people one route through the boundless possibilities that actually exist. Following plans needs a keen eye for the opportunities that might not have found their way onto the map, but which hold wonders and interest for us all.

Wieck, K. (1994) 'Cartographic Myths in Organisations' in Tsoukas, H., *New Thinking in Organisational Behaviour,* Butterworth-Heinemann, Oxford.

A small Hungarian detachment was on military manoeuvres in the Alps. Their young lieutenant sent a reconnaissance unit out into the icy wilderness just as it began to snow. It snowed for two days, and the unit did not return. The lieutenant feared that he had dispatched his people to their deaths, but the third day the unit came back. Yes, they said, we considered ourselves lost and waited for the end, but then one of us found a map in his pocket. That calmed us down. We pitched camp, lasted out the snowstorm, and then with the map we found our bearings. And here we are. The lieutenant took a good at the map and discovered, to his astonishment, that it was a map of the Pyrenees.

Karl Weick

Summary

My interest is in the future, because I'm going to spend the rest of my life there.

Charles Kettering, Chairman of General Motors

This chapters has made the following key points:

➤ That meeting productivity can be enhanced through defining purpose, planning and managing the process.
➤ That planning processes can contribute effectively to organizing self and others.
➤ That planning can also reflect a bureaucratic approach that restricts creativity and opportunity.

Further reading

R. Kliem and I. Ludin in *The Noah Project* (Gower, Aldershot, 1993) give an interesting view of the project planning process through an entertaining novel about a zoo. The novel deals with many management issues in the process of relocating animals as a result of the zoo being sold. The novel approach brings humour and reality to planning issues.

References

Bennett, R. (1989) *Personal Effectiveness*, Kogan Page, London.

Hannaway, C. and Hunt, G. (1992) *The Management Skills Book*, Gower, Aldershot.

Mintzberg, H. (1989) *Mintzberg on Management: Inside Our Strange World of Organizations*, Free Press, New York.

Miller, D. (1990) *Icarus Paradox: How Excellent Organizations Can Bring About Their Own Downfall*, Harper Business, New York.

Pascale, R.T. (1990) *Managing on the Edge: How successful Companies Use conflict To Stay Ahead*, Viking Penguin, London.

Sherman, J. (1991) *Productive Planning*, Crisp Publications, London.

Stacey D.R. (1993) *Strategic Management and Organisational Dynamics*, Pitman, London.

Tsoukas, H. (1994) *New Thinking in Organisational Behaviour*, Butterworth-Heinemann, Oxford.

Part Three

Organizations

16

A strategic perspective

Our most significant strategic decision was made not in response to some clear-sighted corporate vision but by the marketing and investment decisions of front-line managers who really knew what was going on.

Andy Grove, CEO of Intel

Objectives

By the end of this chapter you will be able to:

➤ describe the conventional approaches to strategy making
➤ evaluate the assumptions upon which these approaches are based
➤ describe an alternative perspective to the process of generating strategy
➤ explore some of the processes that support alternative perspectives

Introduction

Designing strategy has long been a purpose of senior managers, and one that has been inextricably bound up with planning structures and systems to deliver an ideal future for organizations. As the scope of organizations grows wider, with global markets and increasing numbers of distinct product niches, it has become more important to make strategic plans that will help achieve an effective fit between the organization and its operating environment. Yet growing complexity has also emerged in the modern world of business, with global infrastructure and technology overtaking some of the traditional stability in which organizations operated. As strategic plans have become more open to the shocks produced in a dynamic and interdependent environment, the process of designing strategy has become increasingly reliant on sophisticated analysis of ever-more complex variables. Worse, the plans that the process has formulated have become less reliable, with detailed strategies falling foul of the vagaries of geopolitical, economic and social change, and with generalized statements of strategic intent often too vague to drive the decisions and vision of people on the front line of organizational action. This chapter explores the conventional approach to strategy, questions the assumptions that underpin the concept of intended corporate direction, and proposes alternatives that challenge the central tenets of strategic purpose.

A conventional approach to strategy

Strategic management is the way in which organizations identify and pursue the activities that make up their overall purpose. Rather than being concerned with the day-by-day operational decisions, it is designed to provide the plan which successfully unifies all of the organization's activity. Further, because investment decisions, mergers and strategic choices inevitably have long-run consequences, the process of strategic management concerns both the present state and the desired future state of the organization. In addition, the process involves matching the organization's activity to the environment in which it operates, taking account of markets and political, economic and social factors, both now and for the future. Strategic management also involves matching these activities to the resource capability of the organization, and making plans to adjust the resource capability to meet anticipated changes in activity.

However rationally or carefully they approach the task, such a process is inevitably affected by the values and expectations of those who have power within organizations. The success of strategic decisions is dependent on the interaction of many variables – the response of competitors, political changes, the level of economic activity or consumer values and expectations to name a few. As a consequence, designing strategy involves people in power making judgments about patterns and events, and these judgments are inevitably based on expectations and values. For example, there will be different strategic responses within UK businesses to the possibility of an incoming Labour government in the late 1990s, according to the perspectives that people hold on the policies that the new government may pursue. Of course, those policies will themselves be partly driven by the strategies that firms adopt – widespread efforts to avoid tax by using offshore tax havens may lead to regulations that affect the movement of capital, for example. Strategic decisions are therefore enacted against a dynamic environment, where the decisions taken themselves shape and change the background factors that led to the original strategy.

Galbraith, J. (1977), *Organisation Design*, Menlo Park, California, Addison Wesley and Galbraith, J. and Nathanson (1978), *Strategy Implementation: The Role of Structure and Process*, St. Paul, Minnesota, West Publishing Company.

Strategy involves decisions and plans that have a fundamental impact on the organization design. One way of examining this impact is through looking at an adaptation of Jay Galbraith's model of organization design, which identifies six key variables of design through which strategic decisions take effect. Galbraith argues that the specific actions which make up strategy must have an effect on the organization through these variables, including the organization's:

- Task
- Structure
- Information and decision processes
- Reward and recognition systems
- People and skill requirements
- Values and culture.

The interesting thing about the model is the interdependence of the variables. An organization that pursues a strategy that involves a change to the organization's task, such as restructuring its product portfolio, will find that this has implications for its structure. The new pattern of production will need to be supported by a different sales strategy, refocused research and development and an administration system that can move the associated orders, customer service and invoicing effectively. In turn this will alter the requirements

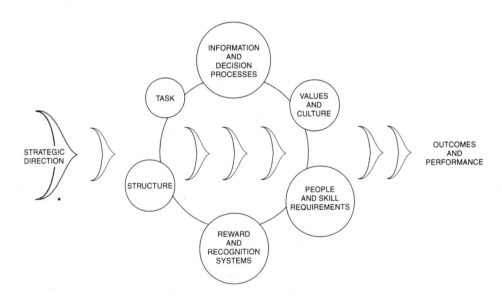

Fig. 16.1 Strategy and the impact on organisation design.

for information and interfere with the established flow – the changes themselves will demand new information and feedback channels if the organization is to understand the dynamic implications that the strategy has in its markets. Further, different portfolios imply changing roles for people, and these changes also demand quality information and structural shifts to allow involvement and participation. The organization may need to adapt its reward system to provide new incentives to help meet different goals. Almost inevitably, the changes make demands on people to work differently, and these need to be supported by developing new skills, values and cultures that enable the strategy to take effect.

Changes in strategic direction must impact on the organization's design and the interdependence of design variables makes the ultimate impact difficult to assess. Changes to any one of the variables will operate through any or all of the others in a complex chain of cause and effect, where reactions are not mechanistically determined but are based in part on the values and emotional responses of people to change. This means that strategic plans operate in an environment that is interdependent and where changes will have unpredictable effects that are sometimes contrary to expectations.

System complexity

An easy way to illustrate how complexity escalates in systems is to look at what happens in a model with six basic variables. If we assume that these are the only six variables of organization design, in itself a simplification, we can link these six variables to each other by the simplest possible cause and effect chain. We can draw this as a line from each variable to each other incorporating a switch. If the switch is open, then the effect of a change in the source variable produces a negative effect upon the target variable. If it is closed, then a positive effect is felt. In either case, our simple switch tells us nothing about the magnitude of the effect. This simple system is represented in Figure 16.2.

The diagram contains thirty connecting switches, and the system complexity is evidenced by the number of possible states that the system can display. It is revealed by the mathematical expression 2^{30}, which gives over a billion possibilities! If we then consider that the system through which strategy impacts also includes people, and that they are capable of a sophisticated array of responses, the system complexity begins to rise inexorably. Human responses shift dynamically in response to changes in structure, task, information and values, making the state of the system inherently unknowable. Ultimately, strategy impacts through a system which is open-ended, concept-dependent and self-reflective, making it inherently complex and unpredictable.

In attempting to develop a strategic response to the organizational problem of achieving and sustaining success, two broad approaches have evolved. The first has roots in the 'scientific' management principles developed by Taylor in the early part of the century. This approach is known as the 'rational planning'

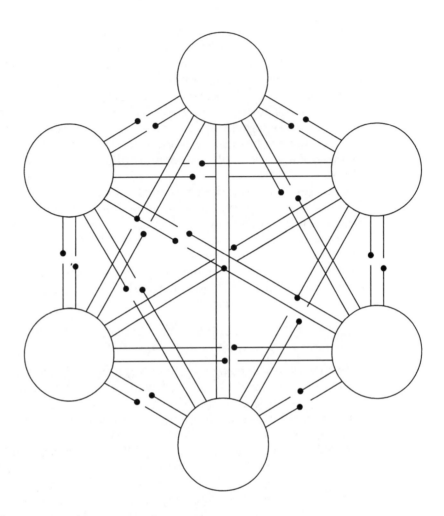

Fig. 16.2 Illustrating system complexity.

approach. The second is based on the work of Peters and Waterman in the early 1980s, and is known as the 'visionary-ideological' approach. Each of these conventional responses to strategy is briefly explored below.

The rational planning approach

Taylor, F. (1947) 'Scientific Management' in *Collected Works of Frederick Taylor.*

The scientific principles of Taylor were a response to the dramatic change that the industrial revolution brought to working life, and were based on the belief that all organizational problems had a technically rational solution that could be scientifically determined. The Henry Ford production lines provide an example of Taylorism being applied to job design, creating work that treated people as resources, and which matched human and non-human resources together in the most efficient way. These roots have led to an approach to strategy based on empirical analysis, founded on the assumption that a technically rational solution exists.

The rational planning approach is based on two key steps. Firstly, it is necessary to specify the corporate financial and operational objectives to be attained in the future. Secondly, it is necessary to define the organizational position that will attain those objectives in the future environment, as some positions that the organization could adopt will not be successful. The objectives established, and the actions necessary to attain the future position, must be acceptable to stakeholders, especially those with a financial stake in the organization. They must also be feasible, in the sense that it is possible to get from the company's current position to the desired future position, despite the actions of competitors or other changes in the operating environment. Objectives must also be suitable, in the sense that the actions required to achieve the objectives are congruent with maintaining balance in the organizational design variables and the external environment.

Once financial and operational objectives are established, the rational

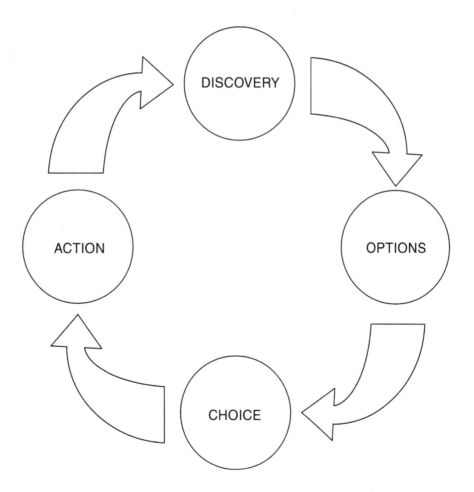

Fig. 16.3 The strategic cycle.

planning model follows a cycle. Objectives lead to options being generated and evaluated, which in turn, using technical analysis, leads to **choice** of the best option. The option is then implemented through **action** and the outcomes are checked to see if there are deviations from the plan. If these occur, they are analyzed as the first step in monitoring the position. This involves a process of **discovery**, leading to further gathering of data which feeds around the cycle into choices over corrective steps.

The rational planning approach is heavily dependent on accurate forecasting, and therefore involves detailed analysis of information in an effort to identify trends and patterns that exist in the organization's performance and in the wider environment. This analysis has to satisfy stakeholders if any strategy is to command support, and therefore commonly has a financial focus. Strategic planning using the rational planning model is typically dependent on demonstrating that the plan will achieve acceptable financial returns. This is achieved through interpreting investment appraisal, cost-benefit analysis, performance benchmarking and through constant reference to key financial indicators. In situations where other stakeholders (employees or outsiders) have particular power, then the financial focus may well be tempered by other concerns. This is exampled by the oil or nuclear industry, which face a vocal environmental lobby and therefore need to present strategies that demonstrate acceptance of environmental concerns and satisfies those power groups.

Case note

Brent Spar

Shell faced a particular environmental issue in the summer of 1995, when they tried to dispose of the drilling rig 'Brent Spar' using deep-sea sinking. This led to worldwide protest, aided by Greenpeace, which subsequently halted the disposal programme. Shell effectively changed their strategy in the face of pressure and direct action from the environmental lobby groups, which was supported by consumer boycotts of their filling stations in Europe. Ironically, evidence has since emerged that the environmental damage of deep-sea disposal would be less than originally expected, and perhaps less than the option of on-shore dismantling and cleaning preferred by lobby groups. Nevertheless, the events illustrate Shell's sensitivity to damage to its environmental image, while also illustrating how technically rational solutions do not necessarily fit well with people's values or expectations.

The rational planning approach has implications for organizations that go beyond the narrow boundaries of designing strategy. As noted earlier, all strategic decisions are enacted through six key variables of organization design. A strategy developed and implemented through rational planning will have significant requirements for monitoring and control, and this is most easily achieved within a framework of clear structure and carefully defined systems.

A strategy that aims to expand the organization's luxury consumer products portfolio is best assessed through a separate division. In this way, inputs and outputs associated with the luxury products, including raw materials, personnel, management time and effort, can be more easily identified, measured and assessed. Similarly, systems that support routine data collection and reporting, especially with regard to financial control data, are a natural by-product of the rational planning approach. To some extent, the rational planning model supports a bureaucratic organizational structure and systems, and these are conventionally associated with slow adaptation to change and feelings of alienation within their embrace.

The visionary-ideological approach

Peters, T. and Waterman, R.H. (1982) *In Search of Excellence*, Harper Collins, New York.

The second approach is more modern in origin and comes from the studies of Peters and Waterman in the early 1980s. This approach rejected the technical-rational model and was based instead on identifying the attributes of successful companies. The study included 43 major American corporations, all of which were identified as excellent according to their adaptability over time and their performance against six financial indicators. The original study was to some extent a reaction to the values underpinning the rational planning approach. The conclusions were that 'excellence' was linked to eight key attributes, and that these could successfully be transplanted into any company as a foundation for an effective strategy and excellent performance. The key attributes were as follows:

- **Stick to the knitting**. Actions in excellent companies followed patterns of building on core strength. This developed in-depth knowledge of business and better ability to predict change.

- **Close to the customer**. By putting quality, reliability and high standards of service at the fore, excellent companies remained in touch with their markets. This again helped them anticipate and respond to change. This closeness was encouraged and rewarded.

- **Productivity through people**. Excellent companies fostered a strong sense of belonging and maintained a concern for the feelings of people.

- **Autonomy and entrepreneurship**. People were empowered to make decisions close to the coal face. This helped to keep organizations flexible and responsive to their environment. It also helped to encourage initiative, creativity and dynamic growth.

- **Hands on, value driven**. Excellent companies allowed their decisions to be driven by values and beliefs. Leaders had an active role in espousing key values and creating harmony in beliefs. The strength of direction was built upon an overarching vision of a future state.

- **Bias for action**. Trial and error action was encouraged as a way of moving through a complex environment. Informal communication channels and task-based alliances were encouraged as a way of forming the political influence to make effective choices. A learning approach to outcomes was highly valued.

- **Simple form, lean staff**. The supporting structure for excellence was based on small, autonomous business units that retained human scale. Authority was pushed down towards the action and flexibility in jobs and roles were encouraged.

- **Simultaneous loose–tight properties**. While structure was fluid and supported autonomy and risk-taking, business units nevertheless operated under tight short-term financial control. Similarly, core values were also protected from contradiction. The contradictions involved in the loose–tight framework were maintained through driving towards shared beliefs.

Under the visionary-ideological approach strategy becomes a process by which top management sets out vision and values, but sets people free to find their own route to achieving those broad aims. This approach assumes that the environment is essentially unpredictable, making stable plans impossible to maintain. As a consequence, a trial and error approach to finding successful strategies is encouraged, driven and controlled by shared vision and tight financial controls. As with the rational planning approach, implementing strategy follows a cycle. A unifying ideology helps bind people together and enables **choice** to be made from a variety of possible actions. These are then subject to trial and error experiment as the primary form of strategic **action**. The fluid structure with lean staffing that remains close to the customer enables **discovery**, leading to rapid learning, new choices and a flexible response to strategic demands.

A conventional model

Both of these approaches accept that the operating environment is full of change. The rational planning model works from the assumption that the change factors can be analysed and predicted using sophisticated analytical tools. This drives a strategic planning process that relies heavily on information, control and structure as a means of moving the organization to a position of best fit. On the other hand the visionary-ideological model assumes that the change factors are too complex and rapid for meaningful analysis. This leads

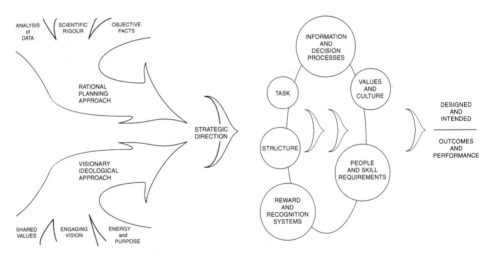

Fig. 16.4 A conventional model of strategy.

to a strategic process that seeks to inspire direction through shared values and an engaging vision, and which builds emotional energy and purpose into organizational aims. This approach involves flexible, motivated staff engaging in a broad range of experimental tasks as a means of working towards a vision of the position of best fit.

Both approaches share some common features, despite their apparent differences. Firstly, both share a belief that strategic direction – the goal or end state of strategy – can be intended by the organization. In the rational planning model, senior managers make analyses, then plan in detail how to reach the intended strategic goals. In the visionary model, the end state is expressed through vision, mission and values, and staff are set free to achieve the intended state through a process of discovery. In both cases, senior managers – as politically powerful stakeholders – intend the strategic goal. Secondly, in both models there is an acceptance that any strategic actions must take place through the organization design variables. Indeed, some examples of the different implications for design have already been mentioned. There is a shared recognition that strategy is enacted through a complex and interdependent set of variables, and that this will lead to adjustments being necessary as the strategy is implemented.

Strategy in practice

Goldsmith, W. and Clutterbuck, D. (1984) *The Winning Streak*, Weidenfeld & Nicolson, London. In an article in *Accountancy*, April 1984, entitled 'Don't let planners meddle with your strategies', J. Argenti reported that only 20% of Japanese companies make use of formal long-term planning. Similarly, in an article in *Long Term Planning*, **19** (2), 1986 entitled 'Does strategic planning improve performance?' G. Greenley found it difficult to establish any link between the use of rational planning and successful performance.

Unfortunately, neither of these approaches seems to be of much value when strategy is put into practice. The visionary approach saw a speedy fall from grace when two-thirds of the 43 companies originally defined as excellent failed to meet the same criteria within five years. A similar grouping of 25 UK companies also proved unable to sustain their excellence.

Any study of the basic rankings of organizations, through the Financial Times top 100, or the Fortune 500, shows up a similar picture of the rise and fall of business success. While the attributes that make up excellence may well be worthwhile business aims, and certainly Peters and Waterman can claim to have focused business thinking on values and culture, they do not appear to be linked to any sustained strategic success.

Similar difficulties occur in looking at the practice of the rational planning approach. Firstly, it is difficult to find companies that practise detailed long-term planning in any case. More often than not, organizations are so immersed in working through the day-to-day problems of organizational life that long-term planning gets very little rigorous attention. Secondly, of the companies that do engage in some long-term planning, less than 15% then used the results as a framework against which subsequent actions were measured. Formal planning appears to have little practical impact on the real strategic patterns that companies adopt, despite the long tradition that it has had as the foundation of corporate progress.

In practice, the conventional models do not appear to hold the key to organizational success. Faced with the problem of designing organizations that can develop and sustain effective strategies, the conventional approaches to strategic management fail to deliver. Instead, the 40-year average life-span of organizations and the four in five failure of business start-ups suggest a picture that raises serious questions about the value of strategic planning. The common response to this view is to blame particular and unpredictable environment factors – oil price shocks, the Gulf War, failing GATT talks or global recession – although it is precisely these type of events that are never far away from making waves in the global economy. Alternatively, management incompetence is blamed, and ever more sophisticated techniques are put forward to enable more efficient precision planning. This is based on the assumption that better plans, followed by the stable pursuit of those plans in an environment of rigorous monitoring and adjustment, will deliver effective strategy, despite whatever levels of unpredictability exist. Yet the assumptions underpinning the conventional approach may well be the core of the problem, in which case managers are not well served by advice to more of the same, but better. The next section explores some of the key assumptions upon which the conventional approaches depend.

Exploring assumptions

The whole concept of strategic planning depends on the assumption that successful organizations are those that are able to move to a position of best-fit in their own particular operating environment. By doing so, they achieve a state where they are in harmony with key aspects of business conditions, where continued operation will be characterized by stability. Resources will be optimized and the organization will be able to exploit its markets to achieve regular and consistent returns on its efforts. However, several factors suggest that this ideal condition is ultimately neither attainable, nor a satisfactory and stable position for organizations to reach.

Firstly, such a process depends on strategy-makers being able to identify the best-fit end state. While it may be plausible that planners could identify a best state given the **present** characteristics of the operating environment, it is misleading to think that this analysis can be extrapolated into the future. The business environment is not static, so any actions taken to implement the strategy will have dynamic effects on the actions of competitors, customers and governments. Further, the impact on the organization itself will be dynamic, affecting the organization design in unpredictable and potential contrary ways. The actions of the organization will shape the characteristics of the operating environment, rather than take place against a static and predictable backdrop.

Miller, D. (1990) *The Icarus Paradox: How Excellent Organizations Can Bring About Their Own Downfall,* Harper Business, New York.

The best-fit state may itself be a misleading concept, regardless of the potential for organizations to move there. In a study by Miller, organizational failure has been linked with building on success. This has been termed the Icarus paradox, whereby organizations typically develop their strengths and extend their specialisms until, like the mythical character, their success leads to their downfall. The study identifies four basic patterns by which organizations pursue strategies based on their existing assets:

- A focusing pattern whereby organizations with strength in engineering and control move towards becoming insular, offering the customer ever more sophisticated and technically perfect products that meet no identified need.

This pattern involves internal focusing on quality, cost, engineering, design and operational strength at the expense of understanding the customer. This is a trajectory by which 'craftsmen' becomes 'tinkerers', and is exampled by periods in the British motorcycle industry, Disney and Caterpillar.

- A venturing pattern whereby organizations with entrepreneurial strengths move towards becoming overstretched, spreading their skills too thinly in the search for growth. This is a trajectory by which 'builders' become 'imperialists', and is exampled by Gulf and Western and Litton Industries.

- An inventing pattern whereby organizations with strengths in scientific and technical innovation move towards the pursuit of far-fetched and resource-hungry projects. This is a trajectory by which 'pioneers' become 'escapists', and is exampled by Rolls-Royce and Apple.

- A decoupling pattern whereby organization with strengths in marketing and branding move towards offering unexciting and uniform products as design issues take a back seat. This is a trajectory by which 'salesman' become 'drifters', overdependent on the brand to shift the product. Proctor & Gamble and General Motors provide large-scale examples of this pattern.

The implication of this study is significant, with Miller identifying that the roots of organizational failure lie in strategies that build on existing strengths. The process by which organizations develop their qualities typically leads to a position of over-reliance on a narrow range of success factors, making them ill-equipped to cope with changing environmental conditions. By focusing on core strengths, organizations come to depend on one unique pattern for dealing with success, and amplifying this pattern exposes the organization in situations where this strategy is no longer adequate. Harmony built on existing success may well be the seeds of downfall, rather than a platform for continued success.

Hamel, G. and Prahalad, C.K. (1989) 'Strategic intent' in *Harvard Business Review*, May–June pp. 63–76.

This idea is reinforced by a further study by Gary Hamel and C.K. Prahalad, which looked at a number of global companies in an effort to distinguish what strategies separated the successful from the less successful. Their conclusions were that the companies that followed the conventional models and which sought to attain strategic fit were those that were less successful. In effect, they tried to build on their existing successes and followed strategies that led to repetition of previous patterns. By contrast, successful organization recognized that previous successes were no guarantee of future sustainability, and they therefore focused on stretching existing resources to widen the core competence of the organization, create new goals and transform the operation to broader goals. Again, best-fit appears to be associated with stagnation, whereas creating new capabilities leads to a transformation that helps equip the organization to make more of the environments that develop.

Secondly, even if it were possible to identify a best-fit end state, strategy-makers would need to be able to identify the steps that would move the organization from A to B. This presumes that organizations are characterized by cause and effect chains whereby particular actions will lead to given outcomes. However, because of the interconnections between the various elements of organization design, these chains are inherently complex wherever they might exist. A plan to restructure departments may have a variety of negative effects on the beliefs of people, for example, that are not held together by some overriding sense of vision. Further, even when the effects are observed and plans are adjusted to take account of the impact on people, it may not be possible to move the organization to the required position. The strategy may depend on people holding certain values (trust or openness for example) that have been irretrievably altered by the implementation of the strategy itself. People themselves are not static, but are shaped and altered by the experiences that they undergo; strategy is an experience that will have dynamic effects on people and their subsequent actions. This might presume to favour a trial and error approach to achieving strategic goals, but even this approach is built on the supposition that a position of best fit exists and is worth attaining. As the analysis above suggests, this assumption is questionable.

In practice, cause and effect in complex systems is a tenuous concept. Actions can lead to a variety of outcomes as the effects transfer through a web of interconnections in the organization. Further, in systems that involve people, the outcomes that emerge may be unintended and opposite to those expected. People learn, and their views shift according to their experience. Just because they respond in one way on one occasion is no guarantee that they will choose the same response in similar circumstances on the next occasion. This effect is something that governments grapple with daily, as policy changes such as reductions in interest rates fail to produce the anticipated rises in consumer confidence and retail spending. Relationships of cause and effect that once held good for the UK economy have been altered by the experience of the Lawson boom, possibly changing people's perceptions of feeling good beyond all recognition. Similar effects exist in organizations, making the concept of pursuing an intended strategy difficult to sustain.

Pascale, R.T. (1990) *Managing on the Edge: How Successful Companies Use Conflict To Stay Ahead*, Viking Penguin, London.

Thirdly, organization success may be linked to factors that are nothing to do with a position of best-fit. Rather than successful strategy being characterized by a rational progression towards some predictable and stable best-fit state, success may be associated with maintaining the ability to break existing patterns and transform the organization. A study by Pascale explores this view by looking at the need for organization to maintain both conventional 'fit', alongside what he terms 'split', or the ability to continuously break down existing strengths and perspectives in the search for something new. Pascale maintains that in order to develop new perspectives and genuine innovation, organizations need to break their existing perspectives, and the structures, systems and values that uphold them, in order to transform their capability and grow beyond the patterns that lead to failure.

This approach brings a significant paradox in that organizations must achieve some level of stability and close fit with their operating environment if they are to succeed in the present. Yet alongside this necessary close fit, they also need to develop the capacity for continual change, with all the breakdown of existing patterns that this implies. Neither of these extremes is an adequate recipe for success, yet neither is a balance between the two extremes attainable – there is no balanced middle ground. Rather, organizations have to work with both ends at once, somehow managing to preserve the value of both without trying to reach a balanced compromise. This is because it is the tension between doing both that leads to contention in the organization as managers grapple with opposing needs and perspectives, and it is this source of conflict that provides the vital spark to generate new strategic postures. Fundamentally, this view challenges the conventional models in that it proposes the creative maintenance of tension across key areas of organization contention. It is an approach that embraces the notion of organizational paradox. and which uses the paradox as a critical source of generating creative transformation.

Porter, M. (1990) *The Competitive Advantage of Nations*,. Macmillan Press, London.

Further support for the idea that success depends on other factors comes from an analysis of the way in which nations build up competitive advantage. Here, although success is in part dependent on the individual strategies that organization pursue, it is also dependent on the self-supporting interactions between suppliers, government agencies, domestic customers and competitors. This effect can be observed in the development of pockets of organizational success within the domestic economy – Silicon Glen as a stronghold of the UK computer industry, for example. The emergence of these regions of advantage is not solely dependent on the internal strategies of any particular firm, but is partly developed by factors in the environment and their interaction to produce conditions of advantage. Critically, success depends upon the actions of others, and the self-reinforcing interaction between demand, supply, government policy and competitor behaviour. In this interaction, an element of chance prevails, as is evidenced by the failed attempts of government regional policy to replicate the conditions for success.

Exploring assumptions: a summary of key points

The analysis of the assumptions upon which the conventional models are built highlights some significant questions. The conditions under which intended strategy might work do not appear to hold good for organizations operating in complex systems; indeed strategic actions may well have unintended and contrary consequences from which there is no retreat. Further, it is questionable whether the very goal of conventional strategy, a stable position of best fit, is a desirable position for organizations to attain. Indeed, there are a number of studies that demonstrate that this may be a step towards failure. Paradoxically, success may well be found in achieving continual fit, while also managing to sustain conditions of breakdown and transformation. This provides a perspective on the strategic process that is fundamentally different from the conventional prescriptions, where strategy is not built on a process of planning or visioning, but instead is generated through the dynamic interactions of people, processes, systems and chance.

An alternative perspective

When organizations are characterized by complex systems, where decisions and actions have unpredictable consequences through an interdependent system of effect, they are operating somewhere between stability and instability. They are not characterized by total regularity, where actions have predictable and reliable consequences, nor are they subject to explosive instability, where the slightest change leads to unbounded and uncontrolled outcomes. Instead, actions have relatively predictable short-term consequences, but long-term outcomes are increasingly unknown, as reactions ripple through the layers of interactions causing amplifying and contrary effects. This state, on the boundary between stability and instability, is characterized by the conditions of chaos. This is a state that allows organizations to transform and move away from stagnating, but does not result in collapse and destruction.

In such conditions a planned strategy cannot succeed. Instead, organizations have to recognize that planning for the future, based on extrapolating past trends, is a meaningless exercise that describes only one of many unpredictable possibilities. Similarly, relying on a binding sense of vision also works counter-productively, tying people to one particular end state amongst many potential possibilities and closing down other options along the way. Control over the longer term is not a function of pursuing an ordered plan, but is instead an outcome of control of short-term changes and patterns that build towards a successful new state. Those changes and patterns occur throughout the organization, amongst the myriad interactions and systemic relationships that take place. They are not the preserve of strategists and planners, but the outcomes of the interactions of the components in the system. Strategy is made through the actions and decisions of us all, operating through a complex web of causality rather than the intended patterns of key agents.

As such, making strategy work is a process of reflective learning, of careful consideration of patterns and consequences as they emerge, a process of shaping and building that depends on the contributions of us all. Faced with conditions of uncertainty, where cause and effect linkages cease to hold predictable answers to the problem of achieving and sustaining success, organizations must come to depend on the ability of people and systems to self-organize. It is through a process of self-organizing, of coming together to make sense of events and outcomes as they emerge, that people shape dynamic, adaptable organizations that transform to conditions that they both meet and create.

New processes

The analysis presents managers with another contradiction. The task of managing itself becomes paradoxical, where managers have to become skilled at maintaining the organization in a situation of best-fit in the present, yet also skilled at managing the conditions that allow the organization to creatively transform. The skills that maintain fit are the preserve of conventional management, with issues such as quality, cost, service and the development of staff all making an important contribution to keeping the organization efficient in its operating environment. An organization that fails to do these things, or does them badly, is one that will be overtaken by leaner and more efficient competitors, better able to control processes in the pursuit of technical efficiency. Yet these skills, fundamentally necessary to the design of effective organizations, are insufficient in situations where adaptation is necessary, and lead along pathways that ultimately signal failure and extinction.

Enabling organizations to transform involves managers in paradox, for they have to provide the conditions where creative challenge of existing views can take place. In doing so, they encourage and allow the organization to be shaped by the responses of people to the contradictions that they face. In meeting these contradictions, such as when faith in a policy of least cost runs up against the hurdle of poor quality, people will engage in dialogue. It is this dialogue, taking place wherever contradiction or anomalies arise, that challenges the existing paradigms and provides an engine for change. Managers therefore have to support both the systems that maintain the existing paradigm and the conditions that will allow it to be altered.

Managers are unable to do this within the formal organization for they are surfacing issues that challenge the frameworks and systems upon which the organization has built its success. In any case, the conventions, values, policies and systems of the formal organization actively work to support and validate the existing view. Instead, these challenges can only arise within the informal organization, as people share their views on inconsistencies or buck against the parts of the system that frustrate their endeavours.

Case note

The power of the formal organization

When working with the managers of a major high street bank, several issues regarding their 'target-driven' environment kept coming to the fore in casual comments and asides. These issues concerned the managers' lack of time for important issues such as developing staff or listening to their concerns. Many felt that the bank's stated concern for staff was cosmetic, and was not supported by the framework in which people had to work. Over several days, the issue kept arising during informal conversations, with many managers feeling that they had to work subversively in order to give their branch staff the attention they felt they deserved. This seemed OK, provided everyone met their targets. As an experiment, towards the end of the course, I asked the managers as a group to think about both the value of the targets and what would change, both positively and negatively, if they were scrapped overnight. Although this was only an academic exercise designed to encourage them to challenge the existing paradigm as well as better understand its rationale, the exercise failed. In the more formal setting of the work group, faced with the opinions of other managers, people avoided bringing up the issues. Further, when pressed, they could only come up with answers that validated the existing paradigm: 'we wouldn't meet the targets anymore' or 'the bank's performance, in terms of the financial measures, would decline'.

Although they informally identified that the targets got in the way of effective performance in many aspects of their work, and provided demotivation to many alongside motivation for a few, the managers would not challenge the paradigm in a formal setting. My attempts to prompt a fresh

> look at the issues, to challenge the measures and to see if effective perform-
> ance could be delivered by other means failed in the face of the power of
> organizational values and beliefs. Informal challenges, in passing comments
> over coffee, were acceptable, but formal threats were not.

Through this process it is the system itself that drives change. In the complex
world of the organization, the ordinary process of working towards goals will
throw up paradox. An organization pursuing sales finds it has lost its way with
quality. An organization driving for profit sees its 'people first' values undermined, or a programme of restructuring delivers technical efficiency at the
expense of morale. By getting to grips with each paradox that emerges, people
build new ideas and perspectives on how the organization should look and
behave. They redefine values and shape new beliefs. In this way, a different
organization emerges, a product of its own, unique history and changed
through the daily effort of people to make sense of what they see. Through a
process of dialogue, common themes are explored and sense is made of inconsistencies. Alliances form around issues, building political strength as a means
of bringing issues forward onto the formal agenda. A voice begins to emerge
from the myriad interactions of people facing the challenges and complexities
of organizational life. Very often, it is the voice of change.

Further reading

Out of Control: The Rise and Fall of Neo-Biological Civilization by Kevin Kelly (Addison-Wesley,
Reading, Mass., 1994) provides an eye-opening view of the characteristics of self-organization
and the natural world of complex systems. A core theme is the ability of nature to produce
order from disorder and to create something from nothing, while there is also considerable
focus on the value of disequilibrium in achieving success.

For those interested in the fascinating subject of chaos, J. Gleick *Chaos: The Making of a New
Science* (Weidenfeld & Nicolson, London, 1988) provides a wonderful overview in a readable
and entertaining style.

References

Bartlett, C.A. and Ghoshal, S. (1994) 'Changing the role of top management: beyond strategy
to purpose' in *Harvard Business Review*, November–December.
Goldsmith, W. and Clutterbuck, D. (1984) *The Winning Streak*, Weidenfeld & Nicolson,
London.
Hamel, G. and Prahalad, C.K (1989) 'Strategic intent' in *Harvard Business Review*, May–June,
pp. 63–76.
Miller, D. (1990) *The Icarus Paradox: How Excellent Organizations Can bring About Their Own
Downfall*, Harper Business, New York.
Mintzberg, H. (1994) *The Rise and Fall of Strategic Planning*, Free Press, New York.
Pascale, R.T. (1990) *Managing on the Edge: How Successful Companies Use Conflict To Stay Ahead*,
Viking Penguin, London.

Peters, T. and Waterman, R.H. (1982) *In Search of Excellence*, HarperCollins, New York.

Porter, M. (1990) *The Competitive Advantage of Nations*, Macmillan Press, London.

Robinson, G.R. (1992) *Managing after the Superlatives*, Tudor Business Publishing, Sevenoaks.

Stacey, R. (1992) *Managing Chao*, Kogan Page, London.

Stacey, R. (1993) *Strategic Management and Organizational Behaviour*, Pitman, London.

Taylor, F. (1947) *Scientific Management, Collected Works of Frederick Taylor*.

17

Management interpreted?

It is not down on any map; true places never are.
Herman Melville, *Moby Dick*

Introduction

In the opening chapter – 'Interpreting management' – we used as our starting point stories related to us by managers about their everyday experience of managing in organizations, 'their managerial reality'. We noted that these stories reflected the richness of our experience of organizational life with all its inevitable ups and downs, the excitement and frustration, successes and blunders, and the laughter and sometimes tears that are an integral part of any human undertaking. We looked also at the value of the many strategies and initiatives that endeavour to improve the way organizations are managed, and the need to focus on the management of people as the key to creating productive, inspiring workplaces and competitive organizations.

Throughout the diverse range of topics covered in previous chapters – from perception to leadership to strategy – we have placed great emphasis on the practical actions and techniques that managers can experiment with in their efforts to design their own effective approaches to management. In doing so we have tried to illustrate how a manager's actions and decisions form part of a web of interdependent and complex relationships. In such an environment, where the effects of actions cannot be clearly predicted, and where the unexpected becomes inevitable, the acquisition of simple management 'skills' alone as a route to managerial understanding, must be questioned.

In striving to expand our understanding and enrich our interpretation of the managerial environment, the development and sound practice of thoughtful management skills and techniques, vital though they undoubtedly are, should not be the 'end' of our voyage. Managers need to move beyond the practice of techniques, and explore ways of grasping the significance and relevance of wider perspectives that help us to understand the complex nature of the social systems in which we work and live.

In this chapter, we revisit this complexity, with the intention of reaffirming the notion of management as a journey, where intuition and humanity have as much to contribute as scientific analysis or rigorous theory. We have drawn into this view the key themes introduced in Chapter 1, in particular the value of learning, and the need to move forward through action and engagement. It is a journey full of hope and excitement, an opportunity to explore wider perspectives and new ways of thinking about the limitations of a static and simplistic approach to managing people and organizations. Furthermore, it is a voyage that creates a particular meaning and direction for each one of us, unfolding as it does in the unique context of our own managerial situation.

Managing complexity

Perhaps the most constructive way of developing our understanding of the value of moving beyond the application of customary management techniques – of adding depth to our interpretation of management – is to work through some common illustrations. We have chosen to look at the difficulties of managing the major dilemma or contradiction between the need for 'stability', structure and systems, and the need for 'instability', change and creativity. This paradox is vitally important both to managing organizations, and to enhancing our understanding of ourselves and others on a more personal level.

If we look at the organizational dimension first, it is easy to be aware of the need for organizations to develop clear aims and objectives, to utilize effective financial procedures, or to support operations with finely tuned systems, for example. In short, this is about creating necessary and technically sophisticated frameworks that provide security and structure for all stakeholders. Of equal importance is the need to foster creativity, innovation and the continual search for the new and the exciting, that is the continual drive for renewal and change. It is the way in which we manage this paradox that helps us to see the value of approaching managerial complexities from a wider perspective. It is the relationships and tensions between these 'opposites' that require exploration and understanding, for they lie at the heart of managing the many contradictions that confront us daily in management situations. We can illustrate this paradox as:

Stability $\prec$ Tension $\succ$ **Instability**

We have referred often in this book to the need to 'manage the tensions' between seemingly contradictory, or paradoxical, views of the same issue – the opposing sides of the same coin if you like. It can be a difficult idea to grasp, in particular for those of us schooled in rational and 'scientific' ways of thinking which demand an absolute 'right' answer one way or another, but it provides an important tool in helping us to understand some of the complex issues and dilemmas that challenge us as managers.

Firstly it becomes clear from the example above that both of the 'opposites' – in this case stability and instability – are equally important and that an organization cannot survive by choosing one or the other. We have discussed many of these 'needs' in more detail in the preceding chapters, but an organization trying to operate without goals or direction, or with no systems at all for dealing effectively with financial information or customer complaints for example, would struggle to survive. It would be difficult for such an organization to manage itself internally and deal reasonably with the demands of partners and its staff. In a situation where no structure exists, the pressures to create systems and 'get organized' are significant, to the extent that people will create their own structures in an effort to meet their needs for order and stability.

Conversely, an organization constructed and run through elaborate systems and procedures will allow little room for innovation, challenge and creativity to blossom. The result may be that people seeking change and stimulation leave, while the organization, failing to adapt quickly enough to a complex and rapidly changing environment, stagnates and dies. The stable organization is equipped to function well only in predictable and static environments, or where it needs to deal with routine work in the short term. While historically businesses operated in reasonably stable environments, the opportunities for doing so today are becoming increasingly rare.

The lesson in this case is that the **management of paradoxes does not respond to simple either/or choices**. One of the key advantages in grasping the idea of paradox is our ability to free ourselves from the anxiety that stems from a narrow focus on either/or choices by moving to an approach that looks for 'both' solutions. A classic example of this dilemma is the apparent conflict between the search for quality and the need for low cost in producing goods or delivering services, which has occupied many Western businesses for years. Trapped in an apparent either/or dilemma, the choice was perceived as being one of high quality/high cost **or** low cost/low quality. The way forward stems from a desire to achieve both sides of the paradox, high quality **and** low cost. The key to handling this paradox is to look for both 'solutions' over a longer-term timeframe, and to acknowledge the complexity of the 'equation'. In this case a focus on quality over time has led to lower costs in terms of reducing the need for inspection, lower customer complaints or less waste, to note just a few examples.

We can use our understanding of paradox to suggest other strategies for managing complex situations. It is tempting to deal with paradoxes, or any other contradictory demands on our energies as managers, by looking for a way to 'balance' the pressures pulling us in different directions – and there is real value in this. In our example above about stability and instability this is a useful approach, particularly when this balance is worked out over a longer timescale. But we can go much further than this in using our understanding of complex systems.

In our example above, managing the stability/instability contradiction suggests the need for managers to make decisions based on their awareness of the tensions and ability to balance conflicting needs over time. In a complex environment, though, this is difficult to achieve as it relies on the manager's knowledge of a vast range of interrelated variables and relationships that are inherently unpredictable and always changing. This view of complex working environments is valuable in helping managers accept a degree of confusion and some unintended consequences. But the management of tensions and contradictions can be made significantly more productive and less frustrating when everyone in an organization or team is involved in the balancing process. In the example above this would be when people are allowed to develop their own structures and 'stability', and to drive their own change and search for excitement. To explore this idea further we need to see how the stability/instability paradox appears not only in organizations, but intrinsically also to the people who work in them. On a personal level this paradox can be simply expressed in terms of seemingly contradictory needs, as the suggestions below show:

Stability   <   Tension   >   **Instability/Change**

Our need for:

Established routines	New challenges and excitement
Familiar surroundings	Growth and development
People we know well	Meeting new people
Clear boundaries	Freedom of action and expression
Consolidation time	Learning new skills

As individuals we all have these paradoxical needs for both stability and instability. Using an example from the above list, each of us needs to have elements of our work that are routine, comfortable and relatively stress-free. We also have the conflicting need for something new and challenging, an opportunity to learn and experiment. These tensions exist in us all as individuals to a greater or lesser extent, and exert pressures that keep any situation dynamic. For instance, too much 'stability' in terms of routine or restrictive systems may result in boredom and apathy, which increases the desire for change, flexibility or challenge. Conversely, constant change and instability can create a growing desire for a period of consolidation and stability. Perhaps the mood of people working in teaching or the health service, for example, reflects this need for stability, after years of new structures, initiatives and changing job roles.

From a management point of view the situation is further complicated in that this paradox will be experienced differently from one colleague to the next. As we have discussed in earlier chapters, people vary greatly in their needs for the safety of structures and routine or the challenge of the new and exciting, so that in any one team of people a manager will experience a range of responses to the stability/instability paradox that also varies over time.

So how does an understanding of this paradox on an individual basis at work help us to manage the tensions it creates? Firstly, as with the organizational perspective noted above, there is the need to accept and work towards satisfying both sets of conflicting needs. Beyond this, though, lies the value of enlisting the potential of every individual in supporting your efforts to create workable balance and to manage tensions. In 'management' terms this includes the processes of enablement, empowerment and involvement. It is about allowing others not just to express their needs (in this case for systems and structure, or change and excitement), but to be overtly involved in creating their own joint solutions to this dilemma on an ongoing basis. This approach reinforces and supports organizational aims in terms of flexibility, innovation and responsiveness in a powerful and meaningful way.

Again paradoxically, freeing people to develop their own solutions and structures can help managers to design new boundaries and control mechanisms that arise from people's need to gain consent and acceptance for their actions or ideas. The need to gain support for a particular idea or initiative provides a system of essentially 'political' checks and balances that effectively prevent extreme or obviously destructive solutions being pursued. In this way the freedoms implied by an empowering environment do not dissolve into a directionless free-for-all or the unconstrained pursuit of personal agendas.

In a team setting, enlisting people in the management of difficult or contra-dictory situations might be expressed in terms of team members creating only the systems or structures they feel meet their own needs for stability and which support, not hinder, the tasks they are undertaking. They may similarly create their own boundaries and opportunities for change and renewal, in their recognition that this instability is also vital for themselves and their organiza-tion. This approach greatly helps the manager to create the balance and manage the tensions inherent in our stability/instability paradox. The 'solution' to the paradox at any one point in time emerges from the joint actions of the team as a whole rather than from the isolated perceptions of the manager struggling with complex and seemingly contradictory situations.

In working through an example, in this case the value of using ideas about complexity and paradox, we can begin to see how adopting a wider perspective can add to our understanding of management. In this case we can see how this perspective supports and amplifies the contribution of the wide range of practical actions and management techniques we have discussed in the preced-ing chapters. In particular it reinforces ideas about the potential contribution people can make to success through their involvement in shaping and changing their working environment. This approach not only provides the best way forward for creating productive and exciting workplaces – with all the benefits that spring from freeing people to explore their potential – it also liberates the manager from the burden of trying to control, organize and manage complex situations that are ultimately beyond the full comprehension of any of us. In short it offers both reassurance and ways forward.

The personal perspective

We have explored the value of wider perspectives such as complexity and paradox as they relate to interpreting some organizational situations. This approach can also be useful in examining the management of relationships and interpersonal issues. It is worth working through a more personal example, one that lies at the heart of many close relationships, working ones as well as social. This is the tension exerted by our hunger for intimacy and our desire for independence.

Intimacy   ≺   Tension   ≻   **Independence**

In this paradox, intimacy relates to our desire to develop and maintain close relationships with others – love, respect and strong friendships – and our fear of being alone or isolated. Independence is clearer, it is our need to break free as ourselves, to be seen as unique and different – to be identified and valued as an individual. In terms of our relationships with others the desire for both intimacy and independence needs no justification, and is particularly recognizable in our closest relationships with partners for instance.

The tensions this paradox creates at work also have real significance in their impact on day-to-day interactions and events. The tensions between our need to 'belong' and to develop relationships with colleagues in contrast to our need to stand out and be valued for our individual talents and contributions are evident in countless workplace interactions. The paradox may find expression in, for example, the conflict between conforming to group norms and 'being ourselves', or wanting to help out colleagues when our own workloads are already stressful. A common dilemma managers often share with us is their concern to develop close relations with their staff which conflicts with their perceived need to maintain some distance between themselves and the people they manage (their independence).

As with the stability/instability paradox, the manager will need to accept that these contradictory needs are equally essential and have attractions for us all. An awareness of this perspective gives depth to our understanding of management issues such as motivation, managing differences and group processes to name but a few. An appreciation of the complexity of managing these 'opposites' needs to be valued in our attempts to understand both ourselves and others.

It is vital that managers recognize that these paradoxes are not 'resolvable' – the contradictions will always be there because both opposing ideas are valuable – in fact they are co-dependent. Paradox becomes a valuable way of seeing some complex work issues as it enables us to recognize such unresolvable tensions, and so manage the conflicting 'pulls' with renewed understanding and a fresh perspective. Ultimately, understanding paradoxes helps us to come to terms with some of the complexities of working situations, and to accept some of the contradictory and often confusing messages we receive from others. More than this it highlights the value of approaching 'messy' and complex issues with a fair degree of intuition and human judgment as opposed to relying solely on attempting to rationalize or analyze your way through them.

Beyond 'skills'

We have tried to illustrate in this chapter the value of considering the complex subject of management from a wider perspective. We have done this by looking at the example of how an understanding of paradox can help us to accept and then manage some of the difficult dilemmas that abound in management practice. There are many other useful ideas that help us to broaden the way in which we choose to interpret our experience of management, some of which we have explored in previous chapters. For example, we have discussed the limitations of 'cause and effect' explanations, the role of confusion (in change), the importance of feedback loops and double-loop learning, or the significance of stories and myths in interpreting our experience of organizational life. All of these ideas and many more have the potential to help us to expand the way we think about things and the limits or restrictions this imposes.

Our view is that this added dimension complements and advances the development and practice of the many management skills we have discussed throughout this book, and which are explored in most management education situations. We can use the wide range of management techniques covered here to develop more effective management styles and greatly enhance the opportunity of creating productive workplaces. We need to continually develop management 'skills' such as:

Understanding and applying ideas about:

- teamworking
- motivation
- leadership
- planning
- empowerment
- communication.

Though the benefits of this approach to management learning are undoubtedly immense, management is about much more than this. We need to develop an understanding of why applying sound techniques can lead to unintended or undesirable consequences, why small interventions can sometimes lead to big successes, or why the unexpected will always happen – in short, to develop a perspective that helps us manage confusion, change and even chaos with panache.

In developing this broader interpretation we have argued that management additionally:

- Demands development of self-awareness
- Positively challenges accepted culture and behaviours
- Creates shared direction, purpose and meaning
- Involves issues about our values, beliefs and world views
- Seeks to replace apathy and cynicism with energy and optimism
- Fosters a unique interpretation of events and actions
- Supports creativity, innovation and continual improvement
- Values diversity and exceptions as a key source of organizational learning.

In summary, our interpretation of management development in terms of learning and applying a simple set of skills needs to be challenged with additional perspectives such as those listed above.

Moving forward

We have explored above the impact that developing practical management skills and a broader understanding of complex interrelationships can have on our interpretation of management. In this last section we need to emphasize the need to take this understanding forward in context – through productive engagement in the management process.

Becoming actively involved in the management process has been one of the recurring themes of this book. At one level this represents the desire to implement and experiment with new perspectives or techniques – to embed learning in day-to-day practice. Also, although reflection and debate are worthy processes in themselves, there is an obvious practical need to realize the benefits of management learning, for organizations as well as individuals, by putting ideas and theories into action. There is much to be lost from an investment in developing skills or understanding that is not then applied in the workplace in a positive effort to improve effectiveness and productivity.

But the importance of immersing ourselves in the action is more fundamental than a return on training investment, or even the need to apply our learning. The very act of engaging in the management process is crucial in reinventing our own unique interpretation of management on a continual basis. It is engagement that provides the primary opportunity to learn, to promote exploration and understanding, and to make sense of the complex social systems in which we work.

Focusing on the need for engagement is not part of a step-by-step process whereby understanding is developed, followed by practice, and then lastly results. The process is circular and continuous, with action generating the opportunities for reflection and learning which conversely provide the basis for new actions. In this respect learning becomes a key strategy, for development, growth and innovation. It is also through this need to take action that learning enables people to find productive outcomes from situations that generate conflict, confusion and the unexpected. Learning becomes one of the key tools in handling such situations as it can provide a valued and accepted focus for dealing with complex or difficult issues openly. A commitment to learning as a primary strategy not only provides opportunities for organizational success in highly competitive environments, but secures a positive approach to personal understanding and survival.

This commitment to learning through engagement creates the opportunity to involve people in the development of solutions to complex issues and opens the door to meaningful empowerment. It provides a framework that allows the free expression of needs, concerns and ideas in the search for ways forward. An important part of this process is to acknowledge that there are no single 'right answers' to difficult or complicated management scenarios, rather that solutions emerge that are useful in the context of the particular situation being faced. This parallels the approach we have taken in this book that sees both the value and dangers of adopting any one particular management idea or technique, particularly in a simplistic effort to solve management problems.

Lastly, the need to become actively engaged challenges an interpretation of the management role as one of helplessness or passive cynicism. This is an easy, and very understandable, stance to take, seeing ourselves as powerless victims of corporate whims or impregnable bureaucracy, but one that condemns us to a fatalistic view of our futures. Management action provides the stage upon which we seek to create meaning and influence others in an effort to change the way we work together for the better. In this way, management becomes the key process in the creation of engaging and purposeful organizations, where people contribute with passion to the shape of their future. It is a journey that is full of hope and opportunity, excitement and interest, wonder and growth. There will always be contention and problems, but by seeking to engage in an effort to find progress, we explore our place in the world. It is a journey that cannot help but bring significance to our lives.

Further reading

There would be more than a little irony in suggesting just one or two books that will help you to explore 'wider perspectives'. The source of ideas and inspiration that you could relate to your experience of management are endless, and definitely not to be restricted to books classified as being about 'management'. Some of the areas that might be worth exploring include obvious ones such as psychology, politics or philosophy, and creative fiction/ literature. Beyond this it is also worth delving into the growing interest in personal development, where there is enormous overlap in ideas about growth and learning, albeit sometimes using very 'non-business' language.

An area we have found of particular value is the current surge in interest in new scientific theory, which has spawned numerous books on subjects like chaos, fuzzy thinking or the parallels between Eastern philosophy and modern physics for instance. Margaret Wheatley's book (see references) is a wonderful example in terms of the links she makes between science and managing organizations, but there are many others. Fritjof Capra's *The Turning Point* (Harper Collins, London 1983) or Roger Lewin's *Complexity* (Orion Books, London, 1993) are useful examples in this area.

On a more specific note, an interesting chapter called 'Why executives lose their balance' by J.R. Kodosimos (in *Managing Learning*, C. Mabey and P. Iles (eds) – see references) explores the intimacy/independence issue further. It looks at the way some executives express their identity through work (independence) at rising cost to their relationships with partners and families, and find in time that their ability to satisfy their need for intimacy becomes impaired by the commitment they have given to their job.

References

Capra, F. (1983) *The Turning Point*, HarperCollins, London.
Handy, C. (1994) *The Empty Raincoat*, BCA, London.
Lewin, R. (1993) *Complexity*, Orion Books, London.
Long, J. (1994) *Rock Junction*, Chockstone Press, Colorado.
Mabey, C. and Iles, P (eds) (1994) *Managing Learning*, Routledge, London.
Peters, T. (1994) *The Pursuit of WOW*, Macmillan, London.
Senge, P.M. (1990) *The Fifth Discipline*, Century Business, London.
Stacey, R.D. (1992), *Managing Chaos*, Kogan Page, London.
Tannen, D. (1992) *That's Not What I Meant!*, Virago Press, London.
Wheatley, M.J. (1992) *Leadership and The New Science*, Berrett-Koehler, San Francisco.

Index